LONGMAN ADVANCED GNVQ

TEST AND ASSESSMENT GUIDE

BUSINESS

Martin Buckley and Bernadette Craven

ADVANCED GNVQ

Longmans Advanced GNVQ
Test and Assessment Guides

Series Editors:
Geoff Black and Stuart Wall

Titles available:
Business
Health and Social Care
Leisure and Tourism

Due for publication in 1995:
Construction and the Built Environment
Hospitality and Catering
Science

Longman Group Ltd,
Longman House, Burnt Mill, Harlow,
Essex CM20 2JE, England
and Associated Companies throughout the world.

First Published 1994

ISBN 0 582 23776 9

British Library Cataloguing-in-Publication Data

A catalogue record for this book is
available from the British Library

Typeset by 23 QQ in 9/11 pt Sabon
Printed in Great Britain by William Clowes Ltd.,
Beccles and London

Contents

Using this book

The first eight units provide you with the vital information and knowledge needed in each mandatory unit, both for passing the compulsory external tests (in seven of the mandatory units) and for completing the various projects and assignments set on those units. You will find many self-check questions at the end of each element in the unit, with answers at the end of the unit. You will also find a unit test at the end of each unit of the type you will face in the external test itself, with answers and examiner comments.

After these eight mandatory units there is a major chapter on the 'Portfolio', helping you develop the skills and insights needed to gain a merit or distinction in your Advanced GNVQ. You will be shown the types of evidence you can present in the portfolio. Actual examples of student assessments are provided together with examiner comments. There is also material in this chapter on what is meant by the core skills in your GNVQ and how these can be demonstrated in your portfolio of evidence.

Introduction: Advanced GNVQ in Business

In order to gain your Advanced GNVQ in Business, you have to demonstrate to your tutors and teachers that you have been successful in meeting the standards for the various units on the course; in other words you will be *assessed*, in a number of different ways, to show that you have reached the required standard for each unit. The bulk of the assessment you will be asked to do will be in the form of **assignments and projects**, set and marked by the staff who teach on your GNVQ. You will also need to pass the **external tests** that are set by business experts outside your school or college. In the case of Business there are currently seven external tests that you will need to pass. An important part of the assessment process for GNVQs is the collection of *evidence* to show that you have successfully completed the different parts of the units. This material is gathered together in a **'portfolio of evidence'**, which is used to confirm that you have covered all the necessary parts of the units and to establish your overall grade for the GNVQ.

Before we can look in greater detail at the different types of assessment in GNVQs, it is important that you understand clearly how the different parts of a GNVQ fit together. You will also need to get used to a lot of new words and phrases, so it's important that you get to grips with these from the outset.

The structure of the Advanced GNVQ in Business
All GNVQs are based on **units**. Advanced GNVQs are made up of 15 units in total, shared out as follows:

- *Eight Mandatory Units* – these cover the fundamental skills, knowledge and understanding related to business. Mandatory means that everybody studying for the Advanced GNVQ in Business must complete these units.

- *Four Optional Units* – these complement the mandatory units and give students the chance to look in more depth at a particular topic. The exact options you will be studying will depend on which awarding body your school or college deals with (BTEC, City & Guilds or RSA), the skills and expertise of your tutors and your own particular interests.

- *Three Core Skill Units* – these help you to develop skills that are vital for anybody wishing to work in business or to go on to study the subject area at a higher level. You will be assessed in *communication, application of number* and *information technology*.

Don't worry if you discover that you are studying more than 15 units on your GNVQ. This is likely to be because your school or college is giving you the chance to develop a broader range of skills or study certain subjects in even greater depth, by offering you *additional units*. Additional units may be necessary for studying certain courses in higher education, at degree or HND level.

Having a number of different units that go to make up the GNVQ award allows greater flexibility in studying. GNVQ will, for many, be on a full-time course of study at school or college; however some students will want to study on a part-time basis, passing one unit at a time. The way GNVQs are designed allows students to build up credit for individual units over an extended period of time.

What does a unit consist of?
At the beginning of this section, we talked about the need to meet the required standard in order to be successful in your GNVQ. The standards for the Advanced GNVQ in Business have been developed by specialists in education and the industry as a way of defining what has to be done by students to achieve the award. The standards are set out as **units**; for Advanced GNVQs these are the eight mandatory, four optional and three core skill units we mentioned above. Figure A overleaf gives a breakdown of a unit (sometimes called a **unit specification**), showing the different parts of a unit and how they link together.

To help you understand even better how a GNVQ unit is structured, an element from the Advanced GNVQ in Business is shown in full in the box below Figure A.

Looking at Fig. A and the box together shows us that each **unit** on the Advanced GNVQ in Business has a number of different components, namely:

1 Elements
2 Performance criteria
3 Range
4 Evidence indicators

We will now look at each of these in a little more detail.

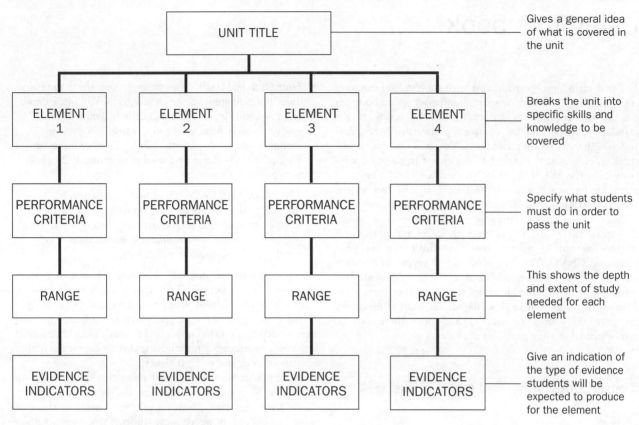

Fig. A The component parts of a GNVQ Unit

The structure of a typical element of the Advanced GNVQ in Business

Unit 1: Business in the economy

Element 1.1: Explain the purposes and products of business

- **Performance criteria**
  1 Demand for goods and services is identified and described.
  2 Demand in relation to a particular product is identified.
  3 Industrial sectors are identified and described.
  4 Products of businesses in different industrial sectors are identified and described.
  5 Purposes of selected business organizations are explained.

- **Range**
  Demand: needs, wants and effective demand; consumption and income; demand and price; elastic and inelastic.
  Industrial sectors: primary, secondary, tertiary.
  Product: goods; services.
  Purposes: profit-making; public service; charitable.

- **Evidence indicators**
  An analysis of selected businesses with an explanation of why businesses exist; an explanation of their products and an explanation of demand in general and demand in relation to a particular product. Evidence should demonstrate understanding of the implications of the range dimensions in relation to the element. The unit test will confirm the candidate's coverage of the range.

---

1 Elements

Each unit in the Advanced GNVQ in Business is broken down into a number of different **elements**, depending on the depth of material included in the unit. The first mandatory unit, for example, 'Business in the economy', is attempting to set business in context and is made up from three elements. Elements are also found in the optional units and core skills units.

In order to be successful in your Advanced GNVQ in Business, you will need to produce evidence to show that you have covered *all* the elements in all the units you are studying.

2 Performance criteria

Each GNVQ element has a number of **performance criteria** related to it. There are five criteria in the example given in the box, but the number will vary between different elements. The performance criteria help to explain what that particular element is all about, by telling you what areas you need to cover to be able to pass it.

In carrying out the different types of assessment for a unit, you can think of the performance criteria as a 'checklist' of evidence that you will need to collect and include in your portfolio to demonstrate that you have successfully met the requirements of the element.

In the course of your assessments, you must show that you have met the requirements of *all* the performance criteria for each element of your GNVQ.

3 Range

You will see in Fig. A that, as well as having performance criteria related to it, each element will identify a **range** associated with it. The range tries to indicate the boundaries that each student will need to work within on a particular element. In the example given in the table, for example, the range states that the student must provide evidence to show that they have considered the following points:

- The demand for a product or service.
- The different industrial sectors that exist.
- The product or service itself.
- The purposes for which businesses exist.

To be successful in an element, the evidence that you collect must show that you have covered *all* the range points included in the unit specification.

4 Evidence indicators

The **evidence indicators** included in the unit specifications give a general idea as to the *sort of evidence* that would be considered suitable for successful completion of the element. In the example shown in the table, a **report** which included an analysis of why a business exists, its product range, and the general and specific characteristics of the demand conditions it faces, would be a suitable type of evidence given that the report also covered the necessary performance criteria and range.

This does not mean that every student studying Element 1 of the Advanced GNVQ in Business will be researching and writing a report to submit as evidence that they have completed all the requirements. Different schools and colleges will tackle the problem in different ways; some may ask students to make a presentation or carry out a survey, both of which are quite acceptable alternative types of evidence.

There are discussions going on at the moment between the different awarding bodies, about the possibility of setting assessments in some units that will be the same right across the country. Even if this does happen, you will still be given assignments and projects that are specific to your school or college, in addition to any national assessments.

Types of assessment

The **assessment** in your GNVQ concentrates on two main areas:

- External tests
- Continuous assessment

The way in which the two main types of assessment link together is shown in Fig. B.

External tests

You will need to sit and pass **external tests**, set by the awarding bodies, before you can be awarded the Advanced GNVQ in Business. Seven out of the eight mandatory units have external tests; Unit 8 Business Planning does *not* have an external test, since it was thought it would be difficult to ask factual questions on that area. You will therefore sit external tests in the following units:

Unit 1   Business in the economy
Unit 2   Business systems
Unit 3   Marketing
Unit 4   Human resources
Unit 5   Employment in the market economy

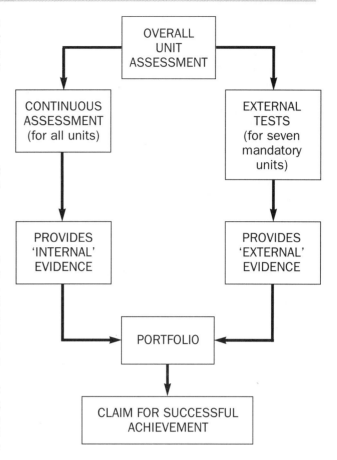

Fig. B: Unit Assessment in the Advanced GNVQ in Business

Unit 6   Financial transactions and monitoring
Unit 7   Financial resources

You will be told the exact dates and times of the tests by your teacher or tutor and will be given the chance to re-sit any tests that you do not pass at the first attempt. Remember, it is essential that you pass all seven external tests in the mandatory units before you can be awarded the Advanced GNVQ in Business. Because it is important that you have a good grasp of the basic knowledge and understanding in each unit, the pass mark is set deliberately high at 70%. All the awarding bodies are planning to mark the tests and get the results back to you in the shortest time possible, so as to provide you with early feedback on your performance.

At present, there are no external tests for the optional or additional units, but, as with any new qualification, changes are being made all the time to GNVQs in response to feedback from students and tutors. To be absolutely sure, you should check with your teacher or tutor what the exact position is regarding tests for your particular course.

Although the seven units listed above are the only units with external tests at the moment, you may find that your particular school or college sets their own tests in some units. This is quite acceptable and will provide you with more evidence to include in your portfolio.

Sitting an external test is a way of showing that you have grasped the essential knowledge and understanding for a particular unit. Some people consider that having tests that are externally set and the same right across the country gives GNVQs more credibility than a qualification based entirely on continuous assessment in school or college.

Passing a test will show that you understand the basic principles of a particular unit, thus providing a good grounding for working in business or going on to study the subject at a higher level.

What are the external tests like?
- Each test will have between 30 and 40 questions.
- Each test lasts one hour.
- You will be asked to fill in your answers on a separate answer sheet, not on the test papers themselves. Don't worry if the answer sheet has more spaces than the number of questions on your test; this is because the number of questions varies between 30 and 40 on different test papers.
- You will not be asked to answer the questions by writing sentences, but will select an answer by writing A, B, C or D on the separate answer sheet. Your answers should be written in soft (HB) pencil only, as the answer sheets are marked by machine.
- You will be allowed to use a calculator in the test, but the memory must be wiped clean before you go into the room where the tests are being taken.
- The questions on the test papers are grouped into 'focus areas' (see below).

- The tests use three different types of questions (see below).
- Tests are taken under secure conditions, on a specified day and at a specified time.

What are 'focus areas'?
You will see from the sample test papers included in Units 1–8 in the first part of this book that the questions are grouped into 'focus areas'. These are simply convenient headings that have been taken from the specifications for each unit. You may find it useful when preparing for tests to structure your revision around the different focus areas in each unit. The focus areas for all seven Advanced Business mandatory units that have an external test are given in the table below.

Types of questions
It is important that you become familiar with three types of question. They are:

1 Multiple choice questions
2 Paired true/false questions
3 Grouped multiple choice questions

Unit	Focus area
1 Business in the economy	1 The purposes and products of business 2 Government approaches and interventions 3 Supply of goods and services 4 Investigating and evaluating
2 Business systems	1 Purposes of administration systems 2 Meeting legal and statutory requirements 3 Evaluating administration systems 4 Communication systems 5 Effects of electronic technology on communication systems 6 Evaluating information processing systems 7 Effects of technology
3 Marketing	1 Research methodology 2 Market research analysis 3 Marketing environment 4 Marketing mix 5 Regulating ethical standards in marketing
4 Human resources	1 Human resource management 2 Employer/employee relations 3 Legal and ethical obligations 4 Types of business and organizational structure 5 Job roles and responsibilities in organizations 6 Recruitment and selection
5 Employment in the market economy	1 Trends and features in employment 2 Business actions and external influences 3 Features of workforce performance 4 Sources of data about workforce performance 5 Analysis and evaluation of workforce peformance
6 Financial transactions and monitoring	1 Purposes of financial transactions 2 Security 3 Accounting information 4 Monitoring
7 Financial resources	1 Sources of finance 2 Cash flow and cash flow forecasting 3 Costs 4 Trial balance, profit and loss statements and balance sheets

We will now look at each of these in a little more detail and study one example of each type.

1 Multiple choice questions

As the following example shows, these have four answer options, only one of which is correct.

Example:

A company has recently purchased an integrated computer system to support its administrative systems.

Which of the following outputs would be most useful for the Accounts Manager?

A pay slips
B staff absenteeism figures
C monthly expenditure reports by each department
D salespeople's performance figures

A correct answer to a multiple choice question is worth one mark.

2 Paired true/false questions

These have two statements introduced by the phrase 'decide whether each of these statements is true (T) or false (F)'. The two statements are labelled (1) and (2) and are always followed by the phrase 'which option best describes the two statements?'

Example:

A company has recently introduced a system to computerize their administration systems. This has become necessary because of the increase in their business and the inability to cope with the amount of paperwork.

Mark each of these statements true (T) or false (F).

1 Using computer-based information processing systems is always more efficient than manual ones.
2 The company should ignore staff complaints following the installation of the new computer system.

Which option best describes the two statements?

A (1) T (2) T
B (1) T (2) F
C (1) F (2) T
D (1) F (2) F

As this example shows, there are four answer options A, B, C or D, only one of which is correct. You would choose:

* Option A if you thought both statements were true
* Option B is you thought the first was true but the second false
* Option C if you thought the first was false but the second true
* Option D if you thought both statements were false.

Take your time when deciding which option to choose; it is easy to make a wrong choice even when you know the right answer. A correct answer to a paired true/false question is worth one mark.

3 Grouped multiple choice questions

These have four answer options A, B, C and D. These are followed by three statements which form the questions. They are numbered as three separate questions.

Example:

Questions 1–3 relate to the following information:

Accounting information is used to produce the following:

A Profit and loss account
B Balance sheet
C Cash flow
D Purchase ledger

Which documents will give information on:

1 Assets
2 Expenses
3 Creditors

You must choose from the answer options A, B, C or D, the correct answer for each of the three questions. For example, the answer to question 1 in the example is the balance sheet, so you would choose option B. Each answer option may be used more than once as a correct answer. Each of the three questions is worth one mark.

Preparing for the tests

You will normally take the unit test towards the end of a period of study of one particular unit. This will make sure that the continuous assessment tasks that you have been set will help to provide information and knowledge needed to be able to answer the test questions. Each unit of this book covers the main *content* you need to know when revising for the test. You will need to spend some time, however, revising specifically for the tests. You may find it helpful to revise with another member of your group, bouncing ideas and questions off each other. Your teachers or tutors may organize revision classes or seminars, which some students find particularly useful. Use the sample tests provided at the end of the mandatory units in the book to practise your test technique, timing yourself to make sure that you are working at the right pace. You are likely to find that there is plenty of time in which to answer all the questions on a test, so rule number one is don't rush!

Once you know the dates of your tests, it is a good idea to draw up a timetable, showing when you will be revising for particular unit tests.

On the day of the test itself, try not to get too worried so that you are able to perform to the best of your ability. Make sure you read each question very carefully before you attempt it and check all answers at the end of the test. If you intend to take a calculator in with you, make sure the batteries will last. Have a spare pencil and rubber with you as well. You shouldn't think of the test as a major hurdle that you have to clear; tests are just one part of the whole assessment process for your GNVQ. Good luck!

Continuous Assessment: The Portfolio

A separate chapter at the end of this book deals with the skills and evidence you need to present for 'the portfolio', with practical examples of student work and examiner comments.

The bulk of the assessments that you carry out on your GNVQ will fall into the category of *continuous assessment*. It can take many forms, including written assignments, projects, demonstrations, presentations and case studies. You will be given a mixture of assessments that will cover all of the elements of the GNVQ units you are studying. This is important, because you must show that you have met the required standard in every unit you are taking before you can be awarded the GNVQ.

An important feature of GNVQ courses is that you will be expected to take responsibility for your own learning and your own assessment. This doesn't mean that you will be setting and marking your own assignments! What it does mean is that your tutors will expect you to come up with good ideas and ways of tackling tasks. They will encourage you to look for information from many different sources, helping you to develop the vital skills that you will need in later life. You probably won't be sitting in classrooms for much of the time that you are studying for your GNVQ. You will often be 'learning by doing' with your tutors providing information, support and advice when needed.

The stages in continuous assessment

Although the exact nature of a piece of assessment work will vary between one school or college and another, there are a number of clearly defined stages that you will go through when carrying out continuous assessment, namely:

Stage 1: Receiving written and/or verbal instructions from your tutor about an assessment that will provide evidence to meet the requirements of a particular element or group of elements.

Stage 2: Discussing the practicalities of carrying out the work with your teacher or tutor and perhaps with other members of your group.

Stage 3: Devising an 'action plan' for the assessment, indicating time deadlines, tasks and sources of information.

Stage 4: Discussing the action plan with your teacher or tutor, who may suggest alterations or improvements to make your task easier.

Stage 5: Carrying out the assessment in line with your action plan.

Stage 6: Having your written and/or oral work checked by your tutor, who will either confirm that it is of the required standard or indicate that more needs to be done to reach the standard.

Stage 7: When completed, claiming credit from your teacher or tutor for the particular element or elements covered, and filing your evidence in your portfolio.

We look at these stages in the portfolio chapter of the book.

What counts as 'evidence'?

You will quickly learn that collecting and presenting evidence is a crucial part of your GNVQ course; in fact, if you are studying for your GNVQ on a full-time course, by the end of the two years you will have heard the term 'evidence' enough times to last you a lifetime! Most of the evidence that you collect will revolve around the assignments that your tutors give you from time to time, for the different units and elements of the GNVQ; e.g. reports, letters, projects and case studies. Evidence can come from a number of different sources, however, and can be concerned with many different activities, including:

- Questionnaire surveys
- Reports of observations
- Photographs, audio and video-tapes
- Computer-generated material
- Role playing
- Organizing an event or service
- Demonstrations and discussions
- Presentations and displays
- Tests set by your tutors
- Notes from lectures or classes
- Activities carried out on work experience
- Records of visits to business organizations
- References and certificates from previous work or study
- Log books and records of achievement

Again, the final chapter of this book will help you develop many of the skills required for the portfolio, giving examples of actual assessments and showing you what is required for a merit or distinction.

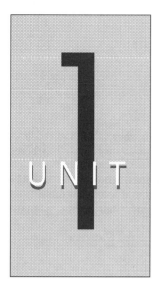

Business in the Economy

Getting Started

This unit provides an introduction to the subject of business and is the foundation on which all other units are based. In the UK there are over 2 million different organizations operating to satisfy the consumer's demand for goods and services. We will look at the different areas of the economy in which they work, and whether these organizations form part of the *private sector* – providing goods and services with the aim of making a profit – or part of the *public*

sector, having wider economic and social objectives. The unit also looks at the kind of economic system within which these organizations work, how prices are determined and the constraints the state imposes upon their freedom of action.

Some of the key terms used in this chapter are defined in the box below. An outline of the *types* of business organization is given in Unit 4 (pages 97 – 103).

Aggregate demand The total demand for goods and services.

Aggregate supply The total output within an economy

Central planning An economic system in which the state decides the three major economic questions – what to produce, how to produce it and how it should be distributed.

Deflation The process of reducing aggregate demand through monetary or fiscal measures.

Demand The quantity of a product that will be bought at different prices.

Fiscal policy Policies designed to change the level of economic activity through the government taxation and expenditure plans.

Free enterprise An economic system in which individuals or groups of individuals are free to undertake economic activity. The role of the state is minimal.

Inflation The process of rising prices.

Market A market's function is to enable the exchange of goods and services to take place. It may be a particular location where buying and selling takes place or, more generally, any way in which the process of exchange is carried out.

Mixed economy An economic system in which some central control is exercised over business and the economy but much is left to private enterprise.

Monetary policy Policies designed to control the supply and price of money in the economy

Monopolistic competition A form of imperfect competition where a large number of producers try to obtain some control over the price of their product by branding or differentiating it from other similar products.

Monopoly A situation in which there is only one producer for a product with no substitute available.

Oligopoly A form of imperfect competition in which the handful of firms that dominate the industry produce and advertise what are claimed to be highly differentiated products in an attempt to obtain brand loyalty and a larger share of the market. Advertising wars are often preferred to price competition.

Private sector The part of the economy which is not owned or controlled by the state

Profit The benefit or reward to owners of businesses in return for risk taking.

Public sector That part of the economy under the control of the state. It includes central and local government operations as well as quango's and public corporations. The term *quango* refers to a non-elected body which often controls large amounts of resources.

Public Sector Borrowing Requirement The amount of money a government has to borrow in order to finance its spending.

Supply In economics the amount that producers are willing to supply at different prices.

Supply side policies Policies designed to help markets work more effectively.

Essential Principles

Goods and services

The fundamental aim of any business is to provide individuals, or other organizations, with **products** which they need. These products may be either goods or services.

The term **goods** refers to tangible products which we can touch or see. Obvious examples include pens, paper, desks and chairs. The term may be divided into *consumption goods* – which will be used or consumed within a short time of purchase – or *consumer durables* where there is a benefit to the purchaser over a period of time. Television sets and cookers are good examples of consumer durables.

The term **services** refers to intangible products. We cannot see or touch intangible products yet they provide some satisfaction or benefit to us. In advanced economies many of the 'products' we buy are services. Thus public transport to and from work or college is one example. Equally car insurance, dental or medical check-ups, banking facilities and even the disco on Saturday night are services.

In practice, it is sometimes difficult to determine whether a 'product' is a good or a service because it has elements of *both*. Thus the mechanic who services your car for you primarily provides a service but, in so far as he has to fit new parts in order to make it roadworthy, is selling goods as well as that service.

The classification of business by economic activity

Traditionally the UK is seen as a manufacturing nation producing a wide range of goods for export as well as home consumption. In practice, manufacturing only forms one part of the UK economy and relies heavily on the output of the other sectors – primary and tertiary.

The primary sector
The **primary sector** has been given this name because it provides the raw materials on which, in some way, all the other sectors rely. It includes any activity which draws natural resources from the earth, for example, mining, forestry, fishing and food.

The secondary sector
The **secondary sector** transforms the raw materials into those finished products demanded by other industries and consumers. It includes the manufacturing, engineering, construction and processing industries as well as the utilities such as gas, water and electricity.

The tertiary (or service) sector
As economic activity has become more complex, firms have become increasingly reliant on other firms to provide specialist services. The **tertiary sector** activities include travel, transport and distribution, wholesaling and retailing, accountancy, law, banking and insurance as well as hotel, catering and leisure activities.

The tertiary sector also includes many of the activities which are undertaken by central and local government, including health, education, defence and public administration.

Did You Know ?

Over the last 25 years, the UK has lost over 4 million jobs in manufacturing. However, it has gained almost 3½ million jobs in services over the same time period.

Changes in economic activity

Fig. 1.1 illustrates the dramatic changes that have taken place in economic activity this century. We can see that the importance of both the primary and the secondary sectors has declined whilst, until recently, economic activity in the tertiary sector (as measured by employment) has been increasing. The experience of the UK is by no means unique, many other industrialized countries have experienced this trend.

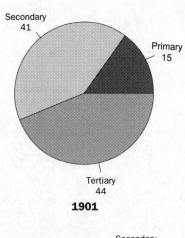

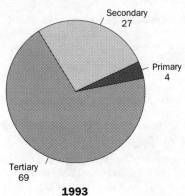

Fig. 1.1 Employment by sector

The decline of the secondary sector and the growth of the tertiary sector has been given the name – de-industrialization. The reasons for **de-industrialization** in developed economies include:

- The impact of technology allowing industry to scale down employment through the use of automation and robotics.
- The growth of manufacturing capacity in developing countries and the consequent increase in world competition, particularly from low cost countries.
- The rise in the incomes of consumers in developed countries which has meant that they are spending proportionately less on basic necessities such as food and clothing and more on service and leisure activities.

The purposes or objectives of business organizations

Businesses come into existence for many different reasons. Often the reason will be economic – that is, to make a profit. Some, though, will have been created so that an individual can pursue an interest or hobby. Others will have been created to provide employment, and perhaps security, for the owner and his family. Public sector organizations and charities will also have very different (and often) complex objectives. In this section we will look at some of the more common **objectives** of organizations.

Survival

At different times in their existence many organizations find that **survival** is the most important objective. Thus in the small firm sector nearly 60% of all firms will cease trading within three years of start-up, many because of financial problems. But financial problems don't only hit small firms. Many large firms will make losses rather than profits in a recessionary situation. They will try to survive by increasing productivity, cost cutting and drawing on reserves of profits from previous years. Survival of the firm may also be threatened by unwelcome predators wishing to take over that firm. In the longer term it is unlikely that a firm's sole objective will be merely survival.

Profitability

Economists would argue that the prime objective of many organizations is to **maximize profits**. In practice it is difficult to know when profits are being maximized and it is more likely that profit-making organizations seek to achieve a *satisfactory* level of profits. For example, many owners of small firms will restrict the size of their operations to avoid working excessively long hours, paying too much tax or employing more people than they can cope with.

Growth

Growth may be pursued as a specific objective by a firm or may arise haphazardly as a result of the firm coming across new and profitable ways of serving the customer. For many firms growth as an objective is an attractive option. It can diversify into new markets and new products and thereby reduce its reliance on one market/product. Managers and employees may feel that their jobs are more secure in a large, growing multi-product business.

Other objectives

So far we have considered the objectives that an organization will pursue in broadly economic terms. We have not considered the impact of different *interest groups* on the workings of the organization. There are many different groups who have an interest in the workings of the organization, such as managers, employees, customers and the local community. In practice we find that firms will often pursue a number of different objectives trying to satisfy the demands of *all* these different groups *subject to the condition that sufficient profits are being made to satisfy the owners/shareholders*. Thus managers may allocate themselves company cars or other fringe benefits; employees may be provided with above average working conditions, healthcare or sports facilities; and customers may be given helpline or other aftersales services.

Within an organization, the groups in control may vary over time, and so the objectives of that organization may vary. For example, in recession the accountants in a firm may have more influence at Board level, so that (say) *maintaining cash flow* may be a primary objective. However, during expansionary periods the marketing/promotional directors may have more influence, so that *growth* may be a primary objective. In other words, the firm's objectives may change through time, depending upon which interest groups have most influence at Board level.

> ### Did You Know ?
> Far fewer shares are now owned *directly* by individuals and far more *indirectly*, via membership of institutions such as Pension Funds, Insurance Companies and Unit Trusts. In 1963 these 3 institutions owned only 18% of all shares, with individuals owning 54%; by 1994 these 3 institutions owned over 58% of all shares, with individuals owning only 20%. Clearly it is the institutions which are now in a strong position to influence the policy objectives of many companies.

Public sector objectives

Government and the **local authorities** provide many services which we take for granted, for example health, housing and education. In providing these services they should ensure:

- The provision of a service which meets the needs of the community.
- The efficient use of the resources at their disposal.
- The meeting of specific targets, such as those laid down in a citizen or consumer charter for that industry (e.g. maximum waiting time for an outpatient, etc.)

Charities

Charities are neither part of the profit-making private sector nor part of the public sector. They are regulated by a Registrar of Charities who ensures that their objectives really are charitable and that dishonest people do not use the charity for their own purposes. Their objective will usually be directed towards improving the welfare of the group or groups for which the charity has been established, for example Age Concern; Child, Poverty Action Group; etc.

The demand for goods and services

We have already noted that the aim of the business organization is to provide people with the goods and services they desire. Precisely what people want or desire is dependent on many different factors such as:

- Where they live.
- What work they do.
- What their leisure interests are.

It will also depend upon the stage of development of the country in which they live. Thus in a subsistence or developing economy, where the standards of living are relatively low, the demands of individuals are likely to be concentrated on very basic items. These basic items, which are sometimes referred to as the 'necessities of life', include such things as food, clothing and shelter. By comparison, in the advanced economies of Western Europe the consumer's demands are likely to be far more varied and sophisticated.

From a business point of view the fact that individuals *want* certain goods or services is not sufficient for those items to be produced. People's wants are relatively unlimited. Unfortunately the *resources* – or money – that they have to satisfy these wants are limited and they must therefore *choose* how best to spend their limited resources. It is those wants (that is, the demand for goods and services) backed up by an ability to pay for them that business is interested in. We term those wants **effective demand**.

Opportunity cost

Because we only have limited resources available to satisfy our wants we have to make choices as to what we buy. In economics the real or **opportunity cost** of buying something is the next best purchase which we have sacrificed. A government, for example, may have a choice between building a new motorway, or a hospital. Firms may also have to choose between competing projects and even as students you may have to decide between buying a textbook or some wallposters for your bedroom or a new CD. In each case the next best option sacrificed – what you go without – is the real or opportunity cost to you.

The role of the market in meeting consumer demand

In a very basic society most of your wants would be satisfied through your own activity whilst the remainder would be obtained through barter (swaps). In a modern society this is not possible and we rely on organizations to provide these goods and services. The mechanism by which consumers and producers are brought together is the **market**. A market is said to exist in any situation where the individual decisions about the amount of a product demanded and supplied *interact* – that is, where buying and selling takes place. It is the interaction of these two forces which will determine the prices we pay and the quantity which firms supply.

The market mechanism is seen as important because:

- It enables consumers to spend money in the way they want.
- It tells the producer what the consumers will buy.
- Competition between producers ensures that goods are produced efficiently.

It is important to understand the principles which lie behind how supply and demand interact to determine prices so that we can analyse the impact of a change in market conditions on prices.

Demand

The term **demand** refers to the amount of a particular product which consumers are willing and able to buy at various prices. It is commonly shown by means of a **demand curve** (see Fig. 1.2). As we can see the demand curve is shown as downward sloping from left to right. In practice the vast majority of demand curves conform to this rule. The demand curve shows that as the price of the product falls the quantity purchased will rise. We can say that the quantity demanded is *inversely related* to the price of the product. This is because the product, when compared with others, becomes relatively more attractive as its price falls. The terms **expansion of demand** and **contraction of demand** are used to signify a change in quantity demanded as a result of a change in price. In other words we use expansion/contraction when we are *moving along* a given demand curve, when only the price changes.

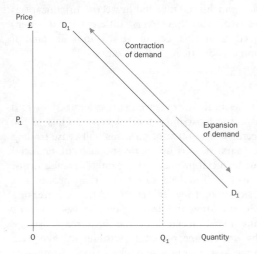

Fig. 1.2 A demand curve

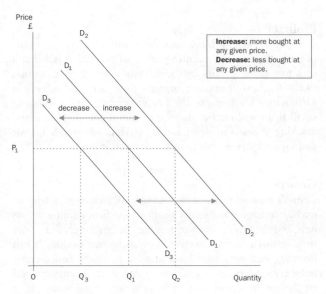

Fig. 1.3 A shift in demand

Sometimes, however, we find that the whole demand curve will *shift bodily* to the right or left of its existing position (Fig. 1.3). This is because factors *other than the price* of the product have changed. These factors are known as the determinants of demand. If the whole demand curve shifts to the right, more of the product is demanded at any price; we call this an **increase in demand**. If the whole demand curve shifts to the left, less is demanded at any price; we call this a **decrease in demand**.

The determinants of demand

A shift in the total demand curve will be caused by one or more of the following:

- *Changes in income.* As incomes rise the demand curve will normally shift to the right (increase) because consumers can now afford to buy more of the item at a given price than before. As incomes fall, demand will normally shift to the left (decrease).

- *Changes in consumer tastes.* Some products are very susceptible to changes in fashion, for example clothes or computer games. As particular clothes become fashionable we will see the demand curve shift to the right, (increase) indicating that more of that item will be bought at any particular price. Conversely as a computer game or other toy loses its appeal we will see the demand curve shifting bodily to the left (decrease).

Did You Know ?

Real expenditure on the product group 'Radio, T.V. and other durable entertainment goods' increased by over 220% between 1981 and 1994, whereas expenditures on 'newspapers and magazines' fell by 10% in real terms. These shifts in consumer tastes have important implications for the pattern of output and employment.

- *Changes in the price of substitute products.* Many products have close substitutes. A fall in the price of a substitute will result in consumers buying more of the now cheaper substitute and therefore less of the orginal product. The demand curve for the original product has moved bodily to the left (decrease). If the price of the substitute rises, the demand for the original product is likely to shift to the right (increase).

- *Changes in the price of complementary products.* Some products are *jointly demanded*; for example the demand for petrol, car insurance and Road Fund Tax arises as a result of the purchase of a car. Where goods are jointly demanded (i.e. are *complements*) a change in the price of one good will affect the demand for the other. Thus a rise in the price of insurance for sports cars may very well cause a decrease in the demand for those cars, that is, fewer sports cars will be bought at any given price (and vice versa).

- *Changes in the population structure.* Changes in the age structure or the size of the population may have a significant effect on the demand for certain goods and services. A fall in the birth rate and an increase in the number of elderly people will result in decreased demand for children's clothes and games but increased demand for retirement facilities.

- *Changes in technology.* The demand for certain products may fall as they are overtaken by other products serving the same purpose but using different technology. Thus the demand curve for cassettes has shifted to the left and sales have fallen as a result of the introduction of compact discs.

- *Changes in government policy.* The government, through varying the taxes on different classes of goods, can affect their demand. For example, if the Chancellor of the Exchequer decides to increase taxes on cigarettes or alcohol this may result in fewer of these items being demanded. Interestingly, if people *expect* these taxes to rise in the budget, expectations about future price rises may result in more than normal being demanded prior to the budget.

Elasticity of demand

Price Elasticity of Demand (PED)

PED for a product measures the responsiveness of demand for a product to changes in its *own* price. We are looking at the way demand expands or contracts as a result of price changes. In other words, with PED we are looking at *movements along* a demand curve. It is calculated as follows:

$$\text{PED} = \frac{\text{\% change in quantity demanded of product X}}{\text{\% change in price of product X}}$$

Strictly speaking, PED is usually a *negative* number, but it is conventional to ignore the negative sign.

PED falls into one of five categories. We may have a situation where:

PED = 0   If PED is *zero*, demand is perfectly inelastic. The quantity demanded is unaffected by any price change.

PED > 1   If PED is *greater than one*, demand is **price elastic**. Thus for any given change in price the percentage change in quantity will be greater. So, for example, if a supermarket faced with a PED of 2 reduced its prices by 5% it could expect its sales to expand by 10% (5% × 2).

PED < 1   If PED is *less than one* demand is **price inelastic**. A given percentage change in price results in a smaller percentage change in the quantity demanded. Thus if a cigarette manufacturer faced with a PED of 0.4 raised its prices by 10% sales would contract by only 4% (10% × 0.4).

PED = 1   If PED is *equal to one*, demand is **unit elastic**. A given percentage change in price results in exactly the same percentage change in the quantity demanded.

PED = Infinity   If PED is *infinity*, demand is **perfectly elastic**. A change in price results in an infinite change in the quantity demanded.

The value of PED is determined by a number of factors. These include:

- *The availability of substitutes.* Demand for a product is likely to be elastic where there are many close substitutes and relatively inelastic where few, if any, substitutes are available.

- *The amount of income spent on the item.* Where an item costs only a small amount and takes up an even smaller proportion of our total expenditure (for example, a box of matches) consumers are unlikely to spend much time searching for an alternative even if the price doubles! Such items are therefore relatively inelastic in demand.

- *Necessities.* Certain basic items such as food, clothing and shelter are likely to be purchased whatever the price. Demand is therefore inelastic.

- *Habit-forming products.* Goods such as alcohol and cigarettes are likely to be purchased in very much the same quantity even though the price rises. Thus demand is inelastic.

Price elasticity of demand and revenue

The **total revenue** of a firm is given by price × quantity. Thus, if I sell, at a price of £20 per unit, 10 units altogether, then my total revenue is £20 × 10 = £200. The total revenue can be shown as an *area* in Fig. 1.4: if at price OP_1 the firm sells quantity OQ_1, then area $OP_1V_1Q_1$ (height × base = area of rectangle) represents the total revenue.

Now a fall in price from OP_1 to OP_2 will affect the firm's total revenue. It will receive less ($OP_1 - OP_2$) on each of the original (OQ_1) units sold. On the other hand it will hope to sell more ($OQ_2 - OQ_1$) units at the lower price. The relationship between *revenue lost* and *revenue gained* will depend upon PED over the relevant range of the demand curve (V_1V_2).

- If PED > 1, then revenue gained > revenue lost. A price cut will *raise* total revenue (Fig. 1.4).
- If PED = 1, then revenue gained = revenue lost. A price cut will leave total revenue unchanged.
- If PED < 1, then revenue gained < revenue lost. A price cut will *reduce* total revenue (Fig. 1.5).

So, if the firm wants to raise total revenue, it should *cut* prices where PED > 1 (elastic) and *raise* prices where PED < 1 (inelastic).

Income Elasticity of Demand (YED)

YED for a product measures the responsiveness of demand for a product to changes in the income of consumers. It is calculated as:

$$YED = \frac{\% \text{ change in quantity demanded of product X}}{\% \text{ change in income}}$$

With YED we are looking at total *shifts* in the demand curve to the right or the left. Most goods will have a *positive* YED indicating that as incomes increase so does the quantity demanded. These are often termed **normal goods**. Where a rise in income is associated with a fall in demand YED is **negative**. Negative YED is most likely to occur with basic products, for example bread or inexpensive cuts of meat. Here, as incomes increase we are likely to buy less of the basic product (e.g. mince meat) and switch to more expensive items (e.g. steak). Products having a negative YED are sometimes termed **inferior goods**.

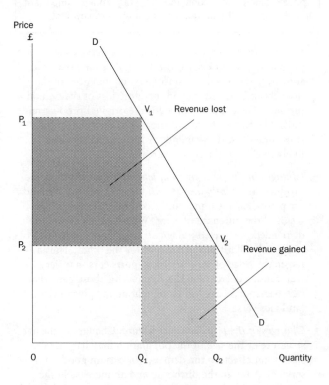

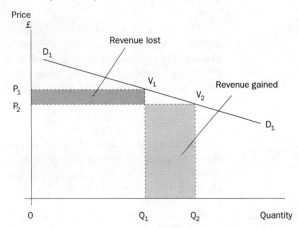

Fig. 1.4 A relatively elastic demand curve. A reduction in price will lead to a *rise* in total revenue.

Fig. 1.5 A relatively inelastic demand curve. A reduction in price will lead to a *fall* in total revenue.

Cross Elasticity of Demand (XED)

XED measures the responsiveness of demand for a product to changes in the prices of related products. It is calculated as:

$$XED = \frac{\text{\% change in quantity demanded of product X}}{\text{\% change in price of product Y}}$$

XED is associated with *shifts* in the demand curve to the right or left as changes in the price of one product influences the sales of another.

Where XED is *positive,* the two products are **substitutes** for each other. Thus a fall in the price of product Y causes a fall in the demand for product X as consumers switch purchases from X to Y.

Where XED is *negative* the two products are said to be **complementary** or dependent on one another. Thus a fall in the price of cars (and the subsequent increase in sales) will cause a rise in the demand for petrol, car insurance and other complementary products.

Self Check ✔ Element 1

1. Give three examples of activities which form part of these sectors:

	Primary	Secondary	Tertiary
(a)			
(b)			
(c)			

2. State three UK industries which are in decline:
   (a)
   (b)
   (c)

3. Give three examples of expanding (sunrise) industries:
   (a)
   (b)
   (c)

4. Describe the changes to the demand curve of each product in the following situations:
   (a) The price of compact discs is reduced.
   (b) Denim jeans are no longer fashionable.
   (c) Petrol, as a result of a rise in the price of cars.
   (d) Restaurant facilities, as a result of a reduction in unemployment.

5. If consumers become more sensitive to 'green' issues what is the likely effect on the demand curves for the following products:

	Demand shifts to the	
	right	left
(a) Fur coats		
(b) Unleaded petrol		
(c) Coal		
(d) Aerosol deodorants		

6. Calculate the elasticity of demand in the following situations. In each case state whether demand is elastic or inelastic:
   (a) When the price of apples rises from 25p to 30p the demand falls by 10%
   (b) When Dave's student grant was £1500 a year he spent £100 on clothes. His grant has been reduced to £1200 and he now spends £80 on clothes
   (c) An increase in the price of butter from 50p to 60p results in Ted buying 2 lb of margarine instead of 1 lb.

1.2. Government Influences on Business

Activities of business organizations do not take place in a vacuum. It is society which provides the inputs which the organization uses and accepts the output. It is society which provides these organizations with profitable opportunities and yet also puts constraints upon the way they can act. This situation, which the business organization faces, is often termed the **environment of business**. For purposes of analysis this environment is often subdivided into four major categories of influence, namely social, technological, economic and political. Our focus in this section is on the economic and political aspects of an organization's environment. The *government*, both central and local, can have an important impact on the economic and political environment within which the firm operates. However, before looking at the influence of government, we briefly consider the social and technological environment.

Social influences

We have already noted that demographic trends (e.g. falling birth rates and an increasingly ageing population) can provide opportunities for, and threats to, the activities of an organization. Equally, social attitudes may also have an important influence on the way an organization acts. These attitudes may be reflected in law (e.g. consumer or employee protection) or in social attitudes (e.g. Sunday trading or smoking in public places). As these attitudes are not constant, the successful firm will be monitoring its activities so as to ensure that 'they move with the times'.

Technological influences

In the last 20 years business has gone through a second industrial revolution based on the micro-chip and electronics. This has had an impact on all aspects of an organization's work, including product design, production processes, the product's technical features, the location of the business and its organizational structure. Successful firms are gaining a competitive advantage over their rivals by incorporating the new technology into all aspects of their work.

Economic systems

Countries, just like individuals, face the problem of scarce resources and choice. It is therefore necessary for each country to answer three questions.

- What is to be produced?
- How is it to be produced?
- Who receives the goods?

These questions can be answered in different ways which will broadly reflect the level of government involvement in decision making. At one extreme we have a free market system with very limited government intervention; at the other extreme we have a centrally planned system where the government takes a major role in decision making.

Free market system

In a **free market** or free enterprise system the government plays as little part as possible in economic decision making.

Instead decisions are left to the market and prices play an important part in the allocation of resources.

- WHAT goods and services are produced will depend on the *prices* people are willing to pay for them. High prices will attract the producer to this market; low prices will encourage him to look elsewhere for more profitable opportunities.
- HOW goods and services are produced will be influenced by *competition*. Competition ensures that goods and services are produced by the *most efficient* (least cost) means available so as to keep prices down. The producer can never be sure of our custom unless he is as efficient as the other producers.
- WHO gets the goods and services depends on who is willing and able to *pay* the price established in the market.

Advantages of free enterprise include:

- People can buy what they want.
- Resources are put to their best use.
- No government interference and costly administrative system.
- The market responds quickly to changes in consumer demand.
- Market forces stimulate competition and therefore efficiency.

Disadvantages of free enterprise include:

- Inequalities of power exist (e.g. monopoly) to the detriment of the consumer.
- Some products produced may be against the public interest.
- Socially desirable goods may not be produced in the right quantity.
- It is impossible to guarantee full employment, stable prices or economic growth.

The centrally planned system

At its most extreme the government in the **centrally planned** system controls the use of all resources and decides the method of production and the allocation of goods and services. It is commonly associated with the Soviet style economies which until recently characterized Eastern Europe.

Advantages of a centrally planned system include:

- Inequalities of power between individuals and firms are less likely to exist.
- More equal distribution of income and wealth.
- Resources used for the community's rather than the individual's benefit.

Disadvantages of the centrally planned system include:

- There is no consumer choice.
- State decisions may not be in the best interests of society.
- Central planning is bureacratic, complex and costly.
- Individual effort and enterprise are not encouraged in the absence of the profit motive.
- Black markets may develop where production is insufficient to satisfy demand.

The mixed economy

In practice the extremes described above are very rare. Most economies exhibit features of *both* the free market and the centrally planned systems – though obviously some come closer to being free enterprise or market economies than centrally planned (and vice versa). The UK and France are often cited as good examples of a **mixed** economy. In such countries many of the decisions relating to what should be produced and how it is to be produced and distributed are taken by the private sector. Yet, through the public sector, the state will intervene where it believes it to be necessary.

Did You Know ?

There is considerable variation in the role of government within the mixed economies. For example, in 1993 the state took 66% of national output in Sweden in tax and social security payments, 43% in the UK but only 32% in Japan, the USA and Switzerland.

One major way in which governments have intervened in the past is through the **nationalization** of important industries. By nationalization we are referring to a policy of taking industry assets into public ownership.

Major **advantages** claimed for nationalization are:

- Left in private hands the firms would not provide sufficient quantity of the product or service or at sufficient quality.
- Substantial cost saving could be obtained by running the industry as one large unit rather than as a number of smaller, and in some cases, competing units.
- Where one firm dominates an industry (a monopoly situation) it can exploit the consumer by charging very high prices. State control prevents this.
- Through state control of industry the government would have greater control over the level of economic activity in a country.

The **disadvantages** of nationalization are:

- Without competition there is greater likelihood of inefficiency.
- Government decisions may not be in the best interests of the industry
- Any losses are borne by the public.
- Government intervention may prevent efficient operation.
- Control may become bureaucratic.

Readers should note that the 'mix' between the public and private sectors may vary over time. For example, in the UK the size of the public sector has been severely cut since the Conservatives came to power in 1979. This has been achieved through a policy of **privatizing** nationalized industries (that is, returning the assets to the private sector) and **contracting out** (outside firms bidding for contracts alongside local authority departments for the right to provide services such as cleaning, catering or refuse disposal).

Did You Know ?

The privatisation programme in the UK has raised over £50 billion of revenue for the government since 1979.

Mixed economies have the advantage that important areas of economic policy are planned and weaker members of society are protected. However, they suffer from the disadvantage that government intervention may prevent individual choice and enterprise. In a mixed economy it is a matter of achieving the most appropriate *balance* between free enterprise and state intervention.

Areas of government intervention

You will find that there are many ways in which the government interferes with the workings of the market in the UK. For example, the state intervenes to provide services that would not normally be provided by the private sector, such as a system of justice, a police force or prisons. It also intervenes to provide goods and services where market provision left to itself may be inadequate – education and healthcare are good examples.

Obviously, it is impossible for us to consider all these different areas. Instead we will look at state intervention in order to manage the economy *as a whole* and then turn to look at how it has intervened in order to solve *specific* problems.

Management of the economy

There are four broad aims which the government is seeking to achieve through its management of the economy. They are:

- High level of employment.
- Low level of inflation.
- High level of economic growth.
- Satisfactory balance of payments and exchange rate.

To achieve these objectives the government has a number of *tools* at its disposal. We will look at each briefly before considering how they could be used to achieve government aims.

Fiscal policy

Fiscal policy involves government revenue and expenditure. Each year the government raises and spends large amounts of money. The money spent is raised through taxes and borrowing. By changing the amount of money it raises or spends from year to year the government can attempt to increase or decrease the level of **aggregate demand** in the economy (that is, the total demand for goods and services). These attempts are sometimes referred to as *demand side policies* or *Keynesian policies* (after the economist J.M. Keynes who first suggested that the budget could be used in this way). However, such policies are more commonly termed 'budgetary' or fiscal policy. Thus if the government wants to encourage a higher level of economic activity it could:

- **Reduce taxes.** In spending the extra money they now have individuals and businesses will increase the demand for goods and services.
- **Increase government spending.** This again will increase demand within the economy.

Should the government wish to encourage a higher level of economic activity it may very well spend *more* money than

it raises. This is known as a **budget deficit**. In this situation it has to obtain the difference by borrowing money, e.g. by selling government bills or bonds. The difference between government spending and revenue leads to a **Public Sector Borrowing Requirement**.

Should the government wish to dampen down economic activity it may spend *less* money than it raises. This is known as a **budget surplus** which arises where the government raises more taxes than it actually spends. It leads to a **Public Sector Debt Repayment**.

> ### Did You Know **?**
>
> In 1994 the Public Sector Borrowing Requirement (PSBR) reached over £40 billion, because government spending exceeded tax revenue. However, as recently as 1989 the government Public Sector Debt Repayment (PSDR) was as high as £15 billion, with tax revenue exceeding government spending.

Monetary policy

Monetary policy involves controlling the *amount* of money circulating in the economy or the *price* (rate of interest) at which it circulates. In this context money is far more than just the notes and coins (cash) in circulation. In the UK it is estimated that over 90% of the money supply consists of bank deposits. Monetary policy is seen as important today because it is believed there is a connection between the amount of money in the economy and inflation. The measures which may be taken to influence money supply include:

- **Interest rates.** Raising interest rates makes borrowing more expensive. Because people borrow less the supply of money in the economy is reduced.
- **Credit control.** By controlling the amount of credit which financial institutions can give or to whom the credit can be given, the money supply can be reduced.

Supply-side policies

The argument goes that when the government tries to encourage growth in the economy there are problems on the supply side which prevent businesses from expanding their output. **Supply-side policies** aim to shift the aggregate supply curve (i.e. the supply curve for *all* goods and services) to the right. As we see on pages 15–19 this will mean more output being provided at any given price. This is done through policies which are designed to encourage competition and to give individuals and businesses greater incentives to work and innovate. In the UK, during the last decade, the following measures have been taken:

- **Reducing taxation.** Taxes on individuals and businesses have been reduced in the expectation that this will encourage individuals to work harder and businesses to be more innovative because they can now keep more of the rewards of their effort.

- **Cutting state benefits.** So as to encourage the unemployed back to work.

- **Encouraging competition.** This has been done in a number of ways such as privatization, contracting out, deregulation of markets and the expansion of the small firm sector. The development of the Single European Market within the European Union is also designed to encourage greater competition.

- **Encouraging training.** To create a better trained and more efficient workforce. For example the government has introduced a number of different educational and training initiatives – one of which is GNVQ!

- **Controlling trade unions.** It has been argued that in the 1980s unions had too much power and were able to stop firms from running their businesses in the most efficient way. Legislation has therefore been introduced to limit the unions' right to take industrial action.

- **Increasing share ownership.** Through privatization and other schemes the government has tried to encourage wider share ownership in the belief that this will make people more aware of, and committed to, the needs of business.

We must now consider how the *tools* or *policy instruments* described above may be used to achieve the *aims* of government economic policy.

Inflation

Fiscal policies to control the level of inflation would centre around reducing aggregate demand. Thus taxes could be raised or state expenditure reduced. Monetary policies to reduce aggregate demand would involve cutting the money supply and raising interest rates to deter borrowing by the public sector.

In the past direct intervention through the use of *prices and incomes policies* has also been used. Here both price and wage increases are pegged to an agreed level or frozen altogether. However, such policies are difficult to enforce except in the public sector and have fallen into disrepute.

Employment

To reduce unemployment through the use of *fiscal policy* the government would aim to increase aggregate demand by reducing taxes, raising public spending and generally aiding business through a system of investment and other incentives. *Protectionist policies* designed to reduce imports and encourage exports could also be used in extreme situations (note that there is always the possibility of retaliation by other countries).

Monetary policy would try to reduce unemployment through increased money supply and lower interest rates. This would have the effect of encouraging borrowing, spending and investment on the part of both individuals and businesses.

Supply side policies could also be used if it is believed that the unemployment is caused by labour market imperfections. Policies used could include controlling union power, devising new training schemes or reducing the real value of state benefits.

Economic growth

To encourage growth, *fiscal policy* would be used in much the same way as for unemployment. By running a budget deficit – reducing taxes and increasing expenditure – a higher level of economic activity can be encouraged.

Aggregate demand can also be increased through *monetary policy,* via raising money supply and lowering interest rates. Lower interest rates will encourage greater borrowing and spending by both individuals and businesses.

Balance of payments

A **balance of payments** problem exists when a country persistently, over a period of time, imports more than it exports. Initially, the policy normally adopted is *deflation.* A series of measures, both monetary and fiscal, is introduced to reduce the level of aggregate demand. These measures may include increasing taxation, reducing public expenditure and raising interest rates.

An alternative measure taken in extreme situations is to *devalue* the currency. Devaluation occurs when the value of the domestic currency is reduced in terms of other currencies. Devaluation aims to :

- Reduce imports by making them more expensive at home.
- Increase exports by making them cheaper abroad.

There are also certain *protectionist measures* which a country may try to solve its balance of payments problems. These include the use of tariffs, quotas and voluntary export restraints. Another option is to prevent capital leaving the country.

Did You Know ?

On only 6 occasions throughout the whole period from 1816 to 1994 has the UK trade in *visible* (tangible) goods been in surplus; i.e. exports greater than imports.

It should be evident from what has been said above that, in practice, it is very difficult for any government to achieve all four policy goals at the same time. This is because the means of achieving two or more policy goals may *conflict.* For example, to achieve a low level of inflation it may be necessary to reduce aggregate demand. Yet this will have the effect of making unemployment worse. In the above situation the present government has chosen to make the control of inflation its primary target.

The conflict in policy objectives has been characterized by a **stop-go cycle.** Thus, in a period of rising demand, inflation would increase and balance of payments problems would arise. To counter this the government would reduce the level of aggregate demand through monetary and fiscal policies. This in turn often led to a period of high unemployment. Eventually public pressure for higher levels of employment would lead to a reversal of the policy measures and a period of rising demand (see Fig. 1.6).

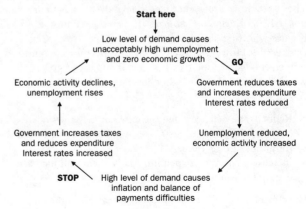

Fig. 1.6 The business cycle and economic policy.

Competition policy

The state is keen to encourage **competition** because of its effect on prices, quality, efficiency and innovation. Yet firms may seek to avoid the impact of, and problems caused by, competition. For example, firms may merge rather than compete. They may make secret agreements on prices and output with their competitors. Alternatively they may restrict supplies to those retailers who are unwilling to maintain pre-set prices. In circumstances such as these the government will step in to protect the public interest.

However, whilst competition in all sectors is the aim of the government, its approach to the problem of monopolies and mergers has been relatively practical. To enforce rigid standards as to when monopoly situations or mergers will not be allowed may deny firms the benefits of economies of scale where no abuse of the public interest exists. The standards which have therefore been used in monopoly and merger situations involve examining:

- The market structure.
- The conduct of individual producers in that market.
- The efficiency of these firms and the whole industry.
- Seeing whether the public interest is threatened.

Under the **Fair Trading Act**, where the **Director General of Fair Trading** believes that intervention is necessary he may refer the suspect monopoly or merger situations to the **Monopolies and Mergers Commission (MMC)** for investigation. He can do this where:

- a monopoly has 25% of the market (note that *local* monopolies may be referred as well);
- a merger will mean that the merged firms now have control of 33% of the market or where the merger involves the taking over of more than £5 million in assets.

The government's attitude to **anti-competitive practices** has been harsher. Collective resale price maintenance (the firm enforcing pre-set prices) was abolished by the Resale Prices Act. This has prevented a group of manufacturers from withholding supplies in an attempt to force retailers to maintain list prices.

Competition policy in the European Union

European Union competition law applies to trade between member states, and overrules national law. There are three broad categories:

- Articles 92–94 of the Treaty of Rome forbids governments to give aid to firms or industries which could distort competition.
- Article 85 bans restrictive practices which allocate markets, limit output or determine prices.
- Article 86 bans abuse of a dominant position. A dominant position will exist if a large firm uses its position to impose unfair terms on suppliers, retailers, competitors or consumers.

Restrictive practices

Restrictive trade practices, that is, any agreements amongst producers regarding prices, output or conditions of sale, have to be *registered* with the Director General of Fair Trading. The **Restrictive Trade Practices Act (1956)** states

that there is a presumption, with all these agreements, that they are against the public interest and therefore illegal. For the agreement to be upheld as being in the public interest the companies wishing to rely on that agreement had to *show* that it had beneficial effects in areas such as employment, exports, research or physical injury.

Under the **Competition Act (1980)** the Director General and the Office of Fair Trading also have the power to investigate and rule on any other anti-competitive practice, such as price discrimination or predatory pricing (selling below cost).

Did You Know ?

Between 1956 and 1994 around 10,000 restrictive agreements have been registered. Most of these have been *voluntarily* dropped, without going to the court. Few companies thought they could win. As well as satisfying *at least one* of eight specific ('gateway') conditions, e.g. protect against injury, prevent local unemployment, etc, the company would also have to demonstrate that the *overall* benefits from the restrictive practice were clearly greater than the costs incurred.

Consumer protection

This is another example of how the state intervenes in the workings of the market. Until this century the attitude of the law to consumer protection could best be summed up by the Latin phrase *caveat emptor*. Translated this means *let the buyer beware*. The assumption was that the parties to a contract were of equal bargaining power. That was not the case then and is not the case now. Quite apart from the problem of imbalance of bargaining power at the time of the contract, consumer protection is also necessary because faults in many products are not obvious at the time of sale and also many consumers don't know their legal rights or how to obtain redress.

As a result, this century has seen the growth of law designed to protect the consumer over the various stages from the initial advertising of the product to the terms on which they contract, including the provision of credit.

Trades descriptions and advertising

It is a criminal offence under the **Trades Descriptions Acts 1968 and 1972** for a trader to give false or misleading descriptions about goods or services on offer. This includes false statements about prices and particularly about price reductions.

The **Advertising Standards Authority** also seeks to enforce a code of practice on all advertisers ensuring that advertisements are legal, decent, honest and truthful.

Contractual terms

Under legislation relating to the sale of goods or services a number of terms are implied into a consumer contract regardless of the wishes of the parties to that contract.

Where there is a **sale of goods** the terms include:

- The goods should correspond with their description.
- The goods should be of merchantable quality.
- The goods should be fit for any purpose the supplier specifies.

Where there is a **contract for services** the terms include:

- The supplier of a *service* will carry out that work with reasonable care and skill.
- That where *goods* are supplied under a service contract the supplier is under a duty to see that they are of merchantable quality and fit for a particular purpose.

Whether the contract is for the sale of goods or services there is also legislation which prevents the seller from excluding liability for any of the points mentioned above.

Consumer credit

The Act is very complex but seeks to ensure that there is *truth in lending.* The Act covers any credit agreement where the borrowing is less than £15,000. It insists that all credit brokers must be registered and that the true cost of borrowing is always stated.

Taking action

In many situations, the supplier of goods or services is only too keen to remedy a problem situation. However, at times it will be necessary to take the matter further. There are several possibilities:

- Trade associations: these sometimes run schemes to help the consumer. However, such schemes are voluntary and the standards laid down by the trade association do not have the force of law.
- The media: consumer problems are the subject of many radio and television programmes. Many firms will go to extreme lengths to avoid trial by mass media.
- Small Claims Courts: if claims do not exceed £1000 a special procedure exists within the County Court. As lawyer's fees are not allowed and many of the normal rules in court are waived (forgone) this is an inexpensive and simple way of obtaining satisfaction. Details of the scheme are available from the County Court or from any consumer advisory body.

Regional policy

For most of this century there have been **regions** of the UK that have experienced far less economic prosperity than other regions. This variation in prosperity can be measured in many ways, for example *regional income per capita* (the average income of an individual in that region) or *regional growth rates*. However, the most common method is to look at *regional unemployment levels*. In most cases the reason for excessively high regional unemployment lies in past over-reliance by a particular region on a specific industry which has now gone into decline; for example shipbuilding on Tyneside, the cotton industry in Lancashire or more recently the coal industry in Lancashire, Wales, Scotland and other regions.

This situation of regional imbalance has occurred in many other countries apart from the UK and most governments have felt it necessary to intervene to remedy the situation. In the UK attempts to address the problem of regional unemployment were first introduced in the 1930s, but despite all attempts the regional problem is still with us today.

There are two broad approaches to the problem.

'Take the workers to the work'

Thus when coal mines in Durham were closed down the miners were offered alternative work in the Yorkshire and Midlands pits. At the present time the government encourages this mobility of labour through retraining, travel and resettlement grants. However, attempts to uproot people and get them to move to a different area have never been particularly successful as community and social ties are so strong. The policy has also been criticized as doing nothing to regenerate employment and prosperity in the depressed area.

'Take work to the workers'

For the reasons above the emphasis in most government's regional policies has been to 'take work to the workers'. In the UK a number of areas have been identified as needing assistance. These have been designated **development areas** or **assisted areas** (see Fig. 1.7). Various incentives are available to firms setting up in these areas, the greater incentives being made available to firms in the 'more needy' development areas. Thus there are grants for new investment projects and for each new job created. Grants are also available for the retraining of new employees.

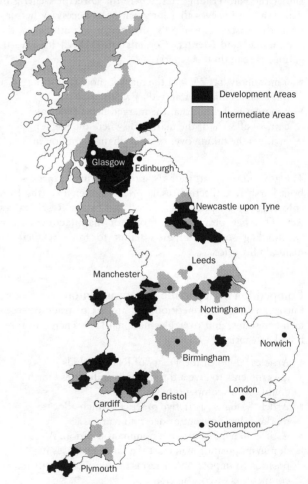

Fig. 1.7   UK assisted areas

It is difficult to assess the success of UK regional policy. The employment and prosperity imbalance between regions still exists. Yet there is also no doubt that it has created many new jobs in these regions and protected even more. However, the policy has been costly – estimates range from

£10,000 to £35,000 for each new job created. This is because much of the new investment was capital intensive and thus expensive in terms of grants but generated only a handful of jobs. Finally much of the investment has been proved to be highly marginal in recessionary periods as parent companies cut back on output, closing even modern regional plants.

Did You Know ?

In the recent recession, the South East region for the first time in 1992 had a higher unemployment percentage than the North West or the Midlands! The latest recession has hit jobs in the service sector even harder than those in the manufacturing sector.

International trade

Without trade the UK, like many other nations, would not be able to enjoy its present standard of living. Without imports from other countries the UK would not have the raw materials on which industry is dependent or the foodstuffs to feed its people. Nor, without exports, would we have the money to pay for these imports. Trade will benefit all countries in the same way.

International trade provides us with those goods which we cannot produce ourselves or choose not to produce ourselves. Trade also expands the size of the market in which we can sell our goods. More importantly trade allows us to concentrate our resources on making what we are best at. The surplus to our own requirements is sold overseas and provides us with the money to buy those goods which other countries produce more cheaply than we can ourselves. Without trade we would have to divert resources to producing goods which we could obtain more cheaply through trade! Thus the prosperity of all industrialized nations depends on free multilateral trade and specialization (in producing those products in which we have an advantage compared with other countries).

Yet despite the obvious benefits of international trade, countries, from time to time, have intervened to limit or change the pattern of trade. Such a policy is termed **protectionist** and the reasons why it may be introduced are:

- It is a means of protecting *infant industries* who, because they are newly established, cannot compete effectively with the older established, lower cost industries from abroad.
- To enable certain industries to exist which may have a *strategic significance*. For example steel is the basis of so many other products that a government may decide that the country needs to have its own steel industry. Only protection may permit such a strategic industry to exist.
- To prevent *dumping*. Surplus goods from one country may be dumped in another country below cost. Dumping has the effect of maintaining the price in the home market but of damaging the industry in the export market.
- To prevent *unfair competition*. This may arise as a result of another state subsidising exports. Developing countries may do this in order to obtain foreign exchange.
- Restrictions on trade may also be introduced in an attempt to *reduce unemployment* generally or in a

specific industry. Thus during the Great Depression of the 1930s world trade was reduced by 67% within four years as a result of 'beggar my neighbour' policies.
- Where a country has *balance of payments problems* resulting from importing too much, restrictions may be placed on the inflow of goods.

Did You Know ?

Trade can be restricted in a number of ways. Tariffs (a tax imposed on imports) and quotas (a quantitative limit on imports) are the two most important. More recently the European Commission has drawn attention to the growing use of administrative barriers. These may take the form of slow customs procedures, the retesting of imports, the deposit of bonds (to be used to cover claims against those goods) and establishing standards different from those used elsewhere.

General Agreement on Tariffs and Trade (GATT)

The experience of the 1930s when international trade was so reduced by protectionist policies prompted the developed countries to set up GATT after the Second World War. It now has over 115 members who, between them, account for 90% of all world trade. The aim of GATT is to promote free multilateral (many country) trade. Members accept:

- They should not discriminate against one another; in other words benefits extended to one country should extend to *all* countries.
- Where protection is necessary it should be by tariff so that the extent of the protection can be seen.
- Further liberalization of trade should be encouraged.
- Developing countries are entitled to a measure of protection until their economies grow stronger.

Members of GATT recognize that trade liberalization is a long-term goal. Since it was set up in 1947 seven **rounds** of negotiations have been ended successfully. The recently concluded eighth set of negotiations – the **Uruguay round** – has been concerned with the reduction of agricultural subsidies and the liberalization of the trade in services.

The European Union (EU)

This was initially known as the European Economic Community (EEC) when it was set up in 1956. The UK joined in 1973. There are now 12 member states:

Belgium	UK
Denmark	France
Germany	Greece
Ireland	Italy
Luxembourg	Netherlands
Portugal	Spain

There are also a number of other countries who may join shortly. These include Austria, Cyprus, Finland, Iceland, Malta, Norway, Sweden, Switzerland and Turkey. The aim of the EU is the creation of a **single market** free from tariff barriers and in which:

- Member states can trade without restriction.
- Free movement of EU nationals is allowed.
- Competitive practices are encouraged
- A common external tariff is applied to imports from non-member states.

In the longer term the EU has as its objective political union between its members. In joining the EU the UK has implicitly accepted a loss of sovereignty. By this we mean that the UK is no longer able to decide policy unilaterally (on its own). Laws that are passed by the EU take precedence over UK legislation where the two conflict. In the past two decades there have been many instances where the UK government has felt that EU policies have discriminated unfairly against the UK or been against our interests. For example in 1984 the UK, despite being one of the poorest members of the community, was required to contribute 20% of the total community budget (this was eventually renegotiated to give the UK a 66% rebate). However, in other situations we have not been so fortunate.

The EU has numerous policies which affect businesses within the Union. We will look at just four.

1. *The Common Agricultural Policy (CAP)*

   At the heart of CAP is a price support scheme which is designed to give farmers a reasonable standard of living. The support scheme requires the Union to set a guaranteed minimum price for all agricultural products and to purchase anything the farmer produces at this price. Whilst it is open for the farmer to sell on the world market, in practice the higher guaranteed price of the CAP has meant that farmers almost always opt to sell to the EU. As a result, the cost of the price support system has been extremely high and we have seen the growth of vast surpluses of foodstuffs. It is estimated that each house-holder pays an extra £14 a week in food prices because of this support scheme.

   CAP was one of the main stumbling blocks in the present round of GATT negotiations. Modest amendments have been made as too speedy an introduction of CAP reforms would have a major economic impact on agricultural and related businesses and could even bring about political crises in some countries more dependent on agriculture than the UK.

2. *Regional development*

   We have already noted that many countries have areas of higher than average regional unemployment. The **European Regional Development Fund** provides money to relieve unemployment and encourage development projects in these less prosperous parts of the EU. The retraining of workers in these areas may also be supported by the **European Social Fund**. Additional finance, at attractive interest rates, may be offered to firms setting up in these areas.

3. *The Social Chapter*

   At the end of 1992 all EU members signed the **Maastricht Treaty**. One part of this treaty was an attempt to harmonize working conditions throughout the EU and give workers certain basic rights. This was termed the **Social Chapter**. These rights included:

   - A minimum wage.
   - A maximum working week of 48 hours.
   - A minimum of four weeks paid holiday a year.
   - The right to proper training.
   - Young worker protection.

The UK obtained an opt-out to this particular part of the treaty because it objected on principle to working conditions being determined by the EU and feared that it would increase businesses' labour costs.

4. *The Single Market*

   The Single Market came into existence at the end of 1992. This was designed to speed up the removal of the existing non-tariff barriers within the EU, establish common technical standards, enhance the free movement of labour and get rid of the remaining controls on the movement of capital.

   Obviously it is difficult to say what the effect of these measures will be. However, supporters claim:

   - They will reduce costs and increase competition and thereby lower prices.
   - Although profit margins of businesses may be squeezed, output is likely to increase (consumers' extra spending power) and thereby offset the loss of profitability.
   - The standards of living for individuals will be improved as a result of lower prices and greater choice.
   - The restructuring of industry will generate an extra 1.3 to 2.3 million jobs within the EU.
   - Individual governments will lose more sovereignty through the harmonization of laws. Moreover, the ability of individual governments to control the national economy through the use of monetary and fiscal policy will be more limited.

Self Check ✔   Element 2

7. The following characteristics are used to distinguish between different types of economic system. Complete the table:

	Market Economy	Planned Economy	Mixed Economy
Role of the state	Minimal		
Right to own and dispose of resources			Yes, subject to some control by state
Existence of profit motive		No	
Allocation of resources through price mechanism			Not always

8. In terms of the characteristics mentioned above state which category of economic system the following countries fall into:

	Market	Planned	Mixed
Cuba			
United Kingdom			
Hong Kong			
France			
China			

Self Check ✔ continued

9. List the major aims of government economic policy:
   (a)
   (b)
   (c)
   (d)

10. Why is it impossible to achieve all these aims at the same time?
   _____
   _____
   _____

11. If a government wished to reduce the level of inflation
   (a) What fiscal measures could it use?_____
   _____
   (b) What monetary measures could it use? _____
   _____

12. Explain the term *supply-side* policy and give two examples of supply side measures.
   _____
   _____
   _____

13. Briefly explain the importance of the following Acts:
   (a) Fair Trading Act _____
   _____
   (b) Restrictive Trade Practices Act_____
   _____
   (c) Competition Act _____
   _____

14. Give three reasons why countries may wish to adopt a protectionist policy:
   (a)
   (b)
   (c)

15. Explain what is meant by a *beggar my neighbour policy.*
   _____
   _____

16. What is the aim of GATT?
   _____
   _____

17. List six members of the European Union: _____
   _____

18. In relation to the European Union explain the term *loss of sovereignty.*
   _____
   _____
   _____

1.3. The Supply of Goods and Services by Business

The supply of goods and services

We have already noted the diversity in the demand for goods and services. The aim of this section is to examine the way in which **suppliers** respond to these demands. In practice the supplier will try to *anticipate* these demands, or changes in demand, and thus by comparing likely costs and prices of supply will seek to maximize profits (or minimize losses).

Some of the information necessary to make these decisions is already held *internally* by the firm. For example it has:

- *Information on past performance*
  sales, costs, profits
  market share
  product life cycle

- *Information on current market position*
  sales, costs, profits
  level of competition
  level of customer satisfaction
  potential substitutes and new products

- *Information on which to estimate future trends*
  sales forecasts
  future production costs
  new competitors
  changing socio-legal factors
  new technology

Other information will be *external* to the firm. The sources of such information include:

- *Governmental*
  Most advanced nations produce a wide variety of statistics on items such as:
      the domestic economy
      markets and market trends
      social trends

- *International*
  Many supra-national bodies such as the European Union (EU), the International Monetary Fund (IMF) and the Organization for Economic Co-operation and Development (OECD) provide data on:
      the world economy
      international trade
      market surveys

- *Trade associations*
  Many firms in well developed markets belong to trade associations. These organizations exist to provide a service for all their members. One such service will be to provide information on:
      the size of the market
      market trends
      potential new markets
      potential new products or new product modifications
      the degree of competition

As we have already noted all these sources of information will be evaluated for their impact on costs, output and prices. From this information the organization will be able to predict the potential:

- *Unit cost of production* $\dfrac{\text{costs}}{\text{output}}$

- *Total revenue*   price × output

- *Profit per unit*   price – unit cost of production

- *Profitability*   total revenue – total costs

Supply

Supply can be defined as the total quantity of a product which the suppliers will produce for sale at a given price. As a general rule we can say that as price rises so does supply. This is because the price rise encourages existing producers to supply more by raising profit per unit and the price rise also encourages new, less efficient, producers (who are *now* able to make a profit) to enter the market. Furthermore producers will now find other products less attractive to produce as a result of this particular product price increase. They will therefore switch resources away from these now less attractive substitute products to the product whose price has risen.

Conversely, should prices fall, suppliers will tend to reduce supply. This is because it is now more attractive for existing firms to produce other goods, inefficient firms will leave the market and even efficient firms will make less profit. Figure 1.8 shows a typical supply curve. *Movements along* this curve caused by changes in price are described as **contractions of supply** or **expansions of supply**.

Just as with the demand curve we find that the supply curve may *shift* its position so that more or less than before is supplied at a given price. The reason for the shift in the supply curve is that one or more of the determinants of supply has changed. If the supply curve shifts to the right, more of the product is supplied at any particular price; we call this an **increase in supply**. If the supply curve shifts to the left, less of the product is supplied at any price; we call this a **decrease in supply**.

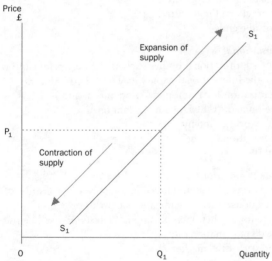

Fig. 1.8   A supply curve

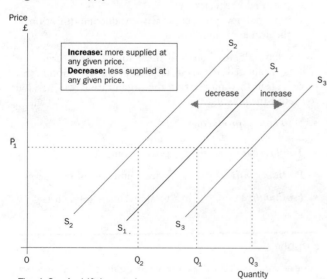

Fig. 1.9   A shift in supply

The determinants of supply

- *Changes in the price of production inputs.* A change in the costs of production, for example an increase in the cost of labour will result in a shift in the supply curve. In the case of higher labour costs the supply curve will shift to the left (decrease) indicating that the firm is willing to supply less output at any price now – see Fig. 1.9 Conversely should the cost of raw materials fall then the supply curve would shift to the right (increase) with more now supplied at any given price.

- *Changes in the price of other goods.* Where goods are jointly supplied, that is, where the production of one is a by-product of another, (for example beef and leather) then an expansion in the supply of beef as a result of a rise in its price will also cause a *shift* in the supply curve of leather to the right (increase).

- *Technological changes.* Where changes in technology lead to better production methods and lower costs for each unit of output then a larger quantity will be supplied at each price. The supply curve has shifted to the right (increase).

- *Changes in taxation or subsidies.* The imposition of a *tax* on a product has the same effect as an increase in the cost of labour or raw materials – it causes the supply curve to shift to the left (decrease). Equally, a *subsidy* for this particular product reduces costs and therefore shifts the supply curve to the right (increase).

> ### Did You Know ?
>
> The impact of technical change can be clearly seen in the manufacture of microchips. Over 1 million components (and therefore computer functions) can now be etched onto a single microchip, cutting the cost per component to less than 0.01% of what it was only 10 years ago. Effectively this is a major shift to the right (increase) in the supply curve for microchips.

Price Elasticity of Supply (PES)

PES measures the responsiveness of supply to changes in price. It is calculated thus:

$$PES = \frac{\%\text{ change in quantity supplied of product X}}{\%\text{ change in price of product X}}$$

PES will fall into one of five categories :

PES = 0	Supply is **perfectly inelastic**. The quantity supplied is unaffected by any price change.
PES < 1	Supply is **inelastic** with a change in price causing a *less than* proportionate change in supply.
PES > 1	Supply is **elastic** with a change in price causing a *more than* proportionate change in supply.
PES = 1	Supply is **unit elastic**. A change in price will cause an *exactly proportionate* change in supply.
PES = Infinity	Supply is **perfectly elastic**. A change in price leads to an infinite change in the quantity supplied

The value of PES is determined by:

- *The time period.* In the short term supply tends to be inelastic because firms find it difficult to respond quickly to any change in price. When the time period is extended, supply becomes more elastic as the producer can switch resources to produce more (if the price rises) of the product, perhaps making use of spare capacity by overtime working or working an extra shift. In the long term supply can adjust more adequately to changes in price with changes in capacity, perhaps by building a new plant or leasing or renting new premises.

- *Mobility of factors of production.* The more mobile are the factors of production (e.g. land, labour, capital) in switching into, or out of, a particular industry, the more elastic (responsive) will supply of the product be to any change in its price (and vice versa).

- *Barriers to entry.* Supply will tend to be inelastic where *new firms* find it difficult to enter the industry, for example because of high capital costs.

Price determination

So far we have looked at supply and demand *separately*. Now, in order to see how **prices** are determined in a free market we need to put them together. The market price for a product is where the quantity demanded is exactly the same as the quantity supplied. In Fig. 1.10 supply and demand intersect at price OP_1. This is known as the **equilibrium price** because the market has been cleared and there is no reason why the price should move from this point. However, let us look at prices OP_2 and OP_3. If we set a price of OP_2 we can see that at this high price supply is greater than demand (excess supply). Put another way, demand is insufficient to clear the market and the excess supply can only be disposed of by reducing the price. How far will prices fall? They will fall to the point (P_1) where supply and demand coincide for, as we have already pointed out, that is the price at which the market is cleared. Note that it is price which acts as a *signal* to producers and consumers in the market to restore equilibrium. As price falls from P_2 to P_1, *supply contracts* as producers find it less profitable to produce this product and *demand expands*, until price P_1 and quantity Q_1 is reached.

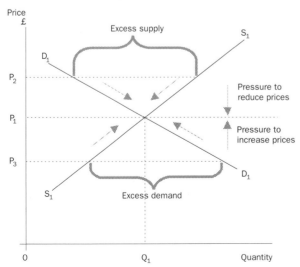

Fig. 1.10   The equilibrium price and quantity.

Conversely, if we set a price OP_3 we have a situation where demand far exceeds supply (excess demand). There will be people who are willing to pay far more than the current price. In effect what happens is that they bid the price up, and as they do so suppliers find it profitable to sell more than previously so that supply expands. Consumers wish to buy less at the higher price, so that demand contracts. The process of adjustment will continue until we reach price OP_1 – the equilibrium price – and quantity OQ_1.

Changes to the equilibrium price

Movements from the equilibrium price that we have talked about above will only arise should one or more of the **determinants** of supply or demand change. For example, let us assume that the Chancellor of the Exchequer decides to impose an additional tax on cigarettes. Producers *would like* to raise the price of their product by the amount of the tax, so that they still receive the same as before having paid this tax to the government. This will have the effect of shifting the whole supply curve upwards by the amount of the tax and to the left, so that less is supplied at any price. The effect, as can be seen from Fig 1.11, is that we have a new higher equilibrium price OP_2 at which a slightly lower quantity is demanded (and supplied). Of course the tax increase that we have talked about could just as easily have been an increase in any of the costs of production.

Note here that the rise in price is less than the tax. How much of any extra tax (or cost) can be passed on to consumers will depend upon the price elasticity of demand (PED). The *less elastic* the demand, the more of any tax (or cost) that can be passed on.

Fig. 1.11   The impact of a shift in the supply curve on equilibrium price and quantity.

The implications of price changes

Price changes affect the overall profitability of the firms and therefore their willingness to compete in a particular market. We can distinguish two situations – a situation of *falling* prices or a situation of *rising* prices.

Falling prices

In the short term the firm will accept the lower prices and profitability. Indeed it will even continue producing in a loss making situation as long as prices cover its variable costs and make some contribution to fixed costs. It will be able to continue in this situation until the time comes for it to renew some of its capital equipment. In the longer term the firm has a number of options. These include:

- Ceasing production.
- Merging with other firms, thus reducing overcapacity in the industry.
- Aggressive price cutting designed to increase customer base and persuade other producers to quit this market. At a later stage prices may be raised.
- Finding new markets where competition isn't so intense and prices are higher.
- Diversifying into the production of other products.

Rising prices

In the short term rising prices, caused by increased demand, will result in increased profitability for the existing producers. Some consumers may attempt to find substitutes as a result of these higher prices. If they are successful in this, the demand curve will shift to the left and prices will fall. However, increased profits may be used to finance advertising that is designed to increase brand loyalty and stop the demand curve shifting to the left.

In the longer term the increased profitability is likely to attract new entrants to the industry, shifting supply to the right and thus driving prices down again.

So far we have looked at rising prices caused by increased demand. If the cause is decreased supply via higher costs, then profitability may not have increased. Here a leftward shift in supply will raise equilibrium price but reduce equilibrium output.

> **Did You Know ?**
>
> Since 1900 the *average* price of a product has risen and costs over 40 times as much today as it did then. However there have been interesting changes in *relative* prices. For example, the price of the cheapest Ford car is lower today, *compared to other prices*, than it was in 1900. What has happened here is that although there has been a huge *increase in the demand* for car ownership, mass-production techniques have so *increased the supply* of such cars that their *real price* has actually fallen. Can you think of other products where this has happened?

Prices and competition

Through the interaction of supply and demand we see how the market price for a product is determined. The assumption behind all this is that the market is free or competitive. Many small businesses find that they are unable to manipulate the prices being charged in their market. We would call them **price takers**. For example, a company producing a can of baked beans has little opportunity to set its prices because of all the competition from other firms. However, other firms *do* have some control over their prices because:

- Consumers don't have complete knowledge of all products and prices in a particular market.
- Firms may find it difficult to enter that market because of start up costs, patents or lack of know-how.
- Firms have the ability to differentiate their product from that of their competitors, for example 'barbecue' baked beans.

In practice we can distinguish a number of different market structures with varying degrees of competition.

Perfectly competitive markets

Sometimes called **perfect competition**, this form of market structure is rare in practice but is admired because it encourages efficiency and keeps consumer prices down. The assumptions on which it is based include:

- Many buyers and sellers, none of whom is big enough to affect market prices.
- All buyers and sellers have complete market knowledge.
- No market barriers to entry.
- All products very similar, that is, undifferentiated.

There are very few markets that conform to these characteristics. It is suggested that the Stock Exchange comes nearest.

Perfectly competitive markets, with their emphasis on efficiency and keen prices, are a good starting point for a study of other market structures. As we will see, once we start relaxing the assumptions made above invariably the consumer suffers!

Monopolistic competition

The major difference between **monopolistic competition** and perfect competition, described above, is that here each organization produces a *slightly differentiated product*. This difference may be *physical* (for example the styling of a car) or in the terms of sale, such as offering superior guarantees or aftersales service. Differentiation may also be more *imagined* than real. This occurs when persuasive advertising, linked to a brand name, is used. As a result of differentiating their product the supplier is not a price taker but, instead, has a limited degree of control over the price he charges.

> **Did You Know ?**
>
> Estimates of *branded*, processed foods put their prices almost 10% higher than 'private label' (i.e. unbranded) equivalents in the UK and US.

However, the firm's ability to control prices is limited by the number of relatively close substitutes available and the ease with which new firms can enter the market. Monopolistic competition exists in industries such as soft drinks, hotels and catering, footwear, carpets and in some forms of clothing.

Oligopoly

Oligopoly exists when a few firms dominate a market and produce a differentiated product. The markets for beer, petrol and detergents are good examples. It is often not apparent that there are only a few producers in the market because they will produce several different products for sale. For example, the detergents market is dominated by two firms, Unilever and Proctor and Gamble, with each making several different brands of washing powders.

Oligopoly is often measured by looking at the *degree of concentration* in an industry. We obtain a *concentration ratio* for an industry by looking at the proportion of total industry sales accounted for by the top five firms. Thus if industry sales were £100 million and the top five firms sold £72 million of this, the five-firm concentration ratio would be 72%. Taking British industry as a whole, the five-firm concentration ratio is now approximately 50%.

Oligopoly, or market domination by the few, may arise in part because of the benefits of *large scale production.* As output is expanded, significant cost savings can be made by utilizing more specialised and sophisticated machinery and production processes. For example, large-scale assembly lines mass producing a common product can substantially reduce costs per unit.

Savings may also be made in the areas of:

* *Purchasing*   e.g. bulk discounts
* *Marketing*   e.g. selling a range of products
* *Finance*   e.g. better credit terms for big firms
* *Managerial*   e.g. employment of specialist staff

Did You Know ?

Some firms have to be extremely large before the *average costs* of production can be reduced to the lowest level possible. A washing machine producer needs to have a plant big enough to produce almost 60% of total UK output of washing machines before its costs fall to the lowest level possible. Some estimates put this *minimum efficient size* at 100% of UK output for volume car production (ie space for only 1 car producer) but below 10% for paint, beer, cement and brick production.

These cost savings are commonly known as **economies of scale.** We would not be concerned about oligopolies if the cost benefits described above were always passed on to the consumer. In practice, though, the consumer may suffer through lack of real choice and also through lack of price competition between the producers. There is often an unspoken agreement that firms will not compete on price (because it might start a price war between them), but instead competition will be limited to areas such as advertising and other sales promotions in an attempt to build brand loyalty. In some industries you may also find:

* One dominant firm becoming the price setter, with everyone else in the industry following suit.
* Firms getting together and fixing prices. This is a restrictive trade practice and is illegal in many countries.

New firms also find it difficult to enter the market even though prices and profits attract them. Barriers to entry may arise because of the large size of the production unit needed so as to compete successfully against existing suppliers. The amount of money needed to be spent on advertising and promotion in order to compete with existing firms may also act as a barrier to entry.

Monopoly

A **monopoly** situation occurs when there is only one firm producing and selling in a particular market. This situation of 'pure monopoly' may occur as a result of the exclusive control of a natural resource, government intervention to create a nationalized industry or patent rights. It results in other firms being unable to enter this market. Monopolists will try to maintain these barriers to entry because it gives

them strong control over the prices they charge for their product. Consumers may lose out because a lack of competition means that the monopolist is not forced to find the most efficient means of production, nor if he did is he forced to pass these benefits on to the consumer in the form of price reductions.

The ability of a monopolist to charge higher prices is often limited by the fact that there are a number of imperfect substitutes available. Thus whilst British Gas may be a monopoly supplier of gas in this country, it does face competition from both the electricity and the oil industry.

What we are describing here is a situation of *pure monopoly.* Remember, the *legal definition* is different. In the UK a legal monopoly situation arises when a firm controls more than 25% of the market.

Self Check ✔ Element 3

19. Explain why the supply curve for a normal good is upward sloping to the right:

    _____

    _____

20. A shift in the Supply curve can only be caused by a change in one of the *determinants of supply*. List 3 determinants of supply:
    (a)
    (b)
    (c)

21. Complete the following statement by inserting the missing words:

    In a free market _____ are determined by the interaction of supply and _____. With given _____ and _____ curves only one price is sustainable. This is the _____ price and is the only price at which _____ and demand are equal.

22. Study the following supply and demand schedules for product A:

Quantity supplied	Price of A	Quantity demanded
80	10	20
70	9	40
60	8	60
50	7	80
40	6	100

    (a) Plot these demand and supply curves on a graph.
    (b) What is the equilibrium price and quantity? Explain your answer.
    (c) Calculate the elasticity of supply when the price moves from £8 to £9.

    _____

    _____

    _____

    (d) Calculate the elasticity of demand when the price moves from £8 to £7.

    _____

    _____

    _____

23. In what circumstances would a firm be unable to influence the price of its product?

    _____

    _____

---

24. The table below summarises the important characteristics of the different forms of competition. Complete the table.

	Perfect competition	Monopolistic competition	Oligopoly	Monopoly
Number of firms	Many	Many		
Barriers to entry				Very great
Influence on price			Usually strong	
Product differentiation		Some branding		Not required (no competition)

25. Define the term economies of scale

_____
_____
_____
_____
_____
_____
_____

26. Give 3 examples of economies of scale:
   (a)

   (b)

   (c)

Unit Test   Answer all the questions

Focus 1

Question 1
Mark each of these statements true (T) or false (F).

(1) Retailing is part of the secondary sector.
(2) Selling coal is an example of a business in the primary sector.

Which option best describes the two statements:

A (1) T   (2) T   Choose this answer if both statements are True.
B (1) T   (2) F   Choose this answer if statement (1) is True and statement (2) is False.
C (1) F   (2) T   Choose this answer if statement (1) is False and statement (2) is True.
D (1) F   (2) F   Choose this answer if both statements are False.

Make sure you choose the answer which represents the correct order of the statements.

Question 2
Mark each of these statements true (T) or false (F).

(1) The term services refers to tangible products.
(2) A telephone is an intangible product.

Which option best describes the two statements:

A (1) T   (2) T   Choose this answer if both statements are True.
B (1) T   (2) F   Choose this answer if statement (1) is True and statement (2) is False.
C (1) F   (2) T   Choose this answer if statement (1) is False and statement (2) is True.
D (1) F   (2) F   Choose this answer if both statements are False.

Make sure you choose the answer which represents the correct order of the statements

Question 3
Mark each of these statements true (T) or false (F).

(1) The key objective of a public limited company is to provide a public service.
(2) The key objective of a private limited company is to make a profit.

Which option best describes the two statements:

A (1) T   (2) T   Choose this answer if both statements are True.
B (1) T   (2) F   Choose this answer if statement (1) is True and statement (2) is False.
C (1) F   (2) T   Choose this answer if statement (1) is False and statement (2) is True.
D (1) F   (2) F   Choose this answer if both statements are False.

Make sure you choose the answer which represents the correct order of the statements.

Question 4
Which is the least likely objective of a public corporation?

A Efficient use of assets
B Profit
C The public interest
D Increased sales

Question 5
Goods may be classified as consumer durable, consumer non-durable or capital goods. Which of these is least likely to be a consumer durable good?

A Car   B Cooker   C Photocopier   D Television

Question 6
Mark each of these statements true (T) or false (F).

(1) Opportunity cost is what you can't afford to buy.
(2) Effective demand is the amount of a good that consumers wish and are able to purchase over a certain period of time.

Which option best describes the two statements:

A (1) T (2) T Choose this answer if both statements are True.
B (1) T (2) F Choose this answer if statement (1) is True and statement (2) is False.
C (1) F (2) T Choose this answer if statement (1) is False and statement (2) is True.
D (1) F (2) F Choose this answer if both statements are False.

Make sure you choose the answer which represents the correct order of the statements.

Question 7
Central government provides many services which we take for granted. Which of the following is least likely to be provided by central government?

A Law and order
B Defence
C Personal services
D Medical services

Question 8
There is a decrease in the demand for lemonade. This can be explained by:

A A rise in the price of orange juice
B An increase in the costs of production
C A decrease in the number of children
D A rise in consumer incomes

Question 9
Mark each of these statements true (T) or false (F).

(1) A shift in the total demand curve may be caused by changes in consumer tastes.
(2) A movement along a demand curve is a reflection of changes in other goods prices.

Which option best describes the two statements:

A (1) T (2) T Choose this answer if both statements are True.
B (1) T (2) F Choose this answer if statement (1) is True and statement (2) is False.
C (1) F (2) T Choose this answer if statement (1) is False and statement (2) is True.
D (1) F (2) F Choose this answer if both statements are False.

Make sure you choose the answer which represents the correct order of the statements.

Question 10
Mark each of these statements true (T) or false (F).

(1) If the price of a substitute product falls sales of a competing product will also fall.
(2) Cars and petrol are examples of complementary products.

Which option best describes the two statements:

A (1) T (2) T Choose this answer if both statements are True
B (1) T (2) F Choose this answer if statement (1) is True and statement (2) is False.
C (1) F (2) T Choose this answer if statement (1) is False and statement (2) is True.
D (1) F (2) F Choose this answer if both statements are False

Make sure you choose the answer which represents the correct order of the statements.

Question 11
The diagram below shows a change in the demand for business computers. This change can be explained by :

A A reduction in VAT
B An increase in business activity
C A fall in the price of raw materials
D More efficient use of business computers

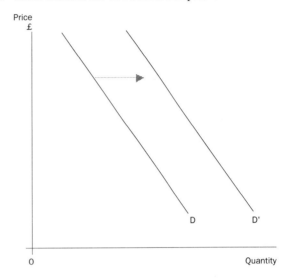

Question 12
Mark each of these statements true (T) or false (F).

(1) Where the market demand for a product is inelastic a reduction in price will reduce total revenue.
(2) Where the market demand for a product has unitary elasticity a change in price will have no effect on total revenue.

Which option best describes the two statements:

A (1) T (2) T Choose this answer if both statements are True.
B (1) T (2) F Choose this answer if statement (1) is True and statement (2) is False.
C (1) F (2) T Choose this answer if statement (1) is False and statement (2) is True.
D (1) F (2) F Choose this answer if both statements are False.

Make sure you choose the answer which represents the correct order of the statements

Focus 2

Question 13
Which of these characteristics does not describe a free enterprise system?

A People can buy what they want
B All products produced are in the public interest
C Market forces encourage efficiency
D The system does not guarantee full employment

Question 14
In a recession the government could use monetary policy to stimulate the economy by:

A Raising interest rates
B Reducing interest rates
C Lowering taxes
D Reducing government expenditure

Question 15
Mark each of these statements true (T) or false (F).

(1) The Public Sector Borrowing Requirement will increase as a result of a government budget deficit.
(2) A budget surplus will have a deflationary effect on an economy.

Which option best describes the two statements:

A (1) T (2) T Choose this answer if both statements are True.
B (1) T (2) F Choose this answer if statement (1) is True and statement (2) is False.
C (1) F (2) T Choose this answer if statement (1) is False and statement (2) is True.
D (1) F (2) F Choose this answer if both statements are False.

Make sure you choose the answer which represents the correct order of the statements.

Question 16
Mark each of these statements true (T) or false (F).

(1) To reduce unemployment and encourage economic growth the government could spend more.
(2) To reduce the level of inflation and balance of payments difficulties the government could spend less.

Which option best describes the two statements:

A (1) T (2) T Choose this answer if both statements are True.
B (1) T (2) F Choose this answer if statement (1) is True and statement (2) is False.
C (1) F (2) T Choose this answer if statement (1) is False and statement (2) is True.
D (1) F (2) F Choose this answer if both statements are False.

Make sure you choose the answer which represents the correct order of the statements.

Questions 17–19 relate to the following information.
Objectives of government economic management include:
A To encourage exports
B To promote employment
C To encourage economic growth
D To control inflation

Which government objectives would be helped by:

Question 17
Higher interest rates

Question 18
Introduction of retraining schemes

Question 19
Joining a trade block

Question 20
Restrictions on trade are not imposed to:

A Correct a balance of payment problem
B Reduce unfair competition
C Control inflation
D Protect infant industries

Question 21
Which international organisation has been set up to encourage international trade:

A U.N.   B. GATT   C IMF   D World Bank

Questions 22–24 relate to the following information:
The European union has numerous policies including :

A Regional Development
B The Single Market
C The Social Chapter
D CAP

Choose the appropriate policy for each of the following :

Question 22
To protect farmers interests

Question 23
To protect employees working conditions

Question 24
To encourage trade

Focus 3

Question 25
The graph shows two supply curves. What is the most likely to cause the move in the supply curve from SS to S_1S_1.

A A change in price
B An increase in raw material costs
C A government subsidy
D Greater competition

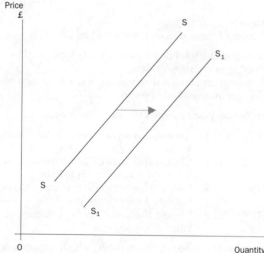

Question 26
Consider the following diagram.

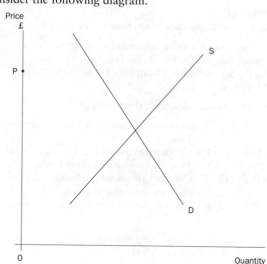

Mark each of these statements true (T) or false (F).

(1) At price P demand is greater than supply and prices will fall.
(2) Prices will fall until supply equals demand.

Which option best describes the two statements:

A (1) T (2) T Choose this answer if both statements are True.
B (1) T (2) F Choose this answer if statement (1) is True and statement (2) is False.
C (1) F (2) T Choose this answer if statement (1) is False and statement (2) is True.
D (1) F (2) F Choose this answer if both statements are False

Make sure you choose the answer which represents the correct order of the statements.

Question 27
Which information is most likely to be found in sources 'external' to the firm?

A Trends in sales
B Trends in production costs
C Trends in consumer income and expenditure
D Trends in competition

Questions 28–30 relate to the following information:
Each month government statistics give information on the state of the economy. Some of the changes identified are:

A An increase in business investment
B The cost of living increases
C VAT on fuel has been introduced
D A fall in the balance of payments deficit

Which of the changes will most affect the following:

Question 28
The demand for consumer products.

Question 29
The demand for bank loans

Question 30
The demand for gas

Focus 4

Questions 31–33 relate to the following information.
A business monitors the following relationship :

A Price and supply
B Price and cost per unit
C Turnover and capital
D Total produced and cost

Which of these relationships will help to forecast :

Question 31
Profit on expected sales

Question 32
Total revenue

Question 33
Unit costs of production

Question 34
The relationship between supply and price can be evaluated:

A By analysing market trends
B In financial terms
C By analysing the level of customer satisfaction
D By analysing market demand

Question 35
An organization's sales are monitored and evaluated to find:

A Competition
B Trends
C Profitability
D New markets

Question 36
Mark each of these statements true (T) or false (F).

(1) Managers make business decisions through an evaluation of costs, supply and price.
(2) An evaluation of trends in prices provides information on the state of the market.

Which option best describes the two statements:

A (1) T (2) T Choose this answer if both statements are True.
B (1) T (2) F Choose this answer if statement (1) is True and statement (2) is False.
C (1) F (2) T Choose this answer if statement (1) is False and statement (2) is True.
D (1) F (2) F Choose this answer if both statements are False.

Make sure you choose the answer which represents the correct order of the statements

Answers to Self-check Questions

1.

	Primary	Secondary	Tertiary
(a)	Fishing	Car making	Catering
(b)	Agriculture	Building	Insurance
(c)	Forestry	Engineering	Retailing

2. (a) Coal; (b) textiles; (c) steel.

3. (a) Computers;
   (b) bio-technology
   (c) satellite TV.

4. (a) This is a movement along the demand curve; demand expands.
   (b) A shift in the demand curve to the left – decrease.
   (c) A shift in the demand curve to the left – decrease (if demand for cars falls so will the demand for petrol).
   (d) A shift in the demand curve to the right – increase – because people have more money to spend on meals out (normal good).

5.

		Demand shifts to the	
		right	left
(a)	Fur coats		✓
(b)	Unleaded petrol	✓	
(c)	Coal		✓
(d)	Aerosol deodorants		✓

6. (a) Demand is inelastic.

$$PED = \frac{\% \text{ change in quantity demanded}}{\% \text{ change in price}} = \frac{10\%}{20\%} = 0.5$$

   (b) Unitary elasticity.

$$PED = \frac{6\frac{2}{3}\%}{6\frac{2}{3}\%} = 1$$

   (c) Demand is elastic.

$$PED = \frac{100\%}{20\%} = 5.$$

7. The following characteristics are used to distinguish between different types of economic system.

	Market Economy	Planned Economy	Mixed Economy
Role of the state	Minimal	Interventionist	Intervenes where necessary
Right to own and dispose of resources	Yes	Only the state	Yes, subject to some control by state
Existence of profit motive	Yes	No	Yes
Allocation of resources through price mechanism	Yes	No	Not always

8.

	Market	Planned	Mixed
Cuba		✓	
UK			✓
Hong Kong	✓		
France			✓
China		✓	

9. (a) Low inflation; (b) full employment; (c) economic growth; (d) satisfactory balance of payments.

10. The means of achieving policy goals may conflict. Thus attempts to increase employment through the use of fiscal policy may worsen inflation or the balance of payments.

11. (a) It should aim to reduce aggregate demand by reducing the budget deficit or running a budget surplus.
    (b) Raise interest rates and limit the amount of credit available.

12. These aim to shift the aggregate supply curve to the right by encouraging competition and giving incentives for people to work. Two examples would be (1) the lowering of income tax and (2) controlling the power of trade unions.

13. (a) **Fair Trading Act:** May be used to refer monopoly and merger situations to the Monopolies and Mergers Commission for investigation.
    (b) **Restrictive Trade Practices Act:** Outlaws agreements between traders regarding prices, output or conditions of sale – unless held to be in the public interest after investigation
    (c) **Competition Act:** Gives the Office of Fair Trading the right to investigate other anti-competitive practices, for example selling below cost

14. (a) To protect new and, as yet, uncompetitive industries.
    (b) To prevent dumping.
    (c) To protect industries having a strategic significance.

15. Restrictions on another country's imports, often imposed as a penalty for restrictions posed on this country's exports.

16. To encourage free multilateral trade.

17. Any six from Belgium, Britain, Denmark, France, Germany, Greece, Ireland, Italy, Luxembourg, Netherlands, Portugal, Spain.

18. The inability of a country to decide policy or make laws which are in conflict with those of the European Union.

19. As the price increases existing producers will be encouraged by the higher revenue to expand production even though costs are rising. Higher prices also encourage less efficient producers to enter the market.

20. (a) Changes in technology; (b) changes in the prices of other goods; (d) changes in the prices of production inputs.

21. In a free market **prices** are determined by the interaction of supply and **demand**. With given **supply** and **demand** curves only one price is sustainable. This is the **equilibrium** price and is the only price at which **supply** and demand are equal.

22. (a), (b) The equilibrium price is 8 and the quantity is 60. This is the point of intersection for the supply and demand curves.
    (c) 1.33.
    (d) 2.66.

23. Under perfect competition.

24.

	Perfect competition	Monopolistic competition	Oligopoly	Monopoly
Number of firms	Many	Many	Few	One
Barriers to entry	None	Few	Great	Very great
Influence on price	Price taker	Not strong	Usually strong	Price maker
Product differentiation	None	Some branding	Keen branding	Not required (no competition)

25. Cost savings made as a result of large-scale production.

26. (a) Discounts for buying in bulk,
    (b) Employment of specialist staff.
    (c) Better rates when borrowing.

Answers to Unit Test

Question	Answer	Question	Answer	Question	Answer	Question	Answer	Question	Answer
1	D	9	B	17	D	25	C	33	D
2	D	10	A	18	B	26	C	34	A
3	C	11	B	19	A	27	C	35	B
4	B	12	A	20	C	28	B	36	A
5	C	13	B	21	B	29	A		
6	C	14	B	22	D	30	C		
7	C	15	A	23	C	31	B		
8	C	16	A	24	B	32	A		

Unit Test Comments (Selected questions)

Question 1 D
Statement 2 will catch many people out. Mining coal is certainly a primary sector activity. 'Selling', though, is an example of a tertiary or service sector activity.

Question 2 D
Services are intangible – there is no tangible product. However, a telephone – rather than the service of the telephone company, is a tangible product!

Question 3 C
You must be able to distinguish between a public corporation and a public limited company. The key objective of a public corporation is to provide a service but the objective of any company (long term) must be to make a profit.

Question 4 B
Profit is the least likely of the alternatives given.

Question 5 C
It is unlikely that many homes will have a photocopier; however, the other items are examples of longer term assets likely to be held by consumers for their personal use.

Question 6 C
Statement 1 is incorrect because the opportunity cost of something is the next best alternative to going without.

Question 7 C
Although medical services can be provided by the private sector they can, and are, provided by the government in many countries. However, personal services such as hair-dressing would rarely be provided by government.

Question 8 C
If orange juice and lemonade were substitute products a rise in the price of orange juice would cause sales of lemonade to rise! Items C and D are both determinants of demand but a rise in consumer incomes would normally result in increased demand for goods. A fall in the number of children is likely to reduce demand for lemonade.

Question 9 B
A movement along a demand curve reflects the quantity demanded at different prices for *this* product.

Question 10 A
In statement 1 if the price of a substitute product falls its sales will rise, having an adverse effect on the sales of a competing product!

Question 11 B
An increase in business activity implies greater spending on the vast majority of goods and services which would shift the demand curve to the right.

Question 12 A
Inelasticity of demand implies a situation where a change in price will have a less than proportionate effect on demand, and in this case a price cut will reduce total revenue. With unitary elasticity any change in price will leave total revenue unchanged.

Question 13 B
In a free enterprise system products which are demanded by consumers will be produced by firms whether or not they are in the public interest (as long as they can make a profit!).

Question 14 B
You must be able to discriminate between fiscal and monetary policy. Options C and D refer to fiscal policy and are therefore automatically excluded. Option B – reducing the cost of borrowing – stimulates demand for investment monies and therefore the level of economic activity in the economy.

Question 15 A
A budget deficit means that the state spends more than it receives in revenue – the remainder it borrows, thereby increasing the PSBR. A budget surplus takes money out of the economy as tax revenue exceeds state spending and therefore has a deflationary effect on the economy.

Question 16 A
This is basic fiscal policy. Pumping money into the economy will encourage business activity and therefore economic growth and employment. Taking money out of the economy by cutting government spending reduces the demand for goods and services and therefore inflationary pressures and also imports.

Question 17 D
Higher interest rates discourage borrowing and spending and therefore curb inflationary pressures. The higher interest rates would *discourage* exports (raise costs of investing, financing borrowing etc), *discourage* output and employment and therefore *discourage* economic growth.

Question 18 B
Main *direct* impact will be in making labour more employable.

Question 19 A
Main *direct* impact will be to provide a (protected) market for exports. Only then will employment and economic growth tend to increase.

Question 20–23 See Answer Grid

Question 24 B
The Single Market established in 1993 is designed to increase trade between member states.

Question 25 C
The shift in the supply curve shows that more is supplied at all prices which is most likely to be the result of a government subsidy.

Question 26 C
Look carefully at the diagram. You will see that, by dropping a vertical line from where the price line intersects the demand and supply curve, demand is less than supply. Excess supply will cause prices to fall; supply contracts and demand expands until we reach equilibrium.

Question 27 C
Trends in consumer income and expenditure would not be available from the everyday activities of the firm.

Question 28 B
An increase in the cost of living means that our money 'won't go as far' as it used to and demand for consumer products will fall.

Question 29 A
Demand for bank loans is closely linked with business investment.

Question 30 C
VAT on gas, a fuel, will shift supply upwards, raise equilibrium price and reduce demand.

Question 31 B
The difference between price and cost is profit! Profit per unit × units sold gives us the profit on sales.

Question 32 A
The equation becomes clearer if we talk about price × quantity supplied.

Question 33 D
Costs divided by total produced gives us the unit cost of production.

Question 33–36 See Answer Grid

UNIT 2

Business systems

Getting Started

Within any type of organization there will be a number of activities, both routine and non-routine, that need to be carried out. An organization structures itself around the type of activities carried out and it will set up **systems** to deal with information that comes in and flows out. Every business system will have four common features. It needs to be:

- **Planned** – what needs to be done.
- **Organized** – ensuring required resources are available.
- **Executed** – actually carried out.
- **Monitored** – ensuring that things happen as planned.

Often information needs to be *communicated* to others. **Communication** is all about passing on information. Organizations have to communicate with people both inside and outside the organization. For an organization to run efficiently it is vital that it has *formal* communication systems set up. Formal communication systems exist where proper procedures are set down. An effective communication system is needed:

- To handle the flow of information inside and outside the organization.
- To assist in decision making.
- To measure business performance.

Communication has been greatly improved by the advances in technology over recent years. The consequences for business organizations are that a great deal of their information can be processed electronically.

In this unit we will be concerned with the information generated by an organization, the systems it sets up to organize this information and how it communicates it. We will concentrate on the systems it sets up and how it makes use of technology to do this.

Communication and information technology are both core skills and you will find this chapter particularly useful for the development and understanding of these skills.

Database   A collection of files or records stored manually or electronically.

External communication   Takes place outside an organization, for example with customers.

Formal communication   Set procedures are followed and a written record is kept.

Hierarchy   A ranking of people or functions in some sort of order.

Informal communication   Does not follow set procedures and does not require written records; takes place as and when appropriate.

Information processing   The gathering, sorting, storing, analysing and passing on of data.

Internal communication   Takes place within an organization, for example between staff, departments etc.

Non-verbal communication   Written communication, for example letters, memos, reports, minutes etc.

Spreadsheet   Application carried out on a computer that allows arithmetical calculations, for example preparation of budgets.

Verbal communication   Spoken by a person, for example on the telephone, face-to-face.

Essential Principles

In this element we will examine the **administration system** of an organization. We will look at how the system is set up to meet the needs of the organization and to support the various functions within it. To do this we must be able to:

- Explain the different organizational structures.
- Explain the purposes of administration systems in business organizations.
- Describe the different administration systems within an organization.
- Describe how legal and statutory requirements determine how the administration systems are organized.
- Evaluate the effectiveness of administration systems in supporting the functions of a business organization.

Organizational Structure

Before we look at administrative systems in an organization it is important to understand how an organization is **structured**.

The structure of an organization is how it is designed. It describes the size of the organization, what roles people fulfil and what their relationship is with other people within the organization. A formal structure is very important so that people can identify their role within the organization and see how it relates to other people. Staff need to know who they are responsible for and also who they are accountable to.

Hierarchies

A **hierarchy** exists where there is 'a system which is ranked in some kind of order'. In Unit 4 we will look at organizational structures in more detail. However, the different type of structures are now briefly discussed.

Organizational structures are usually hierarchical. They are made up of several layers or tiers of management. A hierarchy can be either 'tall' or 'flat'. We will look at both types:

Tall (vertical) structure

You can find a diagram showing a tall structure in Unit 4, Fig. 4.5 (p. 103). The features of a 'tall' structure are:

- These are usually found in large organizations i.e. limited companies.
- They are made up of several layers of management where each level is controlled by the one above.
- At the top level is the managing director who is responsible for the control of the organization.
- Most of the power and responsibility lies with the people at the top of the organization.

The main problems with this type of structure are firstly that communication can be a problem as the managers at the top of the structure become remote from the other employees. Secondly staff can become very demotivated as they see little prospect of any promotion.

Flat (horizontal) structure

You can find a diagram showing a flat structure in Unit 4, Fig. 4.6 (p. 103). The features of a 'flat' or 'horizontal' structure are:

- There are few layers of management but usually more departments or divisions.
- They tend to be more democratic, i.e. decision making is shared amongst the managers rather than one person making the decisions.

Many large organizations are restructuring themselves into flat structures dividing the company up into smaller operating units. Each unit is given more autonomy, i.e. power.

The main problems associated with this type of structure are that communications tend to be poorer across the organization. There is also a lack of control by the top management as they have a wider span of control.

Factors affecting organization structure

The structure of an organization will depend on several factors including:

- **The aims and objectives of the organization.** For example, in a manufacturing firm the production department is likely to be the largest.

- **The number of employees.** This will determine to what extent specialization can occur. In a large organization there are likely to be many specialist roles whereas in a small organization people are more likely to take on a number of roles.

- **What the business does.** Whether it is a manufacturing firm or a selling firm.

- **Where the organization is located.** It may have several plants, branches throughout the country or it may be situated in just one location.

All these factors will influence the type of organizational structure appropriate to the business.

> **Did You Know ?**
>
> Less than 20% of UK firms now regard themselves as 'manufacturing' firms. Around 97% of all UK firms employ less than 20 people, and 86% actually employ less than 5 people.

Types of organizational structure

Within every organization many different **activities** are carried out. The organization has to divide up these activities and link them together into a **structure**, putting a manager in overall charge.

There are several different ways of dividing up the activities of an organization as follows:

- Division by function
- Division by product

- Division by process
- Division by geographical area
- Division by customer

We will look at each one in turn.

Division by function

The most common way of dividing up an organization is to do it by **functional** areas. Large organizations will employ many specialists whereas in smaller organizations people tend to have a wider range of responsibilities. The structure of an organization where division is by function will look something like Fig. 2.1. Later on in this chapter we will look at the responsibilities and administrative activities of each of these functions.

Division by product

Where an organization offers several products it may divide its activities into separate divisions according to the **product** (Fig. 2.2). For example a pharmaceutical company may have separate divisions for medicines, cosmetics and toiletries.

Division by process

The manufacture of many goods involves several stages or **processes** (think about car production). Each separate stage often involves different labour, equipment and machinery and it is carried out in different locations. Each process is frequently allocated to a separate department (Fig. 2.3).

Division by geographical area

Many organizations operate in different locations both at home and abroad. Often they are divided into separate divisions with complete autonomy, reporting to a board of directors (Fig. 2.4).

Division by customer

Many firms sell to *consumer* markets and *industrial* markets. Often these two types of customer require different treatment and so the organization creates two separate divisions to cater for their individual needs (Fig. 2.5).

Fig. 2.1   Division by function

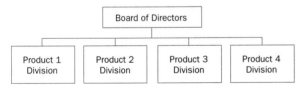

Fig. 2.2   Division by product

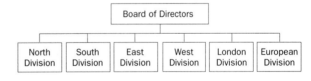

Fig. 2.4   Division by geographical area

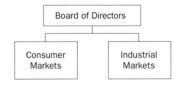

Fig. 2.5   Division by consumer

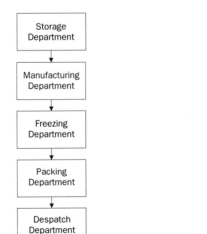

Fig. 2.3   Division by process in the manufacture of frozen foods

Did You Know ?

Around 4,500 firms operate worldwide, with major parts of their operations located in several countries. These are called 'multinationals' and the largest of these have turnovers greater in value than the National Income of many countries. For example, Exxon, Ford and General Motors of the USA each have a turnover larger than the GNP's of all but fourteen countries!

A typical administration system

In a large organization it is common to find specialist functions as outlined below.

Function	Activities
Accounting	A key function of a business responsible for the financial affairs of the business including financial record keeping, recording money coming in and going out of the organization, the preparation of final accounts and management accounts including preparation of budgets. Much of the work is done on computer
Personnel	Responsible for the recruitment and training of staff, the induction of new staff, staff appraisals, industrial relation matters including health and safety and staff welfare
Marketing	Responsible for finding out what the customer wants and then satisfying their needs. To find out what the customer wants they have to carry out market research and work very closely with the sales department
Sales	Responsible for persuading the customer to buy the organization's products. Usually a sales force is employed to go out and sell the products
Purchasing	Responsible for the purchase of all materials and equipment throughout the organization from raw materials to office supplies
Production	Responsible for producing the goods to be sold. Have to ensure that all goods meet the right quality standards. Liaise closely with sales and marketing and purchasing departments to ensure that they have the right materials for production and are on schedule to meet orders
Distribution	Responsible for ensuring that the goods reach the customer on time and in the right condition. Warehousing, storage, stock control and despatch are also the responsibility of distribution
Support services	An extremely important function within the organization responsible for holding together the organization. The types of services include cleaning and maintenance, catering, computer services, reprographics and printing

Table 2.1 The most common functions found within an organization

Functions (purposes) of administration systems

The *functions* of any administration system fall into two categories.

- **Routine functions.** These are the functions which are carried out on a regular basis. For example a routine function of an accounts clerk in the Accounting department might be to record the petty cash on a weekly basis.

- **Non-routine functions.** These are any other functions *not* carried out on a routine basis. For example the accounts clerk above may be asked to analyse petty cash on a departmental basis – information not normally generated by the organization.

The existence of administration systems means that anyone within the organization is able to carry out routine functions.

What would happen if administration systems were not in place? The answer is that chaos would probably reign!

Did You Know ?

There has been a huge increase in the volume of information a firm must process. The OECD has estimated a sevenfold increase in the past twenty years.

Need for Administration Systems

Administrative systems are needed in organizations for the following reasons:

- *So that the organization operates efficiently and effectively.* For example when a salesperson makes a sale, certain documentation and paperwork will need to be completed. An order form will be generated and copies of that form will need to go to the customer and various departments within the organization. A system will have to be in place to ensure that the above procedure is followed. It is also vital that everyone within the organization knows who is responsible for what.

- *So that an organization can record and monitor its business performance.* Organizations are constantly setting aims and objectives and as a consequence they need to monitor their progress. It is usually the role of management to control and monitor performance and they will request certain information on a regular basis to do this (see Table 2.2).

Function	Example of Information Produced
Accounting	Monthly profit and loss accounts Monthly budgets comparing forecast figures with actual figures
Personnel	Figures on staff absenteeism, staff turnover Staff appraisals
Marketing	Customer feedback on new product
Sales	Sales performance figures compared with targets
Purchasing	List of suppliers of raw materials Purchase orders
Production	Figures on machine output per hour Wastage levels in production process
Distribution	Customer feedback on quality of distribution service provided
Support services	Employee feedback on services offered by the staff canteen, contract cleaning, reprographics and other support services

Table 2.2 Information produced by the different functions within an organization to monitor its performance

- *So that resources employed within an organization can be supported.* These resources are described in Table 2.3 and can be divided into three main categories – human, financial and physical.

Type of resource	Examples of administration systems which support it
Human	Staff training and development Wages and salaries Services such as canteen facilities
Financial	Systems for recording transactions, receipt and payment of cash etc. Staff training to provide suitably qualified staff
Physical	Services such as maintenance of premises and equipment System for purchasing equipment and assets

Table 2.3 Examples of administration system provided to support the resources of an organization

Within *every* administrative system there exist four functions which are:

- **Planning** Deciding what needs to be done; usually carried out by senior management.

- **Organizing** Ensuring adequate resources, for example staff, are available; usually carried out by middle management.

- **Monitoring** Ensuring that things happen as they were planned; usually carried out by lower management.

- **Executing** Actually carrying out the particular activity; usually carried out by staff.

Legal and statutory requirements

So far we have seen that administration systems are necessary to ensure the smooth running of the business – to meet its *internal requirements*. In addition to these internal requirements every organization, large or small, has to fulfil certain **legal and statutory requirements**, that is, it has to comply with the law. For example, an organization must ensure that it provides a safe place of work for its employees. To meet these legal requirements it has to have administration systems in place. Someone has to take responsibility for ensuring that the requirements are being met, that the necessary documentation is in order.

Did You Know ?

Over 3,500 government regulations affect UK business operations. Apart from all the other administrative needs, firms must ensure that they comply with these regulations. In 1993 a 'Deregulation Taskforce' was appointed to simplify and remove unnecessary regulations.

Figure 2.6 highlights some of the most important legal requirements that an organization has to meet. These are described in more detail later in this section.

Fig. 2.6 The legal requirements of a business

Health and Safety Legislation

There are three main Acts with which every organization has to comply. These are:

- Health and Safety at Work Act 1974
- Factories Act 1961
- Offices, Shops and Railways Premises Act 1963

We will look at the main principles of each act in turn.

- *Health and Safety at Work Act 1974 (HASAWA)*
  This Act covers all places of work and its purpose is to protect employees and the public from health and safety hazards which may arise. It is not, however, solely the responsibility of the employer to provide a safe place of work. The Act places obligations on the employees, manufacturers, designers, suppliers of materials and those in control of premises to ensure a safe working environment (see Table 2.4).

- To maintain and improve standards of health, safety and welfare of people at work

- To protect visitors to the premises and other people against risks to health and safety from work activities

- To make proper provisions for the use, control and storage of dangerous substances

- To control certain emissions into the atmosphere from certain premises

- To provide proper training and instructions on health and safety issues

---

Table 2.4 The main aims of the Health and Safety at Work Act

To achieve the above aims employers have a legal obligation to provide the following:

- *Hygiene facilities.* That is, toilets, cloakrooms, washing facilities

- *Written safety policy.* This should include written procedures on the maintenance of equipment and machinery, arrangements for control, use and storage of any dangerous substances and procedures to be followed in the event of an accident. Safety representatives should be appointed who will sit on the organization's health and safety committee.

- *Safety devices and clothing.* Some jobs require special protective clothing to be worn, for example safety goggles.

- *Safe working environment.* Adequate space, heating, lighting and ventilation should be provided for employees.

Organizations in the UK are also bound by EU law. Many Directives have been issued by the EU in relation to health and safety in recent years. An example of these are the regulations relating to people who work with VDUs, that is, computer screens. Strict guidelines are laid down as to the length of time people should work with them; for example it is recommended that breaks of 10–15 minutes are allowed every two hours. The Directive also makes recommendations as to how the working environment should be laid out; for example VDUs should be placed at a sufficient distance from the operator to reduce eye strain.

The Health and Safety Commission was established by the Health and Safety at Work Act 1974. It is a government organization responsible for securing the health, safety and welfare of people at work. It makes the decisions and the Health and Safety Executive is responsible for carrying out these decisions. It appoints a number of inspectors who visit organizations to ensure that the legislation is being adhered to.

> Both the employer and the employee are responsible for health and safety within the workplace.

- *Factories Act 1961*
  This Act is concerned with organizations that use mechanical equipment. The main provisions of the Act are concerned with toilet and washing facilities, heating, lighting and ventilation, and guards for machinery and equipment.

- *Offices, Shops and Railways Premises Act 1963*
  This Act is mainly concerned with the working conditions of people in offices and shops. It is primarily concerned with temperature levels, heating and lighting, floor space and toilet and washing facilities.

Any organization which does *not* abide with the above legislation could be subject to severe penalties. It is, therefore, of the utmost importance that it is complied with and that proper records are kept. Table 2.5 indicates the administrative systems that *must* be in place.

Legislation	Administration Systems Required
Health and Safety at Work Act 1974	Written health and safety policy outlining procedures to be followed in event of accidents; guidelines on how to handle dangerous substances; guidelines on maintenance and operation of machinery
Factories Act 1961	Written health and safety policy; guidelines on how to operate machinery and equipment
Offices, Shops and Railways Premises Act 1963	Written health and safety policy; regular maintenance and inspection of premises

Table 2.5 Systems that must be in place to support health and safety legislation

Employment Legislation

Employees are protected by various Acts of Parliament which exist to give them certain rights. We have already looked at the Health and Safety at Work Act which protects an employee in terms of health, safety and welfare. We will now look at other items of legislation which exist to protect the employee in terms of employment and discrimination on various grounds. These areas are discussed in more detail in Unit 4.

Employment Protection (Consolidation) Act 1978

Within 13 weeks of starting a new job every full-time employee is entitled to a contract of employment. This must be a written statement outlining the terms and conditions of employment. In particular it should contain the following:

- Names of employer and employee.
- Job title.
- Date of commencement of employment.
- Rate of pay and frequency of payment, i.e. weekly, monthly.
- Hours of work.
- Holiday entitlement.
- Sickness benefits.
- Pensions.
- Grievance procedure and disciplinary rules.
- Length of notice required.

Not all the above information is always given directly to individual employees. It may be contained in a 'Conditions of Service' booklet which must be available and accessible to employees at all times.

Equal Pay Acts 1970 and 1983

These Acts state that women are entitled to the same rates of pay as men when carrying out the same or similar work.

Sex Discrimination Act 1975

This Act makes it unlawful for an employer to discriminate against an employee on the grounds of sex. Men and women should be treated equally in employment as they should in education, advertising and in the provision of housing, goods and facilities.

Race Relations Act 1976

This Act makes it unlawful for an employer to discriminate against an employee on the grounds of race, colour or ethnic origin. Irrespective of a person's race, colour or ethnic origin they should be treated equally in employment, education, advertising and in the provision of housing, goods and facilities.

The administrative systems that are necessary to support such employment legislation are identified in Table 2.6.

Legislation	Administration Systems Required to Support Legislation
Employment Protection (Consolidation Act) 1978	Written contracts of employment; Conditions of Service booklet including terms and conditions of service, grievance procedure to be followed
Equal Pay Acts 1970 and 1983	Written equal opportunities policy
Sex Discrimination Act 1975	Written equal opportunities policy
Race Relations Act 1976	Written equal opportunities policy

Table 2.6 Administration systems required to support employment legislation

Company legislation

Documentation and records

All limited companies are regulated by the Companies Acts 1985 and 1989. These acts place obligations upon the organization in terms of the **documentation and records** it should produce and keep. On the formation of a limited company it has to register with the Registrar of Companies based in Cardiff at Companies House. In order to do this it must produce two documents which are considered further in Unit 4:

1. **Memorandum of Association.** Outlines the constitution of the company, its name, purpose and what it does.

2. **Articles of Association.** The 'rulebook' outlining the internal rules regarding meetings, voting, names of directors and other internal matters.

In addition to this documentation a company must also adopt the following procedures:

- *Keep formal records.* Names of directors, details of their shareholdings and minutes of meetings

- *Send to Companies House annually a copy of their annual accounts.*

- *Return annually to Companies House Form 363.* This contains details of directors, directors' shareholdings, share capital issued and any company property mortgaged for borrowing.

All the above records can be accessed by any member of the public for a fee.

Many large organizations appoint a *Company Secretary* who is responsible for the above procedures and documentation.

Financial obligations

Under the Companies Acts an organization also has a number of **financial obligations** to meet. The *accounting function* is responsible for the administration of these. These obligations are:

- Production of annual accounts and a record of all financial transactions.

- Maintenance of VAT records and accounts.

- Maintenance of payroll records, deduction of income tax and National Insurance from employees.

- Administration of pension arrangements.

We will look at each of the above in turn:

Accounting records and financial transactions

Corporation Tax

Limited companies have a legal obligation to pay corporation tax, that is, a tax on their profits. A company must therefore keep proper accounting records so that their liability for tax can be assessed by the Inland Revenue. Sole traders and partnerships are liable for the payment of income tax, that is, a tax on their personal income. They too must therefore keep proper accounting records and details of all their financial transactions.

Value Added Tax (VAT)

VAT is a government tax on spending which is added to the purchase price of goods sold. The current rate of VAT is 17.5%. Companies with a sales turnover (the value of sales) *above* the amount that qualifies for VAT must register with the Customs and Excise. The minimum turnover required (called the *VAT threshold*) is revised from year to year by the Chancellor of the Exchequer in the annual December budget. Having registered for VAT a company is issued with a VAT registration number. This can be found on the company's letterhead. HM Customs & Excise are responsible for the collection of VAT. The amount of VAT payable is calculated by:

Amount of VAT collected (output tax)
less
Amount of VAT charged to them (input tax)

If the amount charged to the company is greater than the amount collected, a refund is payable by HM Customs & Excise.

VAT returns are made every three months on Form VAT 100. Smaller companies may make their return on an annual basis.

> ### Did You Know ?
>
> Corporation tax, VAT and other (e.g. excise duties) taxes on business profit or business output generate around 40% of total government receipts.

Pay As You Earn (PAYE) System

The PAYE system is used by employers to make a number of deductions from employees pay as outlined in Table 2.7 (see page 34).

The employee receives a payslip which contains details of their pay and any deductions.

The administration of the above can be very complicated, especially for large organizations. It is therefore vital that organizations keep proper, detailed payroll records. Many organizations have a computerized payroll procedure although small organizations may still operate a manual system.

Type of deduction Description

Income Tax	A personal tax based on the level of income earned by an individual less allowances. The Government uses income tax to pay for public spending on health, education, defence etc.
National Insurance	A tax deducted from an employee's earnings and used by the Government to pay for benefits and State pensions
Statutory Sick Pay	Payable to full-time employees who are off sick for between four days and twenty eight weeks
Statutory Maternity Pay	Payable to full-time pregnant employees when they are off work to have a baby. Payable for a maximum of eighteen weeks.

Table 2.7 Deductions made from pay under the PAYE system

Did You Know ?

Income Tax and National Insurance contributions recorded under the PAYE system generated over £100bn of revenue for the government in 1993/94. This was around 45% of total government receipts.

Pensions

A further deduction from an employee could be an amount for a pension scheme. A pension is a form of saving for retirement whereby a deduction is made from an employee's pay on a regular basis and upon retirement a lump sum is paid out or a regular income is paid (or both).

There are different types of pensions as follows:

- *State pension.* A State benefit payable to men over 65 and women over 60. This is funded by National Insurance contributions as discussed above. It is a flat rate which usually goes up each year in the budget, announced by the Chancellor of the Exchequer.

- *Contributory Pension.* Both the employer and the employee contribute to this type of fund.

- *Non-contributory Pension.* Only the employer contributes an amount to this type of fund.

- Formal records of directors shareholdings
- Minutes of meetings
- Annual accounts
- VAT records and accounts
- Payroll records i.e. deduction of income tax, national insurance
- Pension records

Table 2.8 Information required under Companies Acts 1985 & 1989

Consumer Legislation

To ensure survival it is vital that businesses listen to what their *customer* wants and then try to satisfy those needs. Consumers are protected by law and a business must also be aware of the many Acts of Parliament which exist to protect the consumer.

The table highlights some of the main ones.

Acts of Parliament	Main Provisions of Act
Sale of Goods Act 1979	Goods sold must be: • Fit for the purpose for which they are generally used • be of merchantable quality • meet the description applied to them
Supply of Goods and Services Act 1982	Extends the provisions of the Sale of Goods Act to services such as work carried out by builders, decorators etc.
Trade Description Acts 1969 and 1972	Traders must not apply false descriptions to goods, e.g. a jumper described as 100% wool must be just that
Consumers Protection Act 1987	Introduced a framework of strict liability for defective products. If a product is defective and causes injury or damage then the manufacturer, producer, importer or supplier can be held liable

Table 2.9 Main items of consumer legislation

Customer Care Schemes

If organizations are to be successful they need to listen to the needs of their *customers* and then aim to satisfy them. A **customer care scheme** should include the following:

- A written customer care policy setting down the standards to be met.
- Staff training – all staff need to realize the importance of customer care and the benefits to the organization and its personnel.
- Systems to gain customer feedback should be in place, e.g. questionnaires about products and/or services.

Quality Assurance

One way in which an organization can ensure that it does not break the law is to have **quality assurance** systems in place.

Quality assurance systems are a common feature of many organizations. A quality assurance system exists where standards are set and then performance is measured against these standards. For example a company manufacturing clothing garments should have a quality assurance system in place to ensure that all the garments are properly stitched and made up. One or more quality control inspectors will be appointed to carry this out.

The purposes of quality assurance systems are:

- To prevent any errors being made.
- To detect any errors or faults.
- To correct any errors or faults that might have been made.

- To ensure high standards of performance.
- To measure the quantity and quality of work produced.

The results of quality assurance systems can be:

- Improved quality of goods and services.
- Satisfied customers.
- Increased sales and profits due to increased customer satisfaction.

> ### Did You Know ❓
>
> Studies of UK exports have suggested that *product quality* is even more important than price in determining export penetration of overseas markets.

British National Standard BS5750

British National Standard BS5750 is the standard for quality systems. It is a document which sets down the requirements and criteria which an organsation must meet to ensure the highest quality products. Organizations are audited to ensure that they are meeting these standards and if they are awarded the standard their goods may carry the Kitemark symbol. It helps organizations to retain and gain customers who, as part of their quality system, want to trade with people who have been awarded this standard.

Total Quality Management (TQM)

The principles of TQM have been adopted by many organizations. It is a system adopted by management which aims to ensure that everyone within the organization from the Directors to the shop floor workers has a commitment to quality work. Organizations who are implementing TQM will have written quality statements outlining the policies and procedures to be adopted to ensure that the highest levels of quality are achieved.

> Quality assurance is the responsibility of everyone in the organization, not just the people who manufacture the products. All staff should be trained in quality assurance so that they can realize the importance of it and the impact it has upon customer satisfaction.

Evaluating administration systems

Management within an organization will often look to *evaluate* the effectiveness of its administration systems. Regular checks need to be carried out to monitor their effectiveness and to ensure that:

- The system is operating efficiently.
- The system is achieving its objectives.

Many organizations will have internal control systems set up to monitor the effectiveness of administration systems. For example, a suggestion box may be in existence for staff to comment upon the services offered by the staff canteen and to make recommendations on how they could be improved.

Table 2.10 gives examples of several functions and how their effectiveness might be measured.

Functions	Measure of Effectiveness
Quality control	The number of complaints received from customers about faulty and defective products
Recruitment and selection	What is the rate of staff turnover?
Staff canteen	Number of complaints received from staff about the service provided
Budgetary control	Are the targets set being adhered to or is expenditure above the budgeted figures?
Credit control	Are our customers paying on time?
Staff appraisal	Are staff satisfied and highly motivated?

Table 2.10   Examples of how the effectiveness of functions within an organization might be measured

> ### Self Check ✔ Element 1
>
> 1. Name the department which would be responsible for carrying out each of the following routine functions:
>   (a) Recording the levels of staff absenteeism.
>   (b) Monthly profit and loss account and balance sheet.
>   (c) Monthly sales figures.
>   (d) Questionnaire on customers' reaction to a new product.
>   (e) Purchase of raw materials for production purposes.
>
> 2. You have just set up a catering business. You cater for a wide range of functions including small dinner parties, buffets for weddings etc. You employ three other people. What *activities* will need to be carried out as part of the daily running of the business?
>
> 3. Decide whether each of the following statements is true or false.
>   (a) The production manager calculating monthly bonuses of the machine operators is carrying out a non-routine function.
>   (b) The accounts clerk checking calculations on purchase invoices is carrying out a routine function.
>   (c) The personnel manager investigating unusually high staff absenteeism is carrying out a routine function.
>   (d) The accounts manager preparing monthly profit and loss account and balance sheet is carrying out a non-routine function.
>
> 4. Decide whether each of the following statements is true of false.
>   (a) All accidents in the workplace must be recorded in an accident record book
>   (b) All organizations must have a written health and safety policy.
>
> 5. Which of the following must legally be written into a contract of employment?
>   (a) Period of notice.
>   (b) Rate of National Insurance contributions.
>   (c) Rate of pay.
>   (d) Disciplinary rules.
>   (e) Description of main duties.

Self Check ✔ *continued*

6. Which one of the following is a compulsory deduction from wages?
   (a) Union membership fees.
   (b) National Insurance contributions.
   (c) Hospital fund contributions.
   (d) Payments to the SAYE scheme.

7. Which Act(s) of Parliament will influence each of the following administration systems in an organization:
   (a) Submission of annual accounts to Companies House.
   (b) Written equal opportunities policy.
   (c) Procedure to be followed in the event of an accident.
   (d) Issue of written statement of terms and conditions of service to new employees.
   (e) Production of minutes of board meetings.

8. Decide whether each of the following statements is true or false
   (a) The reprographics function can evaluate its effectiveness by the turnaround time of its reprographic requests.
   (b) The efficiency of the production department can be measured by the level of wastage.

2.2 Communication Systems

In this element we will explore **communication systems** in an organization. We will look at both internal and external systems and identify the type of communication system most appropriate for carrying out various functions and activities. We will look specifically at:

- The purposes of communication systems.
- Different types and methods of communicating.
- Effect of electronic technology on communications.
- The factors to consider when selecting a method of communication.

Did You Know ?

80% of management time is spent communicating with others in the process of controlling and directing the activities of the organization.

Purposes of communication systems

When looking at communication in an organization we need to consider:

- Why does an organization need formal communications systems?
- Who does an organization communicate with?
- How do they communicate?

In the course of one day you will probably have many conversations with different people. Some may be for a specific purpose, for example telephoning a friend or colleague to

arrange what time you will meet them. This is known as *formal communication*, when you have a 'plan of action' behind your communication. Other conversations may be on a casual basis whilst standing at a bus-stop or in a queue. This is known as *informal communication*, that is, there is no set procedure. It takes place on a spontaneous and *ad hoc* basis. An example of informal communication in an organization would be a colleague calling into another colleague's office, without prior arrangement, to discuss a particular issue.

Communication is all about the 'passing on of information and ideas'.

Did You Know ?

Non-verbal means of communication, involving posture, gesture, dress, tone of voice, facial expression, eye-contact, etc all deliver a message. In fact psychologists suggest that 70% of all communication is of this kind.

Formal Communication systems

In the previous Element we looked at administrative systems in organizations and saw that in large organizations there are many specialist functions e.g. personnel, finance, sales, production. These functions do not, however, work in isolation. For example the sales department will have to work closely with production to tell them what future sales are likely to be so that they know how many units to produce. In other words, they will have to communicate with one another. To do this efficiently and effectively proper procedures will have to be set down. It would not be efficient for the sales manager to pass on information about future orders to the production manager by word of mouth. This information needs to be written down and properly recorded.

The need for **formal communication systems** in an organization arises for the following reasons.

- *To handle the flow of information*
  A tremendous amount of information passes through an organization from people both within and outside. For example, an organization that is involved in the buying of goods or services will have many financial transactions to record. In Unit 6 we will be looking at the different types of documentation necessary for such a transaction. These documents must be passed on, i.e. communicated to the necessary parties. Limited companies have to publish annual accounts for public inspection. Organizations will have to keep internal records, for example sales figures, personnel records. Many people could be involved in the preparation of these records. Each person needs to know who to ask for certain information and where to send it.

- *To aid decision making*
  Many decisions will be taken on a daily basis in an organization. Effective communication systems will be needed initially to help the decision maker. For example the manager who is preparing a budget for the forthcoming year will want to look at the previous year's

figures. Then people within the organization involved in implementing these decisions will need to be kept informed.

- **To measure business performance**
  A business needs to know how well or how badly it is doing. It will use much of its recorded information to monitor its performance. For example, one way of monitoring an organization's sales is to monitor past performance against current performance. To do this a record of past sales figures must be kept.

Who does an organization communicate with?
We have already said that organizations communicate with people both inside and outside the organization and that proper systems must be set up for both.

Did You Know ?

Some large offices process over 20,000 items of information each day.

- **Internal communication** is concerned with communication within the organization for example between people within different departments. As highlighted above, formal communication systems are necessary for internal communication.
- **External communication** takes place with people outside the organization. An organization will have to liaise with many people outside the organization as Table 2.11 illustrates.

Good communication skills can be learnt and developed. An organization should provide training in communication skills.

Group of People	Information They Might Need
Customers	Sales catalogue, price list, order forms, sales invoice
Bank manager	Financial information, e.g. copy of accounts
Inland Revenue	Copy of accounts
Shareholders	Annual report and accounts
Public	Annual report and accounts, information about jobs, e.g. job advert
Supplier	Payment for goods

Table 2.11 Examples of external groups of people with whom an organization might communicate

Methods of communication
Whether an organization is communicating with people inside or outside the organization the main *forms* of communication possible are:

- Written communication
- Verbal communication
- Electronic communication

The factors to consider when selecting a *method* of communication include the following.

- Is a written record necessary?
- What is the cost of the method used?
- How secure is the method?
- How accurate is the method?
- How efficient is the method?
- When is the information required?
- The distance involved.

We will look at each form of communication in turn with a description of the different methods that can be employed.
Table 2.12 is a summary of the different methods that we will look at.

Internal	External
Written communication	
Reports	Letters
Memorandum	Business documents
Notice, agenda and minutes	Sales catalogue
Staff newsletter	Advertisements
Suggestion boxes	Press releases
Notice boards	
Verbal communication	
Face-to-face	Meetings
Meetings	Telephone
Telephone	
Electronic communication	
Computer networks	Computer networks
Electronic mail	Electronic mail
Facsimile	Facsimile
Computerized Automatic Branch Exchange (CABX)	Computerized Automatic Branch Exchange (CABX)
Integrated Services Digital Network (ISDN)	Integrated Services Digital Network (ISDN)
Combined photocopier/fax/ telephone	Combined photocopier/fax/ telephone

Table 2.12 Summary of main forms and methods of communication used by an organization

Written communications
There are many different methods of **written communication** that can be used to communicate both internally and externally. The main advantage of written communication is that a permanent record exists which can be stored and referred to at a later date. The other advantages and reasons for using written communication are:

- It enables difficult and complex information to be sent, e.g. statistical information.
- People who are located at a distance can communicate.
- It can serve as a reminder to people.

Did You Know ?

An indication of the growth in *written* communication is the fact that the stock of books has doubled every 20 years or so since 1831.

Internal written communications
Reports
Written reports are widely used in organizations for the following reasons:

- To present the findings of an investigation.
- To fulfil legal requirements; for example a limited company must publish an annual report and accounts for shareholders.
- To present statistical information.
- To recommend changes within an organization.

A GUIDE TO REPORT WRITING

1.0 Terms of reference

This should state why the report was written, who requested it to be written, what it will cover and the date when it is to be completed.

2.0 Procedure

This section of the report should outline the procedure that was followed in compiling the report, i.e. how the information was obtained, e.g. by questionnaire, interviews, desk research etc.

3.0 Findings

3.1 Subtitles

This section contains the bulk of the report. It outlines the findings from your research and investigations. Subtitles should be used; for example if you were writing a report on health and safety within the organization, one subtitle could be 'Fire Procedures'.

3.1.2 Subheadings

The report could be further subdivided using subheadings. All the paragraphs should be numbered so that when someone is reading a report or referring to a report it is easy to find specific sections.

4.0 Conclusions

This section should be a summary of the main points. For example the report on health and safety could conclude 'Following the health and safety inspection it was reported that several areas need to be improved upon.'

5.0 Recommendations

These may or may not be included in the report depending upon whether or not they were requested. They should always be numbered for easy reference, as below.

5.1 Recommendations in the health and safety inspection should be followed up immediately.

5.2 All staff should receive training on health and safety matters within the organization.

Signed:

Date:

Fig. 2.7   A guide on how to write a report

An *informal report* is usually shorter and less structured than a *formal report* which is longer and more detailed with a set structure as outlined in the example (Fig. 2.8).

A REPORT ON HEALTH AND SAFETY

1.0 Terms of reference

On Wednesday 2nd March 1994 the Managing Director requested a health and safety inspection be carried out and a report written highlighting areas for action.

The report was to be submitted by Wednesday 23rd March 1994.

2.0 Procedure

2.1 An inspection of the premises was carried out by the Health and Safety Officer.

2.2 All staff were sent a questionnaire and asked to highlight any areas of concern.

3.0 Findings

3.1 Many of the word processing operators complained of increased headaches and back strain.

3.2 Much of the carpeting throughout the organization is old and frayed. The mat in the reception area was frequently cited as an example which has already tripped several staff up.

3.3 Several staff commented upon the inadequate outside lighting.

3.4 In spite of a 'No Smoking' policy being adopted by the office staff several staff appear to be ignoring this.

3.5 Several staff noted that the First Aid boxes were very poorly stocked.

3.6 About 50% of staff do not know the procedure to be followed in the event of an accident whilst at work.

4.0 Conclusions

The principal conclusions drawn were that there are several areas of concern and that many staff are ignorant of health and safety issues and legislation.

5.0 Recommendations

5.1 A health and safety representative should be appointed for each department within the organization.

5.2 All staff should receive training on health and safety and this should be updated on a regular basis.

5.3 Attention should be given immediately to the areas of concern highlighted in the findings of this report and regular health and safety inspections should take place.

Fig. 2.8   Example of a short formal report

Memorandum
Often shortened to 'memo' this is an *informal* written document which is frequently used within an organization. It will often be attached to some other information which the recipient needs to look at. Other reasons why a memo might be sent are:

- To remind someone of something.
- To confirm a verbal message.
- To ask for information.
- To pass on instructions.

Memos are usually written on pre-printed paper. Each organization will adopt its own 'housestyle' and layout (Fig. 2.9). Note: A memo may or may not be signed.

```
                    MEMORANDUM

To:      Departmental Managers      Date: 3 March 1994
From:    John Robinson              Ref:  JR/dp
         Training Officer

SUBJECT:  STAFF TRAINING

Please note that there will be a training session for all departmental
managers on Tuesday 22 March commencing at 9.00 am at Head
Office.

The subject of the session is 'Improving your communication skills'. A
copy of the programme for the day is attached.

If you are unable to attend please let me know.

I look forward to seeing you.


enc
```

Fig. 2.9 Example of a memorandum

Notice, agenda and minutes

Meetings are a common feature of modern business life. Managers spend a large part of their time attending meetings on both a formal and an informal basis. Formal meetings require certain written documentation to be issued before and after the meeting, as follows:

Notice. This will be sent out prior to the meeting to inform the participants of the date, time and venue of the meeting.

Agenda. This is a list of items to be discussed at a meeting and it is often combined with the notice, as in the example in Fig. 2.10.

```
          NOTICE OF THE FINANCE COMMITTEE
        A meeting of the Finance Committee will be held on
             Friday 4th March at 2.00 pm in the Boardroom

Any additions to the Agenda should reach me by Monday 28th
February
Agenda
1.  Apologies for Absence*
2.  Minutes of the last meeting*
3.  Matters arising from the minutes*
4.  Finance Director's Review
5.  Annual Budgets
6.  Refurbishment of Staff Canteen
7.  Any other business*
8.  Date of next meeting*


D Fox
Secretary
```

Fig. 2.10 Example of a Notice and Agenda

Minutes. These are a written record of what was discussed at a meeting. They are written by the secretary and sent out to members. At the next meeting the members will formally approve the minutes and they will be signed by the Chairperson.

In-house newspaper/staff newsletter

It is common for many organizations nowadays to publish, on a regular basis, an in-house newspaper or staff newsletter. The main purpose of this is to keep staff informed of what is happening within the organization. It also allows staff to contribute articles of any interest. The types of information which might be included are:

- Appointment of new personnel
- Introduction of new products
- Opening of a new branch/factory/store etc
- Public relations activities
- Forthcoming staff social events
- Review of past staff social events

Notice boards

Look around your college or your place of work and you will probably find one or more notice boards. Notice boards are used in organizations to display general information to all staff. They should not be used to display vital information which all staff should see as many people may not take the time to read it. Types of information which could be displayed include:

- Sports information
- Job vacancies
- Union news
- Classified information, e.g. 'for sale' adverts
- Health and safety notices

Suggestion boxes

Many organizations nowadays are keen to involve their employees and increase their sense of belonging in the firm. One of the ways in which they try to do this is through the introduction of a suggestion box. Employees are encouraged to put forward any ideas which they feel will improve the organization, increase its efficiency etc. Many organizations offer a reward for the best ideas.

External written communications

Letter

The letter is the most commonly used form of external communication. There are many reasons as to why an organization might send a letter including:

- Letter of enquiry to a supplier
- Letter of complaint to a supplier
- Letter to customer confirming order
- Letter to job applicants to confirm interview details
- Letter to job applicant to confirm offer of job
- Standard letter advertising goods/services

Can you think of any others?

> **Did You Know ?**
>
> Over £4 billion is spent each year on sending letters and parcels to and from businesses. Over 1 million business premises are served by the letter service.

A letter is usually written on the organization's own letterhead and each company will adopt its own housestyle, i.e. way of setting out the letter.

The letter in fig. 2.11 is written in the fully blocked style – all lines begin at the left margin with no indentation and there is open punctuation, i.e. there are no punctuation marks at the end of short free-standing lines. The main body of the letter does have punctuation. This style is the one adopted by most organizations today.

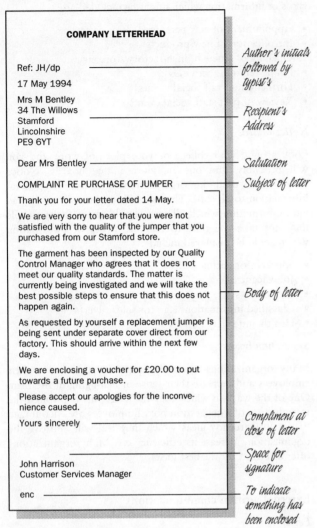

Fig. 2.11 Example of a business letter

Business documents
In Unit 6 you will be looking at the business documents necessary for financial transactions when organizations are involved in the buying and selling of goods and services. These are necessary to keep a permanent record of the transaction so that each party knows how much is owed etc. Examples of business documents include invoices, sales orders, purchase orders, statements.

Annual report and accounts
It is a legal requirement for public limited companies to publish an annual report and accounts for their shareholders. These are usually printed on glossy paper with many photographs, charts and tables included.

Sales catalogues
These will contain the goods or services that a firm sells. Sales catalogues are produced by an organization to send out to customers and prospective customers.

Advertisements
Advertising is a form of communication used to inform people about goods and services and to persuade them to buy. It is a multimillion pound industry and up to a fifth of the cost of a product can be attributed to advertising. We will look at advertising in more detail in Unit 3.

Press releases
A firm will use press releases as part of its public relations activities. They are articles of interest about the company and could include:

- Opening of a new branch, office or factory
- Appointment of new personnel
- Launch of a new product or service
- Sponsorship of an event

An organization often uses press releases as a means of 'free' publicity.

Verbal communication

This is communication by the spoken word and can include face-to-face communication, speaking on the telephone or at meetings.

> ### Did You Know ?
> The average person speaks only for a total of ten to eleven minutes each day.

Face-to-face
During the course of one day we probably all take part in several conversations with people. Some of these may just be a casual 'hello' or a brief conversation to pass the time of day. Some may be more formal to discuss a particular issue.

In an organization people will come together in the staff canteen and probably discuss both work and non-work issues. This is face-to-face conversation on an *informal* basis. People may attend a meeting to discuss a particular issue or they might have to attend a disciplinary meeting or interview. This is face-to-face conversation on a *formal* basis.

Non-verbal means of communication involving eye contact, body posture, gestures and so on play an important part in face-to-face conversation.

Meetings
We have already mentioned **meetings** and looked at the documentation involved in setting up a meeting. Meetings are an example of formal face-to-face conversation. All staff at some time will probably have to attend meetings which serve a wide variety of purposes including:

- To pass on information.
- To make decisions.
- To make recommendations.
- To negotiate, for example a pay award.
- To solve an issue or a problem.

Meetings can take place on either an informal or a formal basis. An *informal* meeting will be a gathering of two or more people to discuss a certain issue and it will not involve any formal written documentation.

A *formal* meeting is one that has set procedures laid down in a written constitution. It will have officials, for example a chairperson and a secretary, and formal documentation. Some meetings are a legal requirement, for example limited companies must hold an annual meeting – the Annual General Meeting (AGM) – by law.

Meetings are held both internally and externally. An example of an internal meeting could be the Board Meeting or Staff Social Club Meeting. External meetings could be held with prospective customers.

Telephone

The **telephone** provides a very common method of verbal communication within organizations. It enables communication between people within the organization on a local, national or international basis. Later on in this unit we will see how advances in technology have brought about enhanced telephone systems. The main advantages of using the telephone as a means of communication are that quick and instant feedback is possible. The main disadvantage is that a written record of what was discussed is not provided. Also important aspects of non-verbal communication e.g. facial expression, gestures, are lost in telephone communication.

Portable telephones/pagers

Portable telephones or 'mobiles' are very common today. Many people, especially those in business, possess one. They are particularly useful for people who travel a lot in their job. They can be either totally free-standing or car-based.

A pager is a 'bleep' device often used by doctors and people on 'call'. It is activated by a radio signal and prompts the carrier to telephone head office or wherever 'base' might be.

Electronic communication

In recent years there have been huge advances in **electronic communications** enabling speedy communications to take place on a worldwide basis.

The 'electronic office' is now widespread with many organizations having introduced computers and electronic equipment to process their information. The impact of the electronic office has brought about changes in the preparation of documents and written material, the storage and retrieval of documents and the transmission of information. Below is an outline of the main methods of electronic communication commonly used in many organizations.

Computer networks

A **computer network** exists where a number of personal computers (PCs) are linked together using an internal telephone line or simple cable. Two types of network exist, a *local area network* (LAN) where computers in one

building or location are joined together, and a *wide area network* (WAN) where computers in different locations are connected.

A computer network allows computers to share resources and information so that they can 'talk to one another'. For example, when goods are received into an organization it is normal practice for a goods received note to be completed and then distributed to the appropriate departments. If a network has been installed, however, the information can be entered into the computer and then accessed by the appropriate people, saving the amount of paperwork normally generated by such a procedure. Clearly there is need for security and confidentiality to be taken into consideration with a network system. This can be overcome by installing passwords and restricting access to certain information by authorized users only.

There are two main types of network, the first being a 'star' network where there is *one* central CPU (central processing unit) linked to a number of terminals each with their own monitor but sharing a disk drive and printer. The other type of network is a 'ring' network where *each* computer has its own CPU so that it can operate either independently or as part of the network. There will be one or more printers attached to the network. Fig. 2.12 illustrates the two types of network.

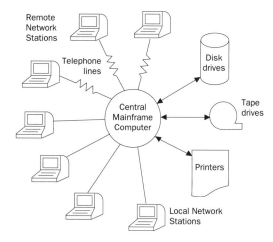

A Star Network

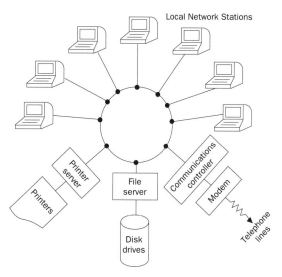

A Ring Network

Fig. 2.12 Star and Ring Networks

The advantages of a network are as follows:

- Communication within the organization is improved as information processed by one computer user can immediately be communicated to someone else on the network system.
- The sharing of resources means that money can be saved.
- A network system reduces the amount of paper within an organization as documents and information can be transferred electronically.

Did You Know ?

Most of these developments in electronic communications have been built on the *microprocessor* – the computer on a chip. The microprocessor is essentially the whole of a computer – logic, memory and control – etched on to a chip of silicon about 1 cm square and 0.5mm thick.

Electronic mail

As the name suggests this allows computer users on the same network system to send messages to one another via their computer terminals. The same message can be sent to a number of different people. If a user's terminal is switched off then the message will be stored and forwarded once the system is switched on. When the message has been read it is automatically acknowledged so that the sender knows it has been received. Sending messages electronically is quick although it relies on the receiver having his or her terminal switched on. It also reduces the amount of paper although if necessary the messages can be printed out.

Telephone systems

We have already seen that the telephone is a very common means of communication used within a business to communicate with people both inside and outside the organization. Technology has had a tremendous impact on telecommunications and expanded the use of the telephone, enabling worldwide communication by telephone cable, satellite or microwave link.

CABX (Computerized Automatic Branch Exchange)

Most organizations have a 'switchboard' which links the telephone network. A 'switchboard' will have several outside lines and internal extensions to which calls are directed. This has traditionally been known as the PABX (Private Automatic Branch Exchange). However, most modern switchboards are now computerized and as a result can perform a number of more advanced functions including:

- Instant dialling of numbers frequently used.
- Play music to waiting callers.
- Three-way conversations.
- Dialling of numbers without lifting the handset.
- Automatic redialling.
- Providing a record of calls made, by whom, the date and time (a printout is available).

Facsimile transmission

Commonly known as the 'fax', information is sent electronically via the telephone lines locally, nationally or internationally. Written information, figures, diagrams and pictures can all be sent. Thus if a document is required urgently, the sender does not have to rely on the post but can fax it to the recipient, subject of course to them having a fax machine. Provided the recipient's fax machine is switched on the information can be sent at any time of the day. This is particularly important when information is being faxed to someone who operates in a different time zone.

Portable 'mobile' telephones

These are commonly used by business people today especially if their job entails a lot of travelling. Mobile telephones enable them to be contacted wherever they are. The phones are either totally free-standing or car-based.

Integrated services digital network (ISDN)

This is a sophisticated system developed by British Telecom which makes use of fibre optic cables to transfer signals. It enables subscribers to make use of the following facilities:

- *Data Transfer.* Information stored on a computer can be transferred quickly and cheaply. For example a printer located in Edinburgh might want to transfer information to a publisher in Leeds.

- *Desktop Conferencing.* Users in different locations can share information on a computer screen and then discuss it, thus saving the time and expense of travelling to different locations.

- *Videoconferencing.* The system allows people in different locations to talk over the telephone and view one another on screen. As with the above it saves the time and expense of travelling.

Prestel

This is a public viewdata system operated by British Telecom which gives organizations and individuals access to a wide range of information on a variety of services such as British Rail, airlines, share prices, exchange rates etc. The information is received on a computer which is linked to a telephone line. As a subscriber you have to pay a quarterly charge plus the cost of each telephone call that you make. Each prestel terminal has a mailbox which enables users to send messages to one another.

Combined photocopier/fax/telephone

One of the most recent developments in electronic communication is the combined photocopier/fax/telephone. The individual items of equipment will soon be replaced by a personal computer (PC), a scanner and a printer. This will enable the user to type a document onto the screen, make photocopies from the screen, and fax it to someone from the screen using the Windows operating system. Documents not stored on the computer can also be scanned and then photocopied or faxed. Incoming faxes will be stored directly onto the screen where they can be read and printed if desired. One obvious advantage is that the quality of the paper will be much better as faxes will be printed out on plain paper as opposed to fax thermal paper.

Table 2.13 provides a useful summary of the various methods of electronic communication.

Method	Description
Computer networks	A number of PCs are linked together using an internal telephone line or simple cable
Electronic mail	Computer users on the same network system can send messages to one another via their computer terminal
CABX (Computerized Automatic Branch Exchange)	A computerized 'switchboard' which can perform a number of advanced functions
Facsimile	Allows information (written, graphical etc.) to be sent electronically via the telephone lines
Portable 'mobile' telephones	Totally free-standing or car-based phones which are commonly used by business people who travel a great deal
ISDN (Integrated Services Digital Network)	A sophisticated communications system which makes use of fibre optic cables. Enables the transfer of data to different locations, sharing of information on computer screen and videoconferencing
Prestel	A public viewdata system whereby a subscriber can access a wide variety of information via a computer terminal
Combined photo-copier/fax/telephone	One PC plugged into a telephone line together with a scanner and a printer replaces the individual items of equipment. Using the Windows operating system all of these functions can be carried out from the one terminal

Table 2.13 Summary of methods of electronic communication

The widespread use of electronic technology in organizations has brought about a great many benefits. There are, however, drawbacks as outlined in Table 2.14.

Advantages	Disadvantages
Speed Information can be transmitted in an instant from one side of the world to another	*Cost* Cost of electronic technology can be considerable. In addition to the initial capital outlay there are installation costs, running costs and costs of training staff to consider
Cost effective In spite of the often expensive initial investment in the long run it is more cost effective to use electronic technology	*Security* Widespread use of computers has raised concern about security and confidentiality – can be overcome by installing passwords restricting access to certain information by authorized users only
Accuracy Less human involvement is necessary which cuts out error	*Breakdown* If there is breakdown of equipment it can hinder progress, costing the organization lost time and possibly business
Reliability Electronic equipment is more reliable than manual equipment and unlike human beings it does not get tired or distracted	*Staff resistance* Many staff do not like change and find it difficult and stressful adapting to new methods of working

Easier access to information A wide range of information can be quickly and easily accessed

Better quality Word processors, desktop publishing and sophisticated printers produce information to the highest standards

Health Research has shown that extensive use of VDUs (visual display units) can damage eyesight and may be harmful to an unborn child

Table 2.14 Advantages and disadvantages of electronic technology

Factors to consider when selecting a communication system

We have seen that there are many alternative methods of communication available to an organization. The most sophisticated method might not always be the most appropriate. The requirements of a business will depend, amongst other things, on its size, location and nature. Table 2.15 provides a summary of the factors to consider.

Speed	How quickly is the information required?
Who is it for?	Is the information for people inside or outside the organization? Is it local, national or international?
Cost	How much will it cost to transmit the information? For example it would be cheaper to fax a document from Manchester to London rather than use the services of a courier
Security	How confidential is the information?
Is a written record needed?	Widespread use of computers means that information can be stored on disk. A telephone call would not be appropriate if a written record was needed

Table 2.15 Factors to consider when selecting a communications system

Self Check ✔ **Element 2**

9. Why is it necessary for business organizations to have formal communications systems?
10. In each of the following cases state what method of written communication could be used:
    (a) Inform staff of a social event organized by the staff social committee.
    (b) Confirming a job interview to an external applicant.
    (c) Announcing the sponsorship by the company of a local football team.
    (d) To remind all senior managers that monthly reports are due by the end of the week.
    (e) Record what was discussed at the monthly Staff Social Committee.

Self Check ✓ **continued**

11. Complete the gaps in the following statements:
Communication by the spoken word is known as
———— communication. It can include ————
conversation, speaking on the ———— or at
————.

Meetings are an example of verbal communication.
Meetings can be held either ———— or ————.
A ———— meeting is one that has set procedures laid
down in a written constitution. Limited companies
must by law hold an ———— ———— ————.
The telephone provides a common method of verbal
communication. Its main advantages are that it is
———— and instant ———— is possible. Its main
disadvantage is that a ———— record of what was
discussed is not available.

12. What method of electronic communication could be
used in the following circumstances:
   (a) Quickly sending a message to senior managers.
   (b) Typing a standard letter.
   (c) Sending a document required urgently overseas.
   (d) Leaving an urgent message for the Sales Director
who is out visiting.
   (e) Linking up three people in Manchester, Edinburgh
and Southampton.

13. Decide whether each of the following statements is
true or false.
   (a) A major disadvantage of a computer network is
the problem of confidentiality.
   (b) Operating a VDU could be harmful to your health.
   (c) Fewer errors are likely to be made using non-
electronic communication methods than electronic
methods.
   (d) Staff resistance to the introduction of electronic
technology can be overcome by staff training.

14. A small manufacturing firm is considering installing a
computer network to assist with its administration.
   (i) What advantages would there be to the
organization of carrying this out?
   (ii) What other factors should they take into
consideration before going ahead?

2.3 Information Processing

In this element we will examine the **information processing**
systems of an organization. We will look at the purpose of
information systems and the different types of systems
adopted within organizations. In particular we will:

- Explain the purposes of information processing systems
used by a business.
- Describe various types of information processing
systems.
- Evaluate the effectiveness of information processing
systems in supporting the functions of business organizations.
- Identify and explain the effects of legislation upon
information processing systems.
- Look at the effects of computer technology on the users
and operators.

What is an information processing system?

All organizations have to deal with a great deal of information on a daily basis. In Element 1 we looked at how
people within organizations communicate with one another.
We saw that communication is all about the passing on of
information which is essential if organizations are to function efficiently and effectively. Before the information is
'passed on' it has to be gathered, sorted and stored, i.e.
processed.

> Information processing is the activity of gathering, sorting,
> storing data and then passing it on.

Purposes of information processing systems

Information processing systems can be either *manual* or
computer based. The great advances in technology in the
last decade have seen many of the more traditional methods
of information processing being replaced by computerized
methods. Whatever method is used, however, the *purposes*
of information processing systems are:

- To store information.
- To distribute information.
- To use information.
- To communicate information.

Fig. 2.13 outlines the functions of any information processing system.

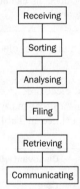

Fig. 2.13   The functions of information processing

We have already said that information can be processed
either manually or by the use of electronic methods. In this
unit we are going to concentrate primarily on electronic
means of processing information. Before we do that let us
compare traditional methods with computer-based methods
(Table 2.16).

Electronic methods of information processing

As can be seen from Table 2.16 the traditional methods of
information processing have been replaced by information
technology. The use of **information technology** in organizations is now widespread and includes both large and small
businesses. We will look later on in this unit at the benefits
new technology has brought to organizations. Before we do
that, however, we will look at some of the more common
electronic systems available. The use and development of
information technology skills is a requirement of your
GNVQ course and it is likely that you will already have
used some of the following:

Function	Manual	Computerized
Receiving	Delivered by the postal system	Information stored on computer can be transmitted from one terminal to another in different locations
Sorting	Carried out manually by clerical staff, e.g. customer details could be sorted by area	Customer records stored on a database can be stored quickly by a simple command
Analysing	Managers manually analyse information, e.g. statistics	Information stored on computer can be analysed at high speed, e.g. financial ratios
Filing/ storing	Stored on paper in filing cabinets, in card indexes or filmed copy, e.g. microfiche	Computerized electronic filing of records is possible. Using a network system these can be accessed by many different users within the organization. Information can be stored on floppy disk and hard disk
Retrieving	Paper-based documents and records manually retrieved from filing systems	Information stored on computer can be accessed speedily and updated if desired, e.g. customer account details, stock position, reports stored on computer disk
Communicating	Typing of reports, letters etc. by secretaries	Word processors, fax machines, electronic mail are some of the means by which information can be electronically processed and communicated

Table 2.16   Comparison of manual versus computerized methods of information processing

Word Processing

This is the most common form of information processing found in modern offices today. **Word processors** have replaced typewriters in the production of textual information. Letters, memorandums, reports and other written forms of communication can be quickly produced on a word processor. They can be stored in the memory and amended as required. Word processing offers many features which can be used in the production of documents. The following is a list of just a few of these features:

- Blocks of text can be copied and moved around the screen.
- Text can be enhanced by the use of emboldening, underlining, different font sizes and styles, e.g. italics, shadow, superscript, subscript etc.
- The mailmerge feature allows standard letters to be produced from a list of names and addresses.
- Tables and graphics can be incorporated into the text.
- Text can be produced in columns as in a newspaper format.
- The spell checker facility will highlight any words incorrectly spelt.
- Words and phrases can be searched for and either removed or replaced with an alternative.

The main advantages of word processing are that standard documents and letters can be stored and easily and quickly amended.

Did You Know ?

92 million paper documents are produced each year. The files of paper documents kept by world businesses are doubling every $3\frac{1}{2}$ years.

Desktop Publishing (DTP)

This is a sophisticated word processing system which is capable of producing very high quality documents. **DTP** programs allow text to be arranged and graphics to be incorporated. The whole of one page can be viewed on screen. Books, magazines, newspapers etc are all produced using DTP.

Some of the many features of DTP are highlighted in Table 2.17:

- A number of different text styles can be used, e.g. typeface, size, enhancements
- Diagrams can be placed on pages with text flowing around them
- Detailed vertical and horizontal ruler guides allow extremely accurate placing of text and graphics
- Graphics can be manipulated to make them larger or smaller, to reposition them, to 'crop' them, i.e. only show part of them
- Graphics can be superimposed over or under text

Table 2.17   Some of the features of DTP

Databases

A **database** is a collection of files or records which can be stored either manually or electronically. A database could be used by an organization for a variety of different purposes. These might include:

- Records of employees.
- Details of customers.
- Details of stock.

The advantages of a computerized database are that once the information has been input into the computer it can be retrieved, amended and sorted easily and quickly. Searches of the database can be made for specific information.

For example imagine that you held all your customer details, i.e. customer name, address, telephone number, account details, on a database. You are asked to provide a list of the names and telephone numbers of all customers in the Manchester area. If the records were kept on card index this would be a time consuming and laborious task as a manual search would have to be made. However, with a computerized database this information could be made available very quickly by virtue of a simple command. Printed copies can be made available by sending the data to a printer.

A set of *terminology* exists which is common to all database programs:

- *File*   A collection of records, e.g. all employees details.

- *Record* An individual record, e.g. details of one employee.
- *Field* One item of data contained in a record, e.g. surname of employee, initials of employee, address, telephone number, department.

Before any information can be input into the database the fields have to be created stating what type they are, e.g. character, numeric etc, and the width of the field has to be specified, e.g. 15 characters. Table 2.18 illustrates a database record for an employee.

SURNAME	Harris
FORENAME	William
ADDRESS	10 Acacia Way, Knowle, Bristol BS6 8TU
TEL NO	0272 668903
DATE OF BIRTH	18/04/49
DEPARTMENT	Production
SALARY	£15,500

Table 2.18 Example of a record contained in a database of employee details

In addition to being able to search for information and select certain records a database can also:

- Carry out numerical calculations, e.g. calculate total sales to a customer
- Sort records alphabetically, numerically and in date order.
- Export data; e.g. customer names and addresses could be exported to a word processing file to enable the 'mailmerge' function.

Any organization which stores computerized information is governed by the principles of the Data Protection Act which is discussed later on in this unit.

Did You Know ?

It has been estimated that over 40% of employees in the advanced industrial countries are now employed in the 'information sector'. In other words their main activities involve producing, processing, transmitting and storing information.

Spreadsheets

A **spreadsheet** is a powerful application that can be used to carry out a number of mathematical calculations. It can carry out simple arithmetical calculations such as additions, totals, percentages, and proceed to more complicated automated calculations and analyses.

Spreadsheets are found in both large and small businesses and can be used for a variety of purposes. They are very useful for providing *accounting information*, including:

- Cash flow forecasts
- Trial balances
- Preparation of final accounts
- Projecting budgets
- Calculation of production costs
- VAT and tax returns

A spreadsheet is a grid consisting of rows and columns into which data is entered and stored. *Data* can be:

- **Numeric** Numbers which will form the basis of the calculations.
- **Text** Words and headings.
- **Formulae** Instructions which make the computer perform numeric calculations, e.g. addition, subtraction, percentages etc.

Some of the *terminology* of spreadsheets is explained below:

- **Rows** Each horizontal row is given a number.
- **Columns** Each vertical column is given a letter.
- **Cells** Each box is known as a cell which is identified by its column letter and row number, e.g. D5. The cell into which data is entered is known as the 'active cell'.

Most spreadsheet packages consist of several hundred columns and several thousand rows. Only a part of the spreadsheet can thus be displayed on the screen at any one time. An extract of a spreadsheet is shown in Fig. 2.14.

	A	B	C	D	E
1	XYZ LTD				
2	BUDGET FOR JAN–MARCH				
3		JAN	FEB	MAR	TOTAL
4	RECEIPTS	£	£	£	£
5	Sales – Cash	3000	3250	3500	9750
6	Sales – Credit	4250	4250	4500	13000
7	Total Receipts	7250	7500	8000	22750
8	PAYMENTS	£	£	£	£
9	Purchases	2500	2600	2750	7850
10	Wages	1500	1500	1500	4500
11	Overheads	1000	1000	1000	3000
12	Total Expenses	5000	5100	5250	15350
13	Total Profit	2250	2400	2750	7400
14					

Fig. 2.14

The different **types** of data which can be entered into a spreadsheet are:

- *Labels* Text entries in the spreadsheet, e.g. headings in columns and rows are known as labels.
- *Values* These are numbers which are input into a spreadsheet, e.g. the value entered into B5 is 3000 which represents cash sales for January.
  B7, B12 and B13 are not values but totals calculated by the means of formulae.
- *Formulae* These carry out mathematical functions. A formula is an equation which is entered into the spreadsheet which then performs a mathematical calculation, e.g. B7 represents total receipts. The formula entered into this cell would be B5 + B6.
  If the values in cells B5 or B6 were altered the result in cell B7 would automatically change.

Other formulae can be entered to carry out divisions, multiplications, percentages, averages, square roots etc.

Once data have been entered into a spreadsheet they can be **edited**. The *functions* which can be carried out include:

- Column headings can be aligned to the left, right or centre of a cell.
- Text can be emboldened or underlined.
- Columns and rows can be inserted or deleted.
- Numbers can be displayed as whole numbers or decimals.
- Blocks of data can be copied or moved to other areas of the spreadsheet.
- Spreadsheets can be exported to other applications, e.g. the spreadsheet above could be exported to a file that has been word processed.

Another very useful function is the use of graphs which can be produced directly from a database. For example a graph showing the profit in each of the three months January to March could be produced from the information shown in Fig. 2.14.

Spreadsheets are thus very powerful tools which can be used by management to assist them in their decision making.

Integrated software programs

Many organizations use a *combination* of different applications. For example, correspondence will be prepared on a word processor, budgets prepared on a spreadsheet and customer details kept on a database.

As a result of this, **integrated software programs** have been developed. These programs incorporate the three functions mentioned above.

The main advantages of these integrated programs are that they provide cost savings and data can be easily transferred from one program to another. Integrated software packages are very useful for the small business with few specialised computer personnel to draw on.

Accounting/bookkeeping packages

Accounting programs are widely used in many organizations nowadays. They are capable of carrying out a variety of *functions* including:

- The recording of routine financial transactions in the ledgers.
- Preparation of business documents, e.g. sales invoices, statements etc.
- Preparation of payroll and payslips.
- Production of figures for final accounts.

The advantages of these packages are that they have removed much of the manual recording of figures and accounts.

Facsimile transmission (fax)

We have already discussed **facsimile transmission** earlier on in this unit as a means of communicating information.

A facsimile machine enables the transmission of information via the telephone lines at any time of the day or night.

The fax machine has a number of advantages including:

- They are easy to operate.
- A fax can be sent at any time of the day or night.
- Written information, pictures, graphics, maps and other documents can be sent.
- Many fax machines double up as photocopiers.

Electronic mail

As we saw earlier in this unit **electronic mail** is the transmission of a message by electronic means via a computer network. Its main advantage is that it allows documents to be sent (letters, memos, reports etc.) from one computer terminal to another, eradicating the need for paper.

Messages can be sent within the organization via the local area network (LAN). They can also be sent externally to other organizations provided that both parties subscribe to an E-Mail system such as the BT Mailbox Service (formerly known as Telecom Gold). This service allows subscribers to send messages to one another via the public telephone network system.

Electronic filing systems

The installation of **computerized filing systems** is becoming more and more common. The main advantage of such a system is that vast amounts of information can be stored on disk thus reducing the amount of paper within an organization. Computerized filing systems can be either centralized or decentralized.

In a *centralized* system everyone within the organization has access to information and files via the network. Access to files can be reduced by means of a password.

In a *decentralized* system files are stored on PCs and access to the file is restricted to certain people, e.g. one department.

As with all computerized systems, backup systems are needed to insure against the loss of any information.

Did You Know ?

Survey evidence suggests that over one in ten *paper-based* documents or files are lost forever due to careless filing techniques and practices.

Optical disk technology

Information can be stored **optically**, the most popular form at the moment being the CD-ROM (which stands for Compact Disk Read Only Memory). They look like the CDs purchased from music stores. Information is written onto them which cannot be removed – hence they are described as 'read only'. They are used for storing vast amounts of information, usually reference material. Examples of the type of information stored are back-dated copies of newspapers, company information including their annual reports, information on countries, dictionaries etc. The disk is fed into the computer and the information can be printed out. Many libraries now have this facility and it could be a very valuable source of information for your GNVQ assignments.

Table 2.19 highlights the advantages and disadvantages of electronic filing systems.

Advantages	Disadvantages
Quick to set up – files can be created very quickly	Electronic systems are expensive to install
Information can be accessed very quickly at the touch of a button	Staff resistance has to be overcome when any new technology is introduced and new methods of working are required
Information can be transferred very quickly between departments, offices and even overseas provided that a network system is in operation	As with any computer-based system it is subject to breakdown. If the system 'crashes' this can be particularly inconvenient and expensive in terms of lost time etc.
They require much less space than paper-based systems. Filing cabinets are bulky whereas disks are easily stored	Security can be a problem when access to information is widespread. As discussed the installation of passwords can overcome this
Provided proper back-up systems are in place and access to confidential files is restricted by use of passwords, electronic systems are very secure	
In the long term electronic filing systems are cost effective	

Table 2.19   The advantages and disadvantages of electronic filing systems

Effects of electronic technology on information processing

We have looked at the main electronic information processing systems available which many organizations, large and small, have adopted. It is essential that organizations keep up with new technology in order to remain competitive. For example if a company abroad requests a quote it is no longer advisable to send it by post. Sending it by fax ensures that information reaches its destination in seconds. To delay the information could mean lost business. Speed is just one of the benefits of new technology outlined in Table 2.20.

Speed	Information can be stored, processed, analysed and retrieved in an instant.
Accuracy	Less human involvement means that mistakes are reduced. Provided the information is input correctly then the outputs should be accurate
Costs	The information of new technology means an initial capital outlay. However, the faster processing of information means that less time is used and thus in the long run cost savings are made
Reliability	Electronic equipment is much more reliable than humans and mechanical equipment. However, if one part fails this can cause the whole system to fail
Access to information	Information can be accessed very quickly from a variety of sources
Improved quality	New technology has greatly improved the quality of information produced. Documents can be word processed and, using desktop publishing, text can be greatly enhanced

Table 2.20   Benefits of new technology

The introduction of electronic technology undoubtedly brings many advantages to an organization as highlighted above. However, the introduction of new technology requires thorough planning as there are several important factors to consider when implementing it, including:

- Staff training and consultation
- Efficiency
- Health and safety
- Security

These issues are discussed in more detail below:

Staff training and consultation
The benefits of new technology will only be gained if staff are properly trained in the use of the new equipment. The operation of new technology requires the use of new skills. Organizations must therefore provide proper training and staff development programmes in the use of the equipment and software. Many people are wary of change and frightened of new technology. These fears and worries can be overcome through training.

Prior to the implementation of new systems staff should be consulted about their needs and requirements. It is important that managers listen to the people who will actually be using the systems to identify their needs.

By the same token it is also important that once the system is operational, managers listen to the staff who are using the system. Any complaints should be taken seriously and investigated.

Efficiency
Before investment in new technology is made, a feasibility study should be carried out to ensure that the introduction of new technology will actually improve the system. There is little point in making the capital outlay if efficiency is not going to improve.

When a manual system is being automated it is wise to run the two systems alongside each other for a period of time. The introduction of new technology undoubtedly brings about 'teething' problems. Running the two systems alongside each other ensures greater accuracy as both systems can be monitored simultaneously. If the computerized system fails or 'crashes' there is the comfort of knowing that the information can be retrieved by means of the manual system.

Health and safety

Several studies have been carried out into the long-term effects of working with computers. It has been suggested that working with computer screens or VDUs for long periods of time can cause several health problems including eye strain, headaches, backache, repetitive strain injury (RSI) through intensive rapid movement of the fingers and wrists, and possible damage to unborn children through exposure to radiation emitted from VDU screens.

Because the introduction of new technology has only become widespread within the last 10 years none of the research has yet been proved to be conclusive. However, new legislation has been passed based on European Directive 90/270/EEC which covers minimum health and safety requirements for work with display equipment. An organization which does not comply with the Display Screen Equipment Regulations is subject to a hefty fine. The legislation also sets down standards which must be adhered to when installing computer equipment.

Table 2.21 sets out the guidelines which have been laid down under the legislation. Make sure you are familiar with these guidelines.

- Computer screens must not flicker or jump and it must be possible for users to adjust the brightness and contrast

- Staff using VDUs all day should be entitled to regular eye tests paid for them by the employer

- Keyboards should be legible, tiltable and separate from the rest of the system

- Software should be suitable for the task and adequate training should be provided

- Chairs should be provided which are adjustable and have backrests

- Employees who use VDUs should be provided with adequate breaks and rests away from computer screens, e.g. carrying out other activities

- Lighting should be arranged to reduce the glare and reflections from the screen. If this is not possible anti-glare screens could be fitted to each VDU

- The rooms should be adequately ventilated as computer equipment radiates dry heat

- Noise pollution should be reduced to a minimum by repositioning equipment or sound-proofing it if it becomes too noisy

Table 2.21 European guidelines on working with VDU's

The Health and Safety Executive have implemented widespread publicity campaigns to ensure that all organizations are aware of these regulations. It is the employer's responsibility to ensure that they are adhered to and that adequate protection is given to users of computer equipment.

Security

The widespread use of information technology has raised serious concerns about security. There are three main issues with regard to security as follows:

- Access to information
- Loss of information due to system failure
- Computer viruses

One of the benefits of new technology is the greater access to information. Computer networks mean that many users can have access to a central bank of information, e.g. customer details. This widespread access to information has obvious benefits but it also has serious implications from a security point of view. There needs to be some control over who can access certain information. Confidential information, e.g. staff records, can be restricted to authorised users only by the use of a password system.

We have already seen that large amounts of information can be stored on computer. If the computer 'crashes' all the information could be lost and the consequences for the business disastrous. Because of this steps must be taken to provide proper back-up systems. Organizations must ensure that proper back-up systems are in place. Valuable information should be stored on floppy disk with back-up taking place at the end of each day. These disks should then be stored away from the main computer system, preferably in fireproof cabinets.

Another threat to security is that of computer viruses. These are written by unlawful individuals and embedded into a program's code making them almost invisible. The whole contents of a hard disk can be destroyed by a computer virus – with serious consequences for an organization. These viruses can be spread when programs are copied from one system to another. Floppy disks can also become infected and if they are inserted into a machine can spread the virus to that system. Programs called vaccines or disinfectants have been written to counteract computer viruses and checks should be carried out regularly to prevent their spread.

- *Data Protection Act 1984*
  This Act was passed following growing concern that holding personal information on individuals on computers could cause a threat to personal privacy. The Act sets down guidelines for both *data users* (those who store the information) and *data subjects* (those about whom the information is stored).

  - **Data users,** that is, those who record and use the personal information, must comply with a set of Data Protection Principles, outlined below. They must also register with a Data Protection Registrar who is appointed by the Home Secretary.
  - **Data subjects** have the right to access any personal information about them which is held on computer. If any damage is caused by unauthorized disclosure of this information, or if the information is inaccurate, they are entitled to seek recompense.

The main principles of the **Data Protection Act** are outlined in Table 2.22. Make sure you are familiar with these.

The data must be:
- Obtained lawfully
- Only used for lawful purposes
- Accurate and up-to-date
- Made available to the individuals concerned on request
- Safeguarded by adequate security measures
- Relevant to the purpose for which it is held

Table 2.22 The data protection principles

The Act only applies to information which is stored on computer and does not apply to information stored in paper-based files.

The Act states that data used in the following circumstances are exempt from the registration rule:

- Data used in payroll programs
- Data used in mailing lists
- Data concerning personal, family or household affairs
- Data kept by clubs and charities

Any organization which does not comply with the Act is subject to a hefty fine. If in doubt, the data user should contact the Registrar. This involves the completion of a form and payment of a small fee.

A final note of caution! Electronic technology might not always be the answer. Before committing itself to the expense of installing new technology an organization should always conduct a thorough investigation and feasibility study to assess whether there will be overall benefits to be gained by installation of the technology.

Self Check ✔ **Element 3**

15. Describe the main functions of information processing.

16. Decide which electronic information processing system(s) would be most suitable for an organization in each of the following situations:
    (a) Storage of customer records.
    (b) Preparation of departmental budgets.
    (c) Information search on a number of companies.
    (d) Sending a standard letter to all customers.
    (e) Preparation of company newsletter.
    (f) Office in Japan requires a document urgently.

Self Check ✔ *continued*

17. Which of the following is *not* an advantage of an electronic filing system:
    (a) Provided proper back-up systems are in place they are very secure.
    (b) There is quick access to information.
    (c) They are expensive to install.
    (d) An electronic filing system reduces the amount of paper in an organization.

18. Decide whether each of the following statements is true or false:
    (i) Mechanical equipment is much more reliable than electronic equipment.
    (ii) The quality of information produced using new technology is far superior to that produced by other means.
    (iii) In the long run the installation of new technology brings cost savings.
    (iv) The introduction of new technology has slowed down the processing of information.

19. Carlux Ltd has recently installed a new computer system and a number of concerns have been raised including the following:

    (i) The number of complaints from staff about general health problems including eye strain, headaches and back strain.
    (ii) Information has frequently been 'wiped' due to a virus in the system.
    (iii) The widespread access to information by many staff, a great deal of which is confidential.
    (iv) Increased staff absenteeism with 'stress' being quoted as the reason.

    What action should be taken by the company to overcome each of these problems?

Unit Test

Completion guide: 1 hour plus 5 minutes reading time
Answer all the questions.

Administration Systems   5 marks

Questions 1–3 share answer options A–D

The following are examples of departments found in large organizations:

A Personnel   B Accounts   C Production   D Sales

Select the department which would carry out the following routine functions:

Question 1
Implementation of an induction programme for new staff

Question 2
Payment of suppliers

Question 3
Quality control of goods

Question 4
The functions of any administration system can be either routine or non-routine.

Decide whether each of the following statements is true (T) or false (F).

(i) The accounts clerk recording petty cash expenditure is carrying out a routine function
(ii) The personnel manager monitoring unusually high staff absenteeism levels is performing a non-routine function.

Which option best describes the two statements?

A (i) T   (ii) T
B (i) T   (ii) F
C (i) F   (ii) T
D (i) F   (ii) F

Question 5
A company has recently purchased an integrated computer system to support its administrative systems.

Which of the following outputs would be most useful for the Accounts Manager?

A Pay slips
B Staff absenteeism figures
C Monthly expenditure reports by each department
D Salespeople's performance figures

Legal and Statutory Requirements   4 marks

Question 6
PAYE is a statutory deduction from an employee's wages and is sent monthly by the company to:

A Inland Revenue
B Local Authority

C Companies House
D HM Customs and Excise

Question 7–9 relate to the following information.
An organization has the following administration systems:

A First aid training programme for all staff
B Written customer care policy
C Monitoring of the ethnic origin of staff recruited
D VAT returns

Which of these systems will be influenced by the following:

Question 7
Race Relations Act

Question 8
Health and Safety at Work Act

Question 9
Sale of Goods Act

Evaluating Administration Systems   4 marks

Questions 10–12 share answer options A–D

The following administration systems are used to support and monitor business:

A   Quality control
B   Staff suggestion box
C   Budgetary control
D   Sales performance figures

Which of the above would management use to ensure:

Question 10
The staff canteen is satisfying the needs of employees

Question 11
Departments are keeping within agreed expenditure figures

Question 12
Goods produced comply with consumer legislation and meet customers' needs

Question 13
Organizations must continually evaluate their administration systems to check their effectiveness.

Mark each of these statements true (T) or false (F).

(i) The effectiveness of a production department can be assessed by the amount of wastage.
(ii) The effectiveness of a marketing department can be measured by obtaining customer feedback on products.

Which option best describes the two statements?

A (i) T   (ii) T
B (i) T   (ii) F
C (i) F   (ii) T
D (i) F   (ii) F

Focus 4

Communication Systems   4 marks

Questions 14–17 relate to the following information:

The following are examples of communication methods used in a business:

A   Written correspondence
B   Facsimile transmission
C   Face-to-face conversation
D   Telephone

Select the best communication method used for:

Question 14
Sending an urgent document overseas

Question 15
Confirming job interviews with candidates

Question 16
Checking with a colleague on another site the time of a meeting to be held that day

Question 17
An organization has recently installed a fax machine. Decide whether each of these statesments is true (T) or false (F).

(i) The recipient of the fax must be available at the other end to receive the fax as it is sent.
(ii) A disadvantage of the fax machine is that only textual information can be sent.

Which option best describes the two statements?

A   (i) T   (ii) T
B   (i) T   (ii) F
C   (i) F   (ii) T
D   (i) F   (ii) F

Focus 5

Effects of Electronic Technology on Communication
Systems   9 marks

Question 18–20 share answer options A–D.

A firm has recently installed a new computer system and is experiencing the following problems:

A   The printers are faulty
B   Many staff are complaining of frequent headaches
C   Lack of data security
D   Staff complain that they do not understand the system

Identify which of the above problems could be remedied by:

Question 18
Staff training

Question 19
Introduction of passwords

Question 20
Hardware suppliers

Question 21
Which of the following is *not* an advantage of sending a fax?

A   It is quick
B   It is easy to send

C   It can be sent at any time of the day or night
D   It is always cheaper than posting documents

Questions 22–26 relate to the following information:

A company has recently introduced a system to computerize their administration systems. This has become necessary because of the increase in their business and the inability to cope with the amount of paperwork.

Question 22
Mark each of these statements true (T) or false (F).

(i) Using computer-based information processing systems is always more efficient than using manual systems.
(ii) The company should ignore staff complaints following the installation of the new computer system.

Which option best describes the two statements?

A   (i) T   (ii) T
B   (i) T   (ii) F
C   (i) F   (ii) T
D   (i) F   (ii) F

Question 23
Mark each of these statements true (T) or false (F).

(i) Efficiency will automatically improve due to the installation of the new system.
(ii) Staff will need to be trained to use the new system.

Which option best describes the two statements?

A   (i) T   (ii) T
B   (i) T   (ii) F
C   (i) F   (ii) T
D   (i) F   (ii) F

Question 24
There has been increasing concern about confidentiality in the organization since the introduction of the system. What should be done to overcome this?

A   Install a password system
B   Restrict the number of staff who use the system
C   Always switch the computers off when not in use
D   Make sure that only management have access to the computers

Question 25
Mark each of these statements true (T) or false (F)

(i) The new system will create more jobs in the organization.
(ii) It will be more cost effective in the long run for the organization.

Which option best describes the two statements?

A   (i) T   (ii) T
B   (i) T   (ii) F
C   (i) F   (ii) T
D   (i) F   (ii) F

Question 26
Mark each of these statements true (T) or false (F).

(i) Invoices produced by the system will always be accurate.
(ii) The system could allow all staff to check on customer account details.

Which option best describes the two statements?

A   (i) T   (ii) T
B   (i) T   (ii) F
C   (i) F   (ii) T
D   (i) F   (ii) F

Focus 6

Evaluating Information Processing Systems   6 marks

Question 27
A computer software package which can be used to prepare sales invoices would be of particular benefit to the:

A   Production department
B   Accounts department
C   Marketing department
D   Purchasing department

Questions 28–30 share answer options A–D

The following are the most common forms of information processing carried out in the office:

A   Databases
B   Spreadsheets
C   Word processing
D   Desktop publishing

Select the most appropriate process to carry out the following:

Question 28
Production of company newsletter

Question 29
Preparation of departmental budgets

Question 30
Standard letters to be sent to all customers

Question 31
A computer software package which can be used to analyse customer questionnaires would be of particular benefit to:

A   Personnal department
B   Production department
C   Sales department
D   Marketing department

Question 32
Following a feasibility study a firm has decided not to introduce a computerized system but to continue with its manual systems for processing information.

Which of the following is an advantage to the firm of continuing with the present manual system?

A   It will improve access to information
B   It will be more cost effective in the long run
C   It will increase the firm's competitiveness
D   Re-training of staff will not be necessary

Focus 7

Effects of Technology   6 marks

Question 33
The Data Protection Act was introduced to protect the rights of individuals by placing certain obligations on data users when handling personal information.

Mark each of these statements true (T) or false (F).

(i)   Everyone who holds personal data on computer should register with the Data Protection Registrar.
(ii) If unauthorized disclosure of information occurs individuals can seek compensation.

Which option best describes the two statements?

A   (i) T   (ii) T
B   (i) T   (ii) F
C   (i) F   (ii) T
C   (i) F   (ii) T

Question 34
Mark each of these statements true (T) or false (F).

(i)   Staff training is essential when introducing new technology.
(ii) A computer-based system is always more secure than a manual system.

Which option best describes the two statements?

A   (i) T   (ii) T
B   (i) T   (ii) F
C   (i) F   (ii) T
D   (i) F   (ii) F

Question 35
Data input clerks have complained of frequent headaches and eye strain. How might this problem be best overcome?

A   Relocate them to another department
B   Ask all staff to undergo a medical examination
C   Vary tasks and allow frequent breaks
D   Put them on a shorter working week

Question 36
As from 1 January 1993 new EU Directives have been introduced which relate to all new computer installations.

Mark each of these statements true (T) or false (F).

(i)   Employers must provide regular free eye tests for all computer operators.
(ii) It is compulsory for anti-glare screens to be fitted to all computer screens.

Which option best describes the two statements?

A   (i) T   (ii) T
B   (i) T   (ii) F
C   (i) F   (ii) T
D   (i) F   (ii) F

Question 37
Mark each of these statements true (T) or false (F).

(i)   Sound-proofing equipment should be provided if equipment is noisy.
(ii) Employers must provide adjustable chairs with backrests.

Which option best describes the two statements?

A   (i) T   (ii) T
B   (i) T   (ii) F
C   (i) F   (ii) T
D   (i) F   (ii) F

Question 38
Mark each of these statements true (T) or false (F).

(i)   Computer viruses are inevitable in a computer network.
(ii) Floppy disks are immune from computer viruses.

Which option best describes the two statements?

A   (i) T   (ii) T
B   (i) T   (ii) F
C   (i) F   (ii) T
D   (i) F   (ii) F

Answers to Self-check Questions

1. (a) Personnel department
   (b) Accounts department
   (c) Sales department
   (d) Marketing department
   (e) Purchasing department

2. Does your list include any of the following:
   - Ordering of food supplies, equipment, office supplies etc.
   - Financial record keeping.
   - Payment of suppliers.
   - Payment of wages.
   - Ensuring that health and hygiene regulations are being adhered to.

3. (a) False – production workers are often awarded a bonus for achieving certain levels of productivity. These will be one of the routine functions of a production manager.
   (b) True – checking of invoices is a routine function of an accounts department.
   (c) False – recording staff absenteeism levels is a routine function but this is a special investigation due to unusually high levels of absenteeism.
   (d) False – preparation of accounts is a routine function of an accounts department (Note: they may be prepared on a monthly basis or less frequently, e.g. three monthly.

4. (a) True – under the Health and Safety at Work Act all accidents which occur in the workplace must be recorded in an accident record book.
   (b) True – it is a legal requirement that all organizations have a written health and safety policy.

5. (a) Period of notice – legal requirement.
   (b) Rate of National Insurance contributions – not a legal requirement
   (c) Rate of pay – legal requirement.
   (d) Disciplinary rules – legal requirement (if not written in the actual contract there must be reference as to where they can be found and this must be accessible to all staff).
   (e) Description of main duties – not a legal requirement (job title must be stated but duties are usually outlined in the job description).

6. (a) Not compulsory – membership of a trade union is voluntary.
   (b) Compulsory – National Insurance is a compulsory deduction used by the government to pay for benefits and state pensions.
   (c) Not compulsory – membership of a hospital fund is totally voluntary.
   (d) Not compulsory – some firms offer SAYE (Save As You Earn) schemes whereby money is deducted from wages and put into a savings scheme but membership is voluntary.

7. (a) Companies Acts.
   (b) Sex Discrimination Act/Equal Pay Act/Race Relations Act.
   (c) Health and Safety at Work Act.
   (d) Employment Protection (Consolidation) Act.
   (e) Companies Acts.

8. (a) True
   (b) False

9. To handle the flow of information that an organization has to deal with from both within and outside the organization. To assist those responsible for making decisions. People within an organization are interdependent which means that they rely upon one another for information e.g. the production manager will need to liaise with the sales manager to find out how many units of a good to produce. To measure business performance – an organization will need to use recorded information to ascertain how well or how badly it is doing.

10. (a) A notice board would be the most appropriate means of communicating this information to all staff. It is general information of relevance to all staff.
    (b) A letter would be the most appropriate means.
    (c) A press release would be an appropriate means of communicating this information. It would be a good public relations exercise for the organization to show that they care about the local community and its activities. It could also be published in the staff newsletter.
    (d) A memo which serves as a reminder would be an appropriate means of communicating this to senior 8managers.
    (e) Minutes should be written up to record what was said at the monthly Staff Social Committee.

11. Communication by the spoken word is known as **verbal** communication. It can include **face-to-face** conversation, speaking on the **telephone** or at **meetings**.
    Meetings are an example of verbal communication. Meetings can be held either **internally** or **externally**. A **formal** meeting is one that has set procedures laid down in a written constitution. Limited companies must by law hold an **Annual General Meeting**.
    The telephone provides a common method of verbal communication. Its main advantages are that it is **quick** and instant **feedback** is possible. Its main disadvantage is that a **written** record of what was discussed is not available.

12. (a) Electronic mail allows a message to be sent to many people at the same time via a computer terminal.
    (b) The document should be faxed overseas. This is a quick means of sending information abroad, taking only a matter minutes depending upon the length of the document.
    (c) The message should be left on a pager so that the Sales Director can return the call at a convenient moment.
    (d) The three people could be linked by video-conferencing which allows people in different locations to communicate with one another whilst viewing one another on computer screen, saving them the time and expense of travelling.

13. (a) True – the problem can be overcome by installing passwords to restrict access to certain information by authorized users only.
    (b) True – research has shown that using computers for long periods of time can damage eyesight and may prove harmful to an unborn child.
    (c) False – the use of technology cuts down the chances of human error, although mistakes can still be made!
    (d) True – when change of any sort is being implemented, including the introduction of new technology, staff should be properly trained in its usage.

14. (i) Communications within the organization would be improved as information processed by one computer could be accessed by a number of people.

    It would be cost effective as resources could be shared, e.g. one printer could be shared by several computer terminals.

    It would reduce the amount of paper within the organization as information could be accessed via the computer terminal.

    (ii) Cost – in addition to the initial capital outlay the costs of installing and running the equipment and training of staff should be considered.

    Security – a network means that many people can have access to the same information. If the information is highly confidential this can be a problem but it can be overcome by installing passwords to restrict access to authorised users only.

    Staff resistance – the organization should ensure that all staff are properly trained in the operation of the equipment.

    Health and safety – consideration should be given to health and safety issues. Guidelines relating to VDU's should be followed.

15. Purposes of information processing systems are to:
    1 Store information
    2 Distribute information
    3 Use information
    4 Communicate information

16. (a) Database
    (b) Spreadsheet
    (c) CD-ROM
    (d) Word processing
    (e) Desktop publishing
    (f) Facsimile machine or electronic mail if there is a WAN

17. (a) This is an advantage of an electronic filing system and therefore is not the correct answer.
    (b) Electronic filing systems do provide quick access to information and therefore this is not the correct answer.
    (c) The cost of installing new technology is expensive therefore this is the correct answer.
    (d) Electronic filing systems do reduce the amount of paper in an organization as information can be stored on disk and transferred via the computer and therefore this is not the correct answer

18. (i) False – mechanical equipment requires more human involvement and thus more mistakes are likely to be made.
    (ii) True – applications such as desktop publishing produce high quality information.
    (iii) True – although it is expensive to install new technology, in the long run cost savings are made as information processing is speeded up, fewer staff are required and the amount of paper is reduced.
    (iv) False – new technology has speeded up the processing of information as large amounts of information can be stored and accessed very quickly.

19. (i) The company should follow the guidelines laid down by the EU Directive which states that employees who use VDUs should be provided with adequate breaks and rests away from computer screens to carry out other activities.
    (ii) Regular checks should be carried out using an anti-virus program on computers.
    (iii) Access to confidential information can be restricted by installing a password/restricted access system.
    (iv) The stress is probably caused by a lack of understanding of how to use the equipment. Proper training should be provided for all staff.

Answers to Unit Test

Question	Answer	Question	Answer	Question	Answer	Question	Answer	Question	Answer
1	A	9	B	17	D	25	C	33	C
2	B	10	B	18	D	26	C	34	B
3	C	11	C	19	C	27	B	35	C
4	B	12	A	20	A	28	D	36	B
5	C	13	A	21	D	29	B	37	A
6	A	14	B	22	D	30	C	38	D
7	C	15	A	23	C	31	D		
8	A	16	D	24	A	32	D		

Unit Test Comments (Selected questions)

Question 1.
The personnel department have the responsibility for the design and implementation of induction programmes for new employees. It is part of the training function. The most appropriate answer is A.

Question 2.
The accounts department are responsible for the recording of receipts and payments including payments to suppliers; therefore B is the correct answer.

Question 3.
The production department are responsible for ensuring that the quality of goods produced is of an acceptable standard. A quality control person is usually appointed. Option C is correct.

Question 4.
B is the correct answer. The recording of petty cash by the accounts clerk is a routine function. However, the investigation into absenteeism will not be a routine function of the personnel department. B best describes the two statements.

Question 5.
Option C is the correct answer as the Accounts Manager will have overall responsibility for monitoring expenditure by the different departments. Options A and B will be of most use to the personnel function and D to the Sales Manager.

Question 6.

A   YES   PAYE deductions include income tax and National Insurance which are sent to the Inland Revenue on a monthly basis.

B   NO   The local authority are responsible for the collection of the business rate.

C   NO   Companies House is where a limited company has to file its financial statements and an annual return giving details of directors and shareholdings etc.

D   NO   Although you may have been tempted to put this. Businesses registered for VAT have to pay it to the VAT authorities, i.e. HM Customs and Excise Department.

Question 7.
The Race Relations act makes it illegal for employers to discriminate against anyone on the grounds of race. Many organizations monitor the ethnic origin of staff recruited. C is the correct answer.

Question 8.
The HASAWA 1974 puts an obligation upon the employer to provide a safe workplace and includes a provision for a number of staff to have proper first aid training. Option A is the correct answer.

Question 9.
The Sale of Goods Act states that all goods sold must meet certain criteria, e.g. they must be of 'merchantable quality'. Any organization with the customer at the heart of its operations will have a written customer care policy pointing out to the customer their rights. Option B is the correct answer.

Question 10.
Option B is the correct answer. A suggestion box is a means of gaining feedback from employees on a range of matters.

Question 11.
Option C is the correct answer since each department will agree a budget and expenditure against this budget will be monitored on a regular basis.

Question 12.
A quality control person will be appointed to ensure that the goods produced are of the right standard and meet the requirements of, for example, the Sale of Goods act. Option A is the correct answer.

Question 13.
A is the correct answer. Both statements are true. The less wastage there is the more efficient a production department will be deemed to be and, if there is high customer satisfaction, the marketing department must have correctly identified what the customer wants.

Question 14.
The fax would ensure that an urgent document could be sent overseas in a matter of minutes; therefore option B is correct.

Question 15.
Confirmation of job interviews is best done in writing by letter outlining the date, time and place etc. Option A is correct.

Question 16.
D is correct since the telephone provides a quick means of checking certain information.

Question 17.
A fax machine can be left on overnight so that correspondence can be received at any time without the recipient having to be there and graphs, pictures, photographs, drawings etc. can be sent. D is the correct answer as both of these statements are false.

Question 18.
Staff cannot be expected to use new technology unless they have been properly trained in the use of it. Option D is the correct answer.

Question 19.
Option C is correct since access to information can be restricted by installing a password system. This should increase data security.

Question 20.
Option A is correct. If there is a problem with any of the equipment itself, i.e. the hardware, the suppliers should be contacted to remedy the problem.

Question 21.
A, B and C are all advantages of sending faxes. However, it is not always cheaper to send a fax. The distance and amount of information to be faxed must be taken into consideration. D is the correct answer.

Question 22.
Statement (i) is false – although there are many advantages of computer-based systems it does not always follow that they are more efficient than manual ones. In addition an organization should always listen to its staff and take on board any comments or complaints. This feedback is particularly important when introducing new systems. Statement (ii) is therefore false. Option D best describes the two statements.

Question 23.
Efficiency will depend upon many factors including the suitability of the system for the operations and how well the staff have been trained in the use of the system etc. Further, the training of staff is vital when new systems are being introduced. Therefore, C best describes the two statements – (i) is false and (ii) is true.

Question 24.
A   YES A password system will mean that only authorized people will be able to access the system.
B   NO As it would be too difficult to monitor who was using the system.
C   NO Since anyone could quite easily come in and switch on the machine and access the information.
D   NO This is not the correct answer as the role of managers is to control and co-ordinate activities. They require staff below them to provide them with the information. It would not be practical or cost-effective for managers to spend all their time on routine activities within the business, e.g. production of invoices.

Question 25.
It is likely that the introduction of new technology will mean fewer jobs as machines replace people. This does not always follow, however. This statement is false. However, although there is the initial capital outlay or purchasing the equipment, in the long run cost savings should be made through reduction of staff, less paper and improved efficiency and this statement is true. Therefore option C best describes the two statements.

Question 26.
C is the correct answer.
(i) False – the accuracy of the invoices produced will depend upon the accuracy of the information input into the computer by staff.
(ii) True – if the system was networked then all staff would be able to access customer account details provided they were on the network.

Question 27.
Option B is correct since the accounts department is responsible for the production of invoices.

Question 28.
The use of desktop publishing would be the best means of producing a newsletter as it allows different sized fonts, graphics etc. Option D is the correct answer.

Question 29.
B is the correct answer. A spreadsheet is an ideal application for the preparation of budgets as it is capable of carrying out calculations automatically.

Question 30.
A word processor means that the details only need to be typed in once and then they can be merged with names and addresses of customers. Option C is therefore correct.

Question 31.
Option D is correct – the marketing function is all about satisfying customer needs. Customer questionnaires are part of the market research function.

Question 32.
Option A, B and C are all disadvantages of continuing with the manual system as opposed to introducing a computerized system. D is the correct answer.

Question 33.
The Act does not apply to data of a personal nature, e.g data concerning personal, family or household affairs, clubs and chairities etc. This statement is therefore false. However, statement (ii) is true – if individuals can prove that they suffered loss or damage as a result of the disclosure of information they can claim damage; e.g. disclosure of medical records could harm someone's chances of getting a job. C is the correct answer.

Question 34.
Option B best describes the two statements. Statement (i) is true – staff must be given proper training to deal with new systems and procedures. However, statement (ii) is false – the widespread use of computers has caused great concern about security. Measures can be taken to overcome the problem.

Question 35.
A   NO The company would still need to have data input clerks who are likely to complain of the same problem.
B   NO All staff are complaining and thus the problem is with the working methods used. A medical examination may diagnose the problem but not solve it.
C   YES The EU directive introduced from 1 January recommends this.
D   NO It might reduce the headaches and eyestrain but additional staff would have to be recruited to ensure that the work is carried out.

Question 36.
B is the correct answer.
(i) True – the Directive states that employees working with new installations should be provided with free eye tests and provided with glasses if necessary.
(ii) False – the Directive states that artificial light must not have a detrimental effect on screen displays. This could be overcome by fitting an anti-glare screen but it is not compulsory.

Question 37.
Option A is the correct answer as both statements are true. Personal computers should not interfere with the user's concentration. If this occurs they should be sound-proofed. In addition, chairs with backrests should be provided where the height and back of the chair can be adjusted.

Question 38.
D is the correct answer. Computer viruses can be avoided if sufficient care is taken and counter-measures adopted. Floppy disks can certainly be infected.

Marketing

Getting Started

It used to be the case that businesses could operate quite happily on the basis of 'selling what they make'. Those days are over, even for companies in the mass production industries such as car manufacturing. Today companies are increasingly faced with the situation that they must 'make what they can sell'. As a result of this **marketing** becomes the central function of the organization. Its major concerns are to:

- Identify suitable markets.
- Identify customer requirements.
- Evaluate the organization's ability to produce what the customer wants.
- Communicate those requirements to other functions within the organization and work with them to ensure that they are met.
- Monitor the market constantly.

Competition based pricing Pricing methods based on competitors' pricing strategies.

Cost based pricing Pricing methods which are based on the firm's costs.

Demand orientated pricing Pricing methods based on conditions in the market. Also known as market orientated pricing.

Demography The study of populations and their characteristics.

Desk research The study of published information which may be internal or external to the organization. It is also referred to as secondary research.

Discretionary income The amount of money consumers have left after paying essential bills.

Extension strategies Methods used to extend the product life cycle.

Field research The collection of data *which do not already exist*. It is also termed primary research.

Informative advertising Advertising which seeks to inform the consumer of the existence and nature of a product.

Institutional advertising Advertising which aims to promote the firm rather than a product.

Marketing mix Elements in the firm's marketing strategy – product, price, promotion, place. Often referred to as the four 'P's.

Marketing research The systematic gathering, recording and analysis of data about problems related to the marketing of goods and services.

Market orientated pricing Pricing methods based upon conditions in the market. Also known as demand orientated pricing.

Market orientation An approach to business which places consumers at the heart of the decision making process.

Persuasive advertising Advertising which aims to persuade customers to buy a particular brand of product.

Primary research The collection of data that does not already exist. It is also termed field research.

Product life cycle The different stages into which the life of a product can be divided, namely introduction, growth, maturity and decline stages.

Product portfolio The particular group or mix of products which the firm is marketing.

Promotion mix The various methods used to bring a firm's products to the attention of the customer.

Reference group A group which has some influence over a person's attitudes and behaviour.

Secondary research Research from data which are already available – this may be internal or external to the firm. It is also termed desk research.

Segmentation Breaking a market down into sub-groups which have similar characteristics.

The Chartered Institute of Marketing defines marketing as 'the management process responsible for identifying, anticipating and satisfying customer requirements profitably'.

In this unit we will first look at how marketing research and sales forecasting can be used to identify suitable markets and customer requirements before considering how other marketing activities ensure that what the organization makes it can sell.

Essential Principles

3.1 Market Research

With the growth of large organizations, international markets and sophisticated techniques for distributing and selling goods, the direct relationship between the business and its customer has disappeared. As a result information on customer requirements may never get to those parts of the organization which need to act upon it. Thus business decisions can be made on inadequate information and unsound assumptions. In such a situation the likelihood of making the wrong decision is high.

The performance criteria we will consider here are:

- Relevant sources of information are identified which establish potential market need.
- Appropriate research methods are identified and the criteria for selection explained.
- Research instruments to collect data are described.
- Data are analysed and conclusions drawn.
- A report on the findings of market research is prepared.

Marketing research aims to provide the business with information on which to make decisions about the organization's future activities and thereby reduce the risks associated with these decisions. It has been defined as **the systematic gathering, recording and analysis of data about problems related to the marketing of goods and services.**

We can draw several points from this definition regarding our approach to marketing problems:

- **Systematic.** Marketing research should be undertaken systematically. Picking up relevant information by chance will not be sufficient for the firm's purposes – it should be an ongoing activity.
- **Gathering.** Identify what information the organization needs for successful decision making.
- **Recording.** Recording of information should also be undertaken systematically so as to ensure that relevant information can be referred to at a later date.
- **Analysing.** Information needs to be analysed so that important trends can be seen or conclusions drawn.

The scope of marketing research.

The term **marketing research** covers a whole range of different areas on which information will be required for planning and control purposes (see Table 3.1).

The market
- the size of the market and its nature in terms of sex, income, social status
- the geographical location of customers
- the amount of competition in the market
- possibilities for segmenting the market
- researching the possibility of new markets for existing products

The product
- an analysis of the strengths and weaknesses of products (ours and the competitors)
- assessing the viability / market testing of new products
- assessing the possibility of new uses for existing products

Promotion
- selecting appropriate media
- analysing the effectiveness of advertising or other promotional techniques (ours and the competitors)

The price
- a comparison of prices in the market
- an assessment of the importance of price in purchase decisions
- an estimation of the price elasticity of demand

Distribution
- an analysis of transportation costs
- design of packaging
- effectiveness of distribution channels.

Table 3.1 Types of marketing research

Thus the organization may require information which:

- *Describes* what is happening in its markets, for example who its major competitors are at the moment and what promotional activities they are undertaking.
- *Predicts* what is likely to happen in the future. Thus the organization may wish to analyse past sales as a means of predicting a trend in future sales.
- *Explains* what is happening in its markets, for example why sales of a particular product have risen, and which groups of consumers are making the extra demand for that product.
- *Explores* new possibilities. Firms will be keen to see if there are openings for their products in other markets or whether there are new products which they can develop for their existing markets.

In each of these cases we can see the relevance of market research to the firm in planning and controlling its future activities. Indeed, the more turbulent the organization's environment is, the more important it is to use marketing research as a means of offsetting that environmental uncertainty and of checking that any progress being made is according to plan.

Did You Know ?

It costs 5 times as much to recruit a *new* customer as it does to service and retain an *existing* customer.

Who does marketing research?

Many large organizations will create a specialist department to carry out their *own* marketing research work. This has the advantage that not only are the staff involved marketing research specialists but they also develop considerable knowledge of that firm's products and markets.

For small firms the cost of operating their own marketing research department is often too high and specialist marketing research companies have developed to provide a service. Some of these firms will undertake any kind of marketing research work for their client. Alternatively, there are others who specialize in one aspect of market research work. Thus Mintel produces a monthly journal containing about five or six reports on markets of interest whilst the Nielsen organization produces specialist information on the food and drug industries.

Did You Know ?

For small businesses, the most important ways of finding new customers were:

- Personal recommendation – 73%
- Speculative call – 29%
- Press advertisement – 22%
- Yellow Pages – 15%

Note: Figures indicate percentage of new customers via that method; since sometimes more than one method was used, the total may exceed 100%.

Sources of marketing research information

Desk research (Secondary research)

This is also referred to as **secondary research**. It is research information which is obtained not by undertaking a market research project but by using other sources of information *already in existence*. As such information is readily available and is relatively cheap to obtain. **Desk research** should always be undertaken before field or primary research (we will deal with this later). In practice there are two potential sources for both desk and field research – those which are *internal* and those which are *external* to the organization (see Fig. 3.1).

	Internal	External
Secondary **(Desk research)**	In-house collected for *another* purpose	Public data collected by government or commercial agency
Primary **(Field research)**	In-house collected for *this* purpose	Marketing research undertaken by, or for, *this* organization

Fig. 3.1   Sources of market research information

- *Internal data*
  Most organizations generate large quantities of information that have *not* been gathered for (but could be used for) marketing research purposes. All too often though, the information is unavailable because it is **not**:

  - Recognized as being useful.
  - Accessible to the researcher.
  - Summarized or stored in a form that is useful to the researcher.

When information *is* available, internal data will probably include:

- *Product sales figures.* Our organization would wish to analyse trends in sales figures generally, and if possible derive a break-down of sales into different product and market segments.

- *Sales reports.* The sales force is the organization's eyes and ears in the market place. The information which they record is wide ranging and often the result of hearsay or subjective assessment. Nevertheless, it is often the first notice that the organization obtains about changes in the market place. (Of course there may also be other staff in the organization, e.g. service engineers, who come into regular contact with the customers and discuss their needs, problems, current activities and future requirements.)

- *Stock movements.* These often provide advance notice of important changes in patterns of demand (sales figures come later) and allow the organization to respond more quickly to these changes than its competitors.

- *Relative importance of customers.* Many organizations will find that 80% of their sales come from 20% of their customers (this is an example of the Pareto 80/20 rule). Such analysis ensures that the organization concentrates its resources on those important customers.

  - *Prospective leads.* These are records of opportunities which have not been exploited as yet.

  - *Competitor information.* This may come from their brochures, company reports and accounts or from an industry-wide trade association.

- *External published data*
  There is a wide variety of information available to the researcher. The sources include the following:

  - *Annual Abstract of Statistics.*   Background information on population trends, employment, production, consumption and overseas trade.
  - *Business Monitor.*   Gives published information (quarterly) on market size, exports, imports, employment and price inflation for over 4000 products and services.
  - *Regional trends.*   Shows regional variations in population, employment, housing, production, investment, education etc.
  - *General Household Survey.*   Based on a survey of 15000 households it contains information on household expenditure, housing, employment and education.
  - *Social Trends.*   Published annually this gives

information on trends in population, education, occupations, crime, leisure pursuits, spending etc.

- *Mintel.*   These are privately produced reports. Each month the journal looks at five or six consumer markets in depth. The information includes market size and growth, the market share of the main products, the major competitors, advertising and promotional expenditure.
- *Key Note Reports.*   Reports for business-to-business markets covering much the same ground as Mintel.
- *Audits.*   Retail audits record sales to consumers at a sample of retail outlets. AC Nielsen and Retail Audits, which are the best known, sell this information on a product-by-product basis to both retailers and manufacturers. The information enables them to work out market shares, new product performance or the impact of price changes, sales promotions and advertising campaigns.
- *Trade Associations.*   Many trade associations undertake market research which will be of general interest throughout their industry and sell it to their members.
- *Kompass.*   Provides information on companies, such as their size and activities.
- *McCarthy Information Ltd.*   Provides a clippings service of articles and information on leading companies and industries.

Did You Know ?

Most of the information sources listed here will be available in your college or local library. A list of *specialist libraries* (over 300) with more detailed information is published in the ASLIB, Economic and Business Group, Membership Directory.

Field research (Primary research)

The problem with desk or secondary research is that it is often not quite what is required and is rather out of date. **Field research** is undertaken within the market itself and is designed to obtain specific information that cannot be obtained elsewhere. Although collecting such information is often costly and time consuming it is only the firm collecting it that has access to it. The information may therefore form the basis of a significant marketing advantage over rivals. There are four major methods of obtaining **primary** (or field) **information**: observation, experimentation, discussion groups and surveys.

- *Observation*
  By this method consumers are watched in the process of choosing or buying goods. It is very popular with retail organizations. It is useful in recording details such as:

- How people moved around a store.
- What in-store promotions caught their eye.
- How people scanned shelves (note that shelf space and location are often significant factors in competing brands sales).
- How long people take to make decisions.

There are two major advantages of observation. First, very large numbers of observations can be obtained quickly. Second, observations are objective with consumers being unaware that they are being watched – they are acting normally. However, the major problem of observation arises from this objectivity because while it can tell us *what* people do it cannot tell us *why* people act in this way.

- *Experimentation*
  This is often referred to as **test marketing**. There are two methods. The first is the *laboratory test*. Here the experiment takes place in an artificial but fully controlled environment. An example would be where a group of consumers are brought together and asked to comment on different foods after a tasting session. The second method is where consumer reactions are measured under *normal market conditions*. Such an experiment will have a 'test' or 'experimental' group and a 'control' group. It will often take the form of making a new or improved product (e.g. a new chocolate bar) available in one geographic region alone – this is the *test group* (note that for the results to be valid this test market must be representative of the whole market). In the rest of the country – this is the *control group* – factors remain as before. Thus the difference in sales between the two groups can be explained by the popularity or otherwise of the new or improved product. To be meaningful this test would have to continue for some time to see if consumers repeated the initial purchase (it is the level of repeat sales that will determine whether this product will be a long-term success). Of course during this period it is always open to competitors to try and defeat the objective of the test by changing their prices or promotional strategy in either test or control area.

- *Discussion groups*
  Consumer panels can be appointed consisting of a mix of people similar to those expected to be the main purchasers of the product. They can be questioned about their reactions to new or existing products.

- *Surveys*
  Surveys are often used for obtaining primary information. There are two forms of survey. The first is the *census*. This involves questioning everyone in a particular market. However, as this is only a practical possibility where the market is fairly small it is the second method, the *sample*, that is most popular and widely used. The range of sampling methods is shown in

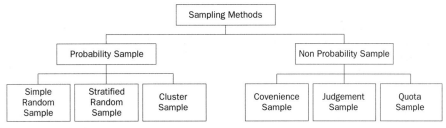

Fig. 3.2   Types of sampling method

Fig 3.2. *Probability samples* have the advantage that by using statistical techniques the researcher can predict how accurate the results obtained from the survey are. We can say that, the larger the sample, the greater the degree of accuracy. *Non-probability samples* are quicker and cheaper to carry out but the results may not be representative of the market as a whole nor can we apply statistical techniques to determine the degree of accuracy.

We now look at **sample surveys** in more detail.

Types of sample

Simple random samples
In **simple random samples** each individual who is a member of the market group being surveyed has an equal chance of being chosen for the sample. The most common way of choosing today is to use a computer to throw out random numbers. This has the advantage that it eliminates any bias in the selection of the sample but assumes (and this is not always the case) that all members of the group are homogeneous (the same). Another method of obtaining the sample is to choose (say) every fiftieth name on a list (this is termed *systematic* random sampling).

Stratified random samples
Results of random sampling may be distorted in markets where some customers are more important than others. In such a situation **stratified random sampling** would be used. Here, the sample would be weighted on the basis of the importance of the different segments in the market. Thus if 20% of customers (e.g. pensioners) account for over half of a firm's turnover they should make up 50% of the sample.

Cluster sampling
The aim of **cluster sampling** is to reduce the cost of marketing research by concentrating the sample on one or more geographical areas. For the technique to be effective the *clusters* chosen must be representative of the whole market. One or more geographical areas will often be selected and *all* the members of the relevant group in that area are sampled, e.g. all engineering firms or all pensioners in one city. For most marketing research purposes the results of cluster sampling are of sufficient accuracy and it is the most popular method of probability sampling.

Quota samples
Quota samples are often used to minimize the cost of fieldwork. The method involves dividing the population up into *segments* based on specific characteristics. The most commonly used ones are age and sex. The interviewer is then told that they must interview a specified number of people from each of the segments which have been identified. Thus they might be told to interview thirty men between the ages of 35 and 50, or forty women between the ages of 50 and 65. The proportions of different groups in the sample will be based on the size of that group in the total population or in the target market. Unfortunately there is no guarantee that the individuals interviewed in this way will accurately reflect the views of the group as a whole because the interviewer merely interviews the first thirty men or forty women in the correct age bands that they meet.

Judgement samples
Here, the people to be interviewed are selected by the researcher in the belief that they are representative of the market as a whole. To a large extent the success or accuracy of the method depends upon the researcher's knowledge of the market.

Convenience samples
This involves gathering information from any convenient group of people.

Types of survey method

Personal interviews
This is a widely used method of obtaining information in which the interview is conducted on a face-to-face basis. These interviews may be structured or unstructured. **Structured interviews** are the product of a formal questionnaire. The interviewer will read through these questions and invite the respondent to make a reply from a limited choice of answers. Structured interviews lead to the collection of *quantitative data* from which specific conclusions can be drawn, e.g. 75% of all men prefer blondes!

Unstructured interviews are very much more like a conversation. The interviewer will have a number of general questions to ask or topics to discuss but allows the respondent to reply and develop their answers as they wish. This kind of interview is used where the researcher wishes to gain '*qualitative*' information.

Advantages:
- Information in depth can be obtained.
- Additional information can be obtained through observation.
- The information is more accurate because clarification of points is possible.
- The questionnaire can be longer than with any other method.
- Relatively high response rates are obtained.

Disadvantages
- They are expensive to administer.
- There is the possibility that interviewer bias may creep into the way questions are asked and replies recorded.
- The method is very time consuming.

Telephone interviews
This is very popular in business-to-business research where it is likely that the target group will have a phone. The method is also becoming more popular in consumer research but its value is limited because there are wide variations regionally and nationally in the number of people who have phones.

Advantages:
- A large number of interviews can be conducted in a short time.

- The information is more accurate because clarification of points is possible.
- The cost per interview is low.
- National and even international surveys are feasible.
- People who are normally inaccessible can be interviewed at a time which is convenient to them.
- Responses can be keyed directly into a computer.

Disadvantages:
- Surveys are limited to respondents with phones (and those who have not gone 'ex directory') and so population coverage is not complete.
- Phone owners may not be representative of the market.
- Cannot evaluate non-verbal communication.
- Response rates are lower than with personal interviews.
- It is difficult to establish a rapport with the respondent over the phone.

Postal surveys

Letters will be sent to the respondents (this involves mailing or door-to-door distribution) inviting them to reply to a questionnaire. The questionnaire is subsequently collected or mailed back. Response rates to such surveys can be as low as 2% and in an effort to improve this firms often offer entry into a free draw for some popular prize. The questionnaire must be short and simple, otherwise people will simply 'bin' it!

Advantages:
- No interviewer bias.
- They are fairly cheap and, within a country, costs do not increase with distance.
- Total anonymity for respondents can be ensured.
- Complex questions can be answered at leisure.

Disadvantages:
- The response rate is generally very low.
- The people who respond may not be representative of the sample as a whole.
- Questions may be misinterpreted resulting in misleading or contradictory answers.
- The amount of information obtained is limited because the questionnaire must be kept short.
- Answers on the return may not be those of the respondents as they may consult with other people before replying.

A summary of the major factors to be considered in choosing between these research methods is shown in Fig. 3.3. It shows that no one method is ideal. However, where a large amount of information is required a postal survey is normally used so as to keep the cost down.

	Post	Telephone	Face-to-face
Cost	low	average	high
Flexibility	poor	good	very good
Response rate	poor	good	good
Interviewer bias	low	average	high
Data collection speed	poor	very good	good

Fig. 3.3 A comparison of post, telephone and personal interview research methods

Panel interviews

This involves a representative group of people being consulted on their attitudes or actions. It varies from the methods used above because the *same group* of people is used over a period of time. There are several types of panel:

- *Consumer purchasing panels.* The panel will report regularly on their purchases, future purchase intentions and their attitudes towards products.
- *Consumer product testing panels.* The panel will be asked to test and comment on new products.
- *Radio and television audience panels.* Participants will record their pattern of listening and viewing. (Audience viewing patterns are used to determine what programmes will be produced and the days and times at which they will be transmitted. Listening and viewing patterns may also be used to calculate the advertising revenue that commercial radio and television companies can obtain.)

Advantages:
- As the respondents remain the same it is possible to research *trends*, for example in buying or viewing habits.
- Factors underlying the trend can be investigated.
- It is the only method which reveals the true extent of brand loyalty.

Disadvantages:
- Composition of the panel will be disturbed if a member leaves.
- Over a period of time panel members' actions and attitudes may become less representative of the whole group.
- It is expensive to maintain a constant panel.

Questionnaire design

A **questionnaire** is simply a tool for the collection of data from respondents. A well constructed questionnaire will aid information gathering because its clarity and simplicity make it easy to answer. A badly constructed questionnaire will lead to misunderstandings, frustration and even antagonism toward the interviewer and the organization he or she represents. However, *designing* the questionnaire is one of the most difficult and critical parts of the survey process. There are a number of *types* of questions which may be asked.

Closed questions

These give respondents a fixed choice of answers. **Closed questions** are often *dichotomous* – by this we mean that they only have two alternatives. Where there are more than two alternatives they are termed *multi-choice*.

An example of a dichotomous question would be:

Have you purchased a sports car before? YES/NO

An example of a multi-choice question would be:

Where did you hear about this holiday offer?
(please tick appropriate statement)
through press advertising
through television advertising
through a travel agent
personal recommendation
other (please specify)

The majority of questionnaires use closed questions because they can be answered more quickly and are easy to analyse.

Open questions

Here the respondents are allowed to answer the question as they think fit. The interviewer will record their reply. An example of an **open question** in a postal questionnaire would be:

Why did you choose this holiday?

_____

_____

Direct questions

These require a specific response. All the questions above are direct questions. They will either require a yes/no answer or provide the structure for making the reply.

Indirect questions

The aim of these questions is to explore an individual's attitudes or behaviour patterns often in circumstances where a direct question might cause offence. Thus our interviewer instead of asking a question such as

Why don't you buy a holiday timeshare unit?

may ask, instead, a series of indirect questions which will build up a picture of an individual's attitude to holiday time-share and the reasons behind that attitude. These questions could include:

What do you know about timeshares?
Why do other people buy timeshare units?
Do you plan to take many holidays when you retire?
What is your experience of package holidays?

Open and indirect questions tend to be used when an 'in depth' study is being carried out. Whilst it is an expensive research method it may reveal fundamental attitudes or changes in attitudes towards products or services which are of importance in planning future products/services.

Did You Know ?

Every word in a questionnaire must be carefully scrutinised in case it 'leads' people into a particular type of response. For example compare:

• Do you think all medical care _should_ be provided free?
• Do you think all medical care _could_ be provided free?

The word 'could' replacing 'should' will produce very different types of responses.

Recording attitudes and opinions

Attitudes and opinions are important determinants of buying behaviour. Thus in our example of timeshare above an individual's experience of high pressure salesmanship from timeshare touts whilst on holiday in Spain may result in negative attitudes toward timeshares in general. Information such as this is vital to the successful marketing of any product.

There are two major techniques for measuring attitudes and opinions. They are **Likert scales** and **semantic differential scales**.

Likert scales

Respondents are asked about the extent to which they agree (or disagree) with a certain statement. They are usually given five or six options ranging from 'strongly agree' to 'strongly disagree'. For example:

Subject Timeshares	Offer better facilities than hotels	Are a good long term investment	Are no more expensive than hotels
Strongly agree	_____	_____	_____
Agree	_____	_____	_____
Don't agree or disagree	_____	_____	_____
Disagree	_____	_____	_____
Strongly disagree	_____	_____	_____

Semantic differential scales

Respondents are asked to rate the variables under consideration on a relative basis using a seven-point scale. Thus our timeshare company may ask you, the holidaymaker, to complete the following form:

Please rate Club La Manga timeshare under the following headings on a scale from 1 to 7.		
Comfortable unit	7 6 5 4 3 2 1	Uncomfortable unit
Excellent cleanliness	7 6 5 4 3 2 1	Unhygienic and dirty
Excellent food	7 6 5 4 3 2 1	Poor food
Courteous staff	7 6 5 4 3 2 1	Rude staff
Good facilities	7 6 5 4 3 2 1	Poor facilities

The information received from each respondent will be aggregated so as to provide a picture of how holidaymakers rate this timeshare. It identifies the strengths and weaknesses of this timeshare and can be used to identify areas in need of improvement.

Self Check ✔   Element 1

1. What do you understand by the term marketing research?
   _____
   _____
   _____

2. Give five examples of marketing information which could be provided by marketing research.
   _____
   _____
   _____
   _____
   _____

Self Check ✔ continued

3. Why is market research important to firms?

_____

_____

_____

4. Distinguish between desk and field research.

_____

_____

_____

5. Give four examples of internal data that would be available for desk research purposes.

_____

_____

_____

_____

6. State two disadvantages of using external published data for marketing research purposes.

_____

_____

_____

7. In relation to field research, what do you understand by the term experimentation?

_____

_____

_____

8. What advantage does a probability sample have over a non probability sample?

_____

_____

_____

9. In what circumstances would you use personal interviews as a means of obtaining primary data?

_____

_____

_____

_____

_____

3.2 Using Consumer Trends to Forecast Sales

Providing the customers with the goods and services they require is central to the success of any business organization. The problem from an organization's point of view is that, over time, the consumers' requirements change. The fact that a company is successfully meeting customer requirements today is no guarantee of success tomorrow. There are many examples of once successful firms that have failed to respond to changes in the market place. Yet in most cases it is possible to discern trends in sales or consumer attitudes which should have given the organization advance warning of changes in its market place. In this section we will concentrate on the *consumers* and the factors which determine their demand for goods and services. The performance criteria we will consider are:

- Characteristics of consumers are investigated.
- Economic information is analysed to identify effects on consumption.

- Economic information and consumer trends are used to predict the demand for products and services.
- Consumer information is used to forecast sales for a business organization.

Economic factors

Income

The firm is interested in people's **real disposable income,** i.e. whether having taken into account the effect of statutory deductions (e.g. taxes) and inflation, people have more or less to spend on goods and services than before. Generally speaking, an increase in real disposable incomes is likely to lead to increased demand for most goods and services.

However, not all goods and services will benefit equally from a rise in real incomes. In fact consumers may actually buy less of some products as incomes rise. Let us take the example of bread or other basic foodstuffs. At very low incomes a large proportion of consumers' income will be spent on bread but as incomes rise they will eat less bread and purchase more expensive foodstuffs. Such goods are said to have a negative income elasticity of demand (see Unit 1) and are often described as 'inferior'.

You may also find that firms distinguish between disposable and discretionary income. **Discretionary income** is often considered to be a better indicator of a consumer's spending power. This is because it indicates the amount of money consumers have left *after* they have paid essential bills on housing, clothing, food etc. You will find that goods and services of an essential nature form little part of our discretionary income and will have a relatively low income elasticity of demand; expenditure on these essential items will not rise in proportion to the rise in incomes. Conversely where goods and services are of a 'luxury' type they tend to form part of our discretionary income and have a higher income elasticity of demand. Consequently as incomes rise there will be a more than proportionate increase in expenditure on these goods and services. This is of major significance to sectors such as leisure and tourism.

Marketers will also be interested in the distribution of wealth within a country. **Per capita income** (i.e. the national income of a country divided by its population) assumes that incomes are shared equally between all members of the population. That is rarely true. For example some African countries with a very low 'per capita income' may be a very good market for luxury items such as whisky or sports cars. This is because whilst the vast majority live in poverty, there are a lucky few who are extremely rich (and have a very high level of discretionary income).

Government economic management

Marketers also need to be aware of the **overall economic environment** within which they are operating. Governments seek to manipulate the economic variables at their disposal in such a way as to maintain low levels of inflation and unemployment, high levels of economic growth and equilibrium in the balance of payments on current account. In doing so, almost inevitably they will affect the level of consumer spending in the economy. The ability to forecast the likely movements in these key economic indicators and the likely government responses to those movements may enable firms to 'place' their business in such a way as to maximise profits or minimize losses. For example:

- Recognition of a likely downturn in growth (and sales revenue) may allow the business to avoid being caught with excessive stocks or too many employees.
- High levels of inflation are likely to lead to increases in interest and mortgage rates which, in turn, will affect (reduce) the amount of discretionary income within the economy. High levels of inflation may also affect a firm's export sales as it finds itself priced out of overseas markets.
- A rising trend of unemployment will signal a possible fall in demand for goods and services generally.
- Changes in public expenditure which are announced each year in the budget may also impact upon sales revenue. Thus in an effort to cut public expenditure the government may slash capital expenditure programmes (note the highly directional impact on the construction industry), limit rises in the state sector wage bill and reduce social security spending (note the impact on both discretionary income and the demand for basic goods).
- Finally, changes in personal taxation and VAT will also affect both disposable and discretionary income and therefore the demand for goods and services.

Demographic factors

Demography is the study of populations in terms of their size and characteristics. There are several aspects of demography which are of interest to marketers, including the size and growth of population and its age structure. Changes in household structure may be influenced by demographic changes but are also influenced by **social** attitudes and patterns of behaviour.

Did You Know ?

Basic demographic characteristics such as age, sex and ethnic grouping are often closely related to *consumption patterns*. Marketers therefore find this a useful method for distinguishing between the needs of different groups – this is known as *market segmentation*. Demographic segmentation has been used as follows:

Variable	Used to segment
Age	Holidays, clothing, insurance
Sex	Cosmetics, alcohol, magazines
Ethnicity	Food, music, clothing

Note that by targeting our consumers in this way we can ensure that our marketing efforts are more clearly directed toward these consumers.

In Table 3.3 below we see another method of market segmentation that is often used.

Population size and growth

Globally the **population** is expanding rapidly. In 1962 world population stood at approximately 300 million but is expected to have doubled by 2001. Population growth has been strongest in the Far East and South America. By contrast population growth in Western Europe has been very small with some countries actually experiencing a decline in population levels.

It would seem from what we have said that the greatest business opportunities in the future are likely to occur in Asia and South America. In practice, at present, opportunities are limited for all but basic goods because of the low gross national product (GNP) of these countries. (In some African countries, growth in GNP is not keeping pace with population growth so that GNP per capita is actually falling.)

Age structure

Because different **age groups** will buy different products the age distribution of the population is highly significant to the marketer. Within the UK a number of different trends are apparent.

- First, the birth rate has been declining since the 1960's and consequently the youth market is contracting. Thus any firm which concentrates on this market is going to have to rethink its long-term strategy. (This could be to identify new markets for its existing products or new products for existing markets).
- Second, there is a bulge in the population between the ages of 25 and 45. This is due to the high birth rate during the 1950s and 1960s. This group, often married and with children, will require very different products and services from the youth market. But whilst demand for goods and services may be high at the moment, overall demand is likely to fall in the future owing to the smaller numbers in the present youth market.
- The one group which is showing strong growth at the moment is the 'over 55s'. This is partly due to a declining death rate caused by improvements in medical science. Many of the group will be married but with children who have left home. Over 30% will have a high level of discretionary income. Again the demands of this group will be very different, with significant opportunities for leisure providers.

Did You Know ?

By the year 2011 it is estimated that 17% of the population of the UK will be aged over 65 years, compared to only 11% in 1951 and 15% today. As many as 20% of all *females* will be aged over 65 by 2011.

Household structure.

By looking at Table 3.2 we can see some trends in **household structure** which are of great significance to business. These include:

- Fewer married couples with dependent children.
- An increase in married couples with no children.
- A doubling of lone parents with dependent children.
- A doubling of one person households.

	1960 %	1990 %
Married couple with dependent children	52	42
Married couple with no children	18	23
Married couple with non dependent children	11	11
Lone parent with dependent children	3	6
One person household	4	10
Other	12	8

Table 3.2 Types of Households

To these we can also add:

- A trend for women to have fewer children.
- A trend for women to have jobs/careers.

Geographic distribution

The UK has a **population density** of approximately 230 people per square kilometre. This is one of the world's highest population densities. It makes the UK a very attractive market because it is easier and less costly to penetrate than a less densely populated country, such as France.

However, the UK population is still distributed very un-evenly throughout the country and there is a slow but con-tinued movement from rural to urban areas by young people. The movement of population from countryside to town will be of great significance to large retailers when determining the location of their retail outlets. The trend toward an ageing rural population has also had an impor-tant influence on the products and services offered there.

Social and cultural factors

Whilst economic and demographic factors may explain many differences in patterns of human consumption, many more can be explained by social and cultural factors. For the most part these factors are outside the control of the organization yet an understanding of them may enable the firm to design, promote and price the product effectively.

Social class

Society can be divided into broad groups of people who share certain common features. These features include occu-pation, income, education, wealth and lifestyle. The differ-ent groups distinguished in this way are commonly termed **social classes**. Marketers are interested in these classes because class is seen as a major determinant of buyer behaviour.

The most widely used technique is to classify people according to the **occupation** of the head of the household (see Table 3.3).There is a lot of evidence which suggests that the occupation of the head of the household has a major influence on consumers' buying behaviour. More impor-tantly this buying behaviour will change as individuals move from one class to another.

Group	Description	Typically	Percentage of population
A	Upper middle class	Higher managerial or professional	3
B	Middle class	Intermediate managerial or professional	11
C₁	Lower middle class	Supervisory and clerical staff	22
C₂	Skilled working class	Skilled manual workers	32
D	Working class	Semi-skilled and manual workers	23
E	Pensioners and unemployed		9

Table 3.3 Socio-economic classification

Reference groups

This is a group which has some influence over a person's values, attitudes, opinions and behaviour. The individual may be a member, or aspire to be a member, of the group. These groups include the family, work based groups, trade unions, religious groups as well as leisure clubs and societies.

Whilst the individual may not be influenced by, or accept, all the attitudes of a reference group, the fact that influence occurs at all makes it important for the marketer to identify the **reference groups** operating in their target markets. They will also try and identify those people within the group who are particularly influential and target their marketing efforts toward these *opinion shapers* or some-times even pay the opinion shaper to endorse their products (e.g. the use of sports stars to endorse a range of sports goods).

Cultural influences

By **culture** we are referring to a set of values, attitudes, beliefs and customs which shape the way we view and inter-act with the rest of society. This culture which is passed down from generation to generation and is learnt as a child within the family and other institutions (e.g. the school) is an important influence on our behaviour. Culture is impor-tant to the marketer because it:

- Determines what products are acceptable and will be purchased.
- Determines the kind of marketing message that will attract the group.
- Determines who is the purchaser (and therefore whom the message should be aimed at).
- Determines what colours are acceptable (e.g. the colour for mourning varies between cultures).
- Determines how and in what circumstances a sale takes place (in some countries/cultures bribes are acceptable).

Did You Know ?

Black Label scotch sold poorly in Greece because status-conscious drinkers thought that the (dark) bottles could not be seen in night clubs.

Both social and cultural influences will vary over time. Marketers must be alert to spot the trends in order to exploit new opportunities. Here are a few of the more im-portant trends that marketers have exploited in recent years:

Changes	Response
• concern for healthy living	natural foods, low fat products, keep fit centres
• concern for the environment	recycled products, environment-ally friendly products
• changing role of women	child care facilities, conveni-ence foods, labour saving devices
• single person family units	smaller houses and flats, singles holidays, smaller food portions
• greater life expectancy	a whole range of products and services catering for the elderly

Segmentation

Market segmentation is the process by which a total market is broken down into separate groups of customers having identifiably different product needs. Segmentation has the advantage of enabling the marketer to devise a marketing strategy which will appeal to these individual segments of the market. We have already noted a number of ways in which groups of customers can be distinguished and a market can be segmented, for example by:

* Age
* Sex
* Income
* Household structure
* Social class
* Cultural factors

To these we must now add several more.

Benefit segmentation

Some markets can be segmented on the basis of the *benefit* sought by the customer. Thus the travel market could be segmented on combinations of benefits such as speed, comfort, cost, frequency of service and personal safety.

Behaviour segmentation

Consumers may be segmented by their *behaviour*, such as frequency of purchase or level of loyalty. Alcohol and cigarette markets are often segmented into heavy, medium and light users.

Geo-demographic segmentation

As its name implies this is a combination of geographic and demographic segmentation. The most popular of these methods is ACORN which stands for A Classification Of Residential Neighbourhoods.

ACORN is based on the belief that certain neighbourhoods will not only have similar housing but the residents will display similar demographic and social characteristics and will have similar lifestyles. They will also, consequently, have similar *purchasing* patterns. With the use of computers and postcodes this is a very powerful tool for the marketer because he can target potential buyers in a very precise way. This explains the growth in direct mail promotions in recent years.

Lifestyle segmentation

Sometimes called *psychographics* this refers to the distinctive patterns of living adopted by different groups of people. It encompasses their values and attitudes, their day to day routines, leisure interests and work patterns. If **lifestyles** can be accurately described and quantified, organizations can develop and market products targeted specifically at a group with a particular lifestyle.

There have been numerous attempts to allocate consumers to lifestyles. One of the more popular is that of the Taylor Nelson market research company. This is shown in Table 3.4.

* **Self explorers.** They are motivated by self-expression and self realisation. They are less materialistic than other groups and have higher tolerance levels (16% of the population)
* **Social resistors.** A caring group with strong views on social values and fairness. Often considered to be intolerant and highly moralistic (11% of the population)
* **Experimentalists.** They are individualistic, materialistic, pro-technology, anti-traditional authority and motivated by fast moving enjoyment (14% of the population)
* **Conspicuous consumers.** They are materialistic and pushy, motivated by acquisition, competition and getting ahead. They are pro-authority and law and order (19% of the population)
* **Belongers.** They seek a quiet undisturbed family life. They are conservative and rule-followers (19% of the population)
* **Survivors.** Strongly class conscious and community spirited. Their motivation is to 'get by' (16% of the population)
* **Aimless.** Comprises two groups (1) the young unemployed, often anti-authority, and (2) the old whose motivation is day-to-day existence (5% of the population)

Table 3.4 Lifestyle categories

Segmentation has become increasingly important since the 1960s. Mass marketing techniques are no longer considered appropriate for anything other than a homogeneous or undifferentiated product. This is because as people in the West have become increasingly affluent they have been willing to pay a higher price for a product that meets their *precise* requirements. Whilst this has created problems for marketers in determining the precise needs of these groups, it has also created opportunities for product diversification.

The growth of small specialist or 'niche' markets has also been of major importance to the development of small firms. In many cases they have been able to meet the needs of these specialist markets more effectively than the large firm. This is because the segment is too small for the large firm to service profitably but is a sufficiently worthwhile opportunity for the smaller firm.

Self Check ✔ **Element 2**

10. Explain how income distribution and discretionary income could affect marketing decisions.

_____
_____
_____
_____
_____

11. Give two examples of how government demand management could affect the sales of a product.

_____
_____
_____
_____

12. Explain the term market segmentation.

_____
_____
_____
_____
_____

13. State five different ways that demographic factors could be used to segment a market.

_____
_____
_____
_____

14. State two ways that a building products firm might segment its market.

_____
_____

15. Give two examples of a niche market.

_____
_____

3.3 Investigating Market Activities

In this element we will consider the following performance criteria:

- Objectives of marketing activities are explained.
- Marketing activities for competing products are compared for effectiveness in achieving objectives.
- New product developments and life cycles are identified.
- Marketing mixes used by organizations are identified and explained.
- Ethical considerations of sales and marketing activities are explained and authorities to ensure ethical standards are identified.

So far we have looked at one of the major marketing functions -- marketing research. In this part of the unit we will be directing our attention to another four major marketing functions, namely:

- Producing the right product.
- Promoting the product.
- Pricing the product.
- Placing (or distributing) the product.

These four functions are normally grouped together and called the **four 'P's** of marketing or, more popularly, the **marketing mix**.

Product	Product range
	Product features
	Product quality
	Packaging
Price	Price levels
	Price discounts
	Credit policy
	Price strategy
Promotion	Advertising spend
	Advertising copy
	Suitable media
	Advertising scheduling
Place	Channels of distribution
	Stock levels
	Delivery

Table 3.5 Aspects of the marketing mix

The marketing mix is a key concept. It refers to the factors which may be varied (see Table 3.5) by the marketer in an attempt to offset environmental uncertainty, gain a competitive edge over rivals and thereby achieve marketing objectives such as

- To maintain or increase market share.
- To become the recognized market leader.
- To target a new market or market segment.
- To develop a new range of products.
- To maximize profits.
- To be the recognized innovator or technical leader in the market.
- To improve the image of the product or company.

Of course, many of these objectives will be pursued at the same time, but some may conflict. For example, maximizing profitability may be inconsistent with producing the best quality product.

We will now explore the various items of the marketing mix in detail.

Product

The term is used to cover not only goods but also services. Even pop stars can be 'products' in the sense that we can buy their CDs and go to their shows. A **product** can be considered at three different levels:

- _The core product._ This is the major function or benefit that the product user obtains. In many cases this is very obvious, for example the function of a washing machine is to clean clothes. In other situations the function or benefit is not so obvious. Take toothpaste. Is the function to clean teeth or to ensure fresh breath?

- _The tangible product._ These are the physical features of the product – the size, colour, shape of the product together with styling, packaging and overall quality.

- _The augmented product._ This includes other benefits that can be obtained with the purchase of that product, e.g. delivery, installation, guarantee and aftersales service. It could also include branding or the image created by ownership, e.g. a sports car.

The product mix

This is also sometimes referred to as the **product portfolio**. It is the total number of product lines that an organization has to sell to the public. Most firms will have a number of different product lines – a typical supermarket will have over 20,000 different product lines!

A _product line_ consists of a group of products that are closely related because they are intended for the same end use, are sold to the same customer group or are part of a particular price range.

There is often a conflict of opinion within the organization over the size of the product portfolio. The _marketing department_ will want as many lines as possible so as to maximize sales. They will argue that the successful lines can carry the unsuccessful ones. Conversely, the _production department_ will want to reduce the number of lines in order to cut production and stockholding costs. The present day trend is for firms to reduce the size of their portfolio by divesting themselves of those lines which do not form part of their 'core' activities.

Product portfolio analysis

The longer term survival of the firm requires it to have a number of products at *different stages* of development (see Product life cycle below). Ideally these should also be selling in different markets. The **Boston matrix** (it is now sometimes referred to as the **product matrix**), so called because it was developed by the Boston Consulting Group in the USA, is an attempt to rate the firm's portfolio in terms of sales growth and market share. The Boston Group argue that these two variables are closely related to profitability. As we can see from figure 3.4 there are four segments to the Boston matrix.

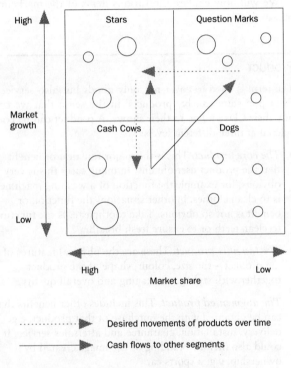

Fig. 3.4 Boston Consulting Group matrix (or product matrix)

- *Question marks* are products where the market growth rate is high but the market share is low. Firms will often invest large sums of money in these products because of the attractiveness of the market. At the present time, however, the product is unlikely to be profitable. Question marks are sometimes related to the introductory stage in the product life cycle.
- *Stars* are products which have a high market share in a fast growing market. Despite large sales the product will only just break even or make a small profit because of cash needs for development and promotion. Stars are sometimes compared with a product in the growth stage of its life cycle.
- *Cash cows* are those products which have been on the market for some time and enjoy a high market share in a low growth market. Because market growth has slowed down there is less need for investment and these products are very profitable. In terms of the product life cycle they are in the maturity stage.

- *Dogs* are products where both market share and growth rate are low. Previously they may have been cash cows but have now moved into the decline stage of the product life cycle. Such products may still be marginally profitable and therefore will be retained. Once profits cease or the costs of managing the product become too high, it will be quickly withdrawn from the market.

In Fig. 3.4 we see a reasonably balanced product portfolio with a number of 'question marks' and 'stars' which we hope will become tomorrow's 'stars' and 'cash cows'. The investment needed in these products is provided by the profits generated by the 'cash cow' products.

Of course it is always possible that the 'question marks' will not become 'stars' nor the 'stars' become 'cash cows'. Either or both could move to the 'dog' segment. Whilst it is unlikely that all a firm's products will follow the pattern shown in Fig. 3.4 it would be worrying if too many failed as this would threaten the long term viability of the organization.

The product life cycle

This extremely important concept, its characteristics and possible strategies are illustrated diagrammatically in Fig. 3.5. It suggests that all products brought to the market follow a pattern which is described as a **life cycle**. This life cycle is normally said to have four stages.

- *Introduction*
  This is a stage where the product is relatively unknown, sales are low and profits are not yet being made. The promotion strategy will be designed to inform people that the product is available. The product would normally be stocked at a limited number of outlets but we would try to ensure that there was maximum exposure at these points of sale. Price would be relatively high at this time owing to lack of competition.

- *Growth*
  In this period there is extremely rapid growth which attracts the first competitors to the market. Prices are likely to be lowered to attract a wider base of customers and the number of outlets is increased. We will be seeking the new products that will replace this one or the modifications to the existing product that will extend it's life cycle. The profits which are starting to be made can be used to support such investment.

- *Maturity*
  The majority of sales are now repeat orders rather than first time purchases. Fierce competition forces the firm to reduce prices further. Advertising seeks to persuade customers to buy this, rather than some other, brand of product. The firm will be looking to see if the product can be sold in other markets – often abroad. Refinements and cosmetic changes are introduced to provide a competitive edge and maintain sales levels. Replacement products are likely to be introduced. Economies of scale resulting from large volume production will help to keep unit costs low and profits high.

- *Decline*
  As sales decline, advertising and promotion ceases. Prices are reduced as much as possible to keep at least some sales. Eventually, as the product moves into loss it is withdrawn from the market.

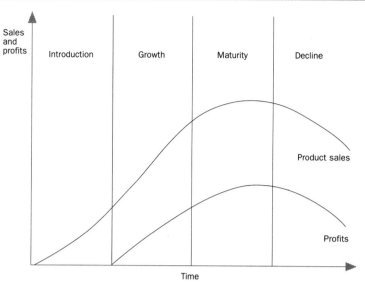

INTRODUCTION

Characteristics
- High failure rate
- Little competition
- Frequent modification
- Make losses

Strategies
- Create product awareness
- 'Skim' pricing or penetration pricing
- Shake out policy – quickly drop unsuccessful products.

GROWTH

Characteristics
- More competitors
- Rising sales
- Possibly acquired by larger company

Strategies
- Promote brand image
- Acquire outlets
- Obtain economies of scale.

MATURITY

Characteristics
- Sales increase at reduced rate
- Product line widened
- Prices fall as market share is lost
- * Profits fall as competition grows
- Difficult for new entrants
- Marginal producers drop out

Strategies
- Encourage repeat buys
- Seek new customers by repositioning
- Seek to hold or increase market share by greater efficiency
- * Use price discounting to hold or win market share
- Hold on to distributors.

DECLINE

Characteristics
- Falling industry sales
- Falling product sales
- Some producers abandon market
- Falling profits

Strategies
- Reposition in niche markets
- Strict cost control
- 'Run out' sales promotion to get rid of stocks prior to introduction of replacement.

Fig. 3.5   Stages in the Product Life cycle

Although it is widely accepted that most products do have a life cycle, the nature and duration of the life cycle is likely to be different for every product. The life cycle for many commonplace items, like soap, will be long. For others, like high technology products, it may be very short. Life cycles of other products – we call them 'fads' – are extremely unpredictable. Sales will increase dramatically and there may very well be difficulties in meeting this upsurge in demand. Equally suddenly the craze will die leaving manufacturers and retailers with unsaleable stock on their hands (Remember Ninja Turtles! Even dinosaurs have lost popularity). Fig. 3.6 illustrates the life cycle for a typical fad product.

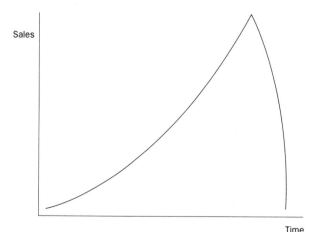

Fig. 3.6   Lifecycle of a 'fad' product

Criticisms of the product life cycle

Some writers have argued that the concept of the product life cycle has been over-used. Their criticisms are:

- The four phases are not clear cut and the particular phase for the product itself may be determined by marketing strategies.
- Many products can survive for years with modifications (see *extension strategies* below).
- Other products seem impervious to the life cycle (e.g. the board game Monopoly).

Extension strategies

You will find that many firms attempt to prolong the life of a product by using 'extension strategies'. Indeed, this may be a far safer option than introducing a completely new product to take over from the existing product. For example, when Ford replaced the very successful Cortina with the very different looking Sierra it took them five years to re-establish leadership in that market segment (a position they had held with the Cortina for over a decade). Extension strategies include:

- Find new markets for existing products – perhaps overseas.
- Find new uses for the product.
- Develop the product line.
- Modify the products appearance or packaging.

The effect of extension strategies is shown in Fig. 3.7.

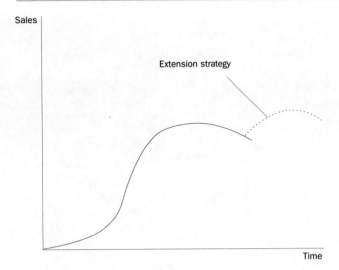

Fig. 3.7 Impact of an extension strategy on the product life cycle

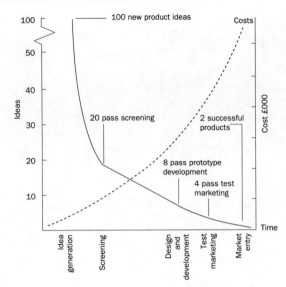

Fig. 3.8 Stages from idea generation to market entry

Many new or even improved products fail to gain market acceptance. One of the major reasons for this is that they fail to possess any significant features or characteristics different from other products. These 'significant' differences are sometimes referred to as **unique selling points** (USPs) and are much sought after by marketers. USPs may be as simple as the hole in the Polo or the characters in a coffee commercial. With more complex products, though, it is easier to identify and establish a USP. But, whatever the USP is, it is the key to being different, recognizable and successful.

Product development

Unfortunately product modification only puts off the evil day when the original product has to be replaced. **Product development** – that is, the process of bringing a new product to the market – is therefore essential to a firm's long-term survival. Product development involves the following steps:

- Identifying a customer need which the firm can respond to profitably.
- Generation of new ideas. Product ideas may range from the entirely 'new', to being 'significantly different' from the existing product, or being the 'me too' imitation of a product already on the market.
- Assessment of new ideas. This should take account not only of market demand but also of the resources (capital, spare capacity, technical expertise) that are available within the organization.
- Market and product testing. *Product tests* are designed to iron out problems in the functioning of the product. *Market tests* establish how acceptable the product is to the public and whether any modifications are needed.
- Market entry. Before entry, a marketing strategy will have to be devised; the plant and machinery necessary for production will also have to be identified.

Of course not all new products are successful once they enter the market. Many will be withdrawn within a few months of being launched. Moreover, as Fig. 3.8 shows, many new ideas for products don't even get beyond the *screening stage*. You will also note from Fig. 3.8 that development costs rise significantly after the screening stage.

Branding

Many products today are mass produced and standardized with very few true distinguishing features. **Branding** is a means of identifying such a product from its competitors by creating a name, term or logo (symbol). This is usually registered so that it can't be used by anyone else.

The major benefit that arises from branding is that the owner of the brand name saves on advertising costs as the product becomes 'known'. Branding enables the manufacturer or retailer to build up brand loyalty so that when customers go into a shop they buy Maxwell House not coffee. Brand loyalty also has the effect of making the product less susceptible to a fall in sales after a price increase.

Apart from the brand name that stands alone with no reference to the maker's name, for example Daz or Tide, there are also:

- *Family brands.* These carry the name of the company, e.g. Heinz, Del Monte, Amstrad, Ford. This 'brand stretching' as it is called, increases the cost-effectiveness of advertising as one successful product promotion rubs off on the other products. Of course the reverse is also true in that one product with a bad reputation can pull the others down.

- *Multiple branding.* This is also known as multi-branding or product segmentation. It involves selling a number of similar products under different brand names in the same market segment. The hope is that when consumers switch products the firm has an additional chance of its products being selected. It also increases competition within the firm between the different brand managers.

- *House branding.* Many retailers have goods made for them which they then sell in their own name, for example Boots, or some chosen alternative name, for example St. Michael (Marks and Spencer). These *house brands* are becoming increasingly important. Consumers see them as having the quality of the famous brands but at a lower price (e.g. Sainsbury's 'classic cola' or 'gold choice' coffee). From the retailers point of view they enhance the store identity as well as create product loyalty.

Packaging the product is not just about protecting the product. It is also about promotion. Packaging on the product is the last chance the producer gets to persuade the consumer to buy *his* product. In a supermarket where many similar products are sold it tends to be the product that is noticed which is sold, for example the shape of a Coca Cola bottle is virtually world famous.

Not only does the packaging have to have 'visual appeal', it must also put across the right image. The marketer will have to experiment with shape, colour, size, ease of use and many other factors. It is not easy to convey the right image but tests have shown that when faced with a new or untried product it is precisely these features that will determine the purchase decision.

Pricing

In Unit 1 we have already looked at the economists' approach to how market price is determined. In a *fully competitive* market the ability of the marketer to exploit the price element of the marketing mix will be distinctly limited – yet as we also saw in Unit 1 there are a variety of market structures ranging from highly competitive to uncompetitive. Where, as in most cases, markets are *imperfectly competitive,* the organization has some discretion over the price it charges.

There are three major ways in which prices can be determined:

- What it costs to produce.
- What the competition is charging.
- What customers are prepared to pay.

We will look at each in turn.

Cost-orientated pricing

There are two major methods. One method is **mark-up** or **cost plus pricing** which involves calculating the average cost per unit produced and adding a mark-up for profit. This is a quick and simple way of setting a price and will be used by firms dealing with many products where it would be too costly to price each item separately. The major disadvantage is that it takes no account of market demand nor is any attempt made to allocate indirect costs to specific products.

A second method is **target return pricing** which involves calculating a selling price which yields a particular return on capital. It has often been used by public corporations to ensure a reasonable return on money borrowed. It is calculated as follows:

$$\text{price} = \text{product cost} + \frac{\text{desired \% return} \times \text{investment}}{\text{volume of product sales}}$$

Both methods suffer from the problem that prices are based on historic cost information. Sudden and unanticipated increases in costs may turn a profit making price into a loss making price. This is a particular problem for the package tour industry where holiday brochures will be prepared up to a year in advance. It is for this reason that tour operators reserve the right to raise prices should, say, fuel prices rise significantly.

Demand-orientated pricing

There are several forms of **demand** (or market) **orientated pricing**. For new products it will take the form of penetration or skim pricing. For other products it may involve psychological pricing or discriminatory pricing.

- *Penetration pricing*
  This involves setting a low price for a new product in order to reach a large market quickly. It can be used where the product is price sensitive (high price elasticity of demand) or when you wish to discourage early competition from other firms. By building up market share and limiting competition the firm hopes to have more control over prices in the longer term (note that there are dangers with this strategy if the product lifecycle is short because there may not be time to recoup development costs).

- *Skim pricing*
  A high price is set for the new product which allows for the early recovery of development costs. Prices may be lowered at later stages in the product lifecycle but the reduced profit margin from a lower unit price will then be offset by lower unit costs via economies of larger scale production. For skim pricing to work there must be buyers prepared to pay the initial premium price and the product must be protected by patents to stop competitors entering the market.

- *Psychological pricing*
  There are two different aspects to consider. First, many products will be priced at £2.95 or £295 rather than £3.00 or £300 because consumers will then tend to place it in a lower, rather than a higher, price band.

  Consumers also use price as an indicator of quality. This is particularly true of luxury products or highly technological products where the consumer has little real understanding of the value of the different features the product has. The manufacturer of these products may therefore set prices far in excess of the real value of the product.

- *Discriminatory pricing*
  This is a situation where different prices are charged for the same product. One example is British Rail's policy of charging higher prices for early morning inter-city travel than throughout the rest of the day. The student or shopper going to London won't be prepared to pay as much as the businessman going to a meeting. Thus by charging a lower price to students but requiring them to avoid the early morning rush-hour trains British Rail has effectively segmented its market and gained revenue which would otherwise have been lost. Other examples of discriminatory pricing are British Telecom's daytime and evening phone rates and the practice of many package tour operators to charge more during the school holidays.

  The examples so far have all been *time based* but price discrimination can also be *market based*. One example of this is students, families or senior citizens being given discounts on rail travel.

For discriminatory pricing to work:

- The market must be segmentable. In other words be capable of being split up into segments, each having different demand characteristics.
- The different segments must be unwilling to pay the same (high) price. In other words, price elasticity of demand must differ between the various market segments.
- The high price segments must not be able to obtain the product or service at a lower price. In other words there must be barriers to prevent people transferring from the high to low price segments.

Competition-orientated pricing

In this situation it is the prices charged by competitors that have a major influence on the prices set by a firm. Generally speaking, competition-based pricing is likely where there is:

- A homogeneous (identical) product with little opportunity for differentiation.
- A mature industry in which there is spare capacity.
- A market similar to the oligopoly model.

- *Follow-my-leader pricing*
  This is sometimes also referred to as 'going rate' pricing. Many firms are reluctant to use prices as a means of gaining a competitive edge over their rivals because it might start a price war (and they doubt their ability to survive!). In these circumstances they will choose a price which is broadly in line with the market. In some markets it is common for one firm to become the acknowledged *price leader* with the others acting as price followers.

> In a highly competitive situation many firms will not adopt a single price but will identify a *price range* within which prices may move. Such a policy gives the firm a flexibility that is not normally available in the short term. Thus prices can be altered quickly to prevent a competitor obtaining a short term tactical advantage over your product or for you to achieve that tactical advantage yourself.
>
> For a supermarket or other retailer, loss leader pricing is a good example of what is generally known as **tactical pricing**.

- *Loss leader pricing*
  It is hoped that by selling some goods below the normal price people will be enticed into the shop and will purchase other items as well.

- *Discount pricing*
  Some shops have a reputation for 'value for money' by selling products slightly cheaper than elsewhere. They are able to do this by using cheaper premises, carrying fewer product lines, demanding cash and paying less attention to presentation.

- *Destroyer pricing*
  This involves setting a price which is designed to drive other firms out of the market. Some people argue that Laker Airways was forced out of business by other transatlantic airlines using this method. One major problem for the 'destroyer' firm is that it too may be weakened in the conflict and thus lay itself open to a takeover bid.

- *Tendering*
  This is common in the construction industry and the public sector. Sealed bids for a contract are submitted by interested parties. The contract is normally awarded to the lowest bidder.

> **Did You Know ?**
>
> Discount stores such as Aldi of Germany and Costco of the US are gaining market share in the UK. However at present, discount stores have less than 10% of total UK food sales, compared to 25% in Germany and 20% in Belgium.

Promotion

By **promotion** we are referring to attempts by a firm to draw the attention of potential customers to its products or services. Promotion has the aim of:

- Making customers aware of a product or service.
- Reaching customers that are geographically dispersed.
- Increasing awareness or reminding customers of a product or service.
- Indicating that a product is better than the competitors'.
- Improving the image of the firm.

The promotional mix

This refers to the combination of techniques which are available to the firm in promoting its products. These techniques which may be combined in different ways are:

- *Advertising.* Defined as non-personal purchased communication using the mass media.

- *Sales promotion.* This includes activities such as money-off coupons, sponsorship, in-store displays and exhibitions

- *Personal selling.* Defined as direct face-to-face communication and persuasion

- *Public relations.* Defined as those activities designed to create and maintain a positive and beneficial corporate image.

The precise nature of the promotional mix will be determined by the nature of the product and the market which is being targeted.

Advertising

Advertising is often referred to as 'above the line' promotion. It refers to all mass media advertising where a large audience is reached easily. 'Below the line' promotion may therefore include some advertising but commonly is taken to refer to sales promotion, personal selling and public relations.

Advertising falls into three broad categories, namely:

- *Informative.* This will be used where a new product is brought to the market or where products (or services) are complex in nature and a large amount of technical information has to be digested. Many industrial products will fall into the latter class.

- *Persuasive.* This is often used in the maturity stage of the product lifecycle for consumer goods, particularly when there is spare capacity in the industry. The aim of such advertising is to create an element of brand loyalty and thus give the firm more control over prices. An economist would say the firm is trying to make the demand curve facing the product less elastic – see Fig. 3.9.

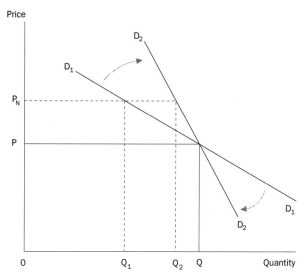

Fig. 3.9 Impact of advertising to create a more inelastic demand curve

In Fig. 3.9 we see what the firm hopes to achieve through persuasive advertising. The original demand curve D1 has been replaced by the more inelastic D2. As a result when prices rise from P to PN the fall in quantity associated with the inelastic demand curve is far less (Q to Q2) than that associated with the elastic demand curve (Q to Q1).

- *Institutional.* The aim of such advertising is to improve the public standing of the advertiser in the community rather than to sell a particular product.

The choice of advertising media

Although this is very important it is pre-determined, to some extent, by the size of the advertising budget. Thus few small firms would be able to consider television advertising – even though it might be the most suitable for their purposes. Apart from cost the other major considerations in the choice of media include:

- *The market segment.* The aim is to find the medium through which the firm is most likely to reach its target audience.

- *The size of the market.* Where the firm is trying to reach a national market the media it uses will have national coverage. Equally, if the market is local or regional the firm will use local media .

- *The nature of the product.* Specialist products, e.g. sports guns, are best advertised in the appropriate specialist magazines. Other products, for example sports goods, are best seen in action to have the greatest impact – this would suggest the use of television.

- *The law.* Some products can't be advertised in certain media. For example, tobacco products can't be advertised on UK television.

The main advertising media

- *Printed media*
  This includes local and national newspapers and magazines together with specialist magazines. It is considered to be one of the cheapest ways of reaching a mass market. It may also be used to target specific customer segments through specialist magazines in a cost effective way. In some magazines the advertisement may be read repeatedly (e.g. the Radio Times). It is also possible that the target audience might fail to notice it amongst all the other advertisements!

- *Television*
  Television is the most powerful media channel with some TV audiences regularly topping 12 million viewers. It is an effective way of reaching a mass audience in a region or nationally. Continuous advertising, particularly of a creative nature, can build and maintain consumer awareness. It is possible to 'put over' complex information through the unique combination of colour, sound and movement.

- *Commercial radio*
  It is a cheap form of advertising for local business. It is said that radio advertisements are poor on impact because people are rarely listening carefully. Repetition is therefore essential.

- *Cinema*
  This is an effective way of targeting the teens and twenties market. Over 75% of the audience fall into this age range. However cinema audiences have been declining owing to the competition of TV and video rentals. To be successful, cinema advertising depends on the quality and popularity of the films being shown.

- *Outdoor*
  This includes posters, hoardings, neon signs, and

electronic screens. This is a very cheap form of communication but depends for its effectiveness on situational impact.

Advertising and society

Because it is virtually impossible to avoid exposure to advertisements in day-to-day life the impact of the advertising industry on individuals is great. We must therefore consider whether advertising needs to be controlled. Advertising is said to confer certain benefits on society. These include:

- Advertising ensures the level of sales necessary for large-scale production and economies of scale.
- The ability to maintain and expand sales gives the worker security of employment and the investor confidence to invest in that firm.
- The public has information on products which would otherwise be difficult to obtain.
- The public can make more informed consumption decisions.
- Advertising enables other products, e.g. newspapers, to be provided at a lower price.
- The advertising industry is a major employer.
- Advertising encourages competition, resulting in better products at a keener price.

However, against these benefits of advertising we must put certain criticisms. These include:

- It increases costs.
- It may be misleading, wasteful or offensive.
- It may be used to prevent new firms entering the market.
- It encourages consumption that isn't really necessary.
- It generates desires for things which we can never hope to achieve.

- *Controls on advertising*
  Because of the kinds of concerns which have been noted above there are certain controls on the use of advertising. For example:

  - *Trade Descriptions Act 1968.* This states that goods for sale must be as they are described. Descriptions of services must also be accurate. Complaints by a member of the public to Trading Standards Departments may result in the offender being prosecuted.

Trading Standards Officers will investigate complaints regarding misleading statements made about goods or services offered for sale, misleading statements about prices, inaccurate weights and measures as well as consumer credit.

  - *Monopolies and Restrictive Practices Act 1948.* High levels of spending on advertising may constitute anti competitive behaviour if it acts to prevent other firms entering the market.
  - *The Advertising Standards Authority (ASA).* This body is responsible for ensuring that advertisers conform to the British Code of Advertising Practice. This code requires all advertisements to be 'legal, decent, honest and truthful'; advertisements must also

not 'cause grave or widespread offence'. Where the ASA deems that an advertisement does *not* meet these requirements it will not be handled by the media.

  - *The Independent Television Commission (ITC).* This is responsible for controlling advertising on television and radio.

Other forms of promotion

- *Public Relations*
  All firms are affected by their external environment. It is therefore necessary for the firm to pay attention to the attitudes and views of those groups of people that form its 'public'. The aim of the public relations department in a large firm, or the marketing manager in a smaller firm, is to maintain or improve the image of the organization in the eyes of its public. This is done by drip feeding the media with 'good ' news or news that shows the firm in a positive light (e.g. donations to local charities). It is also important that the firm is able to put its point of view when bad publicity occurs. The methods used to create this positive image include

  - Press releases and conferences
  - Participation in exhibitions or trade fairs
  - The sponsorship of sport or other events
  - Company literature, e.g. recruitment literature, employee magazines, the annual report and accounts

- *Sales promotion*
  There are a wide variety of techniques available, which include:

  - Immediate incentives – free samples, trial packs, bonus value (i.e. more product for your money), price reductions, competitions.
  - Delayed incentives – 'money off next purchase' coupons, mail-in cash refunds, mail-in give away offers, competitions.
  - Point of sale displays.
  - Exhibitions and trade fairs.
  - Sponsorship.

Sales promotion techniques are widely used in both the consumer and industrial markets. Firms working in markets where there is intense competition, e.g. tobacco, alcohol, petrol, are likely to use sales promotion techniques as part of their wider promotional strategy.

- *Personal selling*
  Most medium- and large-sized firms will employ a salesforce, though its importance will vary according to the markets served. In the industrial market, where potential buyers are often limited in number and the size of the average orders are large, it is cost effective to employ a salesforce. Personal selling is less important in the consumer market, though there are exceptions, e.g. insurance and double glazing. The main advantage of personal selling over other forms of promotion is that the 'message' can be tailored to the needs of the individual (compare that with the advertisement which gives the 'standard' message to 'Mr Average'). There are also other benefits which include:

  - The sales team is a valuable source of marketing research information.

- The sales team can identify new, potential outlets which reflect the company image.
- The sales team help to maintain a direct link with the customer rather than relying on intermediaries, thereby ensuring that the firm's products are brought to the attention of the customer.
- The sales force will promote new products more effectively than will intermediaries.
- The established personal relationship is more likely to generate repeat sales.

Did You Know ?

Cutting customer loss by 5% can increase profit by between 25% and 85%, depending on the sector in which the firm operates.

Distribution (Place)

Channels of distribution provide the link between production and supply. They are an important part of the marketing mix because until the product is in a position to be sold, all previous work is of no effect whatsoever. In choosing a channel of distribution the firm will seek to ensure that:

- The channel gives access to the customer segments targeted.
- The channel meets the firm's objective in terms of market share.
- The channel is relatively cost effective when compared with others.
- The channel allows the firm to compete on equal terms with other similar products.

In practice there is no reason why a firm should limit itself to just one channel of distribution. Thus toys may be sold through intermediaries, direct to a retailer or direct to the customer through advertisements in the press. In fact by using different channels of distribution the firm may find that it is reaching different segments of the market.

The channels of distribution

We will look at the three channels shown in Fig. 3.10. It is also possible to consider *franchising* as another potential channel, but this is dealt with in Unit 4.

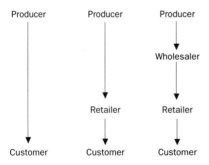

Fig. 3.10   Channels of distribution

- *Direct selling*
  There are many examples of selling direct to the customer. It is common in business markets when the product is of a technical nature. Amongst consumer products sold direct to the public, *Avon* and *Tupperware* are always mentioned but the list could also include insurance and double glazing firms. There are several *advantages* of direct selling. They are:

  - Using your own staff you can make sure your product is properly promoted.
  - It is possible to establish a good relationship with the customer.
  - Sales staff can be a good source of marketing research information.
  - It cuts out the costs of the middlemen.

  But there are also *disadvantages*:

  - Direct selling costs are likely to be high.
  - It is often difficult to display the products in a way that a retailer would do. Some customers will be reluctant to buy on the basis of catalogue pictures and descriptions.

- *Producer to retailer*
  If the firm is not to sell direct to the consumer this method has the advantage of minimizing the loss of contact with the customer and maximising control over the retail outlet. For example the retailer and producer may co-operate over matters such as store display, promotional activity and the training of sales assistants. This is a channel that is often adopted by large firms having a number of products which can be sold through the same retail outlets.

Another decision related to distribution is the number of outlets – wholesalers and shops – that are required. There are three possibilities:

- *Maximum distribution* will be required for everyday goods having no distinctive identity of their own. Cigarettes and many foods come into this category.
- *Selective distribution* gives the producer some control over the outlets selected. It enables him to see that the product is sold in outlets that conform to the image the firm requires. Additional outlets can be added should the producer wish to expand in this market.
- *Exclusive distribution* arises when a producer gives sole rights to sell the product in an area to one dealer. Such agreements limit the availability of the product in the market place. However, limiting the product's availability may actually improve its image in the market and therefore allow the producer to make higher profits on each sale. Franchises are also examples of exclusive distribution deals.

- *Producer to wholesaler*
  This channel tends to be chosen by smaller firms who do not have a complete product range and are not able to afford the luxury of an extensive distribution network and large salesforce. Its advantages include:

  - Lower distribution costs. The producer sells in bulk to the wholesaler and does not have to deal with small orders.
  - The wholesaler has contacts and expertise which the producer does not have.

- Early sale reduces stockholding costs.
- There is very little risk of payment delay or default since the reputation of the wholesaler is known.

There are major problems associated with this method, however. For example the producer has no control over who stocks his products – or how they are displayed. Second, new products do not get the attention they deserve. Finally, profit margins tend to be lower than with other methods of distribution.

Self Check ✔ Element 3

16. State three typical marketing objectives.

17. Why is the marketing mix an important concept?

18. Describe briefly the four stages in the product life cycle.

19. How can a firm extend the life cycle of a product?

20. Explain why product development is so important to a business.

21. Explain one method of cost-orientated pricing.

Self Check ✔ *continued*

22. Why might a firm use penetration pricing rather than skim pricing?

23. In what circumstances can a firm charge different prices for the same service?

24. Explain the term *promotional mix*.

25. Distinguish between 'above the line' and 'below the line' promotion.

26. What method of advertising or promotion would be best for each of the following:
    To sell a second-hand car

    A new cut price restaurant for students

    A new brand of chocolate bar

    A bank's new savings scheme

27. What are the most appropriate distribution channels for the following:
    Package tours overseas

    The sale of textbooks

    The sale of specialist equipment

    Products aimed at a fragmented market

Unit Test Answer all the following questions.

Focus 1

Question 1
Mark each of these statements true (T) or false (F).

Primary research for a newsagent would involve:

(1) Asking existing customers what magazines they read
(2) Asking competitor's customers why they don't buy from him

Which option best describes the two statements:

A (1) T (2) T Choose this answer if both statements are True.
B (1) T (2) F Choose this answer if statement (1) is True and statement (2) is False.
C (1) F (2) T Choose this answer if statement (1) is False and statement (2) is True.
D (1) F (2) F Choose this answer if statement (1) is False and statement (2) is False.

Question 2
Mark each of these statements true (T) or false (F).

(1) Primary data are always external to the organization.
(2) Primary data may be obtained by observation.

Which option best describes the two statements:

A (1) T (2) T Choose this answer if both statements are True.
B (1) T (2) F Choose this answer if statement (1) is True and statement (2) is False.
C (1) F (2) T Choose this answer if statement (1) is False and statement (2) is True.
D (1) F (2) F Choose this answer if statement (1) is False and statement (2) is False.

Questions 3–5 relate to the following information.

A company has identified the following research methods:

A Postal questionnaire
B Desk research
C Interviews
D Observation

Which should it use in each of the following situations?

Question 3
To ask why consumers buy a specific product.

Question 4
To discover the size of the market.

Question 5
To discover consumers' reaction to a point of sale display.

Question 6
Which of these is not an example of secondary research material?

A Retail audits
B Salesforce reports
C Panel interviews
D Official statistics

Questions 7–9 relate to the following information.

Criteria for research method collection include:

A Cost
B Response rate
C Data collection speed
D Accuracy of information

Which of these criteria relate to the following research methods?

Question 7
A telephone survey

Question 8
A postal questionnaire

Question 9
Electronic monitoring

Question 10
Mark each of these statements true (T) or false (F).

A firm regularly uses face to face interviews to obtain research data because

(1) Detailed information can be obtained.
(2) The cost per interview is low.

Which option best describes the two statements:

A (1) T (2) T Choose this answer if both statements are True.
B (1) T (2) F Choose this answer if statement (1) is True and Statement (2) is False.
C (1) F (2) T Choose this answer if statement (1) is False and statement (2) is True.
D (1) F (2) F Choose this answer if statement (1) is False and statement (2) is False.

Focus 2

Question 11
Survey, observation and experimentation are ways of obtaining primary research information.

Mark each of these statements true (T) or false (F).

(1) Experimentation is often referred to as test marketing.
(2) The census is a widely used form of survey.

Which option best describes the two statements:

A (1) T (2) T Choose this answer if both statements are True.
B (1) T (2) F Choose this answer if statement (1) is True and statement (2) is False.
C (1) F (2) T Choose this answer if statement (1) is False and statement (2) is True.
D (1) F (2) F Choose this answer if statement (1) is False and statement (2) is False.

Question 12
To save time and money quota samples are often used

Mark each of these statements true (T) or false (F).

(1) A quota sample is an example of non-probability sampling.

(2) In consumer markets the most common strata used for quota sampling are age, sex and income.

Which option best describes the two statements:

A (1) T (2) T Choose this answer if both statements are True.

B (1) T (2) F Choose this answer if statement (1) is True and statement (2) is False.

C (1) F (2) T Choose this answer if statement (1) is False and statement (2) is True.

D (1) F (2) F Choose this answer if statement (1) is False and statement (2) is False.

Questions 13–15 relate to the following information.

There are several kinds of survey based on sampling techniques, for example:

A. A postal questionnaire
B. The sample is selected by the interviewer
C. Every 10,000th person is interviewed
D. A survey is weighted according to the proportion of turnover different customer groups buy

Which of the above descriptions relate to the following?

Question 13
A random sample

Question 14
A cluster sample

Question 15
A stratified random sample

Questions 16–18 relate to the following information.

A supermarket chain divides the country into 4 regional areas. It has produced the following information:

	sales by value %	sales by volume %
A	36	26
B	25	25
C	28	40
D	11	9

The chain is now planning to increase its promotional budget. Which area should it concentrate on if it wishes to :

Question 16
Maximise sales revenue

Question 17
Increase the value of sales in its largest market

Question 18
Increase revenue and sales equally

Question 19
A study of social trends would not reveal information on :
A Unemployment figures
B Inflation figures
C Crime figures
D Household expenditure

Questions 20–22 relate to the following information.

Demographic segmentation uses various criteria for distinguishing different groups including:

A Age   B Sex   C Household structure   D Ethnicity

Which of the above criteria would you use to segment the following markets?

Question 20
Food and music

Question 21
Pensions and holidays

Question 22
Toiletries and magazines

Question 23
Mark each of these statements true (T) or false (F).

(1) ACORN is an example of behaviour segmentation.
(2) Marketing cars on the basis of reliability, miles to the gallon and comfort is an example of benefit segmentation.

Which option best describes the two statements:

A (1) T (2) T Choose this answer if both statements are True.

B (1) T (2) F Choose this answer if statement (1) is True and statement (2) is False.

C (1) F (2) T Choose this answer if statement (1) is False and statement (2) is True.

D (1) F (2) F Choose this answer if statement (1) is False and statement (2) is False.

Question 24
Which of the following is not an extension strategy?
A Finding new markets for a product
B Developing the product line
C Developing another product
D Finding new uses for a product

Question 25
Which of the following is not a marketing objective?
A To improve product quality
B To improve productivity
C To improve product sales
D To develop a new range of products

Questions 26–28 relate to the following information.

The following are all forms of advertising media.

A Television
B Cinema
C National newspaper
D Commercial radio

Select the most appropriate media for the following products:

Question 26
Children's toys

Question 27
A new brand of cigarettes

Question 28
Fashion clothing for young men and women

Question 29
The maturity stage of the product life cycle will have been reached when:

A Sales are falling
B Sales have stopped rising
C Sales are increasing slowly
D Sales are increasing rapidly

Questions 30–32 relate to the following information.

These are four methods of demand-orientated pricing:

A Penetration
B Skim
C Psychological
D Discriminatory

Which form of pricing would be appropriate when:

Question 30
People use price as an indicator of quality

Question 31
Introducing a product, faced with a price-inelastic demand curve to the market

Question 32
The firm faces a large, but segmentable, market with very different levels of buying power

Question 33
The Advertising Standards Authority will ensure that advertisements:

A Are legal, decent and truthful
B Are legal, decent, honest and truthful
C Cause no offence
D Are in the public interest

Question 34
The Trading Standards Department would not investigate complaints about:

A Inaccurate weights and measures
B Inaccurate statements about prices
C Consumer credit
D Unhygienic storage

Question 35
Mark each of these statements true (T) or false (F).

(1) The Advertising Standards Authority supervises all advertising.
(2) The Trading Standards Department forms part of the local authority.

Which option best describes the two statements:

A (1) T (2) T Choose this answer if both statements are True.
B (1) T (2) F Choose this answer if statement (1) is True and statement (2) is False.
C (1) F (2) T Choose this answer if statement (1) is False and statement (2) is True.
D (1) F (2) F Choose this answer if statement (1) is False and statement (2) is False.

Answers to Self-check Questions

1. It is the systematic gathering, recording and analysis of data about problems related to the marketing of goods and services.

2. The size of the market
Possibilities for segmenting the market
Appropriate media for promotion purposes
Comparison of prices in the market
Analysis of transportation costs

3. It provides them with information on which to base their marketing decisions.

4. Whilst desk research uses information already in existence, field research generates information that is obtained from the market itself by observation, experimentation, survey or discussion groups.

5. Sales reports, stock movements, product sales figures, competitor information.

6. It is very general in nature and often out of date.

7. It is sometimes called test marketing and involves testing the consumers reaction to new or improved products.

8. With a probability sample you can predict how accurate the results are likely to be.

9. Where the interviewer requires the respondent to develop their answers or the interviewer needs to ask supple-mentary questions.

10. The distribution of income within a country or the amount of discretionary income that different groups have indicates the potential size of the market and therefore whether it is worthwhile targeting that market.

11. In an attempt to control inflation the government could introduce higher taxes or higher interest rates. Both have the effect of reducing the consumers' spending power and therefore the level of sales.

12. This is the breaking down of a large market into smaller markets where groups of customers have identifiably different product needs.

13. Age, sex, social class, household structure or lifestyle.

14. By type of customer
By region

15. Handmade shoes
Personal tailoring

16. To increase market share
To become market leader
To find new markets for products

17. An understanding of the concept enables the firm to manipulate the four 'P's in such a way as to reduce environmental uncertainty.

18. The introductory stage is a period when the product is introduced to the market, sales are low and losses are made.
As the product moves into the growth stage sales increase rapidly and the first signs of competition emerge.
In the maturity stage sales will level off, competition becomes much fiercer and the firm looks to introduce the replacement products – 'tomorrows winners'!
During the decline stage prices are reduced to a minimum, promotion ceases and as the product moves into a loss-making position it is withdrawn from the market.

19. By product modification
By finding new uses for the product
By finding new markets for the product

20. Accepting the fact that products do have a life cycle it is necessary to introduce new products to ensure the long term survival of the organization.

21. Cost plus is the most common method. Under this method the firm will calculate the average cost of a product and then add a margin to it.

22. These are both methods used in the pricing of new products. If the firm believes that a significant level of competition is going to emerge quickly it might sell at a relatively low price in an attempt to dissuade competitors from entering the market.

23. There are three conditions: the market must be segmentable, different segments must be unwilling to pay the premium price and the higher priced segment must be unable to obtain the product or service at the lower price.

24. This encompasses all forms of promotion including advertising, sales promotion, personal selling and public relations.

25. Above the line promotion refers to any advertising designed for a mass audience. Below the line promotion refers to other methods of promoting the product or service, including sales promotion, personal selling and public relations.

26. To sell a second-hand car: a local newspaper
A new cut price restaurant for students: some form of student press (cinema??)
A new brand of chocolate bar: national TV
A bank's new savings scheme: personal selling

27. Package tours overseas: producer to retailer (direct selling??)
The sale of textbooks: producer to wholesaler
The sale of specialist equipment: direct selling
Products aimed at a fragmented market: producer to wholesaler

Answers to Unit Test

Question	Answer	Question	Answer	Question	Answer	Question	Answer	Question	Answer
1	C	9	D	17	C	25	B	33	B
2	A	10	B	18	B	26	A	34	D
3	C	11	B	19	B	27	C	35	C
4	B	12	A	20	D	28	B		
5	D	13	C	21	A	29	C		
6	C	14	A	22	B	30	C		
7	B	15	D	23	C	31	B		
8	A	16	A	24	C	32	D		

Unit Test Comments (Selected questions)

Question 13   C
A random sample occurs when every member of a group which is being surveyed has an equal chance of being chosen.

Question 14   A
A cluster sample occurs when the sample is concentrated on one or more areas (which are assumed to be representative of the market as a whole).

Question 15   D
The difference between a random sample and a stratified random sample is that in the latter the sample is weighted on the basis of the importance of different segments of the market.

Questions 16-18   A, C, B
Note the difference in the columns of the table. The first involves *value* (sales revenue), the second involves *volume* (market-share).

Question 19   B
This is an economic statistic.

Question 23   C
Statement 1 is incorrect because ACORN geo-demographic segmentation is based on the assumption that people living in a particular neighbourhood have similar social characteristics and lifestyles.

Question 24   C
An extension strategy takes an existing product and attempts to extend that product's life by, for example, finding new markets or new uses for it.

Question 25   B
Compared with the other objectives mentioned productivity is a very much more general objective.

Question 26   A
By selecting the right day and time the advertiser can reach large numbers of children. The other media are likely to be little used by children.

Question 27   C
Certain forms of advertising including television are illegal. Of the other forms of advertising media mentioned a national newspaper is likely to give the best results.

Question 28   B
Commercial radio does not have the necessary visual impact that a cinema does. Also, by using the cinema the advertiser is targeting young people more effectively than when using commercial radio where the age range of listeners is likely to be much wider.

Question 31   B
With an inelastic demand curve a reduction in price will lead to a less than proportionate increase in quantity and thus total revenue will fall. It is logical, on the basis of this factor alone, to use skim pricing.

Question 32   D
In a situation such as this it will be worth segmenting the market and charging different prices in each segment because this will increase total revenue.

Question 34   D
This would be dealt with by an Environmental Health Department.

Question 35   C
Advertising on television and radio is controlled by the Independent Television Commission.

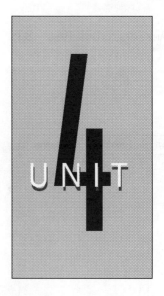

UNIT 4

Human Resources

Getting Started

In this unit we will look at the relationship between an organization and its employees. Labour is the most problematic input into the business process because, unlike other inputs, it has a mind and a will of its own. Individual employees have different skills, motives and aspirations. The ability of the organization to utilize its employees' abilities or skills whilst at the same time satisfying their aspirations and motives for work, is critical to the success of the organization.

In many organizations the relationship with workers is overseen by a specialist department. Traditionally this was known as the Personnel Department but more recently it has become known as **Human Resource Management** (HRM). The change in title is more than just cosmetic and reflects the change in the role of the department from the paternalistic 'welfare' mentality (looking after the workers) to a more objective concern for resource maximization and cost control.

Collective bargaining The process by which workers, through their representatives, negotiate changes in pay and working conditions with their employer.

Contract of Employment A written document given to employees outlining the major terms and conditions under which they are employed.

Co-operative A form of business organization owned and run by its members.

Delegation The process of passing authority to undertake work from a superior to a subordinate.

Franchise A concession given by the owner of patents to another person allowing them to produce and sell those goods/services.

Formal organization The internal structure of an organization.

Induction training Process by which a new employee is introduced to the organization.

Industrial democracy Worker participation in management decision making.

Industrial tribunals System of courts created to deal with cases arising out of employment legislation.

Job description A statement of what a particular job entails.

Joint consultation A discussion between management and employee representatives before a decision is made.

Limited company A business organization that has a separate legal identity from that of its owners. Liability is limited to the amount invested by each shareholder.

Manpower planning The process of determining an organization's future manpower requirements.

Organization chart A diagram illustrating the structure of an organization.

Partnership A form of business organization owned by between two and twenty people.

Person specification A statement of the type of person needed to do a job.

Quango Quasi Autonomous Non-governmental Organization.

Sole trader A business organization which has a single owner.

Span of control The number of subordinates working under a superior.

Trade Unions Organizations created to further worker interests.

Unlimited liability A situation where the owner of a business is personally liable for all the debts of the firm.

Essential principles

Human Resource Planning (HRP)

All organizations *plan*. We look at the process of planning and the development of plans in some detail in Unit 8. In this unit we will look very briefly at how an organization plans to use its **human resources** effectively. In practice there are two aspects to this process.

The first aspect lies in ensuring that the organization has the number and type of employees needed to carry out its activities. This is commonly termed *manpower planning* and must always be distinguished from the term *human resource planning* of which manpower planning is only a part.

The second aspect of HRP is to ensure that human resources are used *efficiently*. Here the **Human Resource Department (HRD)** is concerned with, for example, developing a culture within the organization and among its employees which helps to achieve organizational objectives. It would also be concerned with those aspects of management, for example communication, motivation and leadership, which may affect the morale and productivity of the workforce. (Unit 5 looks at many of these issues.)

In this unit we will consider the following performance criteria:

- Responsibilities in human resourcing are explained.
- Systems for employee relations are described.
- Training and development opportunities are identified.
- Legal requirements regulating employment practices are explained.
- Types of redress available to employees when legislation is not upheld are described.
- Human resource management which improves business performance is identified.

Manpower planning

The process of **corporate planning** is shown diagrammatically in Fig. 4.1. We see that the corporate plan stems from an assessment of the organization's environment and its individual strengths and weaknesses. The aim of a **manpower plan** is to ensure that the longer term labour requirements of the organization are met. This, to a large extent, depends upon the demand for and the supply of the different forms of labour which are required. Important factors which have to be taken into account include:

- Loss of workers through retirement or ill-health in the next few years.
- Loss of workers to other jobs.
- Loss of new workers just recruited.
- Need for new qualified staff.

These calculations may be far more complex than first thought because of changes in organizational goals, technology, competition for labour, or in the population structure. Equally changes in the price of labour caused by trade union negotiation or the imposition of labour taxes by the government may cause the firm to rethink the technology it uses (and therefore the demand for different kinds of labour).

Arising out of these calculations we can see that our organization in Fig. 4.1 has come to certain conclusions regarding the supply and demand for the different categories of labour which it uses. We see that where a *surplus* is predicted it has the options of redeployment and redundancy as well as relying on natural wastage. This is the case with the 'professionally qualified', 'clerical' and 'unskilled' categories of labour. Where a *shortage* is predicted the firm will be looking to recruitment, redeployment and training, as well as to changes in the pay structure to remedy the situation. This is the case with the 'managers', 'supervisors', 'skilled manual' and 'semi-skilled' categories. By these means the HRD will be able to ensure that the future requirements of the organization are met, with the least possible cost to the company and friction to its employees.

Fig. 4.1 indicates that due to changes in the situation facing the firm, manpower planning is an ongoing process. As the situation changes, so does the manpower plan in order to adapt to that new situation.

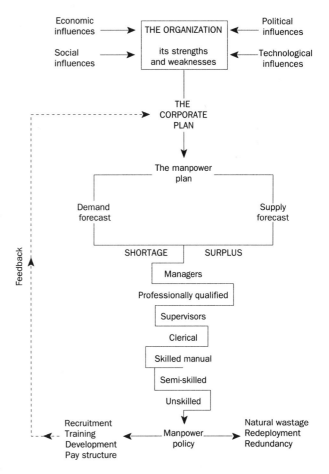

Fig. 4.1 Determining manpower policy with the corporate plan

Labour turnover

Most textbooks will tell you that **labour turnover** is a 'bad thing' and that attempts should be made to reduce it. This is not entirely true; because labour turnover stops a workforce from becoming static and complacent, it is a source of new ideas and may be the only way to avoid an ageing workforce. There are several reasons, however, why the HRD would not want to see *too high* a level of turnover. These include:

- The cost of lost production.
- The cost of recruitment and training.
- The cost of errors made by the new trainee.
- Low morale caused by the break-up of established work groups.

In order to improve the **employee retention rate** the HRD would be looking to :

- Improving the recruitment and selection process
- improving or introducing training courses
- improving pay and working conditions
- improving career ladders and promotion prospects
- introducing job enlargement, rotation or enrichment programmes
- improving the industrial relations atmosphere.

When making a calculation of labour turnover we can also distinguish between voluntary and involuntary turnover. *Involuntary* turnover arises from death, illness, marriage, pregnancy or partner's career. It may also arise as a result of management action – for example, dismissal for disciplinary reasons or redundancy.

Of far greater concern to the organization is the situation where the employee leaves *voluntarily* for reasons such as career development or dissatisfaction with pay and conditions of work. Here the firm is losing a valuable employee, someone in whom it has invested a considerable amount in recruiting and training.

The **rate of turnover** can be calculated as follows:

$$\frac{\text{number leaving} - \text{unavoidable departures}}{\text{average number employed}} \times 100$$

The rate or ratio focuses management's attention on that part of labour turnover which is of most concern – namely *voluntary departures*. Such ratios must be used with caution but where, over a period of time, the percentage rate increases it may be identifying problems such as low morale or uncompetitive wage structures.

Recruitment

Recruitment and selection are at the heart of the HRD's work. Much of the process is routine and yet it is vital to the success of the organization. We will look at the process of selection later in this unit. Here we will touch briefly on the sources of **recruitment**.

Internal recruitment

In many cases it is possible to appoint an *existing employee* to the position. For the individual it may be a promotion or a sideways move. Promotion has obvious motivational

---

Taking on a new employee when a vacancy occurs is the most obvious thing to do, but it may not be the most appropriate. It may be better for the organization to consider one of the following alternatives:

- Reorganize the work.
- Mechanize the work.
- Use overtime.
- Stagger the hours of other workers.
- Make the job part-time.
- Subcontract the work to another firm.

---

advantages and sideways moves can be an effective means of broadening an individual's experience. Internal recruitment has several *advantages*:

- The person appointed and the organization know each other.
- The costs of advertising, recruitment, induction and training are reduced.
- It can improve the morale and motivation of other employees.

Against these we must put the *disadvantages*:

- Without 'new blood' the organization can stagnate.
- Promotion can cause friction amongst other staff who believe their claims have been overlooked.
- Promotion or sideways moves only transfer the recruitment problem elsewhere.

External recruitment

There are numerous sources available to the firm. In practice firms will have established methods of obtaining different categories of staff.

- *Government employment agencies*
  Job centres are the place where those seeking work, as well as those wanting workers, go.

- *Commercial employment agencies*
  In large cities these are often used for hiring clerical staff and 'temps'. There are also a number of specialist agencies, for example for nurses. A commission is charged to the hirer.

- *Management selection consultants*
  These are used for more senior positions within an organization. The consultant will advertise the vacancy (often without revealing the name of the firm) in the trade and national press.

- *Executive search consultants*
  In a situation where people of the right calibre are rare, it may be necessary to appoint an organization to seek out potential applicants and persuade them to change jobs. This is commonly termed 'headhunting'.

- *Universities, schools and careers service*
  Many organizations satisfy their need for graduates and other trainees through the universities' and schools' careers services.

The advantages and disadvantages of each recruitment method are shown in Table 4.1.

Advantages	Disadvantages
Government Employment Agencies	
• Wide range of potential recruits • Service is quick • Cuts recruitment cost	• Matching of applicants to vacancies is limited • Applicants normally drawn from unemployed only • Staff recruited may only stay for a short time
Commercial Employment Agencies	
• Can provide a large number of applicants with the right skills • Reduces employers' administrative burden	• Staff recruited may only stay a short time
Management Selection Consultants	
• Applicants can state organizations they don't wish to work for • The organization can maintain anonymity • The organization can use experience of the consultant to find right employee	• Internal candidates may be excluded • High cost
Executive Search Consultants	
• People of the right calibre can be approached directly • Useful where firm has little experience of these kinds of appointments	• Candidates not part of the headhunter's network are ignored • May be headhunted again after appointment • High cost
Universities' and Schools' Careers Services	
• Relatively inexpensive • Can be targeted towards areas of shortage • Regular yearly flow of applicants	• There are more enquirers rather than true applicants • People often more interested in occupations than organizations

Table 4.1 The advantages and disadvantages of recruitment sources

Recruitment advertising

Unless an organization is prepared to pay a specialist to recruit the employees it needs it will have to undertake its own recruitment advertising. The major options available are advertising in the national, local or specialist press. Information on circulation and readership of papers and magazines can be obtained from a number of sources. The organization can also monitor the response rate to its advertisements in different publications by using codes to be quoted on application forms or through asking a direct question on the application form.

- *National press.* Advertising in the national press is used primarily for managerial or professional appointments. Such advertisements will be seen by many job applicants; however, obviously far fewer will be interested in the vacancy. Some national newspapers, though, may be the recognized way of finding new job opportunities. For example the *Guardian* on Tuesday advertises many educational vacancies. Depending upon the newspaper and the size of the advertisement, the cost may be high.

Many organizations will use the services of an advertising agency in drafting advertisements and placing them in suitable publications. The agency will:

- Draft layout and typography
- Read and correct proofs
- Book space in the appropriate publications
- Check that the right advertisement has appeared in the right publication at the right time

For many organizations who do not have the necessary expertise in-house, this is often the cheapest option available.

- *Local press.* Many employers will use the local press to advertise manual, clerical and supervisory vacancies. Whilst the circulation is more limited it is targeted at those people who are only likely to be seeking local employment. It is far less expensive than the national press.

- *Specialist press.* Advertising in the technical or specialist press is a cost efficient way of communicating a job vacancy to those people with the specific skills the organization requires. However, such magazines and journals may only appear monthly, or even less frequently, which will obviously delay the recruitment process. Specialist press advertisements are often expensive and may also be less effective if a number of specialist publications exist in the same field.

Drafting the advertisement

We have already seen that all matters relating to the advertisement can be left to an advertising agency. Alternatively the work may be done in-house. Either way, the decision as to what to include in the advertisement is critical because of the importance of attracting attention whilst at the same time controlling costs. Research has shown that the size of the advertisement is less important than presentation. Visual layout, however, *is* important and many organizations have a logo which the public associate with them.

In addition to the problems associated with presentation the advertisement must also provide information so that potential candidates can gauge whether they are interested and whether they stand a realistic chance of obtaining the position. At all times the organization should ensure that it is being honest about the job advertised. A new employee who discovers that the job applied for is significantly different from the one he now faces will quickly become disillusioned, infect others with his disillusionment and very soon leave. Every job advertisement should contain:

- The name and brief details of the employing organization.
- Job title and a description of duties.
- Key points of the person specification – age, minimum qualifications, experience etc.
- The rewards and other conditions of work.
- How to apply.
- An equal opportunities statement.

Induction, training and development

All organizations will undertake some form of training with their employees. It is seen as being a sound business investment because :

- Training helps employees learn their jobs quickly and with a minimum of mistakes.
- Employee productivity is improved.
- Training increases staff flexibility by enabling the employee to undertake a wider range of tasks.
- Training can reduce accidents and potential liability for injuries caused at work.
- Labour turnover amongst new staff may be reduced dramatically by a well developed induction programme.
- Labour turnover amongst existing staff can be reduced through training which provides opportunities for promotion within the organization.
- A company with a reputation for good training is likely to attract a better class of applicant.

For training to be effective it needs to be part of a co-ordinated plan which fits in with the manpower plan. The training plan will identify:

- The links between the manpower plan and training to be undertaken.
- The training priorities.
- Who is responsible for the training.
- The method of training.

The plan also needs to be flexible enough to take account of operational problems, e.g. new training requirements caused by a sudden and unexpected change in circumstances. It would also be no good scheduling a course in customer care for a retail organization's sales staff in the week before Christmas or during the January sales period.

The process of training may be expressed diagrammatically as in Fig. 4.2.

Induction Training

Labour turnover statistics from many firms indicate that many new employees, for a variety of reasons, will leave the firm within a short time of joining. This is often termed the 'induction crisis'.

Induction training is undertaken by organizations to ease the entry of the new employee into the organization. Special attention should be given to the school leaver and other groups who may have particular difficulties settling in. How the induction programme is carried out will depend to a certain extent on the size of the firm. However, the objectives remain the same:

- To welcome the new employee and help them settle down.
- To familiarize the new employees with the organization, their department and their job.

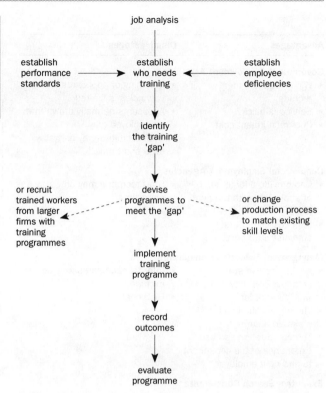

Fig. 4.2   Developing a training programme

- To pass information on organizational policy, rules and regulations, e.g. health and safety.

Large organizations will probably have a formal programme consisting of talks and films. Senior members of staff may be involved. In the smaller firm new employees may just be shown around and introduced to other staff.

Training

- *Shopfloor*
  This will include apprenticeship schemes designed to develop a wide range of skills as well as operative, administrative and clerical training where a far more limited set of skills are taught . Apprenticeship schemes are taught by a combination of 'on the job' training and external courses in local technical colleges. At worst, operative, administrative and clerical training will take the form of watching and imitating experienced workers, but larger firms will often have Training Departments with well developed programmes for these workers.

Training courses may be run by the firm itself or by some external body. Where a course is run 'in house' by the company itself there are a number of advantages such as cheapness and the course being tailored to the precise needs of the employee. Whilst it would be impractical to run certain courses, e.g. induction, outside the organization there are others where the organization may not have the facilities or the expertise to undertake the training course itself.

External courses have advantages such as providing training not available within the organization, bringing together people from different organizations (who can learn from each other's experience) and being away from the place of work (work-related issues are not as likely to interfere with the training process).

- *Supervisory*
Often referred to as the 'man in the middle' the supervisor is normally appointed for his technical skills. Yet as a supervisor the most important skills he needs are inter-personal and team leadership. These are often lacking. Many colleges offer courses for supervisors. The most popular is the National Examination Board for Supervisory Studies (NEBSS).

Management Development

Management development can be defined as the 'series of activities and event which are designed to improve performance now and develop high calibre managers for the future'. Many universities and colleges offer courses which are designed to develop managerial skills. Larger organizations may run their own courses tailored to their particular needs. These will be a blend of practical training and formal short courses.

Managers and other employees with potential may also be 'developed' through:

- *Job rotation.* Employees undertake a range of jobs in order to widen their knowledge and skills. Young graduates and management trainees will often experience job rotation in an attempt by the organization to identify their particular strengths.
- *Job enlargement.* By widening the number of tasks the employee undertakes within a given job.
- *Job enrichment.* This also involves giving the employee additional tasks. Here, though, the additional tasks are rather more difficult and are designed to test the employee's capabilities. Managers will often give promising employees project work as a form of job enrichment.

Did You Know ?

Other labour-market developments in recent years include *job-sharing*; around 250,000 employees in the UK now work on a job-share basis. There has also been a rapid increase in *teleworking*, with staff working at home using computers and telecommunication technologies.

The role of Training and Enterprise Councils (TECs)

There are 82 TECs. They are led by people with business and industrial experience. Initially they receive money from central government to fund training in their area. They are responsible for schemes such as Youth Training and Training for Work.

The government believes that local bodies such as these will also be able to identify, and provide for, local skill shortages far more effectively than any nationally run scheme. Eventually, the government expects TECs to become self-financing – charging local businesses for their services.

Employee appraisal

By **appraisal** we mean the evaluation of the performance, and sometimes the potential, of an employee. It is sometimes also termed *merit rating*.

Many people think of staff appraisal as an annual event. In practice, it is an everyday part of the manager's job as he decides who to allocate work to on the basis of their known strengths and weaknesses, likes and dislikes.

The *objectives* of employee appraisal are twofold:

- *To provide management information*
  - As a basis for manpower planning
  - As a basis for salary reviews, promotion, transfers or dismissals
  - As a basis for monitoring recruitment procedures or training programmes.

- *To motivate the employee*
  - By helping to identify and communicate individual strengths and weaknesses, thus 'letting the employee know where he stands'
  - By helping to increase job satisfaction thereby stimulating the employee to even better performance and the development of potential.

In the majority of organizations appraisal is carried out by an employee's immediate superior. As the superior is normally in everyday contact with the employee he should be well placed to comment and counsel. There is, however, a potential problem of managerial subjectivity (though this can be overcome by involving more than one superior).

The normal procedure for appraisal is as follows:

- A *report* on the employee is prepared.
- The employee is *interviewed* with the report acting as the basis for discussion.
- *Action* relating to that employee is taken on the basis of the report and the interview.

In some companies use has also been made of appraisal by colleagues ('buddy rating') or by subordinates. The US armed services, for example, have used appraisal by colleagues to assist in deciding who should be promoted. Several US oil companies have used 'multi-appraisal' techniques – that is, appraisal by superiors, colleagues and subordinates. Other companies have used appraisal by subordinates as a means of improving supervisor performance.

None of these methods has received widespread support because it is believed that the criteria used by colleagues and subordinates may be very different from those used by superiors and will probably not take into account organizational objectives.

Self-appraisal is another relatively new technique and again not very widely used. The major problem is bias. Studies have shown that the self-appraiser consistently gives himself a higher rating than when appraised by his superior! However, self-appraisal does often form part of the normal appraisal process with the employee being asked to provide a written assessment of his own performance. This, together with the superior's report, will then form the basis of the appraisal interview.

Termination of Employment

All contracts of employment come to an end at some stage. In the majority of cases **termination** arises as a result of an employee finding another job, reaching retirement age or retiring on the grounds of ill health. However, an employer may also terminate an employee's contract on the grounds of redundancy or because that employee's work is no longer satisfactory.

Dismissal

An employee may be *fairly* dismissed in the following circumstances:

- *Misconduct.* This would cover situations such as not obeying lawful instructions from the employer, practical jokes, physical abuse of another employee or theft. Rudeness to customers and lack of care of company property have also been held to be sufficient for dismissal on the grounds of misconduct.

- *Inability to do the job.* This would cover situations such as where the employee does not have, or loses, the qualifications necessary to do a job, e.g. a travelling salesman losing his driving licence. Prolonged illness, where there is no likelihood of recovery is also sufficient

Whilst dismissal for severe cases of misconduct may be immediate, in many other cases the employer is required to go through a formal process designed to allow the employee the opportunity of mending his ways. The Advisory, Conciliation and Arbitration Service have issued a Code of Practice outlining three stages. They are:

- *Informal stage.* The employee is counselled and warned that if his behaviour does not improve, then further disciplinary measures may be taken. Most problems are sorted out at this stage.

- *Formal stage.* Where, after a period of time, there is no improvement in the employee's behaviour, e.g. poor attendance, the Personnel Department will become involved. There will be a formal investigation into the nature and seriousness of the problem followed by discussions between the employee, his manager and the Personnel Department and a *first written warning.*

- *Final stage.* Where there is still no improvement in the employee's performance a *final written warning* is issued by the Personnel Department. After a short period the employee may be invited to a *formal hearing* – he is often encouraged to bring a friend, e.g. a trade union official – at which he will be given the reasons for his dismissal.

Did You Know ?

All employees with over two years of employment with the same employer have the right not to be *unfairly* dismissed. A complaint of unfair dismissal does not require the employer to be in breach of the contract of employment. It simply requires the employer to have terminated the contract in circumstances which are unfair within the meaning of the legislation. Unfair dismissal occurs when an employee is dismissed:

- For joining a trade union
- For refusing to join a trade union on religious grounds
- For becoming pregnant or not being taken back on after pregnancy
- For striking when others on strike have not been dismissed
- With the employer not following the procedures for fair dismissal.

Where an employee is unfairly dismissed he is entitled to compensation or re-instatement. Where re-instatement is not possible, having regard to the bad feeling between the employer and employee, this may be taken into account by the industrial tribunal in deciding compensation.

Redundancy

Any employee who has had more than two years of continuous employment with the same employer is entitled to a compensation payment if dismissed on the grounds of **redundancy**. Compensation, as for unfair dismissal, is assessed on a sliding scale which takes into account the employee's length of service, age and rate of pay.

Redundancy is said to occur when the employer closes down his business or part of his business and thus no longer needs certain employees.

For the employer to avoid a claim for unfair dismissal he must consult with the employees affected, or their representatives. Where ten or more employees belonging to a recognized union are involved, a minimum of 30 days' advance notice must be given. Where over 100 employees are to be made redundant within a three month period, 90 days' advance notice must be given. Employees affected by redundancy are also entitled to reasonable time off with pay during the notice period in order to seek other work.

One problem employers face is *who* should be made redundant. Failure to select on criteria which can be seen to be fair may result in a claim for unfair dismissal. The most commonly used method is LIFO or last in, first out. Increasingly, however, employers are using a range of criteria such as competence and attendance record. Many organizations also go to great lengths to avoid compulsory redundancies. Common strategies include not replacing employees that leave, retraining, early retirement and voluntary redundancy.

The organization's responsibility to its employees

Terms and conditions of employment

The law relating to employment is very complex. Much of it is governed by legislation which is designed to give workers a 'floor of rights' and thereby remedy the imbalance of bargaining power between them and their employers. In fact even *before* employment, the prospective employee has rights under legislation. These include:

- The right not to be discriminated against on the grounds of race or sex in advertisements for jobs (e.g. bar staff must wear skirts), or in job offers.
- The right of the ex-offender not to disclose past convictions after a rehabilitation period if no further offences have been committed. The rehabilitation period – after which the conviction is said to be 'spent' – depends upon the severity of the offence and is calculated as follows:

Sentence	Rehabilitation period
Probation	1 year
Fine	5 years
Under 6 months' imprisonment	7 years
Under 18 months' imprisonment	10 years

For juvenile offenders these periods are halved. However, for some occupations the conviction is never 'spent' and there is a requirement to reveal details of any convictions. Workers coming into this category include doctors, policemen and teachers.

- Employers with more than 20 workers are normally required to employ a number of disabled workers – 3% of the workforce. Certain jobs such as lift and car park attendants are also reserved for the disabled.

When the offer of a job has been accepted, a contract of employment has been created. This is really a statement of the points on which the two parties agree to be bound. These points may involve 'express' or 'implied' terms.

Express terms are those points which the parties to the contract will have specifically agreed to. The terms include job title, pay, pay period, working hours, holidays and pension rights. There are, of course, many others. Some will not be specifically stated in the contract of employment. Instead the contract will indicate the *source* of these terms and where they can be found. The two most common sources are:

- A collective agreement between union and employers.
- Company rules – often to be found in an employees handbook.

Implied terms supplement the points on which the parties have expressly agreed to contract. Implied terms are imposed on the parties by law. These terms will arise as a result of legislation or common law (the basic judge-made law of the land).

Common law obligations on the *employer* include:

- To pay wages in cash, when they fall due.
- To make only those pay deductions authorized by the state or explicitly agreed with the employee.
- To provide work.
- To take reasonable care for the safety of employees.
- To obey the law and not require the employee to undertake an unlawful act.

Common law obligations on the *employee* include:

- To undertake lawful and reasonable orders.
- To take reasonable care in doing their job, including using any special skill (e.g. accounting) that they claim to possess.
- To act with honesty and integrity and avoid situations where their interests and those of their employer might conflict.

In addition to these common law rules, a lot of legislation has been passed by Parliament. As we have already noted much of this has been designed to give employees a 'floor of rights'. The more important legislation includes the following.

The right not to be discriminated against on the grounds of race

Direct discrimination occurs where a person is treated less favourably for training, promotion, transfer or other benefit

---

Did You Know ?

In advanced economies, labour costs may be a very high proportion of total costs in an organisation. In *service sector* industries (over 70% of all employment), labour costs (including National Insurance, costs of safety at work, etc.) may be as high as 75% of total cost.

---

than another person on the grounds of race. *Indirect discrimination* arises as a result of applying a condition or requirement to all employees which has the effect of preventing the majority of one racial group being able to comply. Thus a requirement for a 'good command of English' may be indirect discrimination if this is not essential to carrying out the job properly

Lawful discrimination is allowed, though, where there is a 'genuine occupational qualification'. This is sometimes referred to as the 'Indian restaurant' clause and allows employers to demand a person of a particular ethnic group for reasons of authenticity.

The Commission for Racial Equality has power to carry out investigations and issue codes of practice. It also recommends 'ethnic monitoring' with the aim of getting the employer to assess its employment policies toward minorities.

The right to redress

An employee who believes that his (or her) statutory or contractual rights have been infringed can seek **redress** through industrial tribunals or the courts. An employee will use the system of industrial tribunals where he or she believes their statutory rights have been infringed, e.g. sex or racial discrimination. Matters relating to breaches of a worker's conditions of employment are dealt with by the County Court or the High Court.

Industrial tribunals were set up by the state to provide a quick and inexpensive form of justice compared with the court system. Tribunals are also very informal: legalistic language and procedures have been dispensed with and the case will be heard by a panel of three – a trade unionist, a representative of the Confederation of British Industry (CBI) and an independent chairman who is a barrister or a solicitor.

The right not to be discriminated against on the grounds of sex or marital status

The law follows very much the same pattern as with 'race legislation'. Both direct and indirect discrimination are illegal but discrimination may be allowed where there is a genuine occupational qualification. This could include situations such as modelling, acting and even lavatory attendants.

The Equal Opportunities Commission has the power to investigate organizations and may obtain court injunctions to prevent continued discrimination. The Commission recommends that organizations monitor the recruitment and progress of women within their organization.

A summary of the race relations and sex discrimination legislation is given in Table 4.2 (p92).

The right to equal pay

Before 1970 it was permissible for women to be paid less than men for undertaking the same work. Today, the law (Equal Pay Act 1970) requires that men and women are treated equally. The Equal Pay Act stipulates that where women are employed on

- 'like work'
- 'work rated as equivalent' under a job evaluation scheme

then the terms and conditions offered should be equal.

However, in 1983 an amendment to the act meant that

Race Relations Act 1976	Sex Discrimination Act 1975
Direct discrimination This occurs when an individual treats another less favourably on racial grounds, e.g. segregating workers	*Direct discrimination* This occurs when an individual treats another less favourably on the grounds of sex, e.g. different working conditions
Indirect discrimination This occurs when an individual requires another to meet a condition which, as a member of a racial group, is less easily satisfied because: 1. the proportion of the group who can comply with it is smaller and 2. the condition is to the complainant's detriment and is not justified	*Indirect discrimination* This occurs when an individual requires another to meet a condition which, as a member of a particular sex, is less easily satisfied because: 1. the proportion of that sex who can comply with it is smaller and 2. the condition is to the complainant's detriment and is not justified
Victimization This occurs when an individual treats another less favourably because the other has given evidence or information in an action under the Act against the discriminator	*Victimization* This occurs when an individual treats another less favourably because the other has given evidence in an action under this or the Equal Pay Act against the discriminator
Remedies Complaints may be made to the Commission of Racial Equality. The CRE may investigate the discriminatory act and attempt to settle the matter or alternatively institute proceedings. Complaints will be heard by an industrial tribunal who, if a settlement cannot be reached and the complaint is just, may: 1. recommend action to reduce the effect of the discrimination, e.g. training, promotion 2. make an order declaring rights 3. award compensation	*Remedies* Complaints may be made to the Equal Opportunities Commission. The EOC may investigate the discriminatory act and if necessary issue a *non-discrimination notice* placing requirements on the employer. Complaints against this or the original case will be heard by an industrial tribunal which can, if agreement is not reached and the complaint is justified, 1. recommend action to reduce the effect of the discrimination 2. make an order declaring rights 3. award compensation

Table 4.2 A comparison of race relations and sex discrimination legislation

women could claim equal pay for work of 'equal value'. Thus in one printing industry case a woman received an increase of over £100 per week by successfully claiming that her work as a VDU operator was of equal value to that of a male typesetter.

The right to wage protection

Under the Wages Act 1986 conditions for the payment of wages and deductions from wages are stipulated. Wages are defined as any sum paid to a worker in connection with a job and this would include items not normally thought of such as bonuses, gift tokens, sick pay and lunch vouchers. However redundancy payments are not included. The Act allows employers to make certain deductions from wages. These include:

- Those taken by law, e.g. income tax and National Insurance.

- Those shown in the contract of employment.
- Those agreed by the worker in writing.

If there is a breach of these rules or the employer unilaterally makes a deduction from a worker's wages, the employee can appeal to a tribunal.

The right to safe and healthy working conditions

Workers in the UK are covered by the provisions of the Factories Act 1961, the Offices, Shops and Railway Premises Act 1963 or the Health and Safety at Work Act 1974. The provisions of these Acts have already been covered in Unit 2 Element 1. If you are unsure of the content of these acts refer back to this section.

Did You Know ?

There are over 600 deaths a year due to accidents at work. There are also over 400,000 accidents at work every year which result in an absence from work of more than 3 days.

The right not to be unfairly dismissed and the right to redundancy pay

These have been dealt with above (pages 89–90).

Employee relations

Employees have two major concerns arising out of the the work situation. The first is that there is some mechanism through which their collective interests are **represented**. Remember that, as individuals, employees have very little power and it is easy for the employer to ignore their interests and their grievances. In many countries the mechanism used to express, or represent, workers' interests has been the trade union.

By itself, though, representation is insufficient to ensure that the employee's voice is heard and consequently the second major area of concern is that they are **consulted** over matters that are of importance to them and the means by which that is achieved. We will look in turn at the areas of representation and consultation.

Representation

Trade Unions

A **trade union** can be defined as an organization of workers whose principal purpose is to protect and promote the interests of its members. It is argued that the union has much more bargaining power than the individual. Its objectives would include:

- improvements in pay and conditions of employment
- security of employment and income
- protection of members against unfair practices and arbitrary management decisions
- worker involvement in decision making

and on a political level

- improved social security
- fair shares in national income and wealth

- industrial democracy
- a say in government

More recently unions have been offering a wide range of services to their members, including financial advice on insurance, pensions and mortgages, welfare and illness benefits, legal advice, as well as arranging discounts on goods and services.

Types of trade unions

Traditionally unions have been classified into one of four types.

- *Craft unions*
  Membership is based upon specific skills regardless of the industry in which that skill is used. It is one of the earliest forms of association but as new technology has made many of the skills redundant, the number of craft unions has declined. The National Union of Journalists is often cited as an example of a craft union.

- *Industrial unions*
  These unions represent workers, all of whom are drawn from the same industry regardless of their specific occupation. The National Union of Mineworkers is often quoted as an example. Traditionally such unions have been extremely powerful because they have represented a majority of the workers in the industry. However, the decline of that industry will lead to a loss of union power and the possible amalgamation with another union.

- *General unions*
  These unions represent large groups of semi-skilled and unskilled workers regardless of job or industry. They tend to be the 'giants' of the union movement. Thus the Transport and General Workers Union (TGWU) and the General, Municipal, Boilermakers and Allied Workers Union (GMB) both have memberships approaching 1 million.

Staff associations

There is a tradition of staff associations within firms in the finance sector – banks, building societies and insurance. The objectives of these associations are very much the same as those of trade unions when it comes to industrial relations; however, few are interested in the wider political aspirations of the unions. Staff associations are far more popular in the USA where they are often known as 'company unions'. In the past the staff associations have been criticized for relying on the company for their finances which, it has been suggested, makes them more willing to 'take the company line'.

- *White collar unions*
  This is a union which recruits its members from clerical, supervisory, administrative and professional occupations. It has had the most rapid growth in union membership since 1950. An example would be the National Union of Teachers.

In practice it is often difficult to distinguish which category a union falls into and for that reason other forms of classification have been suggested. For example it is possible to classify unions according to their recruitment policy. Thus some, like the craft unions, will only recruit from workers with a particular skill. This would be termed a 'closed' recruitment policy. Other unions are willing to recruit any worker in any industry. Not surprisingly this is termed an 'open' recruitment policy and is often followed by the big general unions.

Trade union membership

In 1979 membership reached a peak of nearly 13.5 million but since that time there has been a downward trend. By 1994 union membership was approximately 7.0 million, down from 50% to 34% of the total workforce. There are many reasons for this including:

- The contraction of the traditional areas of unionism in manufacturing industry
- An inability to recruit in the fast growing service sector
- Women, who form an increasing part of the workforce, are less likely to be union members
- The growth in part-time employment
- Non-union members obtaining the benefits of collective bargaining
- The growth of anti-union legislation

The total number of unions has also been falling. Thus in 1973 there were over 500 unions but by 1994 this had fallen to just over 250. Much of this decline is due to the amalgamation and merging of smaller unions. However, it also reflects changes in the industrial structure of the UK. For example in June 1993 three major public service unions merged. The unions involved were:

- National and Local Government Officers (NALGO)
- National Union of Public Employees (NUPE)
- Confederation of Health Service Employees (COHSE)

They merged and formed a new union called *Unison* with a total membership of 1.4 million.

Did You Know **?**

Most unions are relatively small. Over half the unions today have less than 1,000 members each. However there have been many amalgamations of unions in recent years and the biggest 10 unions, each with more than 250,000 members, have over 80% of *all* union members.

The TUC

The **Trades Union Congress** (TUC) seeks to represent the interests of the individual unions which are affiliated to it and to arbitrate in disputes between the members. The TUC also seeks to establish links with organizations in other countries which have similar objectives. In the UK it has had strong historical links with the Labour Party and some influence over policy within the Labour movement.

Until recently it enjoyed considerable power through its relationship with the government, though today it has been removed from many national decision-making or government advisory bodies.

Employers' Associations and the Confederation of British Industry

Employers' associations were set up in response to the growth of trade unions. They represent an attempt to offset the considerable power of a large trade union by acting on behalf of their members. The Engineering Employers' Federation is the largest employers' association in the UK, covering firms employing nearly 2 million workers.

An association such as this will undertake the following activities:

- Enter into procedural agreements with the union on the way industrial disputes will be resolved.
- Negotiate pay and conditions of work on behalf of its members.
- Advise members on industrial relations strategy, manpower planning or other employment matters.
- Represent their members' interests on government and other national bodies.

To some extent the power of these associations is limited by the fact that very large and very small firms are often not members. Large firms dislike the restrictions placed on them by membership while small firms see membership as costly and the benefits minimal. In recent years the move to bargaining at plant level has also reduced their influence.

The **Confederation of British Industry** (CBI) was formed in 1965. It represents the interests of its members. These include employers' associations, trade associations, and Chambers of Commerce as well as individual employers in both the public and private sector. Its stated objectives are:

- To represent industry's views on a wide variety of issues at a national level.
- To encourage efficiency in British industry.

Consultation

We have already noted that workers wish to be consulted over matters affecting them. The process by which this is undertaken is called **collective bargaining**. Yet in many firms you will find that workers are consulted over matters which are really part of the manager's job. There are several reasons for involving workers in the decision-making process within the firm – it is often termed *industrial democracy* – the most important being:

- Drawing on the workers' skill and experience.
- Improving worker motivation.

Collective Bargaining

Where employees believe that managers are making decisions which are detrimental to their interests it is likely that some form of industrial action will follow. But even if industrial action does not follow, it is likely that the organization will be affected by low morale and motivation as well as by an increase in below-standard performance, accidents, absenteeism and labour turnover. It is in both the employer's and the employees' interests that the causes of the problem are sorted out.

Collective bargaining may be defined as the process by which workers, through their trade union representatives, negotiate changes to their pay and working conditions with the employer or his representative. Nearly 70% of all UK workers have their pay and conditions determined by some form of collective bargaining.

Industrial action

The major *causes* of industrial action are:

- pay and working conditions
- victimization and unfair dismissal by management
- redundancy
- the impact of change on working groups and working practices, often arising as a result of the introduction of new technology.

The following *forms* of industrial action may be used by trade unions:

- overtime bans
- go-slows
- work to rule
- boycott of materials or other workers
- deliberate damage to organization property
- strikes.

Although strikes tend to catch the headlines they are normally a 'tactic of last resort' and other forms of industrial action which don't hit the employees' pay packets are used more often. Strikes are termed 'official' when they are sanctioned by a trade union as a negotiating weapon. Under the Trade Union Act 1984 the strike must also have been approved by the union members in a secret ballot.

'Unofficial' strikes (they are also termed 'lightning' or 'wildcat') are those which have *not* been sanctioned by the union and represent a feeling of outrage on the part of union members at some management action. This could be the disciplining or dismissal of a fellow worker.

Although we always assume that worker discontent will result in industrial action, this is not the case. It can also be seen in situations where there is low morale, inefficient work or a high level of absenteeism, illness or labour turnover.

Employers also have weapons that they can use in an industrial dispute. They include pay deductions, suspensions, lock-outs, dismissals or even closure of the place of work.

Did You Know **?**

Disputes over pay are the most common cause of working days lost, accounting for 41% of the total in 1993; followed by redundancy issues (38%) and working conditions (9%).

Levels of collective bargaining

There are two important *levels* of collective bargaining. At a *national* or *industry-wide level* employers' and employees' representatives may agree a deal which covers all workers in that industry. Many groups in the public sector, e.g. teachers and nurses, have had pay and conditions determined this way.

More recently national agreements have fallen into disfavour as the government has tried to encourage agreements which reflect conditions at a local rather than a national level. At a *local level* negotiations may still take place between representatives of employers and employees but are increasingly dealt with at a 'plant' level by trade unions and the employer. Local bargaining is becoming the 'norm' in NHS Trusts, local authorities and locally managed schools.

The collective agreement

The *agreement* reached by the parties falls naturally into two parts. First there are a number of 'procedural clauses' which cover items such as:

* the members of the negotiating body
* matters which will be dealt with by the body
* the procedure for bargaining and the settlement of disputes.

Second there are the 'substantive clauses' which refer to the employees' actual conditions of employment. These would include items such as:

* basic and incentive payments, overtime pay, pension arrangements
* working hours and days, work flexibility, place of work
* statutory and other holidays
* health, safety and welfare
* retraining, redeployment and redundancy provisions.

Did You Know ?

The UK has had one of the lowest strike records in the last few years. For example, as an *average* over the past 5 years, less than 130 working days were lost in the UK per 1000 employees, compared to 360 working days in Canada, 300 in Italy and 650 in Spain.

The role of the state

The state has tried to avoid intervention in industrial relations believing that this was a private matter which was better left to parties to solve. It has intervened, however, to provide:

* Legislation designed to protect the interests of employees. Examples would include health and safety or anti-discrimination legislation.
* Legislation designed to curb the power of trade unions. Examples would include secret ballots before calling an official strike, restrictions on picketing, making secondary action illegal, imposing financial liability for the acts of its members as well as establishing limitations on closed shops.
* Institutions to arbitrate between conflicting interests. The most important of these are the Advisory, Conciliation and Arbitration Service (ACAS) which is an independent but state-funded service and the Industrial Tribunals which deal with most cases arising out of employment legislation.

Japanese labour relations are often considered to be better than those in most Western counties. A number of reasons have been put forward for this including:

* Rigorous selection procedures even for low level employees.
* Guaranteed lifetime employment.
* Attention to employee welfare and fringe benefits such as housing.
* The absence of organization charts and job descriptions encourages flexibility.
* All Japanese unions are company unions.
* The emphasis on consultation ('*nemewashi*') and collective decision making ('*ringi sei*').

The result of these practices is that the firm is seen as a community and there is a high level of identification with the organization on the part of individual employees.

Industrial democracy

This is a general term used to express the idea that workers should be allowed to participate in the decision-making process of the firm. The idea is to create a platform through which issues of common interest to the employer and the employees can be discussed. We have already noted that by doing this we may improve the motivation of workers and also draw upon a source of knowledge and experience not normally available to management. Worker participation in management may also help workers to understand and accept managerial decisions that run contrary to their interests. There are many ways in which workers can be involved in decision making. We will look briefly at some of the more important methods.

* *Worker co-operatives*
  This is a situation where workers both own and run the organization. Most successful examples are small because once the organization grows beyond about 20 members, some delegation to specialist managers is inevitable. However, large scale co-operative enterprise is possible as the Mondragon Co-operative venture in Spain shows. Here, over 20,000 workers are employed in a variety of co-operative ventures.

* *Worker directors*
  This is a situation where representatives of the workforce sit on the Board of Directors. Whilst in Germany this seems to have worked successfully, in the UK the attitudes of both management and unions has been very negative. Many managers believe that workers have little to contribute to the *policy making* of the firm whilst trade unionists feel that acting as worker directors might compromise their position as representatives of the workers' interests.

* *Collective bargaining*
  As we have already seen this is a situation where employers give up sole decision-making rights in important areas of the business.

* *Joint consultation*
  This, as its name implies, is consultation between workers and management on issues of common interest which fall outside the area of collective bargaining. Joint consultation is widely practised in the public sector but not in the private sector. It is said to provide a two-way communication channel through which:
  * Workers can have a say in decisions which affect them.
  * Management informs workers of progress, new policy and plans.

* *Employee participation*
  This is the approach which has been favoured in the UK. The aim is to harness the energy and knowledge of the workforce in those areas in which they can make the greatest contribution – that is, at the *operational level* of the organization. This may be achieved through the formal joint consultative procedure as discussed above or through the use of:
  * *Semi-autonomous work groups:* Workers in such groups have the power to allocate tasks between members, order materials, control the flow of production and undertake routine maintenance and quality control.

- *Quality circles:* These will meet regularly in company time to discuss quality problems. The group will investigate causes, suggest solutions and, if given the necessary authority, take the appropriate remedial action.

Did You Know ?

Quality circles were first developed in the USA, but failed to achieve popularity until their success had been proved by the Japanese. Today over 10 million Japanese workers are involved in Quality Circles. In the UK, productivity increases of over 30% have been recorded in the automobile component industry through using Quality Circles.

Business performance

The measurement of labour productivity and the methods of improving productivity are dealt with in Unit 5, Element 3.

Self Check ✔   Element 1

1. Distinguish between corporate and manpower planning.

2. Give three reasons why labour turnover is a 'bad thing'.

3. State two reasons both for and against internal recruitment.

4. In what circumstances would you use the national press for advertising a vacancy?

5. State five essential points you would include in a job advertisement.

6. Why is induction training so important?

7. Give two reasons when an employee may be fairly dismissed.

8. State two alternative policies that an organization might adopt rather than compulsory redundancy.

Self Check ✔   continued

9. Explain why legislation designed to give employees rights has been passed.

10. Explain the term 'spent conviction'.

11. Distinguish between express and implied terms of employment.

12. Outline the major differences between an industrial tribunal and a traditional court of law.

13. State two Acts that ensure healthy working conditions.

14. State three industrial and three political objectives of a trade union:
    Industrial objectives

    Political objectives

15. Distinguish between a staff association and a trade union.

16. Give two examples of each of the following types of union:

Craft	Industrial	General	White collar

17. What impact is the growth of female and part-time employment likely to have on union membership?

18. Fill in the gaps in the following sentence:
    _____ bargaining is the process by which workers through their _____ representatives negotiate changes to their pay and _____ with the _____ or his representative.

19. A collective agreement has procedural and substantive clauses. Give two examples of each.
    Procedural clauses

    Substantive clauses

20. Fill in the missing words:
    Industrial _____ is a term which suggests that workers should be allowed to participate in the _____ process in an attempt to improve employee _____.

4.2. Investigating job roles in organization structures

In this element we will be looking at the role of the individual within the organization he or she works for. The performance criteria for this element are:

- Organizational structures in different types of business organizations are described.
- Job roles within structures are described.
- Purposes of job descriptions are explained.
- Purposes of person specifications are explained.

The private sector

The private sector consists of business organizations owned by individuals or groups of individuals. The predominant aim of such organizations is to make a profit.

The Sole Trader

The majority of business organizations will start their life as this. It is the simplest form of business unit and there are very few legal formalities required to start the business. The owner will:

- Provide the capital for the business (though relatives may also contribute and he or she may borrow from the bank).
- Work in the business (though he or she may employ others).
- Make all the decisions.
- Receive profits or bear losses.

Sole traderships tend to be found in industries where there is little advantage in large-scale activities and where personal service and maintaining a good relationship with the customer is important.

However, sole traderships have several disadvantages. By far the most important of these is that the owner has *unlimited liability* for the debts of the firm. In the event of the firm collapsing he may have to sell all his personal assets to meet the debts of the business. Other disadvantages include:

- Often lacks business skills.
- Works long hours.
- Lack of finance limits expansion.

> **Did You Know** ?
>
> In the UK, approximately 40% of all businesses are sole traders. However because they are small, they account for only 3% of business turnover.

Partnerships

The legal definition of a partnership is *'the relationship which subsists between persons carrying on a business in common with a view of profit.'* As a form of organization it is most common in professions such as accountants and solicitors whose rules prevent them from forming companies. Although partnerships overcome some of the problems associated with sole traderships, for example risk and

finance for expansion, it still has the major problem of unlimited liability. Indeed in some ways the position is worse as partners are legally responsible for their co-partner's actions.

It is always desirable that the partners in the firm have a written agreement outlining their rights and their responsibilities. However, this is not a legal requirement and in many disputes the Courts have inferred terms from the partners' actions. In the absence of a partnership agreement the Partnership Act 1890 states that

- Profits and losses will be shared equally.
- Decisions regarding the nature of the partnership require the agreement of all partners.
- Decisions regarding the day to day running of the business do not require unanimity but may be settled by a majority vote.
- All partners may be involved in the running of the business.

> **Did You Know** ?
>
> The 1890 Partnership Act defines a partnership as having between 2 and 20 people. However more than 20 partners are allowed in the case of accountants, solicitors and members of the Stock Exchange. Approximately 25% of all businesses are partnerships.

The limited company

This is a very popular form of business organization because the owners benefit from **limited liability**. Thus, if the business gets into financial difficulties and goes into liquidation, shareholders in the business will only lose their investment. In law the limited company is a *separate entity*, an artificial 'person' capable of suing and being sued in its own name. The creditors of the company are not allowed to sue the shareholders if the company is unable to pay its debts in full.

Limited companies fall into one of two categories:

- *Companies limited by shares.* This is by far the most common form of company and may be subdivided into public and private companies.

- *Companies limited by guarantee.* Company documents state that in the event of the company being wound up (i.e. closed) the individual member will contribute a specific sum. Liability is limited to this amount.

Public and private companies

The Companies Act 1980 defines a **public limited company** (PLC) as one whose Memorandum describes it as a public limited company and which has a minimum share capital of £50,000. **Private companies** are defined as any company which does not conform to the definition of a public company. Private companies cannot advertise the sale of their shares or obtain a stock exchange listing.

The vast majority of the 1.3 million UK companies are, in fact, private companies, often family firms with the statutory minimum of two shareholders. Of course at the other end of the scale we have a small number of national and multinational firms, many of them household names, who will have thousands of shareholders and be registered as PLC's.

Compared with partnerships and sole traders, public limited companies have *advantages* other than that of limited liability. They are:

- Companies can raise very substantial sums of money through share issues to finance expansion.
- Availability of finance allows the company to produce on a large scale, thus obtaining economies of scale.
- The company has a separate legal existence from that of its shareholders and is not affected by changes in its membership.
- The investors' money is not permanently tied up in the company as shares can be sold (or bought) on the Stock Exchange.

They also suffer from a number of *disadvantages*:

- The company's ability to raise money or to contract is limited by its Memorandum of Association (see below).
- Large companies are often more bureaucratic than small firms (this is because of the number of people who are involved in decision making) and are unable to respond as quickly to changed circumstances.
- Smaller firms are able to maintain closer relationships with their clients.
- The divorce between ownership (the shareholders) and control (the managers and directors) may result in a clash of objectives. The objectives of the investor, namely safety of capital, profitability and the marketability of shares, may not be those of the managers.
- The formalities for setting up and running a company are complex. Its relationships with the outside world are governed by its Memorandum of Association, and its internal government is laid down in its Articles of Association (see below).
- There is a legal obligation to disclose certain information, e.g. annual accounts.

Memorandum of association

This deals with the company's relationship with the outside world. The main contents of the memorandum are:

- *The Company's name*: This allows the Registrar to make sure that no two companies are using the same name. A private limited company's name must contain the word 'limited' (or the letters Ltd) and a public limited company's name must contain the letters 'plc'. Dave and Jim who intend to form a company will not be able to use the name 'Cambridge Plumbing and Heating Engineers Limited' if any other company has already registered the name.

- *The Company's address*: This shows where the company has its registered office. Dave and Jim may have premises on a trading estate which includes an office. The address being: 52 The Estate, Highfield, Cambridge CB3 7EQ.

- *The objects of the Company*: This states the purposes for which the company is formed, such as for the manufacture of chocolate or, as in our example, to provide a plumbing and heating service. Future shareholders, therefore, have some idea of what they are devoting their funds to. In practice, such 'objects' clauses usually outline many different types of activity in order to cover any future change which the business might wish to pursue.

- *A statement*: A statement that the liability of the shareholders is limited.

- *The amount of capital*: The amount of capital to be raised by issuing shares and the type of shares, e.g. £100,000 divided into £1 shares. A public company must have at least £50,000 of share capital.

- *An agreement*: An agreement of those who sign the memorandum that they wish to form a limited company and that they agree to purchase the stated number of shares.

Articles of Association

This deals with the internal relationships of the company, that is the day-to-day running of the company.

The Articles cover:
1. The procedure for calling a general meeting
2. The methods of electing directors
3. The rights and duties of directors
4. The borrowing power of the company
5. Rules about the transfer of shares
6. The division of profits

As regards point 5, for a limited company the Articles of Association will contain a restriction on the right to transfer shares.

Once these two documents have been completed they are sent to a Registrar of Companies along with the **Statutory Declaration**. This states that the promoters of the company have complied with the requirements of the Companies Act. The Registrar of Companies will then check the details and make sure everything is in order before issuing a **Certificate of Incorporation**. This sets up the company as a legal entity. It is the 'birth certificate' of the company. The **private** limited company can now commence business.

A **public** limited company also needs a **Certificate of Trading**. This is issued by the Registrar of Companies when he is satisfied the company has raised sufficient finance to cover its proposed plans. The company will have to advertise the sale of its shares, decide on how they are to be issued and then start trading.

Holding Companies

Quite apart from being a company in its own right, a **holding company** owns shares in other companies which are sufficient for it to exercise control. Technically this implies a 50% minimum shareholding, but in practice, be-cause of shareholder apathy, the percentage of shares needed to control the business may be considerably less. Firms under the control of the holding company will con-tinue to trade in their own name and have their own Board of Directors. Holding companies are often used where two firms wish to merge (perhaps for financial or competitive reasons) but see trading advantages in retaining their separate identities. Many of our national and multinational companies will own subsidiaries and thus also come within the definition of a holding company.

Did You Know ?

Due mainly to the Government's privatization programme, nearly 25% of the adult population now owns shares, compared to 7% in 1979. However the *value* of shares in the hands of private individuals has actually fallen, from 50% in 1963 to only 20% today.

Franchises

Strictly speaking a **franchise** is not a form of business organization but more a way of doing business. A franchise operation may be set up as a sole trader, partnership or a company; however, the majority are formed as limited companies. A franchise can be defined as *a concession given by the owner of patents relating to goods and services to another person allowing them to produce and sell these goods or services*. A typical franchise agreement will contain the following terms:

- The **franchiser** agrees to
  - assign an exclusive sales territory
  - allow the use of the trade name
  - promote the use of the trade name
  - provide training and advice on running the franchise
  - provide financial advice or assistance
  - sell goods to the franchise

- In return the **franchisee** agrees to
  - invest capital into the business
  - pay royalties to the franchiser
  - conform to specified standards
  - make purchases from the franchiser
  - only sell the franchiser's products

The British Franchise Association claims that franchising is the safest way to set up business. Put simply, the majority of business start-ups fail within three years but the majority of franchises survive.

The option of franchising is also attractive to the franchiser as it allows him to expand his activities with very little capital investment. Indeed in many cases franchising actually results in an injection of capital into the franchiser's business.

Franchising is said to be the fastest growing part of the retail market. Well known franchises include Benetton, Body Shop, British School of Motoring, Exchange Travel, Knobs and Knockers, Pronuptia and Tie Rack.

Co-operatives

As a form of business organization **co-operatives** are not particularly popular in the UK. Co-operatives developed in the nineteenth century as a means of self-help amongst working class people. In the UK the best known one is the Co-operative Retail Society. There are, however, successful co-operatives in manufacturing and commerce. Worker co-operatives are popular and successful in other parts of Europe (e.g. Spain – Mondragon) but have failed to raise sufficient finance or find managers of the right calibre in the UK. (Many organizations providing finance are reluctant to lend to co-operatives because they are not, primarily, a profit-making organization.) Where worker co-operatives have been successful in the UK they have normally started life as conventional business organizations (e.g. John Lewis Partnership). Most co-operatives are limited by guarantee and will be run by a Board of Directors appointed by the membership. The principles on which co-operative organizations are founded include:

- One member, one vote.
- The business is owned and managed by its workforce.
- The objectives are determined by the workforce.
- Profits are divided amongst the members.

Societies are registered under the Industrial and Provident Societies Acts and submit an annual return and financial statement to the Registrar of Friendly Societies.

The Public Sector

Public sector organizations are responsible to either central or local government, which in turn is responsible for funding them. They tend to provide services rather than produce a product. There are several types of public sector organization.

Public Corporations

Like public limited companies, **public corporations** are a separate legal entity having the right to sue or be sued in their own name. Similarly, like any large company they will have the equivalent of a Board of Directors (though it may not be called this) who decide policy and professional managers to implement that policy. The Board will be responsible to the government minister who appointed them for the overall operation of the service.

We have already noted that many of the nationalized industries which, as public corporations, formed part of the public sector have been returned to private ownership since 1979. Three important public corporations which remain are the BBC, the Bank of England and Nuclear Electric, and for different reasons the government is likely to retain control of these.

Central Government Departments

Government departments are one of the major ways in which government policy is implemented. Some departments are responsible for a specific service throughout the UK; Health and Social Security are good examples of these. Other departments co-ordinate a wide range of activities in a specific area, e.g. Scotland. Finally, there are a few extremely important departments that act as co-ordinators of government policy, e.g. the Treasury. One important feature of UK government departments is the way that they delegate their responsibilities to other bodies, particularly Quangos and local authorities.

Quangos

This stands for **Quasi Autonomous Non-Governmental Organizations**. Quangos are used to implement government policy where it is of a non-controversial nature and requires an expertise that the government does not possess. There are nearly 2000 in existence and they fall into one of three categories. *Executive bodies* such as the British Overseas Trade Board or the British Council provide a specialist service to the public. *Advisory bodies* such as the Advisory Council on Energy Conservation will undertake research and collect information in order to make recommendations about future policy to the relevant minister. Finally the government may appoint *administrative tribunals* to resolve disputes over matters such as rent, employment or social security.

Local Authorities

It would be difficult for any organization to administer services to 56 million people over a very wide geographic area. For that reason central government departments have delegated some of their responsibilities to other bodies far nearer the point of delivery of the services – **local authorities**. The services they supervise or provide include:

- *Protective*
    police
    fire
    consumer protection

- *Environmental*
    planning
    building regulations
    roads and transport
    pollution

- *Personal services*
    education
    careers
    social services
    housing
    recreation

With the emphasis on local management of many government activities, it is difficult for the government to assess how well the service is being administered. In an attempt to overcome this problem and also to make local managers more responsive to local requirements, the *Citizen's Charter* gives individuals far greater right to question and complain. The charter extends to services provided by public corporations (e.g. British Rail) and also companies undertaking work for central government departments (e.g. motorway repair contractors).

The formal organization

The term refers to the structure which the organization adopts in order to meet its objectives. This structure will change over time as the organization expands and also as it adapts to its environment and changes its objectives. You can see the **formal organization** in the way that:

- Activities are grouped into departments like production, finance, personnel and marketing.
- Work is divided so that employees contribute fully using their particular skills.
- Relationships between different employees are defined.
- Procedures for processing work are established.
- Channels of communication for the passing of information are created.

The informal organization

We have seen that the formal organization structure is devised to achieve organizational objectives. However, arising out of the interaction of employees in the work situation we also have an **informal organization**. We see the informal organization in the groups that develop within departments, the people who are drawn together through age, sex or social interests – the people who sit together in the staff canteen or who meet outside work hours.

The informal organization arises because of a person's need for companionship and social relationships. In the context of the organization these informal groups are a double edged weapon. The informal organization may result in higher morale and motivation amongst staff; it will also be used as an additional communication channel and may even result in greater job flexibility as workers help each other in their jobs. Sometimes, though, the objectives of the informal organization are different from those of the organization. For example, employees may restrict output in an attempt to prevent layoffs or redundancies; or employees might form cliques or closed groups, making it difficult for newcomers to be accepted.

The organization chart

You will find that most organizations will describe their organizational structure pictorially. This is because the organizational structure is often very complex and therefore difficult to describe verbally. A typical **organization chart** is shown in fig.4.3. From this chart we can see many of the points made above.

- Activities have been grouped on the basis of *function*.
- Work has been divided so that certain *specialists* can be employed, e.g. the computer services manager.
- The chain of command indicates who is responsible to whom (and the job title indicates in very general terms what they are responsible for). *Broken lines* show that certain departments have a specialist responsibility for a function throughout the organization.
- The *unbroken lines* between different postholders show the formal lines of communication in the organization. What is not shown are the horizontal (and sometimes diagonal) lines of communication which have been developed so that information can be processed quickly and efficiently. Also note that the unofficial, or informal, communication channels are not shown. These may have been created for work-related or social purposes.

Advantages of organization charts:
- Information in pictorial form is easily understood. It may be displayed on staff notice-boards making chains of command (formal) clear to all employees.
- Organizational defects are more easily identified, e.g. areas of conflict or an excessive span of control
- It provides the basis from which changes to the organizational structure will be made.

Disadvantages of organization charts:
- The chart is a picture of the organization at a certain date and will become out of date rapidly as personnel change and the structure is modified.
- The designer faces the difficulty of trying to show the complete organizational structure, in which case the chart is complex and confusing or simplifying the structure and thereby presenting an inaccurate picture.

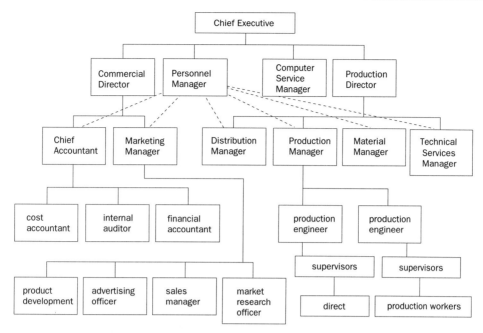

Fig. 4.3   Organizational chart of a typical manufacturing firm

- Organization charts do not reveal the different amounts of responsibility borne by executives.
- The chart does not show the unofficial or *informal* relationships and channels of communication without which the organization would not function properly.

Types of organization structure

In Unit 2, Element 1, we looked at ways of dividing up the activities of the organization by product, function, process or geographical area. In this section we take a rather more theoretical approach and consider how an organization evolves to meet particular problems it faces.

- *Line organizations (activities)*
  This exists where the organization structure focuses on those activities which are essential for the survival of the organization. It will be the structure adopted by all new and small firms. In the case of a *manufacturing* firm, **line activities** would be production, sales and finance – other functions merely exist to improve the efficiency with which line activities are carried out. A *retailing* firm adopting a line organization structure would group its activities around purchasing, sales and finance. As a form of organization it has a number of advantages:

  - The structure is easy to understand.
  - Responsibilities are well defined.
  - There are few communication problems because of the simple structure
  - It develops all-round managers rather than specialists.

  However, against these advantages are the fact that it ignores the benefits of specialists and places a very heavy burden on key personnel.

- *Line and staff organizations*
  The disadvantages associated with a line organization mean that as a structure it is really only suitable for a small organization. As the firm grows we will see specialist departments being created, thus relieving the busy line manager of peripheral responsibilities. Many of

the specialist departments created will have a specialist responsibility throughout the organization. In Fig. 4.3 the Personnel Manager and the Computer Service Manager are examples of specialist departments with organization-wide responsibilities.

Whilst there is no doubt that specialist *staff* giving advice to the *line* managers can improve the efficiency of the whole organization, the relationship between the two groups has always been difficult. This is because:

- Line managers find that their authority is limited by the appointment of specialists. They may feel their status is threatened.
- Specialists are often regarded as senior management's spies.
- Specialists have a narrow outlook and may not fully understand the problems of the line manager.
- Specialists may introduce change to justify their existence.

- *Matrix organization*
  This structure is widely used in the construction and other industries where a high degree of co-ordination is required. The departmental structure still exists but acts as a resource bank for project teams to draw on (see Fig. 4.4). The project team which cuts across functional boundaries is a temporary structure and exists for the duration of the project only. After the project is completed, the team members will return to their parent department until assigned to another project team. Advantages of the **matrix structure** include:

  - Inter-departmental barriers are broken down and a team approach to the work is encouraged.
  - Tighter control of the project is obtained through the co-ordination of the project leader.
  - The client has a point of contact close to his immediate interests, thereby ensuring that his requirements are met.

  Against these advantages we can put the fact that this is a complex organizational structure which may create

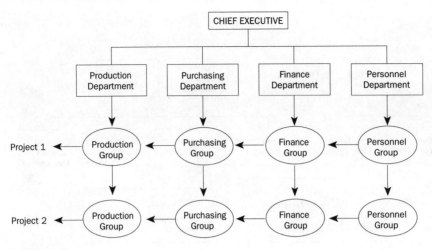

Fig. 4.4   Matrix organization

conflicts of interest (to whom is the team member responsible – the departmental head or the project leader – and what happens if he gets conflicting instructions?). The structure may also result in a less efficient use of resources within the parent department.

Delegation

Whatever form of organization structure is adopted it is extremely unlikely that any manager is going to be able to undertake all the work by himself. To function effectively the manager must **delegate** – by this we mean that certain aspects of the job are given to, and undertaken by, subordinates. This ensures that the manager concentrates on the more important aspects of his job, functions more efficiently and at the same time is training the next generation of managers. An organization chart gives us a broad outline of how work is being allocated or delegated to subordinates. Thus in Fig. 4.3 (p. 101) we see that specific aspects of the Commercial Director's work are being delegated to the Chief Accountant and the Marketing Manager. There are three important aspects to delegation:

- *Responsibility.* In accepting a task the subordinate also accepts the duty to ensure that the task is carried out properly and on time. The responsibilities of the subordinate should therefore be properly defined and documented in a job description.

- *Authority.* For delegation to work the subordinate must be given the necessary authority to carry out his responsibilities. This authority may extend to hiring and firing of staff, access to confidential information, spending money or otherwise using the resources of the organization.

- *Accountability.* Having been given the responsibility and authority to carry out a task, subordinates may be held accountable to the superior for their efforts. There is also another side to accountability though, because the manager who assigns a task to a subordinate will ultimately be held responsible for the actions of that subordinate.

Despite the obvious advantages of delegation you will find that there are circumstances in which work will *not* be allocated to subordinates, for example:

- confidential work
- very important decisions

- where the ability of the subordinate to carry out the work is doubted by the manager
- an unwillingness of the manager to 'let go'
- a subordinate's lack of confidence

The span of control and organizational structure

Another potential limitation on delegation is a managers ability to supervise his subordinates properly. The number of subordinates supervised by a manager is termed his 'span of control'. The main factors affecting the **span of control** are shown in Table 4.3.

Similarity of work	The more similar the work, the wider the span
Geographic proximity	A wider span is possible if the work group is located in the same place
Level of supervision	A wider span is possible where little supervision is required
Level of co-ordination	A wider span is possible where little co-ordination is required
Planning	The less planning a manager does, the wider the span

Table 4.3   Factors affecting the span of control

It has been argued that because of the complexity of his subordinates' work a senior manager should only have a span of control of three to five. The number of subordinates that managers can handle has a significant impact on the shape and the nature of jobs within the organization.

The **tall, hierarchical structure** (see Fig. 4.5) has many layers of management, each with a small span of control. Its major advantage is that all the work is closely supervised and controlled. However, because of its many layers of management it is thought to be unable to respond quickly in periods of rapid change. From the employees' point of view jobs tend to be very specialized and the lack of variety may frustrate some. There are good opportunities, however, for promotion to higher levels in the organization.

A wide managerial span of control will result in a 'flat' organization structure with few layers of management (see Fig. 4.6). Many retailing organizations have this flat structure. Employees may find the wider scope of their work and greater responsibilities give them greater job satisfaction than in the tall structure but there are fewer promotion

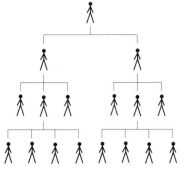
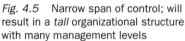

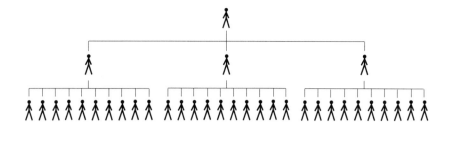

Fig. 4.5 Narrow span of control; will result in a *tall* organizational structure with many management levels

Fig. 4.6 A wide span of control will result in a *flat* organizational structure with few levels of management

possibilities. Because the flat structure tends to push decisionmaking down into the lower levels of the organization, it is considered to be more responsive to environmental change. For this reason many large organizations are moving to this more 'dynamic', structure.

Centralization and decentralization

These terms refer to the extent that decision-making in a business is delegated. In a highly **centralized** organization power and decision-making is concentrated into the hands of a few senior managers. In a **decentralized** organization many of the important decisions will be taken at the lower management level. The benefits and problems associated with each are as follows:

- *Centralised organizations*
  Benefits
  - uniformity of decision-making
  - duplication of effort eliminated
  - highly skilled personnel available to the whole organization, not one unit

  Problems
  - heavy strain on a few managers
  - communication with senior management difficult (lack of time)
  - demotivating influence for all but senior managers
  - senior managers have too much power

- *Decentralised organizations*
  Benefits
  - senior managers workload reduced
  - power is dispersed
  - other managers motivated by more 'important' work
  - decisions made by managers who 'know the situation'

  Problems
  - lack of uniformity in decision-making
  - separate units' efforts unco-ordinated
  - conflict between units may arise

Job roles in an organization

In this section we will look at some of the key *roles* held by people in organizations. Although the term 'management' is commonly associated with business we find managers in all kinds of organizations. Indeed, wherever there is a need for people to work together for a common purpose 'managers' are needed to co-ordinate the inputs of people, materials,

machines and money. Of course not all those people who carry out a management role are called managers. Headmasters, bishops and generals are as much managers as is the marketing manager of a large company. Within most business organizations we can see three broad categories of management (see Fig. 4.7) and we will use these categories to look at managerial roles within an organization.

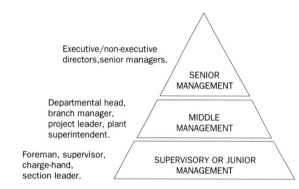

Fig. 4.7 The management pyramid

Senior management

This group, comprising the **senior managers** and the **directors** of the organization, has the most power and responsibility within the organization. It is responsible for determining the long-term objectives of the organization and has a time horizon of over five years. In a company senior management will be responsible to the shareholders for the success of the organization. Due to the complexity of the managers' and directors' work it is likely that they will only have one or two executives reporting to them, but indirectly they are responsible for all employees working under them.

Directors may be executive or non-executive. An *executive director* is a full time employee of the company. He or she will be responsible for the smooth running of a department within the organization as well as being a member of the Board of Directors, contributing to discussions, particularly those involving his or her own functional specialism. *Non-executive directors* are part-time employees appointed to the Board of Directors because of their broad knowledge of industry or political influence. Their knowledge and contacts may be useful in determining policy or in getting contracts. Non-executive directors may also be the representatives of large share-holders who wish to see that their interests are safeguarded. *Worker directors* are another example of non-executive directors.

The role of the manager

It would seem that the job of a senior manager is very different from that of a junior manager. It is – but there are also distinct similarities! All managers, whatever the organization, whatever the level, will carry out the functions of planning, organizing, directing and controlling.

Planning is the starting point for management action. Through planning you establish objectives – which you will later achieve through organizing, directing and controlling the resources at your disposal. Managers who don't devote sufficient time to planning will find that their goals or objectives are not really what are required – or cannot be achieved with the resources available. Senior managers will spend a large amount of their time planning.

Once objectives have been established the manager will develop the necessary *organizational structure*. This may involve the creation of departments, or sections within departments, the division of work to individuals and channels of communication. Although very important, managers spend less time on this than on any other function.

The *directing* function is concerned with the leadership and motivation of the workforce so that they work in a way which contributes toward organizational objectives. Supervisors, with their large span of control, devote the largest proportion of their time to this function.

The *control* function requires the manager to make sure that actual performance coincides with planned performance. Where there is a deviation from planned performance, the manager must take steps to rectify the situation.

Middle management

This group of managers work *within* the policy guidelines laid down by senior management. They are responsible for ensuring that the organization and utilization of resources within their department conforms to these guidelines. Normally their time horizon is one year and they will have between four and nine subordinates reporting to them.

Did You Know ?

Logically we can expect the number of middle-manager posts to decrease:
• In an attempt to save money, and make junior managers' jobs more interesting, responsibility is being pushed further down into line organization
• The use of information technology is reducing the work of many middle managers.

Supervisory management

These are the 'front line' managers who deal with the workers and put plans of senior and middle management into operation. These plans are, by now, essentially short term – perhaps a week or a month at the most. They are also responsible for large groups of workers – a span of control of 20 to 30 is not exceptional. Unfortunately the importance of having good supervisory managers is often ignored. To do their job properly they must not only have good technical skills but also very good inter-personal skills.

The team member

Management is often referred to as 'getting things done through people'. This definition draws attention to the importance of the manager's creating a climate where people believe that they are part of a *team* and their contributions are valued by the organization. The team will obviously consist of the groups that we have discussed above – senior, middle and junior management – but also equally importantly the clerical, administrative and production staff. Today, considerable effort is made by many organizations to make the ordinary worker feel part of the team – an essential and important member. Involvement in decision-making, recognition in company magazines (for social, sports or works-related activities), works outings, Christmas parties and even group gifts on engagements, parenthood or marriages, are all part of the process of team building.

Did You Know ?

There is some form of employee involvement in over 90% of all UK workplaces. *Teamworking* has increased labour productivity and profitability; cost savings of over £2 million have been reported in electrical firms, and cost reductions of 16% in process and material costs in automobile firms.

Job descriptions and person specifications

It is important for any organization to recruit the 'right' person for the job. Failure to do so will result in the person appointed failing to perform adequately. The situation can only be remedied by costly training, transfer to another more suitable job or termination of employment. In each case the cost to the organization in terms of time and money is considerable. Job descriptions and person specifications help to ensure that the right applicant is appointed to the vacancy.

Job descriptions

The aim of the **job description** is to state as clearly as possible the duties and responsibilities of a specific job. Whilst the format of the job description may vary between organizations, the **basic information** that is required is very similar:

• *Basic details.* Title and grade of job, the department concerned.
• *Job summary.* Outlining the purpose of the job, the main tasks and the standards to be achieved. Information on social and work environment.
• *Responsibilities.* Clarifying the position in the organization structure. Who is the job holder responsible to and who is he responsible for?
• *Conditions of employment.* Salaries, pensions, hours of work, holidays.
• *Promotion.* Career structure in the organization, promotion routes, availability of training.

A job description can be used in a number of ways such as:

• the basis for job advertisements
• the basis for deciding the salary to pay
• the basis for devising training programmes

- the basis for person specifications
- the basis for appraisal.

It is important for the organization to keep job descriptions up to date. The characteristics of jobs in most organizations, particularly at a managerial level, are likely to have changed within a few years of the job description being drawn up. Job descriptions should therefore be reviewed and updated at regular intervals.

Person specification

This is sometimes referred to as a **job specification**. However, we use the term **person specification** to avoid any confusion with the term job description. A person specification is a development of the job description and should detail the qualities the ideal candidate should have. Many person specifications are based on the Rodgers seven-point plan. These are as follows:

1. *Physical:* appearance, health, speech
2. *Attainments:* education, qualifications and experience
3. *Intelligence:* intellectual capacity
4. *Aptitudes:* literacy, numeracy, languages, manual dexterity
5. *Interests:* practical, intellectual, social, sporting
6. *Disposition:* ability to work alone or under pressure
7. *Circumstances:* age, mobility, domestic circumstances

When using the Rodgers plan, either to develop a person specification or in an interview situation, managers often identify certain qualities as 'essential' and others as 'desirable'. Many organizations now provide applicants with a person specification as well as a job description. This enables potential candidates to judge more clearly whether or not they are suitable for the job.

Self Check ✔ Element 2

21. The following table details the major characteristics of the different forms of business organization. Complete the table.

	Ownership	Control	Liability	Finance	Formal-ities
Sole trader	One person			Self, relatives, bank, profits	Few
Partner-ship	Two or more partners	The partners	Unlimited		
Company	__ or more share-holders				Complex to form and run
Co-opera-tive	Two or __ members				Some legal require-ments
Public corpora-tion	The state				The Nation-alization Act

22. Explain the term 'franchise'.

_____
_____
_____

Self Check ✔ *continued*

23. Give three examples of areas of business where you are likely to find sole traders:
(a)
(b)
(c)

24. Students often confuse the formal and informal organization. Explain the difference between the two terms.
_____
_____
_____
_____

25. State three features of organization structure that are revealed by an organization chart.
_____
_____
_____

26. Give two examples of staff specialists who may be appointed to help busy line managers.
_____
_____

27. Briefly state the three important aspects of delegation.
_____
_____
_____

28. Senior managers normally have a smaller span of control than junior managers. Why should this be so?
_____
_____
_____

29. Give two examples of people who may be appointed as non-executive directors.
_____
_____

30. The Rodgers seven-point plan is often used as the basis for drawing up person specifications and conducting interviews. What are the seven points?
_____
_____
_____

4.3. Evaluating job applications and interviews

We have already noted the importance of the organization's appointing the right people to its vacancies. It is sometimes said that an organization is only as good as its employees! We have also noted that there are a variety of agencies who can help us in the selection process and the importance of a clear job description and person specification. We now turn our attention to the *means* by which people apply for jobs and the interview. The performance criteria for this element are:

- Recruitment procedures are identified.

- Letters of application are evaluated for clarity and quality of presentation.
- Curriculum vitae are evaluated for clarity and presentation.
- Interviewer techniques are evaluated and appraised.
- Interviewee techniques are evaluated and appraised.
- Legal and ethical obligations in recruitment are explained.

Job applications

There are three major ways of **applying** for a job which we must consider. They are the letter of application, the application form and the curriculum vitae.

The letter of application

This is simply a **letter** which states who you are, what you have done and why you should be considered for the job which has been advertised. It may be used by itself or in conjunction with a curriculum vitae or application form. It may also be used for speculative applications where no vacancy has been advertised. The letter can be presented in any way the candidate thinks fit. A typical letter would have the following sections:

- Why you are applying for the job.
- What contribution you can make to the organization.
- The capabilities you have developed through education, training and leisure activities.
- What special skills and knowledge would enable you to perform well in the job.

Your letter should be concise and to the point. Try to avoid long words or sentences. Ensure that all spellings are correct (if you have a word-processor use the spell check facility) and that the letter is neatly written and well presented. You should keep a copy of all letters that you write.

The letter of application is considered by many people to be a good method of selecting people for clerical and administrative positions. Applicants whose letter of application contains spelling mistakes, grammatical errors and poorly structured points will be considered unsuitable. However, it is wrong to assume that a well written letter of application always means that the candidate is better than another who has submitted an inferior letter, because the former candidate may have been taught the skills of letter writing.

Another disadvantage is that a candidate may not realize that certain skills or experience are important in the job that he is applying for and thus not include them in his letter of application.

The curriculum vitae

Literally translated *curriculum vitae* (it is commonly abbreviated to CV) means 'course of life'. In business terms it is a document which summarizes a candidates personal details and experience. As such it is a very general document and may not relate sufficiently to a specific job. For this reason candidates should always back it up with a letter of application (often referred to as a covering letter) drawing out and expanding on those skills and experiences which they believe to be particularly relevant to the job.

CVs may also be used for very senior appointments where the applicants wide experience renders the standard application form inappropriate.

A CV will normally contain the following sections:

- *Personal details.* Name, age, address, telephone number.
- *Education and Qualifications.* Schools and colleges attended (with dates), GCSEs, 'A' levels, certificates and diplomas obtained (with dates).
- *Training.* Courses undertaken and skills obtained.
- *Career history.* Details of organizations worked for, job titles and responsibilities. School-leavers should give details of part-time and vacation work.
- *Other information.* Items such as driving licence, computing or language skills.
- *Interests and hobbies.* Particularly where there has been some achievement or official position held.
- *References.* Normally you would give your last employer (school-leavers would give the name of their headmaster or some other person who can detail their academic ability and other achievements).

The aim of the CV is to impress the reader. When drawing up a CV you should:

- Ensure that the CV is no longer than two sides of A4 paper. Essentially the CV is a summary. Key points should be expanded in the covering letter.
- Take care with the presentation and ensure that:
  - headings stand out
  - there are ample margins
  - the information is well spaced out
  - spelling and grammar are correct
- Use a short, snappy style of writing.
- Use 'action' words wherever possible. Examples include:

accomplished	achieved	completed
created	delivered	developed
directed	finished	generated
implemented	improved	introduced
pioneered	planned	promoted
re-organized	set up	succeeded

Once you have drawn up your CV it is a good idea to let someone else read through it for mistakes that you have missed. In any case you should also try to edit the CV once or twice by yourself, to ensure that the finished result does you justice.

Application forms

The major problems associated with both letters of application and CVs is that:

- They may omit details which are important to the employer.
- Information is presented in a non-standard way which makes it difficult for the prospective employer to assess the merits of different applicants.

As a result, many employers tend to use **application forms** which they have designed for their own purposes. The function of the application form is to:

- Obtain information on applicants in a standardized and easily comparable format.

- Exclude irrelevant information but also ensure that information relevant to the person specification is collected.
- Provide a basis for shortlisting, interviews and subsequent records.
- Provide a basis for recruiting should a further vacancy become available shortly.

Many firms will often have more than one application form. These will be used selectively for different levels of job. There is no point, for example, in scaring applicants for an unskilled job by insisting they complete a long and complex application form.

Application forms will demand very much the same information that is included in a CV (but, as already indicated, the structure and format may be rather different). However, many application forms will include a section asking open ended questions. It is often the answers to these that decide whether or not an applicant gets to the interview stage. Examples include:

- Why have you applied for this job?
- What objectives would you set yourself, for the first six months, if appointed?
- Why do you think you will be successful in this job?
- Explain how your background would help you in this job.
- Where (jobwise) do you expect to be in five years' time?

Before answering any questions like these you should have a clear idea of what the job entails and the extent to which your background and career history meet the person specification for that job. You should then ask yourself why the employer is asking that question, what your answer will tell the employer about you and whether this is really the impression that you want to give. Finally, make sure you take a photocopy of your application form and covering letter – you will need this information when preparing for your interview.

The interview

This is the most commonly used selection technique. It is also open to more abuse than any other technique. This arises from the incorrect belief that anyone can conduct an **interview**. This is not true and many cases of poor selection arise because the interviewer has not listened to what the candidate has said, nor asked the right questions. In fact preparation for an interview should be undertaken not only by the applicant but also by the interviewer!

Interviews may be conducted on a 'one to one' basis or a panel basis. The panel basis is often used where there are a number of different interested parties. It has the advantage of allowing these different interests to have a say in the final selection decision and eliminating individual subjectivity. However, its disadvantage is that it places the interviewee in a very tense and unnatural situation. For this reason, where candidates and interviewers have time it is better to hold a number of shorter and less formal interviews on a 'one to one' basis.

The interview – the manager's perspective
The objectives of any interview are:

- To assess whether the candidate is able and willing to do the job.

One of the biggest criticisms of interviews is their *subjective* nature. Interviewers may find their judgement affected by many factors:

- *halo effect:* where a particular characteristic (e.g. shared interest in sport) will influence the interviewer's judgement in other areas
- *stereotyping:* where bias arises from the interviewer applying generalisations to a particular characteristic of the interviewee (e.g. male wearing an ear-ring) etc.

For these reasons firms often use other selection techniques, such as 'tests', in addition to (or instead of) an interview.

- To assess whether the candidate will 'fit into' the organization.
- To give the applicant a chance to judge whether the job and the organization are what they really want.
- To give a good impression of the organization (regardless of the outcome) by ensuring a fair and well structured interview.

Personnel managers and many senior staff may have been trained in interview techniques. These are some of the basic guidelines:

- The interviewer should be thoroughly conversant with the job description and the person specification and also have read the candidate's application before the interview session.
- The interview should be properly structured so that each candidate is treated fairly and comparisons can be more easily made. The Rodgers seven-point plan is often used for structuring an interview.
- Interviews should take place in comfortable surroundings where there will be no interruptions or distractions.
- The interview should be started in an easy going , conversational manner before leading on to the more difficult and open ended (i.e. those which can't be answered 'yes' or 'no') questions.
- Allow the candidate to talk freely (ideally the candidate should be talking for 80% of the time) whilst ensuring that the information on which to base a decision is obtained.
- Pay attention (leave note-taking until after the interview) and do not react in a way that shows disapproval or disagreement.
- Always ensure that the candidate has adequate opportunity to ask questions.
- The interview should always end on a friendly, agreeable note.

The interview – the applicant's perspective
Before the interview. If you really want the job that you have applied for you will need to prepare yourself. These are some of the key points:

- Acknowledge the invitation for interview.
- If you have to travel far to the interview, plan your journey in advance and make sure that you get there in good time.
- Wear appropriate formal dress.

- Find out as much as you can about the employer's business.
- Re-read the job description and person specification. Summarize what you consider to be your particular strengths.
- Anticipate and prepare answers to obvious questions.
- List the questions you wish to ask.

During the interview. A typical interview will last roughly 30 minutes. Few people enjoy interviews but during this time you must try and impress the interviewer(s). These are some of the points you should watch:

- On entering the interview room introduce yourself and, if given the opportunity, shake hands with the interviewer. Make sure you smile and appear relaxed. Remember that first impressions count! Interviewers generally make up their minds in the first few minutes about a candidate and then spend the rest of the interview seeking evidence to justify their decision.

- When answering questions you should:
  1. Pause before answering the questions. This shows that you are giving the question proper consideration and not making an 'off the cuff' reply.
  2. Reply to the question asked, not the one you wished they'd asked. If you don't understand a question, ask the interviewer to repeat it.
  3. Recognize the difference between questions requiring short answers and those requiring extended answers. Always try and avoid giving one word answers.
  4. Be honest. If you can't answer the question say so. You will gain more credit that way than giving an answer which is obviously rubbish. You should never lie about your qualifications or experience. This is grounds for instant dismissal if discovered at a later date.

Did You Know ?

Have you ever watched yourself on video and thought '...well I never thought I did that!' Body language, or non-verbal communication, is said to tell us a lot about an individual. In an interview situation the main *negative indicators* are:

- Crossed arms indicate defensiveness.
- Rubbing your nose suggests untruthfulness.
- Constant crossing and uncrossing of legs indicates hyperactiveness.
- Twitchy feet mean boredom or great tension.

There are also some *positive indicators*. You could try practising:

- Gesturing with your hands as you speak. This suggests confidence.
- Leaning slightly forwards when talking to the interviewer. This suggests you are positive and ambitious.
- Maintaining frequent eye contact. This indicates truthfulness and assertiveness.
- Giving a firm handshake on arrival and departure. This suggests confidence.

Whilst positive body language is unlikely to get you the job by itself, a person who leaves the impression of being competent, confident, honest and ambitious is certainly going to be seriously considered.

- Once the questioning has started remember that it is not only your answers that will impress the interviewer but the overall way you conduct yourself. You should:
  1. Look at the interviewer and other members of the panel as you answer questions. Candidates with poor eye contact are seen as unconfident and perhaps even devious.
  2. Make sure you communicate effectively. You should answer questions clearly and concisely. Your voice tone should be varied and different speeds of speech should be used.
  3. Non-verbal communication signs should be positive.

- As the interview draws to a close you will be given the opportunity to ask questions. Some of these you will have prepared beforehand. Other questions asked may seek clarification of points that have arisen during the interview. You should try to avoid asking more than five questions because the interviewers will have a schedule to keep to.
- At the close of the interview thank the interviewer for the opportunity to discuss your application in detail.
- After the interview it is useful to make some notes. What were the difficult questions? Did you handle them successfully? What answers did you give that were unsatisfactory? How could you improve on these?

Legal and ethical obligations

We have already noted some of these obligations. Thus there is an obligation on job applicants to provide full details of their background – education, qualifications and experience – even if this means revealing details which are harmful to your application, e.g. criminal convictions (unless 'spent' under the Rehabilitation of Offenders Act).

Employers also have an ethical obligation to potential employees to ensure that advertising and any other literature relating to the job gives a full and fair picture of the job and the associated conditions of employment.

Legally, there are a number of obligations placed upon employers in the recruitment process. These areas which have been discussed in Unit 2, Element 1, include:

- *Disabled Persons (Employment) Act 1958.* A firm with more than 20 employees has an obligation to employ disabled people up to 3% of its workforce.

- *Employer's Liability (Compulsory Insurance) Act 1969.* All employees must be insured by the employer against accidental injury.

- *Equal Pay Act 1970.* Women have the right to equal pay for equal work (with men).

- *Sex Discrimination Act 1975 and Race Relations Act 1976.* The outlawing of discrimination against potential employees on the grounds of sex, race, colour or ethnic origin.

- *Employment Protection Act 1975 (and Consolidation Act 1978), Employment Acts 1980, 1982, 1988.* New employees have a right to a written statement of the particulars of certain terms and conditions in their contract of employment.

Equal opportunities

It is an unfortunate fact of life that there are always going to be people in our society who are discriminated against because of other people's prejudices and misconceptions. We can see the results of this in the area of employment with many people in these groups finding it difficult to get a job. Yet in many ways the employers who discriminate do themselves no favours because they limit the number of properly qualified people they can recruit from.

Although equal opportunities policies are not required by law they are recommended and the **Equal Opportunities Commission** produces a model policy which can be adapted for the individual organization. The essential features are that there is a commitment *not* to discriminate in the employment sphere and that there is a system to monitor the application of this policy within the organization, together with an established procedure for dealing with grievances and victimization.

Properly administered, such policies can help reduce the incidence of discrimination in the workplace. The policy could also be useful as evidence in cases of alleged discrimination.

Self Check ✔ **Element 3**

31. Why do you think it would be necessary to include a covering letter with a CV when applying for a job?

_____

_____

_____

Self Check ✔ *continued*

32. State two reasons why an organization may prefer to use an application form in a recruitment situation.

_____

_____

33. When conducting an interview what are the interviewer's objectives?

_____

_____

34. Why is non-verbal communication so important in the interview situation?

_____

_____

_____

35. Give examples of *negative indicators* involving non-verbal communication.

_____

_____

_____

_____

36. Give examples of *positive indicators* involving non-verbal communication.

_____

_____

_____

_____

Unit Test Answer all the questions

Focus 1

Question 1
Which of the following is *not* a participative management technique?

A   Quality circles
B   Industrial tribunals
C   Semi-antonomous work groups
D   Joint consultative committees

Question 2
Mark each of these statements true (T) or false (F).

(1) Labour turnover is a bad thing because of the costs involved in employing another employee.
(2) Labour turnover is a good thing because it stops the workforce from becoming complacent.

Which option best describes the two statements:

A   (1) T   (2) T   Choose this answer if both statements are True.
B   (1) T   (2) F   Choose this answer if statement (1) is True and statement (2) is False.
C   (1) F   (2) T   Choose this answer if statement (1) is False and statement (2) is True.
D   (1) F   (2) F   Choose this answer if both statements are False.

Make sure you choose the answer which represents the correct order of the statements

Question 3
Which of the following is not a form of management development?

A   Job rotation
B   Job enlargement
C   Job description
D   Job enrichment

Question 4
Decide whether each of these statements is true (T) or false (F).

(1) An employee may be fairly dismissed on the grounds of gross misconduct.
(2) An employee who has over two years of employment with the same company has not to be unfairly dismissed.

Which option best describes the two statements:

A   (1) T   (2) T   Choose this answer if both statements are True.
B   (1) T   (2) F   Choose this answer if statement (1) is True and statement (2) is False.
C   (1) F   (2) T   Choose this answer if statement (1) is False and statement (2) is True
D   (1) F   (2) F   Choose this answer if both statements are False.

Make sure you choose the answer which represents the correct order of the statements

Question 5
Who is primarily responsible for informing employees of safe methods for handling dangerous substances.

A   The state
B   The firm
C   The Health and Safety Executive
D   The trade union health and safety representative

Question 6
Supply and demand forecasting are an essential part of the manpower planning process. Which of the following factors would affect the demand forecast?

A   Labour market trends
B   Present workforce skills
C   Employee motivation
D   Future expansion plans

Question 7
In law businesses owe certain responsibilities to their workers. The relevant law is :

A   Law of tort
B   Contract law
C   Employment law
D   Criminal law

Question 8
(1) Work study is primarily concerned with improving employee motivation.
(2) Productivity in a workforce can be improved by introducing flexible working hours.

Which option best describes the two statements:

A   (1) T   (2) T   Choose this answer if both statements are True.
B   (1) T   (2) F   Choose this answer if statement (1) is True and statement (2) is False.
C   (1) F   (2) T   Choose this answer if statement (1) is False and statement (2) is True.
D   (1) F   (2) F   Choose this answer if both statements are False.

Make sure you choose the answer which represents the correct order of the statements.

Focus 2

Question 9
Mark each of these statements true (T) or false (F).

(1) White collar unions have experienced rapid growth in membership since 1950.
(2) Since 1979 union membership has fallen substantially.

Which option best describes the two statements:

A   (1) T   (2) T   Choose this answer if both statements are True.
B   (1) T   (2) F   Choose this answer if statement (1) is True and statement (2) is False.
C   (1) F   (2) T   Choose this answer if statement (1) is False and statement (2) is True.
D   (1) F   (2) F   Choose this answer if both statements are False.

Make sure you choose the answer which represents the correct order of the statements.

Question 10
Which of the following is not an objective of a trade union?

A To represent members in a dispute with management
B To obtain improvements in pay
C To improve productivity
D To promote industrial democracy

Question 11
Good industrial relations requires employers to consult and negotiate with employees. Which one of the following would not be part of the selective bargaining process?

A Negotiations to establish a disputes procedure
B Negotiations to obtain an increase in pay
C Negotiations over catering facilities in a new canteen
D Negotiations to redeploy redundant workers

Focus 3

Questions 12–14 relate to the following information.

In a work situation employers are protected by various acts including:

A Wages Act
B Equal Pay Act
C Employees Protection (Consolidation) Act
D Sex Discrimination Act

Under which Act would you have redress in the following circumstances

Question 12
A waitress discovers that her male counterparts earn £10 a week more than her

Question 13
A waitress drops some dinner plates and has some money deducted from her salary

Question 14
A waitress is dismissed when the restaurant at which she works closes down

Question 15
Businesses provide workers with job contracts, pay slips and safe working conditions because:

A It improves morale
B It is part of a collective agreement
C It is the law
D It is good publicity

Question 16
Mark each of these statements true (T) or false (F).

(1) Under the Race Relations Act it is illegal to stipulate 'a good command of English' in a job advertisement for a factory worker.
(2) Under the Race Relations Act it would be illegal for an Indian restaurant to advertise for Indian waiters and waitresses.

Which option best describes the two statements:

A (1) T (2) T Choose this answer if both statements are True.
B (1) T (2) F Choose this answer if statement (1) is True and statement (2) is False.
C (1) F (2) T Choose this answer if statement (1) is False and statement (2) is True.
D (1) F (2) F Choose this answer if both statements are False.

Make sure you choose the answer which represents the correct order of the statements.

Question 17
Which law is NOT designed to ensure that employees doing the same work are treated in the same way?

A Wages Act
B Equal Pay Act
C Race Relations Act
D Sex Discrimination Act

Question 18
Mark each of these statements true (T) or false (F).

(1) If an employee is injured at work as a result of breaches of health and safety regulations he would take his claim to an industrial tribunal.
(2) Industrial tribunals are a quick and inexpensive form of justice dispensing with many of the formalities of a court of law.

Which option best describes the two statements:

A (1) T (2) T Choose this answer if both statements are True.
B (1) T (2) F Choose this answer if statement (1) is True and statement (2) is False.
C (1) F (2) T Choose this answer if statement (1) is False and statement (2) is True.
D (1) F (2) F Choose this answer if both statements are False.

Make sure you choose the answer which represents the correct order of the statements

Focus 4

Question 19
Decide whether each of these statements is true (T) or false (F).

(1) All partners in a partnership must have unlimited liability.
(2) A 'sole trader' is a form of business organization in which the owner works in the business by himself.

Which option best describes the two statements:

A (1) T (2) T Choose this answer if both statements are True.
B (1) T (2) F Choose this answer if statement (1) is True and statement (2) is False.
C (1) F (2) T Choose this answer if statement (1) is False and statement (2) is True.
D (1) F (2) F Choose this answer if both statements are False.

Make sure you choose the answer which represents the correct order of the statements.

Question 20
Which of the following is least likely to affect a manager's span of control?

A Ability of his subordinates
B Manpower planning
C Similarity of subordinates' work
D Geographic proximity of subordinates

Question 21
Mark each of these statements true (T) or false (F)

(1) Line organizations develop all-round managers rather than specialists.
(2) A matrix organizational structure will be used where a

high degree of inter-departmental co-ordination is required.

Which option best describes the two statements:

A (1) T (2) T Choose this answer if both statements are True.
B (1) T (2) F Choose this answer if statement (1) is True and statement (2) is False.
C (1) F (2) T Choose this answer if statement (1) is False and statement (2) is True.
D (1) F (2) F Choose this answer if both statements are False.

Make sure you choose the answer which represents the correct order of the statements

Question 22
Mark each of these statements true (T) or false (F)

(1) All directors own shares in the company they work for.
(2) Directors are responsible to the company's shareholders for their actions.

Which option best describes the two statements:

A (1) T (2) T Choose this answer if both statements are True.
B (1) T (2) F Choose this answer if statement (1) is True and statement (2) is False.
C (1) F (2) T Choose this answer if statement (1) is False and statement (2) is True.
D (1) F (2) F Choose this answer if both statements are False.

Make sure you choose the answer which represents the correct order of the statements

Focus 5

Question 23
Supervisory staff are one level of management within the organization. Which statement below correctly describes their role in the organization.

A To decide policy for the business
B To agree with managers in other departments the flow of work through the organization
C To monitor and control the work of shopfloor employees
D To devise annual and monthly budgets against which performance can be measured

Question 24
Which of the following would not be found in a job description.

A The conditions of employment
B A job summary
C The educational qualifications needed
D The responsibilities of the job

Question 25
The cost accounting department of a firm consists of the manager, two supervisors and eight clerks handling cost accounting information relating to different products.

Mark each of these statements true (T) or false (F).

(1) The task of ensuring the information is entered accurately onto the monthly budgetary control statements is the job of the manager.
(2) The task of writing a report explaining why variances from budget have occurred is the job of the clerks

Which option best describes the two statements:

A (1) T (2) T Choose this answer if both statements are True.
B (1) T (2) F Choose this answer if statement (1) is True and statement (2) is False.
C (1) F (2) T Choose this answer if statement (1) is False and statement (2) is True.
D (1) F (2) F Choose this answer if both statements are False.

Make sure you choose the answer which represents the correct order of the statements.

Question 26
Mark each of these statements true (T) or false (F).

(1) Job analysis provides the information which is the basis for job descriptions.
(2) Job descriptions would be used when a manager appraises his subordinate.

Which option best describes the two statements:

A (1) T (2) T Choose this answer if both statements are True.
B (1) T (2) F Choose this answer if statement (1) is True and statement (2) is False.
C (1) F (2) T Choose this answer if statement (1) is False and statement (2) is True.
D (1) F (2) F Choose this answer if both statements are False.

Make sure you choose the answer which represents the correct order of the statements

Question 27
Which of the following is not the role of senior managers?

A Policy making in the organization
B Determining the structure of their department
C Carrying out appraisals on all the employees in their department
D Maintaining a high level of morale and motivation within their department

Focus 6

Questions 28–30 relate to the following information.

Listed below are four examples of external recruitment agencies:

A Government employment agencies
B Commercial employment agencies
C Management selection consultants
D Executive search consultants

Which agency would you go to for the following categories of staff?

Question 28
A temporary office worker

Question 29
A transport manager

Question 30
An unskilled worker

Question 31
A firm advertising for the post of Research and Development Director is most likely to use

A   Employment agency
B   National press
C   Specialist magazines
D   Local press

Question 32
Listed below are descriptions of activities in the recruitment process. Which is least likely to be the responsibility of the Human Resources Department?

A   Organizing the job advertisement
B   Drawing up the person specification
C   Assessing candidates technical ability at the interview
D   Informing unsuccessful candidates of the result

Questions 33–35 relate to the following information.

You could use any of the following methods when applying for a job

A   Curriculum vitae
B   Telephone call
C   Application form
D   Letter of application

In the following circumstances, which of these methods would you be most likely to use

Question 33
A speculative application where there is no advertised vacancy

Question 34
A clerical vacancy in the sales department of a local company

Question 35
A senior management position in a national company

Question 36
A person specification is used to:

A   Determine the salary to be paid
B   Identify whether a vacancy exists
C   Identify whether a candidate is suitable for the job
D   Explain what the job entails

Answers to Self-check Questions

1. The corporate plan states the long-term objectives of the organization whilst the manpower plan is designed to ensure that the labour requirements of the corporate plan are met.

2. The organization incurs costs in a number of different areas such as lost production, recruitment and training.

3.
For:	Against
lower costs of recruitment	may cause friction amongst staff
improves employee morale	all organizations need new blood

4. When advertising for a senior management position.

5. Name and details of the employing organization
   The job title and a description of the duties
   Key points in the person specification
   The remuneration package
   How to apply

6. It enables the new employee to settle in to the new organization and quickly become an effective worker.

7. Misconduct
   Inability to do his job

8. Strategies would centre round retraining and redeployment, early retirement or voluntary redundancy.

9. It reflects the lack of bargaining power that they have in negotiations with the employer.

10. It is a conviction that does not, in normal circumstances, have to be revealed to a prospective employer because the rehabilitation period has passed.

11. Express terms are those which have been agreed to by the parties to the contract. Implied terms are inserted into the contract as a result of legislation or common law.

12. Tribunals have a limited jurisdiction, e.g. sex or race discrimination, and were set up to provide a quick and cheap solution to employment 'disputes'.

13. Factories Act 1961
    Health and Safety at Work Act 1974

14. **Industrial objectives**
    to obtain better pay and working conditions for their members
    to ensure security of employment
    to protect the employee from unfair action on the part of the employer

    Political objectives
    industrial democracy
    a say in government
    an acceptable distribution of national income

15. A trade union is an organization whose aim is to protect and promote the interests of its membership by industrial or political means. Staff associations, sometimes referred to as company unions, have very much the same objectives but draw their membership from just one firm.

16. **Craft**
    National Union of Journalists
    Musicians Union

    Industrial
    National Union of Mineworkers
    National Association of Colliery Overmen, Deputies and Shot Firers (NACODS)

General
General Municipal Boilermakers and Allied Trade Union (GMB)
Manufacturing, Science and Finance Union

White collar
National Union of Teachers
National Union of Journalists

17. Women and part-timers are less likely to belong to or become involved in trade union activity.

18. **Collective** bargaining is the process by which workers through their **trade union** representatives negotiate changes to their pay and **conditions of work** with the **employer** or his representative

19.
Procedural clauses	**Substantive clauses**
who is involved in the negotiating	pay and conditions of work health and safety
rules for negotiating	

20. Industrial **democracy** is a term which suggests that workers should be allowed to participate in the **decision-making** process in an attempt to improve employee **motivation**.

21.
	Ownership	Control	Liability	Finance	Formalities
Sole trader	One person	The owner	Unlimited	Self, relatives bank, profits	Few
Partner-ship	Two or more partners	The partners	Unlimited	Partners, profits, banks	Few
Company	Two or more share-holders	The directors	Limited	Shares, profits, banks	Complex to form and run
Co-op-erative	Two or more members	The members (workforce)	Limited	Members profits, banks	Some legal require-ments
Public corpor-ation	The state	The dir-ectors	The state	The state	The nation-alization Act

22. This is a concession given by the owner of patents to another person allowing them to produce and sell these products and services.

23. (a) building; (b) catering; (c) retailing

24. The formal organization refers to the structure a firm adopts in order to achieve its objectives. The informal organization refers to the pattern of relationships which develop to meet the social needs of the workforce.

25. It reveals the chain of command, the formal lines of communication and the extent of specialization within the organization.

26. Personnel staff
    Marketing research staff

27. For delegation to work: the subordinate must have respon-sibility to see that the delegated tasks are carried out satisfactorily; the subordinate must have the authority to carry out these duties; the subordinate must be accountable for performing the work agreed.

28. This is because of the difficulty and complexity of their own and their subordinates' work.

29. Senior directors in other organizations
    Individuals with political influence

30.
    | Physical attributes | Aptitudes |
    | Attainments | Interests |
    | Intelligence | Disposition |
    | Personal circumstances | |

31. The CV is a very general document and the covering letter allows you to identify particular aspects of the CV which you feel qualify you for the job applied for.

32. It ensures all relevant information is obtained.
    It ensures that information is presented in a standard form.

33. To see if the candidate can do the job
    To see if the candidate will 'fit in'
    To give the applicant the chance to see if the job is what they want
    To give a good impression of the organization

34. Your non-verbal communication or body language will have an important impact upon the interviewer. It may confirm, detract from or even negate the impression you are trying to put across.

35. See box, p108.

36. See box, p108.

Answers to Unit Test

Question	Answer	Question	Answer	Question	Answer	Question	Answer	Question	Answer
1	B	9	A	17	B	25	D	33	D
2	A	10	C	18	C	26	A	34	C
3	C	11	C	19	D	27	C	35	A
4	A	12	B	20	B	28	B	36	C
5	B	13	A	21	A	29	C		
6	D	14	C	22	C	30	A		
7	C	15	C	23	C	31	C		
8	C	16	C	24	C	32	C		

Unit Test Comments (Selected questions)

Question 1   B
Industrial tribunals are a quick and cheap alternative to the traditional court structure and are used for many employment disputes.

Question 2   A
Statement 2 is true. An injection of new employees from different backgrounds and with different skills may enable existing employees to see work-related problems in a different light.

Question 3   C
Job descriptions are used as part of the recruitment process.

Question 5   B
The firm is responsible for the health and safety of its employees at work. The role of the Health and Safety Executive is to ensure that these responsibilities are carried out properly.

Question 6   D
Future expansion plans will affect the numbers and skills of employees demanded by the firm.

Question 8   C
Statement 1 is false because the main thrust of work study is to improve the efficiency of the work process.

Question 10   C
The major objective of the trade union is to represent the interests of its members. Raising productivity is a matter of interest to the firm but is not necessarily in the interests of its employees.

Question 11   C
The subject matter of collective bargaining is (1) the procedures by which bargaining is carried out or disputes are settled and (2) the terms of employment. Whilst the employees may wish to make their point of view known on canteen facilities this would be done through joint consultation channels.

Question 15   C
It is the law that states employees should have information on their conditions of employment and pay (and more importantly deductions from pay) as well as being provided with safe working conditions.

Question 16 C
Statement 1 is false because 'a good command of English' may be necessary for some jobs.
Statement 2 is true. It is legal for an Indian restaurant to advertise for Indian employees if this is necessary for the purposes of authenticity – a 'genuine occupational qualification'.

Question 17 B
It is the Equal Pay Act which states that the terms and conditions offered to a woman should be equal to those offered to a man applying for the same job.

Question 18 C
An employee will sue in a normal court alleging the employer has been negligent (law of tort).

Question 19 D
Statement 1: The Limited Partnership Act 1907 states that some partners may have limited liability as long as there is one partner whose liability is unlimited.
Statement 2: The sole trader bears all the financial risk himself but may, in carrying out his business, employs others.

Question 20 B
Manpower planning is to do with the forecasting of the supply and demand for future labour.

Question 22 C
Statement 1: Although many directors will own shares in the company they work for, this is not a legal requirement. It is very unlikely that workers or non-executive directors will own shares.

Question 23 C
Supervisory staff are the link between the workers and middle managers. They are sometimes referred to as junior managers and their responsibility is to supervise 'shopfloor' workers.

Question 24 C
The educational requirement needed for a particular post form part of the person specification.

Question 25 D
Routine work is likely to be undertaken by the clerical staff whereas the (more responsible) writing of a report will be undertaken by a more senior person.

Question 27 C
It would be virtually impossible physically, and a very poor use of time, for a senior manager to carry out appraisals on all employees who are responsible to them. It is normally the immediate superior who would undertake the appraisal interview.

Question 31 C
In view of the specialist nature of the position the most likely option is to use the specialist press.

Question 32 C
Whilst HRD staff may be present at the interview to ensure there is no discrimination, it will be the staff from the department concerned who will assess the candidate's technical ability.

Question 33 D
Although it is possible to use a phone call, a letter of application giving details of education and experience is far more likely to be successful.

Question 35 A
It is unlikely that a standard application form would be suitable having regard to the applicant's varied experience.

Question 36 C
A person specificiation is a development of the job description and outlines the qualities the ideal candidate will have.

UNIT 5

Employment in the Market Economy

Getting Started

In Unit 4 we looked at the relationship between employers and employees in some detail. This unit develops the theme of **employment** but in a rather broader context. In particular we will be looking at how wages are determined in a market economy and how the environment influences wage levels. We look at the different forms of wage payment system and their impact upon motivation and productivity. Finally we consider trends in UK employment and unemployment.

Activity rate The proportion of the working population in paid employment.

Core workers Full time employees who are well paid, highly trained and have a permanent contract and career path within the firm.

Cyclical unemployment Unemployment linked to the downswing of the trade cycle and resulting from a fall in aggregate demand.

Derived demand Where the demand for one product or factor of production is dependent upon the level of demand for a final product or service.

Flexible workforce Attempts by an employer to recruit a workforce that can respond to the changes a firm may face.

Frictional unemployment Short term, search related unemployment.

Fringe benefits Non-financial benefits given by some employers to their employees.

Group technology An alternative to assembly line production techniques. It involves workers completing a whole task in teams.

Hawthorne experiments Experiments carried out by Mayo at the Hawthorne plant of the General Electric Company from which he concluded that employees are motivated by social and physiological factors.

Hierarchy of needs Maslow suggests that 'classes' of needs can be placed in a hierarchy. At any one time one need is dominant, but once it is satisfied it is no longer a motivator. Another need in the hierarchy now becomes dominant.

Homeworking The trend for people to work from home, linked to their office through phone, fax and computer terminal.

Job enlargement An employee is given more work of a similar nature to do.

Job enrichment Employees are given greater responsibilities through undertaking tasks of a more demanding nature.

Job rotation An attempt to reduce boredom by requiring employees to switch jobs.

Measured day work Workers guarantee a long term level of output and in return the employer agrees to pay them for this output, despite short-term fluctuations. It offers pay stability where workers are paid on piece rates.

Merit pay Extra pay awarded to employees for above-average performance.

Payment by results Methods of payment that reward employees for the output produced.

Performance related pay An attempt to relate worker productivity to pay.

Peripheral workers Workers having less job security and few career paths whose employment will be increased or decreased according to demand.

Piece rates Employees are paid at an agreed rate per 'piece' produced.

Scientific management A theory, first suggested by F.W. Taylor, that there is a 'best' way of performing tasks.

Seasonal unemployment Unemployment caused by seasonal variations in demand, e.g. building employees or hotel staff.

Structural unemployment An extreme form of frictional unemployment arising from structural changes in the pattern of demand. Often extremely localized.

Time rates Workers are paid according to the hours worked.

Essential Principles

5.1 Investigate Employment in Business Sectors

The population and its structure is the basis of all economic activity. It not only determines what goods and services are produced but also the number of people who are available to produce them and the technology which will be involved. In this element:

- Changing features of employment are identified using a variety of information sources.
- Employment trends in the UK and European Union (EU) are identified and explained.
- Employment trends within different business sectors are investigated and explained.
- Economic relationships are analysed in relation to different business sectors.
- Economic relationships used to investigate employment trends are explained.

Population size

The **UK population** grew rapidly during the nineteenth and first part of the twentieth century but, as Table 5.1(a) shows, has recently experienced much slower growth. The overall size of the population depends on three factors, namely birth rates, death rates and (net) migration.

Year	Population (millions)
1801	10.5
1851	20.8
1901	38.2
1951	48.8
1981	55.9
2001	57.6

Table 5.1(a)   UK growth of population

The **birth rate** (Table 5.1(b)) is measured as the number of live births per 1000 population. Apart from short-term fluctuations we have seen a gradual reduction in the birth rate from the situation in the nineteenth century, when 25% of all families had nine or more children, to today where less than 2% of families have that number of children.

Year	Birth rate	Death rate
1801	37	27
1851	35	23
1901	25	15
1951	16	13
1971	16	12
1991	13	11

Table 5.1(b)   Births and deaths per thousand of population

The fall in the size of the family can be attributed to factors such as the increasing knowledge and use of contra-ception and the decision by many families to limit the number of children because:

- There is a decline in the mortality rate.
- Children are no longer an investment! (note the abolition of child labour).
- Parents want a higher standard of living.

The second major factor in the population size is the **death rate** (Table 5.1(b)). It is measured in the same way as the birth rate. Since 1900 we have seen a sharp fall in the death rate due to improvements in medicine, hygiene and diet. Put into context it means that the life expectancy of a child born today is over 70 years whereas in 1900 it was 50.

To these natural causes of population change we must add **migration**. For most of this period migration from Britain to its colonies and to America has been an important limiting factor on population growth. It has only been in the periods 1931–1951 and 1981–1991 that the level of immigration has exceeded emigration.

Time period	Average annual change in thousands				
	Live births	Deaths	Net natural change	Net civilian migration	Overall annual change
1901–1911	1,091	624	467	–82	385
1911–1921	975	689	286	–92	194
1921–1931	824	555	268	–67	201
1931–1951	785	598	188	25	213
1951–1961	839	593	246	–9	237
1961–1971	963	639	324	–32	312
1971–1981	736	666	69	–44	25
1981–1991	757	654	103	21	124

Table 5.1(c)   Population change in UK (thousands)

The age structure of the population

The changes in the birth and death rate noted above have had a significant effect on the **age structure** of the UK population. Basically, as Table 5.2 shows us, the UK now has an *ageing population*, and more importantly an *ageing workforce*. That trend is likely to continue. The likely consequences of this are:

- A greater burden is placed on the working population. As the dependent population increases, so does the number receiving state pensions and the demands made on state welfare services – particularly health. If living standards of these groups are to be maintained, each member of the working population must pay that much more in taxes of one kind or another.
- An ageing population is less likely to be geographically or occupationally mobile.
- An ageing population is less likely to save as much. This will mean there is less money available for investment in industry.
- Public sector investment undertaken for a generally younger population will not be appropriate to the needs of an ageing population.

Year	Percentage in each age group		
	0–15	16–65	65+
1911	31	64	5
1951	22	64	14
1991	21	64	15
2011	18	66	16

Table 5.2   UK population – age distribution

		16–24 %	25–34 %	35–44 %	45–59 %	60–64 %
1971	Male	82.2	95.4	96.2	94.8	82.9
	Female	65.0	54.1	59.6	62.0	50.9
1991	Male	80.4	93.8	94.6	87.6	54.3
	Female	71.6	69.7	76.4	66.8	23.9

Table 5.3   UK economic activity rates by age group, 1971 and 1991

The working population

The Department of Employment is responsible for the collection of information on the UK labour market. This information will be used for both manpower and economic planning. Information on vacancies available and industries which are expanding will have implications for courses run by further education colleges and training agencies. Equally, unemployment statistics may be used to make a case for giving help to a particular region or group of employees.

As we can see from Fig. 5.1, of the 28.8 million **working population** over 75% are *employees in employment*. The other two main groups are the *self-employed* and the *unemployed*.

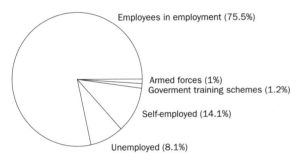

Total workforce 28.8million

Employees in employment (75.5%)
Armed forces (1%)
Goverment training schemes (1.2%)
Self-employed (14.1%)
Unemployed (8.1%)

Fig. 5.1 A break-down (%) of the total workforce

One way of relating labour supply to the working population is to calculate the 'activity rate'. Here we compare the number of people out of a total group who are actually in employment with those who are seeking work. The higher the activity rate, the greater the supply of labour. Out of the total population aged between 16 and 65 years (60 in the case of women) of some 33.5 million, around 4.7 million (15%) are economically inactive, in the sense that they are not seeking paid employment.

Did You Know ?

Women are three times more likely than men to be economically inactive. The major reason for this is that they are looking after the family home and children. The other two important reasons for economic inactivity affect men and women very much the same. They are:

- full-time education
- long-term sickness

From Table 5.3 we can see the economic activity rates for men and women in different age groups. Two trends stand out. First the economic activity rates of men in all groups are falling – young men are staying in education longer and older men are retiring earlier. Second, female activity rates have expanded strongly. In 1961 women formed 32% of the working population compared with 45% in 1994. We will consider the reasons for this below.

Trends in employment

Specialization

Take any job description and you will find that the duties outlined are very specific and limited in scope. Put another way, most of us are **specialists** in our jobs. In fact one of the main reasons for the growth of the UK economy since the industrial revolution has been the increase in job specialization. The advantages of **specialization** include:

- People have different skills. Specialization allows them to concentrate on what they are best at.
- Task repetition improves an employee's skill and efficiency.
- Specialization of task enables sophisticated machinery to be introduced, thus allowing large-scale production and economies of scale

However, specialization does have disadvantages. For example a high degree of specialization may lead to disputes between workers over who should perform a particular task. Another problem is the breaking down of jobs into repetitive tasks. This can cause boredom, low morale and high turnover. As you will see later in this Unit, it is for this reason that many employers are now trying to expand the scope of jobs.

Changes to the UK industrial base

In Unit 1 we noted that the three *sectors* of employment were primary, secondary and tertiary. We also noted that there had been radical changes in the importance of these sectors. Since the industrial revolution the importance of the primary sector as an employer has been declining. By the 1850s the secondary or manufacturing sector was the most important employer. More recently, there has been a shift in employment from the manufacturing to the services sector. This has resulted from increased overseas competition in manufacturing and the use of labour-saving technology and has been termed de-industrialization.

Did You Know ?

Since 1964, the UK has lost over 4 million jobs from the manufacturing sector. However over the same period it has added over 4 million jobs in the service (tertiary) sector. The increase in *unemployment* during this period is partly due to the rise in the number of people seeking a job.

The working week

For many employees earnings are related to the hours worked. For many there is the dilemma that longer working hours produce more money but result in less time in which to spend it. For this reason trade unions have for many years, tried to obtain reductions in the **working week**. Despite a gradual reduction in the working week (approximately 38 hours) the *hours worked* have remained fairly constant, with the displaced hours paid at premium overtime rather than basic rates. From the point of view of the employer this has some advantages, in that there is a built-in flexibility to meet changes in market demand.

Today most employees work a five-day week, though the actual days and hours can vary according to occupation. For example, one of the most important changes in recent years has been the introduction of flexi-time. This is a system by which employees are allowed to vary the hours at which they start and finish work. There is usually a 'core' time – say from 10 am to 4 pm – when everyone is expected to work (apart from lunch!), but the rest of the weekly time requirement can be adjusted to meet the employee's personal circumstances. The great advantage of flexi-time from the employer's point of view is that it reduces absenteeism and improves motivation. Married women with family commitments find the system particularly useful.

Women in the workforce

Perhaps the most significant trend in the latter half of the twentieth century has been the growth of **female employment**. The UK economy has become increasingly dependent on the use of female labour and, for a variety of reasons, that dependence is expected to rise. The reasons for the growth in female employment are many, and include:

- Women have more control over their lives due to contraception. Smaller families and labour-saving kitchen and household gadgets have increased the amount of spare time available to women.

- Social attitudes have moved in favour of the working wife and mother. For many households the woman's wage is an essential part of the family income.

- There has been an increase in one-parent families where the mother has found it necessary to go out to work to support the family.

- There is a trend for women to have children at a later age and to return to their job after the period of statutory maternity leave. This has been made easier through the increased provision of child care.

- Gender discrimination is now unlawful as a result of the Sex Discrimination Act and the Equal Pay Act.

Did You Know ?

Nationality and culture play a large part in determining female employment activity rates. Thus the UK has one of the highest rates in Western Europe, the lowest being recorded by Italy, Spain and Ireland. However, within the UK there are also significant differences. Over two-thirds of white women are part of the working population, compared with only one-third of Asian women.

So far we have looked at the reasons why the *supply* of female labour has increased. The *demand* for women's labour has also increased because:

- Many more young women are going on to further and higher education in order to obtain degrees, diplomas and other professional qualifications, making themselves far more valuable on the labour market.
- The growth of the service sector and more particularly the public sector – health and education – has provided many new jobs suitable for women.
- There has been a growth of part-time jobs. Many women see these as an attractive way of combining paid work with family responsibilities. In 1993 over 45% of all women employees were working part–time (compared with only 6% of men).

Despite changes in attitude toward women in work and anti-discriminatory legislation, women do not earn as much as men; nor (bearing in mind the number of working women) do they hold many of the top jobs in industry or commerce. For example in 1993 women's gross average weekly earnings were less than 75% of their male counterparts – not that different from 1970 when the Equal Pay Act was introduced. Quite apart from sex discrimination, which undoubtedly still exists, there are three major reasons for this earnings discrepancy:

- Many occupations that employ women offer poorly paid and part-time work.
- Women often refuse (for the sake of the family) to work overtime or unsociable hours.
- Women taking career breaks often find that they have to restart their careers on returning to work.

Did You Know ?

In the UK today there are over 5 million female part-time workers, compared to only 900,000 male part-time workers. The large majority (91%) of female part-time workers did not, in fact, want to work full-time. However only 40% of male part-time workers did not want to work full time.

Labour flexibility

Uncertainty about the future is a far greater problem for firms now than, say, 20 years ago. The reasons for this are the rapid changes in:

- technology
- consumer tastes
- economic conditions

One of the responses to this trend is to demand a highly **flexible** workforce. The flexibility that is required is of three kinds:

- *Functional.* The ability to redeploy people between jobs.
- *Numerical.* The ability to hire and fire as market conditions demand.
- *Financial.* The ability to adjust labour costs in line with market forces.

The new employment structure that is developing to meet this requirement for additional flexibility is shown diagrammatically in Fig. 5.2. In this model workers are divided into two groups – core and peripheral. (The key thing to remember is that all the activities undertaken by these workers would previously have been done *within* the firm and most usually by full-time employees.)

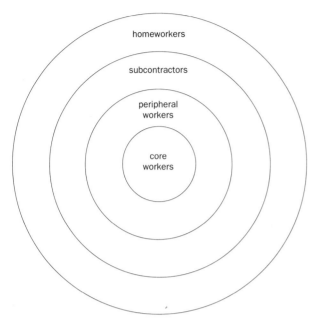

Fig 5.2   A flexible workforce

Core workers

Core workers have the following characteristics:

- small in number
- well paid
- highly trained
- well educated
- permanent contract and career path within the firm

These are the employees, at any level of the organization, who are vital to the firm. Such people will, commonly, be difficult to recruit on the labour market. They are expected, from time-to-time, to switch jobs and even locations. This ensures an element of 'functional' flexibility.

Peripheral workers

All workers not included in the 'core' group are deemed to be **peripheral**. Such workers have the following characteristics:

- less job security
- few career paths
- full time, part-time or temporary contract

The first peripheral group of workers, like the core, is full time. However, unlike the core workers their skills are in plentiful supply on the labour market. The majority of clerical and supervisory workers will fall into this category. As their jobs are routine and offer few career opportunities, labour turnover is quite high, which gives the firm the 'numerical' flexibility it requires.

Still greater functional and numerical flexibility is obtained by the use of *part-time* and *temporary contract* employment, *job sharing* and *subsidized trainees*. Part-time employment, which is the most important of these categories, is widespread in many industries, e.g. retailing,

catering, the teaching and health services. Many clerical and secretarial jobs are also part-time. These jobs often appeal to married women and students.

Subcontracting

As firms have grown larger there has been a tendency to create departments providing specialist help for the organization. A good example would be marketing research. The trend nowadays, however, is for firms to concentrate on their core activities and **buy in** the specialist services they require. In this way considerable savings in overheads and labour costs can be made.

Homeworking

In one way this is a return to the early days of the industrial revolution when certain jobs (which hadn't been mechanized) were put out to domestic workers. Today though, the majority of people working from home whilst remaining employees of the firm are highly skilled and highly paid professionals. Contact with the firm will be maintained by modern communication methods, including phone, fax and computer links. This is another example of the firm trying to limit overhead costs. It also allows women at home with children to continue with their career or rejoin the workforce.

However, despite predictions that this would be a very important trend in future employment patterns, homeworking is less important than anticipated. It is thought that the isolation and lack of human contact has made many people reject this opportunity.

Self-employment

Another major change in employment patterns has been the growth in **self-employment**. From a low of 8% of the workforce being self-employed in 1979, self-employment in 1994 had risen to 14% in the UK or 3.21 million people. This is a larger proportion of the workforce than ever before.

The growth of self-employment, and more generally the small-firm sector, has been a major plank in Conservative policy during the 1980s. The reasons for this are the belief that:

- Small firms are more efficient than large firms.
- Self-employed people are willing to work longer hours for less pay – especially during the early years of their business.
- They adapt to changed business conditions more rapidly than the larger firm.
- They are able to provide goods and services which would be uneconomic for the larger firm.
- They are a source of competition for larger firms.

The growth of self-employment received a major impetus from the recession of the early 1980s when many people were made redundant. Rather than face the 'dole queue' and a long search for alternative employment, many workers used their redundancy pay to set up a small business.

Self-employment also received a boost from firms critically reviewing the extent of their business activities. In many cases they decided to concentrate on 'core' profitable activities. Peripheral activities have been closed down and bought in from subcontractors. Alternatively, these activities have been sold to the employees who sell the service back to their former employer (as well as to other firms). This process of selling part of the business to the employees is commonly termed a 'management buy-out'.

Unemployment

This is one of the major economic problems of the 1980s, with **unemployment** being well over 8% of the working population for much of the period (see Fig. 5.3). If all employees were to experience unemployment equally we would all become unemployed several times in our working lives. In practice that is not the case. During the 1980s the following factors influenced the likelihood of unemployment:

- *Age.* Unemployment hits young people and men over 50 particularly hard.

- *Skills.* Unskilled, manual workers are the most likely to experience unemployment.

- *Ethnicity.* Ethnic minorities are twice as likely to be unemployed as members of the white community.

- *De-industrialization.* Workers in manufacturing industry have experienced greater unemployment than those in the service sector, as manufacturing firms have closed down.

- *Region.* Traditionally, unemployment has been lower in the south-east and higher in the manufacturing regions of the north of England, Ireland and Scotland.

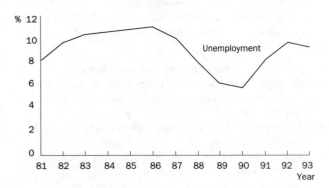

Fig. 5.3   Trends in UK unemployment (as % of labour force)

More recently several other trends have emerged. Thus unemployment caused by the introduction of new technology has begun to hit skilled manual workers. Employees in the tertiary sector and also middle managers have lost jobs as computers have provided a more efficient way of doing their work. Finally the recent emphasis on employee flexibility by firms means that many more employees will be employed on part-time or temporary contracts, thus increasing their vulnerability to unemployment.

Unemployment is classified in a number of ways, for example:

- *Frictional.* This is also termed 'search' unemployment. It is often temporary and occurs in the short time a worker is 'between' jobs.

- *Voluntary.* A situation where unemployment arises because people are unwilling to work at existing wage rates.

- *Seasonal.* The demand for some workers fluctuates with the seasons, e.g. summer work in holiday resorts.

- *Cyclical.* Unemployment caused by fluctuations in the level of economic activity.

- *Structural.* Caused by a change in the *pattern* of demand, this often affects whole industries. It often results in long term and localized (or regional) unemployment. For example, the worldwide decline in demand for merchant ships has been a factor in higher levels of unemployment in the UK shipbuilding industries, causing particular problems in Tyneside, Barrow, Plymouth, Clydeside and other shipbuilding regions.

The impact of technology on employment trends

Changes in **technology** have had a marked influence on employment and employment patterns. The aim here is to summarize some of the more important trends:

- *Productivity.* The increasing use of technology has raised the productivity of workers. Less people are now needed to produce a given level of output.

- *Wages.* Increases in productivity have allowed employers to give higher wages and employees have enjoyed a steady rise in real earnings. However, where wages rise *more than* productivity, labour may price itself out of a job.

- *Wage differentials.* The gap between those with and without skills is widening. Traditional weightings in wage payment systems, example for physical effort, age or experience in the job, are far less important now.

- *Skills.* The level of general education and training required of workers is far greater now. Lower activity rates for young people are a reflection of this need.

- *Security of employment.* Rapid changes in skills requirements lead to a loss of morale and motivation as workers fear for their jobs.

- *Resistance to change.* Employees are likely to resist change because it brings the threat of unemployment; it may very well threaten their status and position in the organization as well as breaking up important social groupings.

- *Retraining.* It is likely that workers will have to be retrained several times in their working life.

- *Unemployment.* There is a mismatch between the skills of the unemployed and what is required by employers. Greater emphasis must be placed on retraining to bring these workers back into the job market.

- *Macro-economic policy.* The use of monetary or fiscal policy to alleviate unemployment may well have little success because of the mismatch of skills.

- *Working conditions.* Initially, technology created many routine, boring jobs.There is now the opportunity to automate those jobs and release the employee for more interesting work. Additionally the physical environment is generally safer. However, nervous strain may increase because of:

  - Lack of control over the pace of operations.
  - The need for constant alertness.
  - Isolation (few other workers employed on the process).
  - Need for shift work (to utilize expensive machinery effectively).

- *Industrial relations.* Potential for conflict is multiplied by rapid change.

Did You Know ?

Every robot employed on automated assembly lines is estimated to replace three workers on average. The current generation of 'intelligent' robots, with heightened sensory powers, is expected to replace between five and ten workers in certain assembly jobs.

Sources of data on the labour market

There is a wealth of data available on the labour market in the UK and Europe. You will find in any research on the UK that the Department of Employment's main publication, the *Employment Gazette,* is a source of regular data on all aspects of employment and unemployment. It often summarizes information from other government departments as well as providing its own survey material. Some of the other more important sources are listed below.

Activity rates

The *General Household Survey* reports show the percentages of economically active persons in the UK by age, sex and, for women, part-time or full-time, by age and according to the number of dependent children.

Similar information, but covering regional trends as well, is given by the *Labour Force Survey.*

Working population

The *Monthly Digest of Statistics* gives details of the working population. It is broken down into male and female employees, the self employed, HM forces and the unemployed.

Seasonally adjusted information is provided in *Economic Trends.*

Employment trends

- *UK National Accounts* estimates employment by sector and industry.

- *Annual Abstract of Statistics* provides information on employees by occupation.

- *Employment Gazette* provides information on part-time employment.

- *Labour Force Survey* provides intermittent information on labour mobility.

Unemployment

The *Employment Gazette* provides the fullest data on a quarterly basis.

The *General Household Survey* reports on the extent of unemployment, the proportion claiming benefit and the reasons they left their last job.

Job satisfaction

The *General Household Survey* provides information on job satisfaction by sex, age, marital status, length of employ-ment and socio-economic group.

Regional Trends in employment

- *Regional Trends*
- *Annual Abstract of Statistics*
- *Scottish Abstract of Statistics*
- *Digest of Welsh Statistics*

Earnings

The *New Earnings Survey* has data on the earnings of people in occupations which demand qualifications and also data on time rates, piece rates and young workers' rates.

The *General Household Survey* shows earnings by highest qualification attained.

The *Reward: Employment Market Survey* shows the earnings of people registered with the Professional and Executive Recruitment Service by age and occupation.

All the sources mentioned above relate to the UK. There are a number of very important other sources. For example, the *Eurostat Labour Force Survey* issued by the Council of the European Commission looks at employment trends within the EU. *Employment in Europe* is a booklet published annually containing articles and statistics on topics of general interest. Finally, both the *Organization for Economic Co-operation and Development* (OECD) and the *International Labour Office* (ILO) provide employment statistics from nearly 200 other countries.

Self Check ✔ **Element 1**

1. What is meant by the term activity rate?

2. Why is an ageing population of concern to a government?

3. Explain the term 'specialization'.

4. From an employer's point of view what are the advantages of flexi-time?

5. State three reasons for the growth of female employment.

6. Employers are demanding far greater labour flexibility. What do you understand by the terms:
   Functional flexibility

   Numerical flexibility

   Financial flexibility

7. Explain the difference between core and peripheral workers.

8. Select an industry of your choice and give an example of a core worker and a peripheral worker.

9. Explain why the government has encouraged self-employment.

10. State one major source of employment information relating to:

    Activity rates

    Employment trends

    Unemployment

    Earnings

    European Union

5.2 Analyse External Influences Relating to Employment

In this element the performance criteria are:

- External influences on business actions relating to employment are analysed and explained.
- Current examples of business actions relating to employment practice are identified.
- Actions taken by business are explained using economic relationships.

The market for labour

In Unit 1 we defined a market as 'the mechanism by which buyers and sellers are brought together'. We also noted that a market exists wherever decisions are made about the quantity supplied and demanded of a product. The **labour market** is no different from any other market – it is the forces of supply and demand which will determine the price of labour.

In practice the market is very complex because

- Workers have different skills and experiences to offer.
- Firms have differing labour requirements (e.g. full-time/part-time).
- Industries are growing or contracting at different rates.
- Labour is often immobile or unaware of job opportunities.
- Trade union activity may influence the level of wage rates in an industry.

The supply of labour

There are many factors which affect the **supply of labour**. We have already noted the importance of the size of the working population, the age/sex composition and activity rates. To these we can also add the length of the working week and the remuneration.

The individual's supply of labour

At an *individual* level the amount of work that a person does is a matter of preference and will be determined by a number of factors such as:

- rates of pay
- levels of expenditure
- lifestyle
- value put on leisure.

It is normally assumed that as wage rates rise, individuals will work more hours. That is not necessarily so. In agreeing to work more hours the individual is in fact saying that the extra pay received is worth more than the leisure time given up (this is an example of opportunity cost). However, as the amount of leisure time becomes increasingly scarce so the value placed upon it becomes higher. Thus workers may reach a stage where they are *not* willing to sacrifice more leisure time whatever the wage rate. In fact, if the wage rate rises beyond this point individuals, having decided to accept this level of income, may reduce the hours actually worked. This is because the workers now earn sufficient from fewer

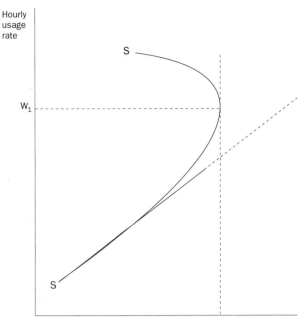

Fig 5.4   Individual Supply (SS) and Total Supply (SS¹) curves for labour

hours, allowing them to work less and take more leisure. This is shown diagrammatically by curve SS in Fig. 5.4. At wages higher than W_1, the number of hours worked (individual's supply of labour) starts to fall.

The total supply of labour to a market

In general terms we can say that the *total* supply of labour to any market will vary directly with the wage rate. At higher wage rates more workers will be available for employment in that market, and vice versa. This is shown by the curve SS^1 in Fig. 5.4 above.

However, in certain circumstances the total supply of labour to a market may be relatively inelastic in the short run. Thus where the nature of the work is highly skilled and requires a considerable period of training, the supply of labour to that market will not rise substantially as wage rates increase. A good example of this is doctors and lawyers. There are other factors which would have the same effect, namely causing a relatively inelastic supply of labour; for example:

* a lack of knowledge
* geographical immobility of labour
* restrictions placed on entry to the trade or profession
* dirty or dangerous jobs

In the *long run*, though, the supply of labour is likely to be more elastic than in the short run, as higher wages encourage people to undertake the necessary training, thus increasing the amount of labour available.

In the case of unskilled labour, supply will tend to be relatively elastic in both the short and the long run because little, if any, training is required.

The demand for labour

The basis on which a firm will decide how many workers to employ is the *demand for the product* which they would be making. Thus, where product demand increases, more workers would be taken on, and vice versa. We can therefore say that the **demand for workers** is a *derived demand* – derived from the demand for the product itself.

Marginal productivity theory

The **marginal productivity theory of labour** suggests that a firm will continue to employ labour until the cost of employing the last, or marginal, worker is the same as the revenue obtained from employing that worker. If we assume that the firm can sell all its output at the market price and that it recruits workers at a constant wage rate, this is easily demonstrated.

Number of workers	Total product (units)	Marginal physical product (units)	Marginal revenue product (£)	Marginal cost (£)	Total revenue product (£)	Total cost (£)	Profit (£)
1	25	25	250	200	250	200	50
2	53	28	280	200	530	400	130
3	87	34	340	200	870	600	270
4	128	41	410	200	1280	800	480
5	174	46	460	200	1740	1000	740
6	215	41	410	200	2150	1200	950
7	248	33	330	200	2480	1400	1080
8	272	24	240	200	2720	1600	1120
9	286	14	140	200	2860	1800	1060
10	289	3	30	200	2890	2000	890

Table 5.4   Various labour market curves (assumption of product price £10, wage £200)

Table 5.4 assumes a constant market price of £10 for the product and a constant wage rate of £200 per week. The second column shows the **total product** or output as a result of employing different numbers of workers. The *addition to total output* arising from the employment of an *extra person* is known as the **marginal physical product** and is shown in the third column. The **marginal revenue product** – i.e. the value of the marginal worker's output – is obtained by multiplying the marginal physical product (the third column) by the product price of £10. The **marginal cost** (fifth column) is the cost of employing the additional worker – in this case £200. The **total revenue product** (sixth column) is the value to the firm of *all* workers' output.

Marginal Revenue Product	=	Marginal Physical Product	×	Price of product

From the table we can see that the addition of subsequent workers after the first adds more to revenue than to costs. As this adds to profits (or reduces losses) it is logical to expand employment. This situation continues until the employment of the eighth worker. The ninth and subsequent workers, however, add more to costs than to revenue, reduce profits and would not be employed.

This may be shown diagrammatically as in Fig. 5.5. For this firm the *marginal cost* line is the **supply curve** which it faces (remember we assumed that the firm could take on as many workers as it wished at a constant wage rate of £200). The downward-sloping part of the *marginal revenue product curve* is the firm's **demand curve for labour.**

At wage rate W_1 the firm will demand (wish to employ) L_1, i.e. the point corresponding to W_1 on the marginal revenue product curve. Only here is the firm maximizing profit with the marginal cost of employing the last person exactly matched by the marginal revenue from employing that person. To employ *more* than L_1 would be to lose money as the extra person adds more to cost than revenue. To employ *less* than L_1 would lose money as the extra person adds more to revenue than cost.

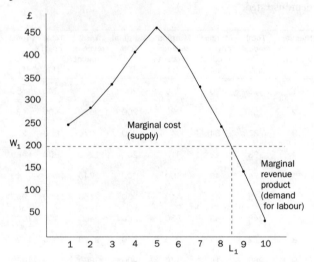

Fig. 5.5   Marginal Revenue Product as the Demand Curve for Labour

The marginal revenue product (demand) curve for labour can, of course, vary in position and shape. Thus a **shift to the right of the curve** – meaning that more labour is demanded at each price – may be caused by:

- An increase in the demand for, and therefore the price of, the final product – remember the demand for labour is a *derived* demand.
- An increase in the productivity of labour, thus raising its marginal physical (and therefore revenue) product.

The *elasticity* of the **demand curve for labour** depends upon:

- *Demand for the final product.* For example, if the demand for the final product is relatively inelastic, so will be the demand for labour. Suppose there is an increase in the wages of skilled workers in an industry providing a basic product such as gas or electricity. This is likely to be passed on to the consumer (rather than leading to a reduction in the number of workers employed) because a rise in the price of this product is not likely to lead to a large reduction in the quantity demanded.

- **The percentage of total costs attributable to labour.** Where labour costs form only a small proportion of total costs, demand for labour will be relatively inelastic. A rise in the price of labour will not, then, result in a large reduction in the quantity of labour demanded. Conversely, where labour costs are a high proportion of total costs, a small increase in the wage rate may have a significant effect on total costs and therefore on the selling price of the product. The firm will therefore look at different production methods, perhaps using more capital to avoid these increases in labour costs. As a result the demand for labour will fall.

- *The ease of substitution.* The extent to which it is possible to switch capital for labour is an important determinant of the elasticity of demand for labour. Thus in the engineering industry, skilled craftsmen earning high wages have been replaced by computerized machines. So far, though, it has been rather difficult to replace the skill, and mechanize the work, of doctors, dentists, lawyers, policemen, nurses or teachers. The demand for the labour of these groups is therefore relatively inelastic.

Wage determination

So far we have looked at supply and demand separately. By combining the two – as we did in Unit 1 – it is possible to see how the **wage rate**, i.e. the price of labour, is determined. Given a free market, as we can see from Fig. 5.6, only one wage rate is sustainable. This is the wage where the supply of labour is exactly equal to the demand for labour (W in Fig. 5.6). Of course that wage will vary in different markets. Thus the higher equilibrium wage rate in one market is due to the fact that at any given wage rate the demand for labour is greater and/or the supply of labour is lower than in another labour market (see Fig. 5.7). The reasons for this are discussed below.

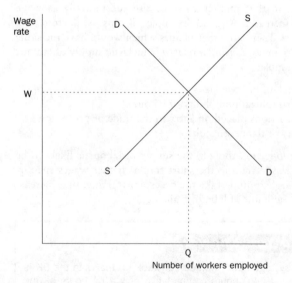

Figs 5.6   Finding the equilibrium wage rate.

In Fig. 5.7 the very low supply curve of labour, S_1, is the main reason why the wage rate W_1 is higher in this labour market.

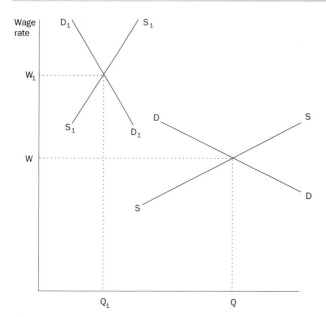

Fig. 5.7 Different labour markets have different equilibrium wage rates.

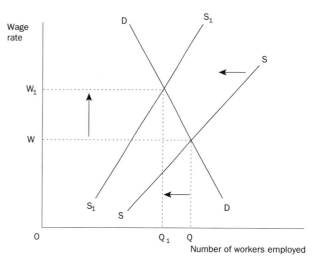

Fig. 5.8 Supply restriction by a union raises equilibrium wage to W_1 but reduces employment to Q_1.

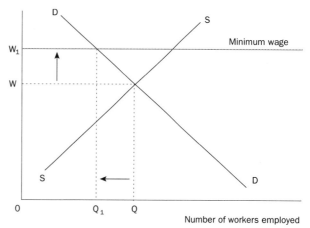

Fig. 5.9 Setting a minimum wage *above* the equilibrium wage; raises wages but reduces employment

Labour market imperfections

If the forces of supply and demand were to work properly we would see wage rates in different occupations and industries rising and falling in response to changes in those forces. We would also see one wage rate for a particular job applying throughout the UK. In practice this fails to happen because of certain **market imperfections**. Some of these imperfections we have already noted. Thus lack of information on job opportunities or family ties (geographical immobility) may result in, say, mechanics *not* moving from low wage regions to high wage regions. Because they do not move, the wage differential can continue. We will consider two sources of labour market imperfections – trade unions and government interference.

The role of trade unions

Trade unions have considerable influence in the labour market. Their behaviour is determined by their objectives. In Unit 4 we saw that two important objectives were to raise the living standards (wage rates) of their members and to increase (or at least maintain) the numbers employed. There are three possibilities – restricting the supply of labour, securing a minimum wage, or shifting the demand curve for labour to the right.

- *Supply restrictions*
  If a trade union or a professional association restricts the entry into that occupation, e.g. by agreements to limit new entrants and to maintain closed shops, then the wages received by its members will be increased. However, the number of members employed in that occupation will be reduced. In Fig. 5.8 entry restrictions result in a shift in the supply curve to the left, from SS to S_1S_1. As a result wages rise from W to W_1 but employment falls from Q to Q_1.

- *Minimum wages*
  Many trade unions negotiate **minimum wage** deals with the employers. If, as in Fig. 5.9, these are *above* the

market equilibrium then the majority of members will benefit from the increase in wages (W to W_1) but a minority will lose their jobs (Q to Q_1).

Did You Know ?

The trade union's power to negotiate successfully on behalf of its members is dependent on:-

- **The elasticity of demand for labour.** The more inelastic the demand for labour, the greater is the union power because higher wages don't result in many members losing their jobs.
- **The ability to recruit and organize workers.** Where union membership is high, sanctions against employers are likely to be more effective.
- **External factors.** These range from the state of the economy to the attitude of the government to union activity.

- *Increased demand for labour*
  Trade unions will support any measures by the employer to improve sales of the product (e.g. an advertising campaign) as this will increase the demand for labour. They may also be prepared to negotiate productivity deals. In an expanding market the trade union not only

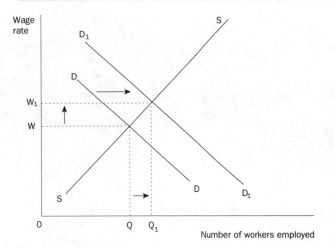

Fig. 5.10 Increased demand for labour raises wages and employment

obtains higher wages for its members but will also obtain new recruits (see Fig. 5.10). The increased demand for labour from D to D₁, raises wages from W to W₁, and raises employment from Q to Q₁.

Government interference

Like trade unions, the **government** has considerable influence in the labour market. For example, health and safety legislation and employment protection legislation significantly affect the environment within which business operates. Even though labour's marginal productivity has not changed, industry's demand for labour has probably fallen as a result of the restrictions on a firm's ability to hire, use and fire labour as it wishes. Equally, taxes on labour such as National Insurance contributions, increase the cost of employment and therefore shift the demand curve for labour to the left.

- *Minimum wage legislation*
  Some economists believe that government attempts to establish minimum wages – through, for example, Wages Councils – are counterproductive. Fig. 5.9 earlier illustrates this point with the minimum wage being above the market equilibrium. As a result the demand for labour and for the final product or service is *less* than in a free market.

- *Unemployment benefits*
  It is sometimes argued that unemployment benefits act as a floor to wage rates. Once again figure 5.9 can be used to illustrate this point. Suppose W₁ this time represents the average level of *unemployment benefits*; it is rational for the unemployed person to refuse any offer of employment which offers a lower wage. In Fig. 5.9,

---

Did You Know ?

The abolition of Wages Councils in 1993, which fixed pay in industries such as catering, retailing, hairdressing and laundering, is likely to lead to a reduction in wage levels in these industries. As these industries are predominantly employers of female labour, still wider wage differentials between men and women may occur. (Out of the 2 million low paid workers, 80% are women.)

---

unemployment benefits would have to fall from W₁ to W if the equilibrium level of employment, Q, is to be achieved. The Conservative government, since 1979, has abolished Wages Councils (which fixed pay for the low paid) and reduced unemployment benefit (in real terms) in an attempt to increase the supply of labour and reduce voluntary unemployment.

Wage differentials

The major reasons for the existence of **wage differentials** are the particular characteristics of individual employees and the industry in which they are working. By **individual characteristics** we are referring to the particular skills and aptitudes each of us has. It's not surprising that the person who has inherited certain skills which are in high demand but short supply, for example musical or sporting skills, should be able to earn a higher wage. Nor is it surprising that people who go to the trouble of acquiring specialist skills should be paid more. People in the top 10% of earners receive, on average, six times more than those in the lowest paid 10%.

The second major reason for the difference in wages is the **industry in which one works**. Industries will expand or contract according to the demand for the products they produce. Employment in the industry will also expand or contract in line with its prosperity. You will also find that as industries expand and their demand for labour rises, so do wages. Conversely, relative wages will fall as the industry contracts.

There are three other reasons for wage differentials which we should mention:

- *Age.* It is generally thought that people get paid more as they get older. That is certainly true for the first 25 years of working life. However, for many employees in mid-life wages reach a plateau and stop rising. For manual workers this may be as young as 40 years, for non-manual workers 50 years.

- *Sex.* As a woman you are likely to earn considerably less than a man in any industry or any occupation. The reasons for this have already been discussed.

- *Region.* On average, wages tend to be highest in London and the South East of England. In part this reflects the difficulty employers have had, in the past, obtaining qualified employees. It is also a result of the industries in this area expanding rather than contracting.

External influences on employment

The government
In 1979 a new, radical Conservative government was elected. Since that time there have been a number of significant changes relating to the employment market. For example:

- The goal of full employment has been abandoned.
- Collective bargaining at a national level is being replaced by local bargaining. Individual pay bargaining has also been encouraged.
- The growth of single union deals, 'legally' binding contracts (including 'no strike' clauses) and pendulum arbitration have been encouraged.
- Employee share ownership schemes have been

encouraged so that employees identify themselves more closely with the organization's objectives.

- The inadequacy of training in British industry has been recognized and various schemes to meet the problems of skill shortages and unemployment have been introduced.
- Privatization has significantly reduced the size of the public sector. The pursuit of efficiency and profitability has reduced the level of employment, and the security of employment, in these industries.
- Public sector pay increases have been squeezed as the government has sought to influence the level of pay deals in other sectors of the economy.
- Attempts have been made to 'encourage' people back into work by reducing the level of unemployment and social security benefits.
- There has been a reduction in 'protective' legislation, particularly as it relates to small firms, in an attempt to encourage the growth of employment in that area.

However, it is in relation to trade unions that the changes have been most significant. The Conservatives came to power in 1979 with a mandate to curb excessive trade union power. Their dislike of unions arises from a belief that they prevent the proper operation of the market for labour and thereby cause unemployment. This may happen in one of two ways:

- By obtaining wage rises for their members above the market rate they reduce the willingness and the ability of the employer to replace employees that leave or to take on extra staff. Politicians claim that British workers are being 'priced out of jobs' or that jobs are being 'exported' to other countries as a result of the high wage demands of unions.
- Trade unions have resisted improvements in efficiency by attempting to maintain existing working practices, closed shops and rigid job demarcation. Whilst these activities benefited their members in the short term, over a longer period they have contributed to higher costs and prices which, in turn, have led to lower sales and employment.

In the last fifteen years there have been a number of Acts which have been designed to curb union power. The major thrust has been to reduce the immunity of unions from legal action awarded by the Trades Disputes Act 1906 and to make unions liable for the actions of their members. The main Acts are described below:

Employment Act 1980
- Picketing, other than at the place of employment, was made illegal.
- Alternative forms of 'secondary' action, e.g. the 'blacking' of goods, were restricted.
- The introduction of closed shops was made more difficult.
- It became more difficult for an employer to sack someone who refused to join a closed shop.
- State funds were made available for secret ballots.

Employment Act 1982
This Act reviewed and limited the definition of a trade dispute and made unions liable for the unlawful acts of their members. In particular:

- Demarcation disputes were made illegal.

- Disputes must relate to 'employment matters' – this was an attempt to prevent political strikes.
- Unions could now be sued in their own name. Previously, it was only union officials who could be sued for organizing unlawful industrial action.

Employment Act 1984
- Union leaders have to be elected (and re-elected) by secret ballot.
- Secret ballots are required *before* industrial action, in order to maintain immunity from legal action.
- Secret ballots are required for expenditure on political activities.

Employment Act 1988
- Trade union members have the right to prevent industrial action where it has not been authorised by secret ballot.
- Union members cannot be disciplined for not taking part in industrial action.
- Enforcing a closed shop by industrial action is illegal.
- Dismissal by an employer for refusing to belong to a closed shop is unlawful.
- Postal ballots must be held for the election and re-election of all union executive members.
- Members can inspect the union's financial records and take legal action to prevent the unlawful use of funds.

Employment Act 1990
- It is unlawful for an employer to refuse anyone employment because they are not union members.
- Unions are legally responsible for unofficial strikes called by any union official.
- All secondary action is unlawful.

Trade Union Reform Act and Employment Rights Act 1992
This gave all employees the right:

- To a written statement setting out the main conditions of their employment.
- Of every woman to 14 weeks' maternity leave and to be protected from losing her job.
- Of all safety representatives not to be dismissed for carrying out their duties under the Health and Safety at Work Act.
- To have disputes with the employer over the contract of employment settled by industrial tribunal.

It also gave trade union members the right:

- To decide which union to join.
- To an independently scrutinized postal ballot before any strike.
- To protection against union funds mismanagement.
- To protection against fraud or abuse in union elections.
  - To decide whether union subscriptions should be collected by automatic deduction from pay.

For many years it was thought that the UK *voluntary* system of industrial relations could not be effectively regulated through *legislation* – that was certainly the message from the Conservatives' ill-fated 1971 Industrial Relations Act. However, the more gradualist approach to legislation taken since 1979 against a background of two recessions has proved very much more successful. If one takes the number of days lost through strikes each year as a measure of success, then during the 1970s nearly 13 million days were lost each year compared with less than 2 million in the period 1986–94.

The European Union (EU)

There are a number of ways in which the EU is affecting employment amongst its members. For example, since 1973 there have been attempts to create extra work in areas of high unemployment. This currently takes a number of forms including:

- The **European Regional Development Fund.** This provides financial help for business and also to local government for infrastructure projects such as road improvements.
- The **European Social Fund.** This provides funds for assisting the long term unemployed, the disabled and young people back into the labour market through training schemes.
- The **European Investment Bank.** This provides loans for firms wishing to set up or expand in depressed areas.

The UK has received nearly £1000 million from the EU in the last five years under these schemes.

The **Single European** Act which came into force in 1993 is also likely to have a wide ranging impact upon employment. This Act is designed to create a single competitive market throughout the EU by reducing physical, technical, administrative and fiscal barriers. It is predicted that:

- The structure of industry will change to reflect the 'specialisms' of different countries. Firms will not be able to rely on a 'soft' home market for survival anymore.
- Many overseas firms located outside the EU will locate production units within the Single Market area to avoid paying the Common External Tariff.
- An additional 1.3 to 2.3 million jobs will be created within the market as a result of efficiency gains and access to an enlarged market.

Did You Know ?

The Single Market in Europe gives companies access to a tariff-free, high income market of over 375 million people (more when the new entrants join the EU). This market is responsible for over 40% of world trade and 30% of world population. All *non-members* face a common external tariff on their sales to the EU.

There is no prediction, though, as to which of the member states is going to gain from these changes (though there is some evidence that the UK is benefiting from foreign business investment).

In 1992 the Maastricht Treaty was signed by all member states. Part of the treaty was termed the **Social Chapter.** Its aim was to standardize working conditions throughout the EU. The UK government was strongly opposed to the basic rights guaranteed by the document and obtained an opt-out clause. Thus workers in the UK are less well protected than their European counterparts. You will find that the poorest workers in this country will be paid considerably less and have poorer working conditions than those in the rest of the EU who are protected by the Social Chapter. However, on the plus side, a low-wage economy may encourage certain low-skill, labour-intensive firms to relocate to the UK.

Did You Know ?

Currently *non-wage costs* per unit of output are three times higher per unit of output in Germany than in the US, and more than twice as high in Germany, France and Italy than they are in the UK. 'Non-wage costs' include the various costs associated with hiring labour *other than* the wage rate; e.g. employer's National Insurance, health and safety, working conditions, etc.

Competition

Competition is one of the cornerstones of free enterprise. It is admired because of its impact on prices, efficiency and innovation. Competition means that no firm is able to control the market and thereby prices and profits. Indeed in an attempt to improve profitability the firm will seek ways to improve the efficiency with which the product is produced. They will also be looking for those new or improved products which will give them the competitive edge in the future. In this way we see that competition also has the effect of making the future (and therefore employment) very much more uncertain than either the firm or its employees would like.

According to M.E. Porter the *level of competition* in an industry depends on five factors. These are:

- *Barriers to entry.* These include economies of large scale production, patents, brand strengths and capital requirements. Most firms will try to create barriers to entry in order to prevent new firms entering the market.

- *Threats of substitutes.* The availability of rival products or the degree of buyer loyalty will determine the extent to which customers will switch to substitute products.

- *Bargaining power of suppliers.* Factors like the availability of substitute *inputs* and the degree of concentration in the industry affect the power that suppliers have over the future of the firms in an industry.

- *Bargaining power of buyers.* Factors like the volume of purchases, the knowledge of and availability of substitute products, determine the degree of influence that *buyers* will have in that industry.

- *Rivalry amongst competitors.* Factors like the rate of industry growth and the extent of product differentiation will determine the level of competition amongst the firms in the industry.

These five forces determine the degree of competition facing any firm. Firms will try to *reduce* competition to an acceptable level in a number of ways. For example the firm may:

- Move into other markets where competition is less intense.
- Integrate 'vertically backwards' and buy one or more of its suppliers so as to guarantee supplies of inputs.
- Integrate 'vertically forwards' and purchase one or more of the outlets for its products, thus ensuring a certain level of sales.
- Integrate 'horizontally' by buying up one or more of its competitors.

Attempts to reduce competition in this manner are limited by the government's and the EU's legislation to ensure competition in all markets. This is discussed in Unit 1.

As an alternative, Porter suggests that the firm must devise a strategy which gives it a *competitive advantage* in the market. He suggests that there are three options:

- *The cost leadership strategy.* This requires the firm to be the recognized cost leader within the industry. Additionally the product must be perceived as comparable with that offered by its rivals. Cost leadership will be obtained through economies of scale, operational efficiency, technological innovation or access to low cost inputs (e.g. cheap labour).

- *The differentiation strategy.* Here a firm seeks to be unique in an industry in ways which are highly valued by its customers. The uniqueness may relate to high quality, superior service, innovatory design or a very strong brand image. The key to success in this strategy is that the attribute chosen must distinguish the firm from its competitors and be significant enough to justify the price premium.

- *The focus strategy.* Here the firm seeks to obtain a competitive advantage through either the cost strategy or differentiation strategy, but in one or a limited number of *segments* in the market. The firm effectively tailors its strategy to *specific* product varieties, end users, distribution channels or geographical locations of buyers.

Porter uses the phrase 'stuck in the middle' to describe organizations that are unable to achieve competitive advantage through one of these strategies. These organizations will find it very hard to achieve long term success. Many small organizations, whose success has been founded on a focus strategy, find themselves 'stuck in the middle' as they grow too big for that strategy and yet are still too small to achieve cost leadership.

However, even successful organizations do not always survive in the longer term. Each year in January the *Financial Times* produces a list of the UK top 500 firms. A comparison of the list today with even ten years ago will show some marked changes.

Our conclusion must be that competition introduces an element of uncertainty into the labour market. Employees cannot, today, be guaranteed long-term security of employment – not just because there is no guarantee of the long-term survival of the firm but also because the firm in its search for success may revise its product lines or its production methods.

Self Check ✔ **Element 2**

11. Explain why, with higher hourly rates of pay, an individual may work fewer rather than more hours.

12. Why is the demand for labour a derived demand? Explain the implications of this.

13. Fill in the gaps in Table 5.5 below. The price of the product is assumed to be constant at £5 per unit.

14. Why is the labour market often described as 'imperfect'?

15. Why would a trade union prefer a situation where the demand for its members' labour was inelastic?

16. Why is it likely that the abolition of minimum wage legislation will adversely affect the average earnings of female labour?

17. Why was the policy of full employment abandoned by the government in 1979?

Number of workers	Total product (units)	Marginal physical product (units)	Marginal revenue product (£)	Marginal cost (£)	Total revenue product (£)	Total cost (£)	Profit (£)
1	18	18	90	100	90	100	–10
2	41	23	115	100	205	200	5
3	70			100		300	
4	106			100		400	
5	147			100		500	
6	190			100		600	
7	220			100		700	
8	241			100		800	
9	255			100		900	
10	261			100		1000	

Table 5.5

Self Check ✔ **Element 2** *continued*

18. State one way in which trade unions are said to cause unemployment.

_____

_____

19. In general terms how has recent legislation curtailed the power of trade unions?

_____

_____

_____

_____

20. Why has the British government been opposed to the Social Chapter of the Maastricht Treaty?

_____

_____

_____

_____

21. In relation to employment, state two benefits and two problems arising from technological change.

_____

_____

_____

_____

_____

_____

_____

5.3 Evaluate the Workforce Performance of Business Sectors

In this element the performance criteria are:

* Features of the workforce performance of different business sectors are identified.
* Data relating to workforce performance of business is accessed from a variety of sources.
* Economic relationships are used to analyse the workforce performance of business.

Motivation

Management writers have been interested for many years in the subject of **motivation**. This is because managers are responsible for a job which is too big for them to undertake themselves. In having to work through other people, it is necessary that managers understand worker behaviour and find ways of persuading them to act positively and for the benefit of the organization. There are a number of *writers* who have made an important contribution.

F.W. Taylor

Working around the turn of the century, Taylor was concerned at the inefficiency he saw in industry. Taylor stressed the importance of the planning, organization and supervision of work by *managers*. He viewed workers as being closely linked to their machines and whose output could be improved by

* Establishing what was the correct way to do the job through work study.
* Motivating them to produce, via high wages and incentive payments.

Whilst Taylor's approach to motivation is seen today as naive, money is an important motivator and the development of incentive payment systems is still often used as a motivator.

E. Mayo

Mayo's great contribution to the understanding of motivation arose through his experiments at the Hawthorne plant of the Western Electric Company in the US. Mayo carried out a study on the link between different working conditions and productivity. The results indicated that there was little in the way of a link between the two. In fact output even rose when conditions were worsened!

Mayo argued that worker attitudes toward employment were more influenced by the *social context* of the job than by money or other incentives. In the study above, he argued that motivation was high because of social and psychological factors. The experimental group of workers not only became good friends as a result of their shared experiences but also felt that what they said and did was recognized as being important. Mayo concluded – very differently from FW Taylor – that:

* People are motivated by social needs.
* Division of labour and specialization had destroyed much of the earlier meaning of work. This was now found in the social context of work.
* Work groups have more impact on employee motivation than organizational incentives and controls.
* In order to harness employee effort to the needs of the organization, the manager must ensure that the workers' social needs are met.

Whilst Mayo's contribution to the understanding of employee motivation should not be underestimated, all too often the improvements in motivation expected as a result of the application of his ideas failed to materialize. The link between motivation and productivity was far more complex than he suggested.

A. Maslow

Maslow argues that workers have a *hierarchy of needs* (see Fig. 5.11). The first three needs – physiological, safety and social – are termed *lower order needs* and are likely to be met from the context within which the job is undertaken. Self-esteem and self-actualization (the realization of one's potential) are very important *higher order needs* and will be met through the content of the job.

At any one time one need is dominant and can be considered as a *motivator*. Once that need is satisfied, though, it is no longer dominant or a motivator. It will be replaced by a higher order need which is still to be satisfied.

For managers, the implications of this theory are that they must try to satisfy the needs of their subordinates within an organizational context. Some examples of how they can do this are shown in Table 5.6.

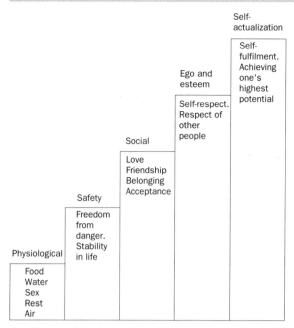

Fig. 5.11 Maslow's hierarchy of needs

Need	Example
Physiological	Pay; rest periods, canteens; holidays
Safety	Health and safety measures; security of employment; pensions
Social	Formal and informal groups; organized social events; sports clubs
Ego and esteem	Power; titles; status symbols; merit awards; promotion
Self-actualization	Challenging work; developing new skills

Table 5.6 Methods of satisfying employee needs

D. McGregor

In analyzing formal organizations McGregor suggested that there were two broad approaches to the motivation of workers which were based on very different assumptions. These he labelled theory X and theory Y. (This model can be very useful to you when visiting and observing an organization.) Theory X adopts a number of rather *negative*

Did You Know ?

You must be able to understand the difference between a *symptom* and a *cause* of poor motivation. The symptom is an outward manifestation of a deeper rooted problem. In a work situation you will often find that absenteeism, sickness, making mistakes, a lack of pride in work and sullen acquiescence to orders are symptoms of the problem. Our reading on motivation should tell us that these are some of the likely causes of poor motivation.

- unsatisfactory pay
- poor working conditions
- boring jobs
- changes in work or working conditions
- unsatisfactory social relationships
- changes in work groups
- poor communication between management and workers

---

assumptions about employees and is based very much on F.W. Taylor's ideas. These include:

- Man dislikes work and avoids it if he can.
- Man wishes to avoid responsibility and prefers to be told what to do.
- Man demands security above all else.

In these circumstances the role of the manager is to direct and control the employees' efforts, ensuring they meet organizational objectives through threats of punishment as well as wage payment incentive schemes.

Contrast this with theory Y which is based on a much more *positive* set of assumptions about workers. These include:

- Man enjoys work and finds satisfaction in it.
- Man accepts and seeks responsibility.
- Man can be committed to work for organizational objectives without the threat of punishment.
- The typical job uses only a small part of the average worker's potential.

The role of the manager here is to provide an environment in which employees can achieve their own goals whilst at the same time achieving organizational objectives. To achieve this the organization would be structured to allow employees to 'manage themselves' and allow more participation in decision making.

However, it is almost impossible to develop an organization where all jobs are challenging and interesting whilst at the same time achieving the high levels of efficiency needed for success. In these circumstances 'theory Y' workers will quickly become disenchanted with the restrictions that are placed on their natural enthusiasm. Poor morale, low motivation as well as absenteeism, high labour turnover and poor industrial relations will result.

Paradoxically, all this negative behaviour would confirm the theory X manager in his belief that he was right to treat these workers according to theory X assumptions. In this way assumptions that managers make about their workers tend to become *self-fulfilling prophecies*!

Money as a motivator

It is not always clear how important **money** is to the individual as a motivating influence. To a young married person with a family it is probably very important. To an older person with few financial commitments there are probably other more important motivators. However, for many firms it is an important part of their motivation package. We will look at the most popular **wage payment schemes**.

Time rates

With time rates, wages are paid on an hourly rate. **Time rates** will be used where:

- High quality work is essential.
- The work cannot be speeded up.
- There is no standard type of work.
- Output cannot be measured.

Time rates have certain disadvantages. For example, there is a lack of incentive for better workers, supervision of workers is usually necessary and output may be limited by 'go slow' or working to rule tactics.

Piece rates

With piece rates, output is measurable and roughly proportional to the amount of effort used. **Piece rates** may be used to reward the individual or a group of workers. The advantages of piece rates are:

- Greater effort is encouraged.
- More efficient workers are rewarded.
- Workers work at a pace which suits them.
- Constant supervision is not needed.
- Output is increased and expensive machinery is used more intensively (thus spreading overheads).

Against these advantages we must put the disadvantages. These include the possibility of workers over-exerting themselves, variations in wages earned being a source of discontent amongst workers, and discontent when workers' output (and therefore wages) is limited due to a fall in product demand.

Measured day work

This is a system where the employer and the employee agree a level of output which both believe can be achieved in the long term. The employer then agrees to pay the worker for this level of output regardless of short-term variations in productivity. Thus, workers are able to predict what their earnings are going to be and the employer is able to predict the level of productivity. Moreover as the employer is paying the 'high rate' regardless of the level of output there is an incentive for him to ensure that machines do not break down.

You should be able to distinguish between the following terms:

- *Wages.* Paid on a weekly basis and calculated on a time or piece work basis.
- *Salaries.* An annual salary is agreed which is then paid on a monthly basis.
- *Earnings.* What an individual takes home after statutory deductions such as income tax. It would also include any bonuses paid.
- *Nominal wages.* The amount of money the worker actually receives.
- *Real wages.* The true value of the wages after taking inflation into account.

Merit pay

Basically, extra money is awarded for what is seen as above-average effort. It has fallen into disrepute because judgements are subjective and difficult to measure.

Performance-related pay

Like merit pay this is another attempt to reward, or motivate, indirect workers whose output is not easily measurable. It is often linked to a system of annual appraisal where a number of measurable objectives are agreed between the superior and subordinate. Increases in pay are

linked to the achievement of these objectives (performance appraisal is dealt with in Unit 3).

PRP, as it is often referred to, has been supported by the Conservative government as a means of moving away from nationally negotiated agreements to a system where contracts are negotiated individually. This system can be used for employees at any level in the workforce.

Profit sharing schemes

Organizations such as ICI or John Lewis give a proportion of their profits to their employees in the belief that it encourages effort, loyalty and co-operation. The main disadvantages are that the system of distribution may not be seen as fair, that the annual reward is too remote to affect behaviour and that profits can be affected by factors outside the workers' control.

Fringe benefits

Some organizations offer non-financial benefits to their employees. These are termed **fringe benefits** or 'perks for the job' and are paid over and above the basic salary. These benefits may include house purchase, life or medical insurance, company cars, loans, subsidized transport, sports facilities, cheap holidays and share option schemes. It is estimated that these benefits constitute approximately 30% of the total payroll bill.

Fringe benefits can be a tax-effective way of rewarding employees as well as increasing loyalty and staff satisfaction. However, the benefits offered may not be appreciated or appropriate to the needs of all employees.

Other steps to motivate workers

Although money is an important motivator for many people our study of motivation would suggest that a good manager could motivate his subordinates in a number of other ways, which include:

- Ensuring that working conditions are adequate.
- Ensuring that the employees have been properly trained for their job.
- Developing (a mutually supportive) team spirit.
- Providing the employee with the means to measure how well he is doing.
- Improving the workers self-esteem by recognizing and celebrating achievement or through involvement in decision making.
- Ensuring good vertical communication both upwards and downwards
- Ensuring the job is challenging (even in routine jobs) by means of job rotation, job enlargement and job enrichment. These are dealt with in more detail below.

The link between job design and motivation

One of the major criticisms of the Industrial Revolution and the growth of large scale or mass production techniques was that it often reduced work to small repetitive tasks. Put another way, the division of labour and specialization of tasks has created many mundane and boring jobs with the result that:

- Workforce potential is not being fully realized.
- The workers gain little satisfaction from their job and in the longer term this may lead to frustration, absenteeism and high labour turnover.

We will look at some of the more successful methods of restructuring work.

Job rotation

This is the most basic form of redesign and involves training staff in a number of different skills so that they can then be rotated between jobs. Whilst job interest is maintained by rotation, too frequent changes may be counterproductive as social relationships are disrupted. **Rotation** is really only of value when other alternatives are not possible.

Job enlargement

This involves widening the duties of the employee, thus making jobs less repetitive. For example, where an operation is divided into a number of small repetitive tasks each undertaken by a different employee it would be possible to ask the worker to carry out a *number* of these tasks. Whilst cynics would argue that you are replacing one boring job by three or four more, there are many examples where 'enlargement' has reduced labour turnover and increased productivity.

Job enrichment

This is significantly different from job rotation and enlargement in that the employee is involved in the planning, organizing and controlling of a task. Thus with **job enrichment** an employee may be given tasks such as:

- planning and prioritising work
- quality control
- being responsible for a particular group of customers
- ordering materials
- maintenance of machinery

These tasks which are a challenge and will develop unutilised skills offer scope for fulfilling Maslow's higher level needs, namely ego/esteem and self actualisation.

Group technology

Initially introduced by Volvo in Sweden to counter labour relations problems, this is now a popular alternative to assembly line production techniques. Under this system **groups of workers** are given a 'whole' job to do, for example building an engine. Management will inform the group what their target is. The group is then left to decide how to plan the work, ensure quality, order materials and maintain equipment. By 1977, just three years after its introduction, the plant adopting 'group technology' was the most efficient of Volvo's Swedish car plants. Labour turnover fell and job satisfaction rose dramatically.

Productivity

One of the major reasons that employers are willing to invest so much time in redesigning jobs is that they believe that a happy or motivated worker is a more **productive** worker. (In practice the link between motivation and productivity is very much more complex.) In a market economy where firms are competing directly against one another, productivity is particularly important. The firm that is highly efficient or productive will be able to provide the product or service to the consumer at a lower price than its competitors. In that way it guarantees its survival and profitability.

Did You Know ?

UK output per person employed in *manufacturing* is today over $2\frac{1}{2}$ times as high as it was in 1964. For *service* industries, however, the productivity gain has been much smaller. However information technology is revolutionising many service activities (e.g. the office) and large productivity gains are now being experienced there.

Measuring productivity

Productivity shows the relationship between the output of the organization and its inputs – labour, capital and materials. It is normally expressed as a ratio:

$$\text{productivity} = \frac{\text{output}}{\text{labour, capital, materials}}$$

This is termed a *multi-factor* ratio and looks at the overall efficiency of the organization.

Of more importance to the organization are the productivity ratios relating to a *single* input. Thus, **labour productivity** could be measured by comparing the output against the number of employees:

$$\text{productivity} = \frac{\text{output per period}}{\text{number of employees per period}}$$

There are many variations on this ratio. For example, where a number of differently priced products are produced it will be the *value* of output rather than physical output which will be measured. Another common variation is to measure the productivity of a *group of workers* involved in a particular operation. Productivity ratios can be used in a number of ways:

- To detect trends in the level of productivity over time.
- To detect trends in the levels of productivity between different plants.
- To use in negotiations with trade unions over wage rates, or with management over extra resources.

Did You Know ?

We can also try to measure the productivity of the *national economy* in much the same way. Thus:

$$\text{productivity} = \frac{\text{gross national product}}{\text{total population}}$$

GNP per head of population is a measure of comparison that is often used to compare standards of living between countries. However, it suffers from the problem that it assumes that incomes are distributed equally throughout the economy. In some countries you will find the bulk of the population living in abject poverty whilst a small elite have very high standards of living.

Calculating productivity is not without problems. Thus, on what basis do we calculate the number of employees? Do we just include direct production workers or do we also include those involved in the maintenance of essential machinery or even the whole workforce? There is also a problem of how to deal with part-time employees or those who are ill for a long period.

Levels of absenteeism are another important way of assessing how effectively we are using our workforce. The absenteeism rate for the total workforce, or for an individual, can be calculated as follows:

$$\frac{\text{number of working days lost (per period)}}{\text{total potential working days in period}} \times 100$$

By monitoring absenteeism on an individual, departmental, or organization-wide basis over time, trends can be established. On a departmental or organization-wide level, increasing levels of absenteeism probably indicate low morale and job dissatisfaction.

On an individual level we often find that the bulk of absenteeism is caused by a small group of workers. Again, by monitoring the situation over a period of time, a pattern of absence which should be investigated may be noted (e.g. the incidence of death in maternal grandmothers whilst England is batting at Lords!). Worker efficiency may also be gauged through statistics such as:

- Spoilt production
- Speed of service
- Customer complaints

Methods of improving productivity

In recent years there have been considerable *improvements* in the productivity of labour. An increase in productivity will occur where:

- Output increases but inputs, and therefore costs, remain constant.
- Output remains constant but inputs, and therefore costs, fall.

This situation has been achieved in a variety of ways. In this unit we have already considered the use of money as well as job rotation, enlargement and enrichment as means of motivating employees. In Unit 3 we also noted that attempts by organizations to involve employees in the decision-making process could improve motivation and the efficiency of that organization. There are also various other ways in which productivity could be raised.

The link between size and efficiency

Large-scale production can reduce the average cost per unit of output. This is in part because the *fixed costs* of production – which don't vary with output – are spread over a larger number of units. It is also, in part, because the *variable costs* per unit of production can be reduced as the size of output increases. This efficiency which comes with the increas-ing scale of production is commonly termed 'economies of scale'.

Technical economies of scale can arise because large-scale operations can make use of more sophisticated, faster machinery. Often the team of men required to operate this machinery is the same size as for less advanced machinery. So for a given labour cost we get higher output per person.

Economies may also be obtained through the linking of processes, which may only be possible when output is large, yielding savings in time, transport or fuel.

Did You Know ?

The car output per year needs to be as high as 2 million vehicles before average costs fall to their minimum. A firm producing 2 million cars per year will have a 34% lower cost per unit than one producing only 100,000 cars per year.

Managerial economies arise because management does not necessarily have to increase at the same rate as output. Moreover as output increases it is also possible for the firm to employ and make full use of specialist managerial staff – e.g. a marketing research analyst.

Trading economies are advantages gained in buying and selling as the firm grows in size. The firm can obtain cost reductions for buying in bulk. Savings can also be made in advertising or distribution costs.

Financial economies arise as a result of the firm's reputation and size. Bankers are more willing to lend, and on better terms, on the basis of a large firm's reputation and the security it can offer. The large costs of a share issue are also less, per pound raised, because of the greater amount that is raised.

Did You Know ?

Large firms also suffer from **diseconomies of scale**. These often arise because the organization structure be-comes very complex as the firms grows and extra costs are incurred to overcome the problems of communication, co-ordination and control.

In the past large-scale production has also led to products becoming standardized. The lack of variety may then lead to lower sales.

Work study

This has been defined as:

A generic term for those techniques, particularly method study and work measurement, which are used in the examination of human work in all its contexts. Work study leads systematically to the investigation of all the factors which affect the efficiency of the situation being reviewed, in order to effect improvement

---

The first known attempts to use **work study** were by F.W. Taylor in America. His attempts to rationalize tasks were given the title 'scientific management'. Although all Taylor's work was directed toward improving efficiency in the factory, the techniques are equally applicable in the office.

Method study attempts to find the right way to do the job. Jobs to be studied will often be chosen because a problem exists – e.g. excessive overtime, bad quality work or production 'bottlenecks'. The present method of doing the job will be carefully analysed and an alternative method is developed. Fig. 5.12 shows a 'critical examination sheet' that is often used as part of this process. Apart from identifying the correct way to do a job, method study may also be used to:

- Minimize employee effort and reduce fatigue.
- Improve workplace layout.
- Improve equipment design.

Present facts		Alternatives	Decision
What is done	Why?	What else?	What should be done
How it is done	Why that way?	How else?	How it should be done
When it is done	Why then?	When else?	When it should be done
Where it is done	Why there?	Where else?	Where it should be done
Who does it	Why him?	Who else?	Who should do it

Fig. 5.12 Critical examination sheet

Work measurement seeks to determine how long a particular task should take. It is necessary that method study is undertaken first in order that the correct way of doing the job is established.

The best known technique for work measurement is **time study**, sometimes referred to as 'stop watch studies'. By this method an operative is repeatedly timed carrying out his job, or part of it. By rating this performance through comparison with other workers, it is possible to establish a standard time for doing this job. Work measurement provides more reliable data for planning and control, it ensures that the organization achieves more efficient planning levels and it establishes a reliable basis for incentive payment schemes.

Operational research

This is a series of statistical techniques which can be used to help managers in planning and decision making. They include:

- **Critical path analysis.** This is a technique which allows a firm to calculate the minimum time needed to complete a complex operation, e.g. building a bridge. It can also help identify those activities which are likely to delay completion of the task.

- **Simulation/queuing theory.** This creates a *model* of what is happening in reality in order to solve problems. For example a supermarket may have problems with queues at particular times of the day. A simulation allows a supermarket to calculate the number of checkouts it must operate at different times of the day in order to keep queues to a minimum.

- **Game theory or competitive strategy.** This allows a firm to *predict* how a competitor will react in a specific situation, e.g. a reduction in prices or an increase in the promotion budget. Anticipating the competitors' response allows the firm to devise a better strategy.

- **Linear programming models.** These are used to solve allocation problems. They are used where there is a directly proportional relationship between certain factors. For example such a model may be used to

determine the number of factories or warehouses that should be built in order to minimize transport costs to different markets.

Operational research techniques can also be used to determine certain outcomes. For example, to reduce the statistical likelihood of a batch of products having more than a certain percentage of defects *below* a specific figure or to minimize the cost of holding stock and yet ensuring that the firm never runs out of those stocks.

Just-in-time (JIT) management

This is a form of production control which aims to reduce costs by cutting stock levels. In essence it requires that:

- The suppliers of materials or parts, supply what is required *just in time* for manufacture.
- The manufacturer produces *just in time* for the goods to be sold.

It has the advantage of not only cutting stock levels but also reducing production delays and linking production more closely with market demand.

JIT leads to a much closer relationship between buyer and supplier. It often results in long term and sole supplier-ship deals and may also lead to special agreements whereby the buyer supervises the quality control operation on the supplier's premises.

On the downside JIT may result in higher ordering and administrative costs, added to which the benefits of bulk buying discounts may be lost.

Quality circles

A **quality circle** is a group of employees who meet at regular intervals to discuss work-based problems. The issues discussed are very varied, ranging from the level of output (or service) rejects, through to safety issues. These circles not only devise ways of overcoming the problem but will also be responsible for the implementation of the solution. In practice, the benefits from using quality circles are as much in the improvements in morale and motivation, from being involved in the decision making process, as in the improvements in productivity, quality and safety.

Total quality management (TQM)

This is a philosophy that is designed to affect all parts of the organization's operations, its employees and suppliers. It aims to create an environment which encourages everyone to *strive for continuous improvement* in all areas of operations so as to *consistently exceed customers' expectations*. The key to the success of TQM lies in changing the organizational culture to one in which all employees strive to satisfy the customer – and in this context a *customer* is anyone they deal with during the day. TQM also emphasizes the idea of *continuous improvement* in the operations of the organization. The contributions of ordinary employees, often through quality circles, are again fundamental to the success of this aim.

Self Check ✔ **Element 3**

22. State the five levels of need in Maslow's 'hierarchy of needs'.

_____
_____
_____
_____

23. What was F.W. Taylor's contribution to motivational theory.

_____
_____
_____

24. Why were the 'Hawthorne' experiments considered so important?

_____
_____
_____
_____

25. Distinguish between time and piece rates.

_____
_____
_____

26. Distinguish between job enlargement and job enrichment.

_____
_____
_____

27. In what ways could the measurement of productivity be used by an organization?

_____
_____
_____
_____

28. Distinguish between work study and work measurement.

_____
_____
_____

29. What is meant by the term 'economies of scale'?

_____
_____
_____

30. Give some _reasons_ for the existence of economies of scale.

_____
_____
_____
_____
_____
_____
_____
_____
_____
_____

Unit Test Answer all the questions

Question 1
Which sector of the economy has lost the largest proportion of jobs in the UK economy since 1960?

A Manufacturing   B Extraction   C Service   D Private

Questions 2–4 relate to the following information:

Organizations have a number of sources of employment information open to them including:

A   Reward Employment Market Survey
B   Employment Gazette
C   International Labour Office
D   Eurostat Labour Force Survey

Which would you consult to find out about:

Question 2
Unemployment trends in the UK

Question 3
Employment trends in Europe

Question 4
Earnings of professional people

Question 5
Many firms provide their employees with a remuneration package including 'fringe benefits'.

Mark each of these statements true (T) or false (F).

(1) Employers see fringe benefits as a way of motivating key workers.
(2) You do not pay tax on fringe benefits.

Which option best describes the two statements:

A (1) T   (2) T   Choose this answer if both statements are True.
B (1) T   (2) F   Choose this answer if statement (1) is True and statement (2) is False.
C (1) F   (2) T   Choose this answer if statement (1) is False and statement (2) is True.
D (1) F   (2) F   Choose this answer if both statements are False.

Make sure you choose the answer which represents the correct order of the statements.

Question 6
Average earnings for women are lower than for men.

Mark each of these statements true (T) or false (F).

(1) Women are paid less than men for the same job.
(2) Many women aren't able to work-full time due to other commitments.

Which option best describes the two statements:

A (1) T   (2) T   Choose this answer if both statements are True.
B (1) T   (2) F   Choose this answer if statement (1) is True and statement (2) is False.
C (1) F   (2) T   Choose this answer if statement (1) is False and statement (2) is True.
D (1) F   (2) F   Choose this answer if both statements are False.

Make sure you choose the answer which represents the correct order of the statements.

Question 7–9 relate to the following information.

In order to analyse employment trends it is possible to consider

A   Activity rates
B   Technological change
C   Hours worked and earnings
D   Unemployment

Which would need to be analysed in order to:

Question 7
Monitor low pay

Question 8
Discover the proportion of 45 to 55 year old men who are working

Question 9
Identify training needs

Questions 10–12 relate to the following information.

Some economic policies pursued by the government are:

A   Encouraging the growth of local pay bargaining
B   Encouraging employee share ownership schemes
C   Encouraging an increased investment in training
D   Privatization

Which of these policies could have the following effect on employment trends?

Question 10
An increase in overall employment

Question 11
Reduce labour turnover

Question 12
A reduction in the rate of growth of average wage settlements

Question 13
Mark each of these statements true (T) or false (F).

(1) An employer can refuse to employ someone if they do not belong to a recognized trade union.
(2) An employee has a legal right to belong to a trade union.

Which option best describes the two statements:

A (1) T   (2) T   Choose this answer if both statements are True.
B (1) T   (2) F   Choose this answer if statement (1) is True and statement (2) is False.
C (1) F   (2) T   Choose this answer if statement (1) is False and statement (2) is True.
D (1) F   (2) F   Choose this answer if both statements are False.

Make sure you choose the answer which represents the correct order of the statements.

Question 14
Mark each of these statements true (T) or false (F).

(1) There must be an independently scrutinized postal ballot of members before a strike.
(2) Employers must provide reasonable assistance to a trade union organizing a secret ballot.

Which option best describes the two statements:

A (1) T (2) T Choose this answer if both statements are True.
B (1) T (2) F Choose this answer if statement (1) is True and statement (2) is False.
C (1) F (2) T Choose this answer if statement (1) is False and statement (2) is True.
D (1) F (2) F Choose this answer if both statements are False.

Make sure you choose the answer which represents the correct order of the statements

Question 15
Mark each of these statements true (T) or false (F).

(1) A firm's demand for labour will fall if the demand for its products falls.
(2) A firm's demand for labour will fall if wage rates rise.

Which option best describes the two statements:

A (1) T (2) T Choose this answer if both statements are True.
B (1) T (2) F Choose this answer if statement (1) is True and statement (2) is False.
C (1) F (2) T Choose this answer if statement (1) is False and statement (2) is True.
D (1) F (2) F Choose this answer if both statements are False.

Make sure you choose the answer which represents the correct order of the statements

Question 16
Mark each of these statements true (T) or false (F).

(1) Wage rates will fall if there is an increase in the supply of labour.
(2) Wage rates will fall if there is an increase in demand for labour.

Which option best describes the two statements:

A (1) T (2) T Choose this answer if both statements are True.
B (1) T (2) F Choose this answer if statement (1) is True and statement (2) is False.
C (1) F (2) T Choose this answer if statement (1) is False and statement (2) is True.
D (1) F (2) F Choose this answer if both statements are False.

Make sure you choose the answer which represents the correct order of the statements.

Question 17
Mark each of these statements true (T) or false (F).

(1) The Social Chapter of the Maastricht Treaty aims to improve the mobility of labour throughout Europe.
(2) The provisions of the Social Chapter do not apply in the UK.

Which option best describes the two statements:

A (1) T (2) T Choose this answer if both statements are True.
B (1) T (2) F Choose this answer if statement (1) is True and statement (2) is False.

C (1) F (2) T Choose this answer if statement (1) is False and statement (2) is True.
D (1) F (2) F Choose this answer if both statements are False.

Make sure you choose the answer which represents the correct order of the statements

Questions 18–20 relate to the following information:

A Trade unions B Competition C Government D Media

Which would be responsible for:

Question 18
Import penetration into the UK car market by overseas producers reducing the demand for car workers in the UK

Question 19
Negotiating with a newspaper firm over changes in working practices designed to improve competitiveness

Question 20
A fall in demand for cars after adverse publicity

Question 21
Which of these is an advantage of specialization?

A Greater job satisfaction
B Employees more flexible
C Output levels rise
D Labour turnover rises

Question 22
McGregor suggested that there were two broad approaches to the motivation of workers which he labelled theory X and theory Y. Which of the following is not consistent with assumptions about a theory Y worker?

A Man enjoys and finds satisfaction in work
B Man wants and accepts responsibility
C Man wants security above all else
D The average job uses only a small part of the employee's ability

Question 23
Which of the following is not an advantage of piece rates?

A More efficient workers rewarded
B Workers work at the pace that suits them
C Greater effort is encouraged
D High quality work is encouraged

Questions 24–26 relate to the following information:

Maslow's hierarchy of needs includes the following

A Social B Safety C Self esteem D Self-actualization

Which need would be satisfied by:

Question 24
Knowing that one has done the best one can

Question 25
Being a member of the staff association

Question 26
Receiving an award for long service

Question 27
Multi-skilling can be considered an illustration of:

A Job specification
B Job analysis
C Job enlargement
D Job enrichment

Question 28

A quality circle is a group of employees that meet at regular intervals to discuss work-based problems. Which of the following would it *not* discuss?

A The level of output from the department
B The level of absenteeism in the department
C The level of rejects from the department
D Safety issues

Focus 2

Question 29

Mark each of these statements true (T) or false (F).

(1) The *Annual Abstract of Statistics* provides the most up-to-date data on employment statistics.
(2) The *General Household Survey* provides information on job satisfaction.

Which option best describes the two statements

A (1) T (2) T Choose this answer if both statements are True.
B (1) T (2) F Choose this answer if statement (1) is True and statement (2) is False.
C (1) F (2) T Choose this answer if statement (1) is False and statement (2) is True.
D (1) F (2) F Choose this answer if both statements are False.

Make sure you choose the answer which represents the correct order of the statements.

Question 30

Which of the following does not provide data about the UK labour force?

A Labour Force Survey
B The labour market
C International Labour Office
D Employment Trends

Question 31

Workforce performance within a company is *not* measured by:

A Output per employee
B Labour cost per unit
C Operational research
D Rejects as a percentage of total output

Question 32

A trade union is most likely to be successful in making a wage claim when:

A Demand for work is greater than the number of vacancies
B Demand for work is less than the number of vacancies
C Supply of workers is greater than the number of vacancies
D Supply of workers meets the demand for workers

Question 33

Many companies have adopted just-in-time (JIT) techniques.

Mark each of these statements true (T) or false (F).

(1) JIT can be described as a 'pull through' system of production.
(2) JIT leads to a far closer relationship between buyer and supplier.

Which option best describes the two statements:

A (1) T (2) T Choose this answer if both statements are True
B (1) T (2) F Choose this answer if statement (1) is True and statement (2) is False
C (1) F (2) T Choose this answer if statement (1) is False and statement (2) is True
D (1) F (2) F Choose this answer if both statements are False

Make sure you choose the answer which represents the correct order of the statements.

Question 34

Mark each of these statements true (T) or false (F).

(1) Race discrimination policies help to ensure that the best use is made of scarce labour resources.
(2) Race discrimination policies have no effect on labour productivity.

Which option best describes the two statements:

A (1) T (2) T Choose this answer if both statements are True.
B (1) T (2) F Choose this answer if statement (1) is True and statement (2) is False.
C (1) F (2) T Choose this answer if statement (1) is False and statement (2) is True.
D (1) F (2) F Choose this answer if both statements are False.

Make sure you choose the answer which represents the correct order of the statements.

Question 35

A company facing increasing competition decides to introduce a policy of total quality management. The company is therefore competing by:

A Giving all supervisors management training
B Providing management with quality information
C Providing a better service to the customer
D Providing all staff with proper training

Question 36

Mark each of these statements true (T) or false (F).

(1) GDP per head of population is measured by total output divided by total working population.
(2) Output per employee is measured by total output divided by working population.

Which option best describes the two statements:

A (1) T (2) T Choose this answer if both statements are True.
B (1) T (2) F Choose this answer if statement (1) is True and statement (2) is False.
C (1) F (2) T Choose this answer if statement (1) is False and statement (2) is True.
D (1) F (2) F Choose this answer if both statements are False.

Make sure you choose the answer which represents the correct order of the statements

Question 37

If wage increases are not matched by productivity increases then:

A Fewer workers are promoted
B Fewer workers are employed
C Fewer workers are made redundant
D Fewer workers are motivated

Answers to Self-check Questions

1. This refers to the proportion of a specific age/sex group who are in paid employment.

2. There are several reasons including that a heavy burden is placed on the working population for state pensions and welfare services. Past state investment is not necessarily appropriate to the needs of an ageing population. Older people save less and therefore there is less available for investment; nor are older people very willing to move for new jobs.

3. Another term for specialization is division of labour. This is the breaking down of a task or a production process into a number of smaller specialist tasks. The aim of specialization is to improve the productivity of the workforce by allowing people to concentrate on what they are best at.

4. By giving workers some control over their hours of work employers hope that absenteeism will be reduced and morale improved.

5. Women have greater control over the size of their family. Society is more willing to accept that women, particularly wives and mothers, should have jobs outside the house. The increase in one-parent families has forced some women out to work. Women are also better educated now and have higher aspirations than before.

6. **Functional flexibility**
Employers want to be able to move employees between jobs rather than have the rigid demarcation of jobs which used to exist. The term multi-skilling is sometimes used to denote functional flexibility.
Numerical flexibility
The demand for labour is a 'derived' demand, i.e. it depends upon the demand for the finished good or service. The employer wishes to be able to adjust the size of his workforce according to the level of demand for his 'product'.
Financial flexibility
Competition in the market place may mean that the employer feels that it is necessary to 'renegotiate' wages with employees. Alternatively, in a free labour market situations may arise, for example in times of high unemployment, where the employer believes that the wages he is paying are too high.

7. Core workers are the key workers within the organization. Their skills are necessary for the long term success of the organization. They will be highly trained, well paid and have a permanent contract. There are several groups of peripheral workers – full-time and part-time. Because their skills are more available on the labour market or are not as crucial to the success of the firm some workers will not be offered as much job security or career paths within the organization .

8. In a supermarket a core worker would be one of the senior supervisors or an assistant to the manager. A check-out operator would be a peripheral worker. In a hotel the head chef would be a core worker and a waiter would be a peripheral worker.

9. It reduces the burden of unemployment on the state. Small firms tend to be very efficient, adapt rapidly to changed market conditions and provide competition for larger firms.

10. **Activity rates** General Household Survey
Employment trends UK National Accounts
Unemployment Employment Gazette
Earnings New Earnings Survey
European Union Eurostat Labour Force Survey

11. You may find it useful to use a diagram. The explanation lies in an understanding of the value an employee places on work and leisure. At low rates of pay the need for money to provide for the essentials of everyday life will probably mean that he or she works very long hours. At higher rates of pay he or she will obtain the same level of income with fewer hours work and *may* decide to take out the extra time as leisure.

12. Labour is only demanded because it enables the employer to provide some good or service which is valued by the consumer. Demand for labour is therefore derived from the demand for the product. It follows that if the demand for this 'product' increases, the demand for labour will, and vice versa.

13.

Number of workers	Total product (units)	Marginal physical product (units)	Marginal revenue product (£)	Marginal cost (£)	Total revenue product (£)	Total cost (£)	Profit (£)
1	18	18	90	100	90	100	–10
2	41	23	115	100	205	200	5
3	70	29	145	100	350	300	50
4	106	36	180	100	530	400	130
5	147	41	205	100	735	500	235
6	190	43	215	100	950	600	350
7	220	30	150	100	1100	700	400
8	241	21	105	100	1205	800	405
9	255	14	70	100	1275	900	375
10	261	6	30	100	1305	1000	305

14. Because wage rates do not respond to changes in the supply and demand for labour. These imperfections may arise from workers not knowing of job opportunities or being unwilling to move away from their present job/home. Further, collective bargaining or social security benefits may both create a floor below which wage rates cannot fall.

15. With an inelastic demand curve, as prices (in this case wages) rise, output falls less than proportionately. Put another way, trade unions can push for large increases in wages knowing that the increases they obtain will not result in many of their members losing their jobs.

16. Female employment, particularly part-time female employment, is concentrated in industries protected by minimum wage legislation. With the abolition of Wages Councils, wage rates in these industries are likely to fall, thus widening the average earnings gap between men and women.

17. In Unit 1 we noted that the instruments (monetary and fiscal policy) used to control the economy worked in different ways on inflation and unemployment. In 1979 the Conservative government took the view that inflation was the greater problem and that monetary and fiscal policy should be used to control this. There was also some doubt about the extent to which unemployment could be reduced by these policy instruments owing to the mismatch of skills offered by the unemployed and demanded by the employers.

18. High wages 'pricing' labour out of a job etc.

19. Made strikes without ballot of members illegal; curbed secondary picketing; etc.

20. Fears that this would make the labour market less flexible and less competitive internationally (outside Europe especially).

21. **Benefits**
Higher productivity of labour and therefore higher wages. Lower costs of production and therefore firm more competitive in market.
Problems
Higher productivity of labour can mean fewer workers needed. Workers need to be retrained.

22. The needs are physiological, safety, social, ego (self-esteem) and self-actualization. The first three are said to relate to the context of the job and are lower level needs whilst the higher two relate to the content of the job.

23. He emphasized the importance of money as a motivator, particularly through the use of piece rates.

24. They indicated that motivating individuals was far more complex than previously thought. In particular the studies indicated the importance of the group upon attitudes to and motivation to work.

25. A time rate is an hourly payment to the worker regardless of the level of output. It would be used where the quality of output was more important than the quantity.

26. Both are attempts to improve motivation by redesigning jobs to make them more interesting. Job enlargement involves widening the workers' responsibilities so that work becomes less repetitive. The criticism of job enlargement, and this is where it differs from job enrichment, is that the work becomes less repetitious merely because he or she now has three or four boring jobs to do. Job enrichment, though, requires the worker to take on 'higher level' responsibilities, e.g. in the planning, organizing or the (quality) control of work, which would be examples of Maslow's higher level needs.

27. Productivity and the efficient utilization of resources can be measured in many different ways. Whatever the method used is though, the value to the organization lies in the fact that the measurement can be used to establish trends. Monitoring of these trends can be a very effective control mechanism for the organization.

28. Work study is the umbrella term used to denote a number of different techniques, all of which are designed to improve the efficiency of the organization's operations. Work measurement is just one of these techniques and is used to determine how long a particular job should take. The results could be used to establish correct manning levels or as the basis of an incentive payments scheme.

29. A reduction in the average cost per unit of output as the size (scale) of output increases.

30. Various reasons:
    * Spreading fixed costs over larger output reduces *average fixed costs*.
    * Various ways may be used to reduce *average variable cost*, e.g. producing more output per unit of labour etc. Technical economies may be found by increased specialisation, better methods of production, use of more advanced equipment, etc. Other non-technical economies may be found, e.g. economies in finance, in management, in trade, etc.

Answers to Unit Test

Question	Answer	Question	Answer	Question	Answer	Question	Answer	Question	Answer
1	A	9	B	17	C	25	B	33	A
2	B	10	C	18	B	26	C	34	A
3	C	11	B	19	A	27	C	35	C
4	A	12	A	20	D	28	B	36	C
5	B	13	C	21	C	29	C	37	B
6	C	14	A	22	C	30	B		
7	C	15	A	23	D	31	C		
8	A	16	B	24	D	32	B		

Unit Test Comments (Selected questions)

Question 1   A
The growth of low cost manufacturing, particularly in Asia, has caused this sector to lose many jobs to overseas competitors.

Question 3   C
The Eurostat labour force survey relates to the European Union alone. The International Labour Office provides wider European coverage.

Question 5   B
Fringe benefits are certainly seen by many employers as a way of motivating employees but you will find that the Inland Revenue does assess the value of the more important fringe benefits for tax purposes.

Question 6   C
Any woman who is being paid less than a man for the same job has a right of action under the Equal Pay Act so this is unlikely to be true. However, many women work part-time in low-paid jobs because it fits in with their other commitments.

Question 7   C
From this information it is possible to calculate an average rate of pay which can be compared over time.

Question 8   A
Each year the government produces statistics on the activity rates of different groups of workers.

Question 9   B
Information on technological change and the skills needed will enable the state and employers to establish the training needs of workers.

Question 10   C
An investment in training will make workers more employable and therefore increase overall employment.

Question 11   B
Employee share ownership schemes are often used as a means of ensuring the continued loyalty of key staff.

Question 12   A
Local pay bargaining allows employers to negotiate settlements which reflect local conditions. National pay bargaining results in some workers obtaining wage increases that are not justified on the basis of local conditions (e.g. lower cost of living or workers willing to work for less).

Question 13   C
(1) This is unlawful under the Employment Act 1990.

Question 15   A
The firm's demand for labour is a derived demand and therefore if product demand falls so will the demand for labour. According to marginal productivity theory a firm will employ workers until the marginal revenue from employing the last worker equals the marginal cost (or wage rate). It follows that if the wage rate rises then the firm's demand for labour will fall.

Question 16   B
Using your knowledge of the price mechanism you should be able to determine the impact of a shift in the supply or demand for labour on the wage rate (i.e. the price). Whilst wage rates will fall if there is a shift in the supply schedule to the right (more labour is supplied at all prices) a shift in the demand curve to the right (more labour demanded at all prices) will result in the price of labour rising.

Question 17   C
The Social Chapter of the Maastricht Treaty was designed to improve the working conditions of workers within the European Union.

Question 19   A
Don't be misled. The key point is not that it is a newspaper firm (part of the media) but that there are negotiations taking place on an employment-related matter.

Question 21   C
The main advantage of specialization is that it improves productivity.

Question 22   C
It is theory X man that demands security.

Question 23   D
In an effort to earn more under the piecework system workers are likely to ignore the need for high quality.

Question 28   B
This is an example of job enlargement because the additional jobs given to the worker are of the same level of difficulty.

Question 29   C
It is the *Employment Gazette* that provides the most up to date information.

Question 30   B
The labour market determines the price of labour.

Question 31   C
The term operational research embraces a number of mathematical techniques which are used to improve the efficiency of operations within the organization.

Question 32   B
If the demand for work by the workers is less than the vacancies available the shortage of workers is likely to put the union in a strong bargaining position.

Question 35   C
TQM encourages everyone to strive for continuous improvement in all areas of operation so as to consistently exceed the customers' expectations.

Question 36   C
Total output is divided by total population to obtain GDP per capita income.

UNIT 6

Financial Transactions and Monitoring

Getting Started

The buying and selling of goods or services in business organizations is often known as a **financial transaction**. Each item bought and each item sold is an individual transaction. Organizations must develop a system that accurately records every single transaction for:

• Keeping records.
• Use by management to plan and control.
• Stewardship purposes.
• Covering legal requirements.

In Unit 2 (Business Systems) we saw how information technology has revolutionized the ways in which financial transactions can be stored on computer databases. But paper **documents** and **recording procedures** are still an essential part of business life. It is important that you are able to:

• Identify what documents are needed.
• Complete the documents.
• Explain and understand 'why' they are used.

The methods used to record financial transactions provide the base information on which to build a system to **monitor business performance**. As explained in Unit 2, this system should enable the manager to *plan* and *control* the organization's activities. To do this, it should be capable of allowing the manager to identify *how well* the organization has done relative to its objectives.

By *objectives* we mean the purposes for which the organization was formed, whether it be to provide a service or to maximize profits. It follows that an organization with the objectives of providing a service will need different methods of monitoring performance from those that have the objective of profit maximization (see Unit 8, page 204).

In this unit we will concentrate on the organizations that exist to make a profit. To be able to monitor the performance of such an organization it is necessary for you to be able to understand the balance sheet and the profit and loss account and it is recommended that this area is covered first (see Unit 7, pages 188 to 194).

Activity ratios Measures of how efficient an organization is in using its current assets and current liabilities. These ratios directly affect liquidity (for example how efficient they are at collecting debts).

Double entry The system under which every transaction transferred to the ledgers is entered in two places.

Liquidity ratios Measures of whether an organization can pay its debts (for example whether the organization has enough cash and other assets that can be converted into cash to pay current liabilities when they are due).

Monitoring performance Having information which can be measured to assess 'how well' or 'how badly' an organization is doing.

Profitability ratios Measures, in percentage terms, of the size of profit made compared with the amount of sales.

Ratio analysis Used to measure and assess performance. Using appropriate percentages and ratios, comparisons can be made.

Targets/budgets Information relevant to managers of the organization. They try to 'meet targets' (for example a target amount of sales will be set for the year) and 'keep within budgets' (for example a set amount will be allocated to purchase materials). Managers monitor regularly whether they have reached their targets and kept within their budgets by comparing actual performance with target/budgeted performance.

Essential Principles

Financial transactions are not limited to organizations – they are made by almost everyone, everyday. When you buy your lunch in the college cafeteria or when you take a bus ride you are involved in a financial transaction. This is because you pay someone money and receive the goods or services in return. As you know, organizations can make numerous transactions every day and there is a need therefore to have a method of *recording* these transactions.

In this element we will explore why organizations need to record financial transactions and the types of documents used. We will identify:

- the purposes of recording financial transactions
- the recording procedures
- the types of purchase and sales documents and why they are used
- the methods and reasons for recording monies paid and received by the firm
- the reasons and types of security checks required

Purposes of recording

Keeping track of financial transactions is an essential function of any organization. It is very easy to ignore 'the paper work' and concentrate on the interesting areas of running a business. However, all organizations need an accurate and efficient system of **recording** for the following reasons:

- *Monitor performance and control costs*
  It is important that *managers* know at any one point in time how many goods have been sold and the cost of making those goods. Managers have to be able to control costs and keep within their targets and budgets. This system provides essential information that allows managers to plan and control effectively.

- *Provide information for the owners*
  Managers have a duty to report to the *owners* of the organization on how well they have been managing the organisation's affairs – how much profits have been made, and how effective they have been. This is called the *stewardship function*. Without accurate records this information cannot be produced.

- *Meet legal requirements*
  All organisations need to keep records and produce financial accounts – for limited companies it is a requirement by law, and for all organizations it is a requirement that accurate records are kept and accounts are produced for taxation and VAT purposes.

Keeping records

Organizations can make hundreds or thousands of financial transactions daily. A good financial transactions system will provide a *permanent record* which can be referred to in the future. The system will record:

- goods bought and sold and the price at which they were bought and sold
- amounts owed to the organization for items sold on credit (debtors)
- amounts owed by the organization for items bought on credit (creditors)
- other items bought (expenses and assets)
- the value of returns of faulty goods to and from the organization.

It is often especially important to keep an accurate record of items bought and sold *on credit*. If you purchase your lunch at the cafeteria, you pay for the goods with *cash*. However, in the business world, it is accepted that items are bought and sold on *credit*. This means that goods are purchased and received by an organization but are paid for at a later date. The period of credit allowed can vary – perhaps between 30 and 90 days, sometimes more.

It is essential that organizations keep track of these transactions so that they have an instant record of:

- credit sales (debtors – how much is owed to the organization and by whom)
- credit purchases (creditors – how much is owed by the organization and to whom).

Credit Control

Allowing credit for businesses means the organization is being deprived of cash for that length of time. It is therefore important that organizations have a good **credit control** system; this is discussed in detail on page 164.

Recording procedures

How and where the information is recorded will vary according to the needs of each organization. However, the **standard accounting procedures** used are described below.

Day books

The **day books** are so called because they are used 'daily' by organizations to list any financial transactions (sales, purchases and returns) by:

- date
- name
- amount

They are also referred to as 'books of prime entry' since they are the first recording place of any financial transaction. Different day books are used to record different types of invoices and are as follows:

Title of day book	Document listed
Sales day book	Sales invoices
Sales returns day book	Credit notes issued
Purchase day book	Purchase invoices
Purchase returns day book	Credit notes received

All day books have the same headings. Using the 'Sales day book' as an example they are shown as follows:

Sales Day Book				
Date	Account name	Net	VAT	Gross

Double entry

Periodically, each invoice entered in the day books is transferred to the ledgers. The ledgers form part of what is known as **'the double entry system'**. It is called 'double entry' because every transaction transferred to the *ledgers* is entered in two places.

Ledgers

A **ledger** is the acceptable method of recording financial transactions. Ledgers in use by organizations are as follows:

Title of ledger	Contents
Sales Ledger	Accounts of debtors by name A record of sales made on credit A record of sales returns A record of payments made by the debtors
Purchase Ledger	A record of creditors by name A record of purchases made on credit A record of purchase returns A record of payments made to creditors
General Ledger	A record of totals for the following: sales; purchases; returns; items of expense; assets bought; capital and VAT
Cash Book	A record of cash and bank receipts and payments made

Debit and Credit

Each ledger contains a DEBIT side and a CREDIT side. These are explained as follows:

- **Debit** (or 'in side'). Recording goods or money coming into the business.
- **Credit** (or 'out side'). Recording goods or money going out of the business.

Example

Laser Enterprises Ltd make a sale of £500 to Buxtod Garden Centre for garden equipment on 1.2.XX. The accounts department of Laser Enterprises will record the financial transaction in the ledgers as follows:

- **DEBIT** (in) the account of Buxtod Garden Centre in the sales ledger to the amount of £500 (since Buxtod Garden Centre have received the goods into their organization).
- **CREDIT** (out) the sales account in the general ledger by £500 (since Laser Enterprises Ltd have sent the goods out of their organization).

This would be shown as follows:

SALES LEDGER

BUXTOD GARDEN CENTRE

DEBIT					CREDIT
DATE		AMOUNT £	DATE		AMOUNT £
1.2.XX	Sale	500.00			

GENERAL LEDGER

SALES ACCOUNT

DEBIT					CREDIT
DATE		AMOUNT £	DATE		AMOUNT £
			1.2.XX	Buxtod Garden Centre	500.00

On 1.3.XX Buxtod Garden Centre pay Laser Enterprises Ltd for the goods bought. The accounts department of Laser Enterprises will now:

- **DEBIT** (in) the bank account (since they have received the cheque into the organization).
- **CREDIT** (out) the Buxtod Garden Centre account in the sales ledger to the amount of £500 (since they have sent the cheque out of their organization).

This would be shown as follows:

BANK ACCOUNT

DEBIT					CREDIT
DATE		AMOUNT £	DATE	PAYMENTS	AMOUNT £
1.3.XX	Buxtod Garden Centre	500.00			

SALES LEDGER

BOXTOD GARDEN CENTRE

DEBIT					CREDIT
DATE		AMOUNT £	DATE		AMOUNT £
1.2.XX	Sale	500.00	1.3.XX	Bank	500.00

Important

- Double entry: for every financial transaction there will be a DEBIT (in) and a CREDIT (out).
- Ledgers: should provide accurate and reliable information.
- Ledgers: information from the ledgers is used as a base on which to make decisions.

Types of purchase and sales documents used

Fig. 6.1 indicates the generally accepted **documents** which flow between the buyer and seller. The *direction of the arrows* indicates the *flow* of the documents.

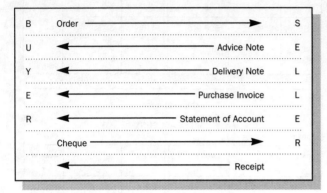

Fig. 6.1 Flow of business documents

Order

After receiving a price list from the supplier (the seller), the buyer will send out an **order form** which indicates :

- Name, address and telephone number of the buyer's business.
- Name and address of the seller's business.
- A reference number to which both buyer and seller can refer.
- Quantity, description, seller's catalogue number and price of the items required.
- Delivery address (this is important as goods may need to be sent to a branch rather than to the invoice address).
- A signature by someone who is authorized to approve the purchase.

In Fig. 6.2, Laser Enterprises have issued an order for the

ORDER			
FROM	Laser Enterprises Ltd 21–23 Barkerend Road Bradstall West Yorkshire WF14 6AY	Tel 0924 603966 FAX 0924 601235 Date 30.11.XX	**Order No** 5601/1
TO	Brixton Engineering Ltd 201 Frampton Court Birmingham B14 2LZ		

PLEASE SUPPLY

Quantity	Description	Your Cat. No	Price Each
600 metres	cable	C2456	£1.00/metre

Delivered by: Road

To: the above address

Signature of approval ....*J. Nicholson*........Buyer

Fig. 6.2 Example of a Purchase Order Form

supply of cable from Brixton Engineering Ltd. Notice that there is an order number 5601/1. This allows both organizations (buying and selling) to 'tie up' the relevant documents used throughout the transaction.

Once the supplier has received the order form, it will:

- Check with the stores department to see if the goods are in stock.
- Inform the production department if they have to be made.
- Inform the distribution department if they have to be delivered.
- Inform the accounts department so that an invoice can be made out.

Advice/Despatch note

Once the buyer has been found to be satisfactory in terms of creditworthiness, the supplier may send out an **advice note**. This generally contains the same information as the delivery note and states when the goods are to be delivered.

Delivery note

The **delivery note** (see Fig. 6.3) is often similar in layout to the advice note and invoice. It is usually packed in with the goods. When the buyer unpacks the items a check can be made to see if the stated items have been received in an undamaged condition.

When the goods are delivered by the seller's own vehicle, the driver will be given a carbon copy of the delivery note and will ask the buyer to sign for the goods. This is to confirm that the goods have been delivered.

```
                    DELIVERY NOTE
                  Brixton Engineering Ltd
                    201 Frampton Court
                       Birmingham
                        B14 2LZ

Tel 021–456 4891                              Fax 021–456 4309

Invoice To    Laser Enterprises Ltd   Deliver To   Laser Enterprises Ltd
              21–23 Barkerend Road                  21–23 Barkerend Road
              Bradstall                             Bradstall
              West Yorkshire                        West Yorkshire
              WF14 6AY                              WF14 6AY

Your order No 5601/1

Delivery No 1256                      Date   14.12.XX

Quantity  | Description   | Cat. No | Price/unit    | Delivery Date

600 metres| cable         | C2456   | £1.00/metre   | 15.12.XX


Good Received by......J.L. BROWN..........................................
Position ..................Stores Manager.....................................
Signature ................J.L. Brown...........................................
```

Fig. 6.3 Example of a Delivery Note

Goods received note

Within the buying organization it is important to have a system for recording and checking all goods which are delivered to the organization.

Once the goods are delivered and have been checked to see if they are in a good condition, it is normal procedure to produce a **goods received note**. This is an internal document that notifies other departments that the goods have been accepted in a good condition.

Once checked, the goods are either put into stock or sent to production. The goods receipt note is produced in triplicate:

- one copy is held by the goods received department
- one copy is passed to the purchasing department
- one copy is passed to the accounts department for processing.

```
                    LASER ENTERPRISES LTD

GOODS RECEIVED NOTE              Blue Copy Stores
                                 Green Copy Purchasing
                                 White Copy Accounts

              NAME              SIGNATURE
Received by   J L Brown         J L Brown
Checked by    A Patel           A Patel
Carrier       Supplier Transport  Date received  14/12/xx

Quantity | Description | Order No | Supplier  | Stores Location

600m     | Cable       | 5601/1   | Brixton   | L31
                                    Engineering

Comments on condition/amount received
         Condition good: amount as per order

Accounts Department

Date Received | Authorisation for payment | Amount of | Cheque No | Payment sent
                                            payment
```

Fig. 6.4 Example of a Goods Received Note

Sales invoice

The seller (supplier) will now bill the buyer using a **sales invoice**. This is the demand for payment of goods supplied. The invoice will state:

- The goods or services supplied
- The quantity supplied
- The cost of each item
- Any discounts being offered (e.g. for prompt payment)
- The total cost payable by the buyer (purchaser) to the seller
- 'E & OE' (see below)

Invoices are very important legal and financial documents:

- The selling organization (if registered for VAT), must state its VAT number on the invoice.
- Both buying and selling organizations must keep all invoices as they are often checked by auditors and VAT inspectors and are proofs of purchases and sales.

The accounts department in the selling organisation will:

- Record the amount of sale and the name of the debtor in the sales ledger.
- Record the value of goods sold in a sales account.

Checking the sales invoice

The buyer will check the invoice against the original order form and goods received note to see if they all agree. If they do, then payment will be authorized.

The accounts department in the buying organization will then:

- Record the amount owed and the name of the creditor in the purchase ledger.
- Record the value of goods bought in the purchases account.

If the order form, goods received note and invoice *differ*, the accounts department will usually ask the supplier to amend the invoice. This is done by means of debit and credit notes.

Debit and credit notes

If the buyer has been asked to pay *too much*, the seller will issue a **credit note** for the difference. The amount on the credit note will be entered by the accounts department into the buyer's account in the purchases ledger. This will reduce the amount owed by the buyer to the organization.

If the buyer has been asked to pay *too little*, the seller issues a **debit note** for the difference; the amount is then entered into the buyer's account in the purchase ledger. This will increase the amount owed by the buyer to the organization.

Fig 6.5 shows the invoice sent from Brixton Engineering Ltd to Laser Enterprises Ltd for the goods supplied. The invoice gives details of:

- Purchase order number so the invoice can be matched with the original order and delivery note.
- Amount and VAT shown separately for accounting purposes.
- Date and terms of settlement (paid within 30 days).

Fig. 6.5 Example of an Invoice

Statement of account

When a customer buys from a supplier on a regular basis using credit, payment will be made on receipt of a monthly **statement of account** from the supplier. Payments made in this way avoid the need to send a cheque for every invoice when it falls due. It also acts as a way of delaying payment, since a purchase of goods which may be made at the start of the month will not appear on the statement until the following month.

The statement will list:

- purchases made during the month
- payments made since the last statement
- the total payment due to be paid
- the balance outstanding.

Fig. 6.6 indicates that Laser Enterprises bought goods in October and, applying 30 days' credit, were due to pay for them in early November. However, as Laser Enterprises pay

Fig. 6.6 Statement of Account

on statement and not individual invoices, the £100.05 would not be shown as due until the November statement was received. This has allowed them a credit period just short of 2 months rather than 30 days.

Payment documents

Providing the invoice has been approved as correct, the accounts department will request authorization for payment from the purchasing department. This is done in the form of a *pay slip*.

Pay slip

The **pay slip** is a security measure used by organizations to ensure that no payments are made before the goods are checked. It takes the form of a simple document which is signed by an authorized person who instructs the accounts department to pay for the goods or services purchased.

This could be in the form of:

- A document which gives details of the goods bought and includes room for the signature of an authorized person.
- A rubber stamp which is placed on a copy of the invoice and is sent to the authorized person for signing.
- A space on the goods received note allowing a signature for authorizing payment (see Fig. 6.4 earlier).

The important detail is that it must be signed by a person with authority before payment is made.

The importance of the cash book

All receipts and payments made by an organization are entered into the **cash book** by the cashier. The cash book is a very important part of the accounting system. Periodically, when a bank statement arrives (see Fig. 6.11), the cashier will make sure all items paid into the bank and all items paid out of the bank 'match' those on the bank statement.

Undetected errors

As with the purchase ledger and stock account, it is essential that the *sales invoice* is entered correctly in the sales ledger and sales account. If errors go undetected it can have the following consequences.

Sales ledger (a record of the amount owed and by whom) will be either:
- *understated* (the sales invoice is too little)
  or
- *overstated* (the sales invoice is too large).

Sales Account (a record of total sales):
- If the amount entered in the sales account is *understated*, this will show a falsely low profit figure.
- If the amount entered is *overstated*, the profit figure will be falsely high.

Both will show false creditors, liquidity and return on capital employed ratios (see Element 6.3).

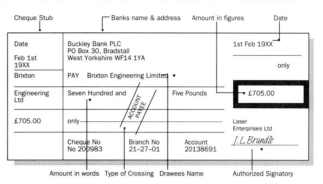

Fig. 6.7 Example of a completed cheque

cheque to the value of £705.00 for goods purchased on the 15 December. Fig. 6.7 shows the cheque and cheque stub made out to Brixton Engineering Ltd.

Payment and receipt of cheques

The payment made by the buying organization will be matched by a receipt in the selling organization. It is important to know what happens in both circumstances.

- *Payment by cheque*
  Most payments are made by **cheque**. Cheques in a large organization are often completed by means of a 'cheque run'. Details of payment and purchase account numbers are fed into the computer system. The system will automatically produce the cheque and deduct the amount owed from the creditors account.

  Cheques in a smaller organization are completed manually and are sent to an authorised person for signing. This person is known as a 'cheque signatory'. The accounts clerk will write the amount of the cheque on the cheque stub and deduct the amount owed to the creditor in their account.

- *Receipt of a cheque*
  Each cheque received for payment from customers is recorded in the cash book by the cashier. This amount is then deducted from the amount owed to the organization by the debtor in their account. Periodically, perhaps once a day, the cashier will enter the total amount of the cheques received onto the paying-in slip (see Fig. 6.10).

- *Examining the cheque*
  On receiving payment by cheque, the following procedures should be carried out to ensure that the cheque clears smoothly:

  - Check that it is signed and dated.
  - Check that the words and figures agree.
  - Check that it is made out to the right organization.

  If the receiving organization is inefficient and does not carry out these checks, it may result in the cheque being returned to the organization's bank after it has been paid in, resulting in delayed payment.

  Laser Enterprises have now received their statement of account for the month of January. They have written a

Cheque crossings

As a security measure to reduce the risk of fraud all cheques now have **crossings** – two bold parallel lines across the face (see Fig. 6.7).

- *Uncrossed Cheques*
  At one time **open** or **uncrossed cheques** were given. An **uncrossed cheque** did not have to be paid through a bank account and payment could be made over the counter. Therefore a person finding or stealing an uncrossed cheque would be able to obtain payment over the counter (it is as though you have cash in your pocket).

- *Crossed Cheques*
  A **crossed cheque** has to be paid into a bank account and cannot be paid directly to the bearer (the person who takes the cheque into the bank). Stolen cheques are less likely to be paid through a thief's account where it can be traced. However, if the person named on the cheque signs the back (endorses the cheque), the bearer can pay the cheque into their own bank account. This meant that fraud could still take place.

- *Account payee or account payee only*
  Today, as a security measure, the Cheque Act 1992 states that all cheques must be crossed with the words '**account payee**' between the lines. The use of these words instructs the bank to direct the funds only to the account of the payee and any endorsement would not be allowed. Variations to these words may be 'a/c payee' or 'a/c payee only'.

The only exception to this rule involves some businesses who may request an alternative crossing.

Petty cash voucher system

Some goods and services need to be purchased using *cash* (usually because they are of such a small value). For example, employees may be asked to buy some stamps or have had to use their own money on travelling expenses for the benefit of the organization. In these situations, employees will need to obtain the cash prior to the purchase or be reimbursed at a later date.

A control procedure needs to be in place for these types of purchase for auditing and VAT purposes and to minimize the temptation of the light fingered. The procedure generally used is **the petty cash voucher system**. Here, a clerk will

Fig. 6.8 Example of a Petty Cash Voucher

have the responsibility for issuing or reimbursing cash to employees.

The employees will be asked to complete a petty cash voucher and have it signed by an authorized person (see Fig. 6.8). On completion of the voucher, the cash will be issued and recorded in the petty cash book.

It is important that the person who is purchasing or has purchased the goods gives a receipt to the clerk for auditing and VAT purposes. This is called a **strict receipt system**.

Other payments

Cash sales

Not all purchases are made on credit. For instance, the customers of retail organizations most often pay for their goods using **cash**. Cash sales include payments made by cheque or plastic card and a company should have a policy for accepting payment using these methods. However, certain basic **security measures** should take place. These are described below.

Payment by cheque

- Ensure that it is filled in correctly (see *examining the cheque* page 151).
- Ensure that it is accompanied by a valid cheque guarantee card.
- Ensure that the signatures match.
- Write the number of the guarantee card on the back of the cheque.
- If the amount of goods to be purchased exceeds the guarantee card limit, check with your supervisor for authorization.

Payment using credit cards (plastic such as Access or Visa)

- Check the card is valid.
- Complete the sales voucher slips and check that the

signature on the credit card matches the signature on the sales voucher.
- Follow company procedure as to the maximum amount allowed *before* authorization is obtained by telephone from the credit card company.

Payment using debit cards (plastic such as 'Delta' or 'Switch')

Debit cards act like a cheque where funds are obtained directly from the customer's bank account (subject to them having sufficient funds). From a seller's point of view, this card should be dealt with in the same way as a credit card.

Electronic Funds Transfer at Point of Sale (EFTPOS)

Credit and debit cards can be used using EFTPOS. This system allows retailers to debit the credit card company or the bank account of the purchaser. This is done electronically at the point of sale and also transfers those funds into the retailer's bank account at the same time. The usual checks on the card and signature must be made. The advantages of this system are:

- Greater efficiency – less time taken with customers to make payment.
- Less cash to handle and therefore fewer security risks.
- Guaranteed payment once acceptance has been made.

Direct debit

If an organization buys regularly from a supplier, it may set up a **direct debit** transfer. Here, approval is given to the bank from the buyer allowing the seller to ask for payment directly into the seller's bank. With a direct debit, the date and amount can vary. This method of payment reduces paperwork and ensures that the amount will be received by a specific date.

Standing order

This is similar to the direct debit but the amount and date are fixed. For example, the buying organization may set up a **standing order** for £200.00 to be paid on the 20th of every month.

Pay Advice

Most organizations will produce a **pay advice** slip for every one of their employees every time they are paid (see Fig 6.9). The employer must keep details of:

- How much each employee has been paid.
- How much tax and national insurance has been deducted.

The employer must then send the amounts deducted in tax and national insurance to the government.

The **pay advice** gives the employee details of:

- tax coding
- gross pay (the amount the employee is paid prior to any deductions)
- tax deducted
- national insurance contributions deducted
- any other deductions
- net pay (the amount the employee actually receives).

LASER ENTERPRISES LTD PAY ADVICE					
NAME	**PAY REF**	**DATE**	**PAY METHOD**	**PAY MONTH**	
B. BROWN	50601	31.12.XX	MONTHLY	9	
PAYMENTS			**DEDUCTIONS**		
BASIC PAY	625.00		INCOME TAX	76.15	
			NAT INS	39.78	
TOTAL PAYMENTS	625.00		**TOTAL DEDUCTIONS**	115.93	**NET PAY** 509.07
ANNUAL SALARY	NI NUMBER	NI TO DATE	TAX CODE	TAXABLE PAY TO DATE	TAX TO DATE
£7500.00	YZ765614A	358.02	344LA	3045.00	685.35

Fig. 6.9 Example of a Pay Advice

The example in Fig. 6.9 shows that B. Brown who works for Laser Enterprises, is identified by payroll number 50601. Brown is paid £625.00 per month and after deductions of income tax and national insurance, the net pay (the actual amount received) is £509.07.

Receipts documents

Receipts are an acknowledgement that you have paid for something. For example, when you take a bus ride, the bus ticket is the receipt that you have paid for the journey. The most usual kind of receipt is a sales receipt.

Sales receipt
Organizations that are registered for VAT must produce receipts that include the VAT registration number, the date of sale and the rate of VAT charged (currently it is 17.5%). Nearly every time you make a purchase you will receive a **sales receipt**.

The next time you buy something keep your receipt and identify:

- VAT registration number
- the date the sale was made
- the amount of the sale
- the amount of the sale excluding VAT.

Calculating VAT
Sometimes a receipt will state the amount of the sale and then add on the VAT to arrive at the total sale. But at other times the receipt will include the amount of VAT. When recording financial transactions it is important to be able to identify the amount of VAT charged so that it can be recorded separately in the accounts.

Assuming a VAT rate of 17.5%, the example below illustrates the calculation of VAT due on a sale of £100.00:

SALE	£100.00
VAT at 17.5% = $\dfrac{100.00 \times 17.5}{100}$	£17.50
TOTAL SALE	£117.50

But if the amount *included* VAT at 17.5%, the calculation would be:

SALE (including VAT at 17.5%)	£117.50
VAT charged = $\dfrac{117.50 \times 17.5}{117.5}$	£17.50
Sale (excluding VAT)	£100.00

As the receipt is a record of what has been paid – by cash, cheque etc. – the amount received is entered by the cashier into the cash book.

Paying-in slip
Periodically (perhaps once a day) the cashier will add up all the cheques received and pay them into the bank using a **paying-in slip**. The paying-in slip (or Bank Giro Credit) is a receipt given by the bank that states the amount of money they have received from you (see Fig. 6.10).

The receipt states:

- the name of the bank and account holder
- the account number
- a signature of who has paid the money in
- a breakdown of the amounts and denominations of money paid in on the reverse of the slip.

The slip is completed in duplicate using carbon paper and both are taken to the bank where it is checked and given an official rubber stamp. The duplicate copy is kept by the organization as a receipt. The back of both the paying-in slip and the carbon copy is also completed. This contains details of each individual cheque paid in on that slip. Fig. 6.10 is a completed paying-in slip for Laser Enterprises. Notice that on the back of the slip each cheque is itemized.

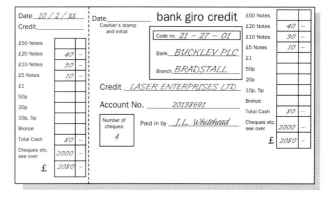

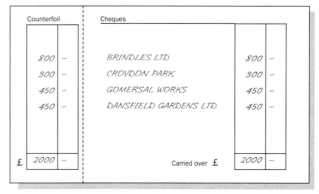

Fig. 6.10 Example of a paying-in slip; front and back

Bank statement
A **bank statement** is a document sent by the bank to the organization at regular intervals. The interval could be weekly/ monthly etc. The document itemizes:

- the amounts paid in using paying-in slips
- the amounts paid in by direct debit or standing order
- the amounts paid out using cheques

- the amounts paid out using direct debits/standing orders
- any deductions for loans
- the amount deducted for bank charges.

The cashier will tick the items on the bank statement with the items recorded in the cash book to make sure that they are correct. This is called a 'bank reconciliation'. An extract of a bank statement is shown in Fig. 6.11.

Buckley Bank PLC ① 　　　　　　　　　　STATEMENT OF
PO Box 30, Bradstall 　　　　　　　　　　　　　ACCOUNT
West Yorkshire WF14 1YA

Laser Enterprises Ltd ② 　　　　　　　Account Number
21–23 Barkerend Rd 　　　　　　　　　　　　20138691
Bradstall
West Yorkshire WF14 6AY 　　　　　③ **Date** 10.2.XX

DETAILS	PAYMENTS	RECEIPTS	DATE	BALANCE
BALANCE FORWARD			4 FEB	1876.50
20138691 ⑤	705.00		5 FEB	1171.50
20138692 ⑤	106.10		6 FEB	1065.40
20138693 ⑤	467.00		7 FEB	598.40
COUNTER CREDIT		⑥ 1060.35	7 FEB	1658.75
COUNTER CREDIT		⑥ 978.75	8 FEB	2637.50
CREDIT TRANSFER		⑦ 500.00	9 FEB	3137.50
DIRECT DEBIT	135.90 ⑧		10 FEB	3001.60 ④

Fig. 6.11 Example of a Bank Statement

The above example identifies the following:

1. The name and address of the bank where the account is held
2. The name and address of the account holder
3. The date on which the statement was produced
4. The amount in the account as at the statement date
5. Details of cheques drawn by number
6. Amounts paid in (counter credit)
7. Amounts paid in by automatic bank transfer (credit transfer)
8. Any amounts paid out into another account (direct debit)

Security measures and consequences

It is very important for an organization to have built-in security measures. This will help to minimize the following:

- pilfering, e.g. goods being bought for personal use or taken from stores
- wasted expenditure – goods being bought that are not really necessary
- errors – in the production of invoices and cheques
- paying for goods or services that are damaged or not received
- unauthorized employees writing cheques for goods
- security against fraud when payment is made by cash.

The security measures used have been discussed throughout this element and are summarized as follows (Fig. 6.12):

STAGE	BUYER	SELLER
ORDER	Issue only with authorized signature	Check for credit worthiness
DELIVERY NOTE	**Stores:** Check goods are not damaged and quantity matches delivery note. If OK, issue a goods received note in triplicate	Ensure it is signed by buyer on delivery
GOODS RECEIVED NOTE	**Stores:** keep one copy as record of goods received into stores **Purchasing:** match goods received note with the original order	
INVOICE	**Accounts:** check invoice against original order, delivery note and goods received note. If they do not match, contact seller to rectify. If matched request pay slip from purchasing	On receipt of signed delivery note, make out invoice, have it checked by someone else before posting
OVERCHARGED ON INVOICE	Ask for credit note, enter into purchase ledger to reduce amount due	
UNDERCHARGED ON INVOICE		Issue a debit note, enter into sales ledger to increase amount due
PAY SLIP	**Purchasing:** if all is correct, authorize payment. Only an authorized person should sign	

PAYMENT METHOD	SELLER
PAYMENT BY CHEQUE FOR ITEMS BOUGHT ON CREDIT	**Accounts:** on receipt of pay slip write out the cheque. Before payment request signature by **cheque signatories only**
PAYMENT BY CHEQUE FOR CASH ITEMS	**Cashier:** do not accept payment unless accompanied by a valid cheque guarantee card. Write the card number on the back of the cheque. The signatures must match. For items over card limit, follow company policy
PAYMENT BY DEBIT CARD FOR CASH ITEMS	**Cashier:** check the card is valid. On completion of debit slip check signatures match. Follow company procedure on amount that needs to be cleared by debit card company

Fig. 6.12 Security Measures

Self Check ✔ **Element 1**

1. In terms of business transactions, a debtor is an organization that has:
   (a) Bought goods for cash
   (b) Purchased goods on credit
   (c) Sold goods for cash
   (d) None of the above

Self Check ✔ **Element 1** *continued*

2. The goods received note is an internal document which:
   (a) Once signed is proof of delivery for the selling organization.
   (b) Notifies other departments that the goods have been accepted in a good condition.
   (c) Is a security measure.

   Which best describes the above?

   (1) (a) only
   (2) All of the above
   (3) (b) and (c)
   (4) None of the above
   (5) (a) and (b)

3. Using invoice No 19501 in Fig. 6.5, when will this amount become due for payment? How many days' credit has Laser Enterprises Ltd received by the due date as per the Statement of Account in Fig. 6.6?

4. What type of crossing have Laser Enterprises used? What does this crossing mean? What are the advantages of using a cheque crossed with 'account payee'?

5. The following is a list of receipts received by Laser Enterprises for items bought out of petty cash. They all include a VAT charge of 17.5%. Calculate the amount of (a) VAT and (b) the sale price exclusive of VAT, both to the nearest pence.

   (1) £20.00
   (2) £13.50
   (3) £86.75
   (4) £ 3.78
   (5) £54.75

6.2 Documents for Financial Transactions are Completed

In this element we will concentrate on the **completion** of the documents explained in Element 6.1. This gives you the opportunity to reaffirm your knowledge and understanding. The answers to these **tasks** can be found on page 172. You will:

- complete purchase documents
- complete sales documents
- complete payment documents
- be aware of the consequences of incorrect completion.

Note: You will not be able to authorize these documents.

Tasks

1. 30.12.19XX: As an employee of Laser Enterprises Ltd, use the blank order form, make out an order from Laser Enterprises Ltd of 21–23 Barkerend Road, Bradstall, West Yorkshire, WF14 6AY, Tel: 0924 603966, Fax: 0924 601235.

   The Order no. is 6603/1 and it is to be sent to Brixton Engineering Ltd, 201 Frampton Court, Birmingham, B14 2LZ. Details of the order are: 300 metres of cable, their catalogue number is C2456 at a price of £1.00 per metre. The cable is to be delivered by road to Laser Enterprises, Unit 6, Grove Industrial Estate, Warefield, West Yorkshire, WF2 3AZ.

ORDER			
FROM		Tel	**Order No**
		Fax	
		Date	
TO			

PLEASE SUPPLY

Quantity	Description	Your Cat No	Price Each

Delivered By: Road

To:

Signature of approval...Buyer

Fig. 6.13 Order Form

2. 3.1.19XX: Complete the Advice Note (Fig. 6.14)from Brixton Engineering Ltd to Laser Enterprises Ltd confirming that 300 metres of cable will be delivered to Unit 6 at the price on the order form on 15.1.19XX. Remember to complete all the details.

3. 15.1.19XX: Working for Brixton Engineering Ltd. The goods are to be delivered on the advice date. Complete the delivery note (Fig. 6.15). The delivery note number is 1256.

ADVICE NOTE

Tel 021–456 4891   Fax 021–456 4309

Invoice To		Deliver To	

Your order No.

Delivery No		Date		
Quantity	Description	Cat No	Price/unit	Delivery Date

Goods Received By ....

Position ....

Signature ....

Fig. 6.14 Advice Note

DELIVERY NOTE

Tel 021–456 4891   Fax 021–456 4309

Invoice To		**Deliver To**	

Your order No.

Delivery No		Date		
Quantity	Description	Cat No	Price/unit	Delivery Date

Goods Received By ....

Position ....

Signature ....

Fig. 6.15 Delivery Note

4. 15.1.19XX: Complete the invoice no. 19901 for the goods delivered to Laser Enterprises (Fig. 6.16).

5. 15.1.19XX: Working for Laser Enterprises Ltd. The goods are delivered on time. After checking, you find the goods are as per delivery note and are of a good standard. The stores location is LS2. Complete the goods received note (Fig. 6.17).

INVOICE
Brixton Engineering Ltd
201 Frampton Court
Birmingham
B14 2LZ

Tel 021–456 4891			Fax 021–456 4309	
To		**Deliver To**		
Your order No		Invoice Number		
Delivery Note No		Date:		
Quantity	Description	Cat No	Price/unit	**TOTAL**
VAT REG NUMBER 398765 567		**VAT AT 17.5%**		
		AMOUNT DUE		
E & OE		**PAYMENT WITHIN 30 DAYS OF INVOICE DATE**		

Fig. 6.16 Invoice

LASER ENTERPRISES LTD

GOODS RECEIVED NOTE		Blue Copy Stores Green Copy Purchasing White Copy Accounts

	NAME	SIGNATURE
Received by	_____	_____
Checked by	_____	_____
Carrier	_____	Date received_____

Quantity	Description	Order No	Supplier	Stores Location

Comments on condition/amount received

Accounts Department

Date Received	Authorization for payment	Amount of Payment	Cheque No	Payment Sent

Fig. 6.17 Goods Received Note

6. 31.1.19XX: Working for Brixton Engineering Ltd, prepare a statement of account (Fig. 6.18) from the following details recorded for Laser Enterprises:

   1 Jan Outstanding balance from previous statement £855.10.
   3 Jan Payment received £150.10.
   15 Jan Invoice no. 19901 £352.50.

7. 3.2.19XX: Working for Laser Enterprises Ltd. Payment is now due for goods bought during December from Brixton Engineering. Complete the cheque and stub below to the amount of £705.00.

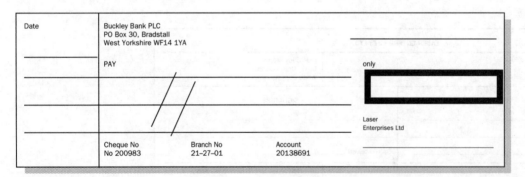

STATEMENT Brixton Engineering Ltd 201 Frampton Court Birmingham B14 2LZ						REMITTANCE ADVICE Brixton Engineering Ltd 201 Frampton Court Birmingham B14 2LZ		
Tel 021–456 4891 Fax 021–456 4309						Tel 021–456 4891 Fax 021–456 4309		
TO		Laser Enterprises Ltd 21–23 Barkerend Rd Bradstall West Yorkshire WF14 6AY				**FROM**	Laser Enterprises Ltd 21–23 Barkerend Rd Bradstall West Yorkshire WF14 6AY	
DATE		ACCOUNT No 168905/1				DATE	ACCOUNT NO 168905/1	
DATE	INVOICE No	ORDER No	DEBIT £	CREDIT	BALANCE £	DATE	OUR INVOICE No	AMOUNT DUE
CURRENT		**DUE**		**60 DAYS AND OVER**				
						AMOUNT DUE		
			AMOUNT DUE			Please return this slip with payment		

Fig. 6.18 Statement of Account

Date	Buckley Bank PLC PO Box 30, Bradstall West Yorkshire WF14 1YA		
	PAY	only	
		Laser Enterprises Ltd	
	Cheque No No 200983	Branch No 21–27–01	Account 20138691

Fig. 6.19 Cheque

Correct completion of financial documents

Financial information is used by managers as a base on which to monitor performance and control costs and it is therefore essential that the financial base from which they extract this information can be relied upon. For this to happen, it is important that the documents discussed in Elements 1 and 2 are completed and checked to ensure that the amounts in the raccounts are accurate. If errors occur and go undetected, the information is not only unreliable but it will also give a false picture of performance.

Consequences of undetected errors

The consequences of **undetected errors** have been discussed throughout Element 6.1. Undetected errors made in the accounts will have effects on:

- the amounts shown in the ledger
- the profit and loss account and balance sheet
- the measurement of business performance ratios (see Element 6.3).

The types and effect of these errors are summarized in Fig. 6.20 below.

ERROR	EFFECT ON LEDGER ACCOUNTS	EFFECT ON YEAR END ACCOUNTS	EFFECT ON PERFORMANCE RATIOS
PURCHASE LEDGER UNDERSTATED	Amount due to creditors too little	Creditors in balance sheet too low	Liquidity ratio too high
PURCHASE LEDGER OVERSTATED	Amount due from creditors too high	Creditors in balance sheet too high	Liquidity ratio too low
SALES LEDGER UNDERSTATED	Amount due from debtors too low	Debtors in balance sheet too low	Liquidity ratio too low
SALES LEDGER OVERSTATED	Amount due from debtors too high	Debtors in balance sheet too high	Liquidity ratio too high
PURCHASES ACCOUNT UNDERSTATED	Amount shown as being purchased is too low	Profit falsely high	ROCE and net profit ratios too high
PURCHASES ACCOUNT OVERSTATED	Amount shown as being purchased is too high	Profit falsely low	ROCE and net profit ratios too low
SALES ACCOUNT UNDERSTATED	Amount shown as being sold is too low	Profit falsely low	ROCE and net profit ratios too low
SALES ACCOUNT OVERSTATED	Amount shown as being sold is too high	Profit falsely high	ROCE and net profit ratios too high
STOCK ACCOUNT UNDERSTATED	Amount shown as being in stock is too low	Profit falsely low	ROCE, net profit and liquidity ratios too low
STOCK ACCOUNT OVERSTATED	Amount shown as being in stock is too high	Profit falsely high	ROCE, net profit and liquidity ratios too high

Fig. 6.20 Consequences of undetected errors

6.3 Monitoring Business Performance

In this element we will explore the ways in which we can **monitor** and measure the business performance of an organization using the final accounts of the company and using the actual performance compared with the budgeted or target performance. To be able to do this we must first be able to:

- Identify the users of accounting information.
- Understand the reasons for monitoring performance.
- Identify and explain what information is needed to monitor performance.
- Examine the information and make judgements about its performance.

Users of accounting information and reasons for monitoring

Various groups of people are interested in 'how well' or 'how badly' an organization has performed. Fig. 6.21 lists the major groups and the reasons for monitoring the performance of an organization. The area of monitoring can be defined in terms of:

- *Profitability.* A measure of the size of profit the company has made compared with previous years or throughout the year when comparing actual results with forecast (expected).

- *Liquidity* (sometimes called Solvency) – A measure of whether the company has sufficient cash to pay its debts when they fall due. Comparisons can be made between years to see whether liquidity is improving or declining, or whether the business is remaining in a solvent state when comparing actual with forecast.

- *Activity.* A measure of how well the company is using its assets. Efficiency is measured by comparing ratios with previous years or comparing actual results with forecast. Activity ratios are closely linked to and directly affect the liquidity of the organization.

USERS	REASONS FOR MONITORING
Owners Sole trader, Partner, Investors, Potential owners	To assess profitability, liquidity and activity last year, now and in the future
All have invested or are considering an investment of capital	How the organization has performed is the responsibility of the management and it is therefore an assessment of their effectiveness
Managers Have a duty of steward-ship (to report to the shareholders and to run the organization in the best interests of shareholders)	Profitability, liquidity and return to shareholders are a measure of how well they have run the organization
	Effective managers will monitor throughout the year by comparing actual results with target/budgeted results. This way they can identify and rectify problem areas and see where improvements in performance can be made
Providers of finance Bank, credit agency, debenture holders, creditor	Interested in whether the organization can repay debts – now and future – especially if there is a need to borrow more, e.g. to expand
Tax authorities Inland Revenue (for tax), Customs and Excise (for VAT)	Interested in correct and accurate records and correct assessment of tax and VAT

Fig. 6.21 Users of Accounting Information and Reasons for monitoring

Key components of accounting information

So far we have identified who uses accounting information and the reasons why they would wish to monitor performance but:

- What information do we need ?
- How do we monitor performance?

One of the main methods of monitoring performance is by the interpretation of accounting information using **ratios**. By converting this information into percentages, comparisons on performance can be made. To do this you must be able to understand the key components of accounting information:

- Profit and loss accounts
- Balance sheets
- Cash flow management

How the profit and loss account and balance sheet are produced will be discussed in Unit 7, page 188. This information will be the starting point of our interpretation, so do check the materials in Unit 7 *before* continuing here.

Effective managers

In practice, managers would not wait until the end of the year to see how well the organization is doing. To help plan and control they would:

- Monitor the performance throughout each year by a comparison of budgeted/ targeted results with the actual results on a monthly, weekly or daily basis.
- If there have been any increases or decreases in the results, effective managers would investigate the causes and try to solve them.
- Monitor regularly in order to identify where improvements can be made.

Nevertheless, managers have a duty of stewardship to report to the shareholders at least once per year. When comparing results on an annual basis, shareholders and other interested parties will expect to see a steady increase in performance. If there is a decrease, the managers should be able to give sound reasons.

Ratio analysis as a means of monitoring performance

It is possible to calculate many **ratios** (percentages) using accounting information but here we will concentrate on the three main areas mentioned on page 159:

- Profitability
- Liquidity
- Activity

> **Important**
>
> The information used as a base for monitoring performance through ratios is obtained via the recording of financial transactions (see Elements 6.1 and 6.2). It is therefore vital that an accurate and reliable **bookkeeping system** is in place.

Now that we know which ratios to produce and how to produce them, the next stage is their calculation and inter-

RATIO CATEGORY AND TYPE	HOW CALCULATED
PROFITABILITY	
Gross profit percentage	$\dfrac{\text{gross profit}}{\text{sales}} \times \dfrac{100}{1}$
Net profit percentage	$\dfrac{\text{net profit (before tax)}}{\text{sales}} \times \dfrac{100}{1}$
Return on capital employed	$\dfrac{\text{net profit (before tax)}}{\text{capital employed}} \times \dfrac{100}{1}$ (capital employed = fixed assets + current assets − current liabilities)
LIQUIDITY (OR SOLVENCY)	
Current ratio	$\dfrac{\text{current assets}}{\text{current liabilities}}$
Acid test ratio	$\dfrac{\text{current assets − closing stock}}{\text{current liabilities}}$
ACTIVITY	
Stock turnover	$\dfrac{\text{cost of goods sold}}{\text{average stock}}$ (average stock = $\dfrac{\text{opening stock − closing stock}}{2}$)
Debtors collection period	$\dfrac{\text{debtors}}{\text{credit sales for the year}} \times 52 \text{ weeks}$ NB: If credit sales are not distinguished from cash sales then assume all sales are made on credit
Creditors payment period	$\dfrac{\text{creditors}}{\text{credit purchases for the year}} \times 52 \text{ weeks}$ NB: If credit purchases are not distinguished from cash purchases then assume all purchases are made on credit

Fig. 6.22 Ratio Categories and Formulae

pretation to determine whether an organization is performing better or worse than last year or better or worse than target/ budgeted performance.

Using the financial accounts of Laser Enterprises for the last two years, turn to page 166 and complete Element 3 Self-Check questions 8–10. We will then analyse its performance. The profit and loss account and balance sheet are shown in Fig. 6.23.

Profitability ratios

The Gross Profit Percentage

This shows how much profit the organization is making as a percentage of sales. The **gross profit percentage** for Laser Enterprises has decreased from 30% to 24% over the two year period:

- For every £100 of sales in the year 1992, the Company has made £30 before deducting expenses.
- For every £100 of sales in 1993 the Company has made £24 before deducting expenses.

A **possible cause** is competition: customers will buy goods at the best possible price. Increased competition will force prices down.

The reasons for the fall in the gross profit percentage could be:

- A reduction in the selling price per unit.
- The selling price per unit remains the same but the cost of goods sold has increased.
- A difference in the type of units sold.

LASER ENTERPRISES SUMMARIZED PROFIT AND LOSS ACCOUNTS

	1992 £000s	1993 £000s
Sales	1500	2000
Less cost of sales		
Opening stock	250	260
Purchases	1060	1770
Less closing stock	(260)	(510)
Cost of sales	1050	1520
Gross profit	450	480
Less expenses	(285)	(310)
Net profit before tax	165	170
Corporation tax	(40)	(50)
Net profit after tax	125	120
Less proposed dividends	(80)	(50)
	45	70
Profit/loss a/c bal b/fwd	200	245
Profit/loss a/c bal c/fwd	245	315

LASER ENTERPRISES SUMMARIZED BALANCE SHEETS

	As at 31.12.92			As at 31.12.93		
	£000	£000	£000	£000	£000	£000
Fixed assets at net book value			1340			1565
Current assets						
Stock		260			510	
Debtors		240			490	
Bank		105			–	
		605			1000	
Less current liabilities						
Creditors	230			510		
Dividend	80			50		
Bank overdraft	–			290		
Tax due	40	350		50	900	
Working capital			255			100
			1595			1665
Less long-term liabilities						
10% Debentures			(350)			(350)
			1245			1315
FINANCED BY						
Authorized share capital 1,000,000 ordinary shares of £1 each			1000			1000
Issued share capital 1,000,000 ordinary shares fully paid			1000			1000
Reserves						
Profit & loss a/c bal b/fwd			200			245
Profit & loss retained			45			70
			1245			1315

Fig. 6.23 Laser Enterprises Ltd Summarised profit and loss account and balance sheets for the year to 31.12.92 and 31.12.93

The Net Profit Percentage

This shows how much profit the organization is making after deduction of all expenses (but before deduction of corporation tax and dividends) as a percentage of sales. The **net profit percentage** for Laser Enterprises has decreased from 11% to 8.5% over the two-year period:

- For every £100 of sales in the year 1992, the Company has made £11 before deduction of corporation tax and dividend payments.
- For every £100 of sales in 1993 the Company has made £8.50 before deduction of corporation tax and dividend payments.

Possible causes are:

- A decrease in the gross profit percentage (as mentioned above)

- A possible increase in the amount of expenses – this can easily be checked by finding the percentage of expenses to sales.

Laser Enterprises: Expenses Percentage

	1992	1993
$\frac{\text{expenses}}{\text{sales}} \times \frac{100}{1}$	$\frac{285}{1500} = 19\%$	$\frac{310}{2000} = 15.5\%$

Laser Enterprises has made less Net Profit in 1993 as a percentage of sales than in 1992 but has been more efficient in the amount spent on expenses – it has cost less in expenses as a percentage of sales in 1993 than in 1992. Therefore the decrease in net profit is due entirely to the decrease in the gross profit percentage.

Return on Capital Employed

There are many different ways of calculating this ratio and each has its benefits. We have chosen a simple method for a limited company.

The ratio compares the amount of profit made per £100 of money invested in the organization.

- Investors would compare the return with the return that might be shown by another company – or even a bank or building society.
- Sole traders and partnerships would compare the return with the amount they might get if they invested in a bank or building society. In comparing the two percentages they may ask themselves whether the return from the business is good enough, taking into account the extra work and risk involved in running their business.

The **return on capital employed** percentage for Laser Enterprises has decreased slightly from 10.3% to 10.2% over the two year period.

- For every £100 of money invested, Laser Enterprises has made £10.30 in profit in 1992, and £10.20 in 1993

Laser Enterprises has therefore earned a slightly smaller return for its investors in 1993 than in 1992.

Liquidity ratios

The Importance of Liquidity

Many businesses measure performance in terms of profitability – they forget about the importance of cash flow. The working capital (or cash flow cycle) is often called the 'life blood' of the business. Without it, the business cannot survive (see Fig. 6.24).

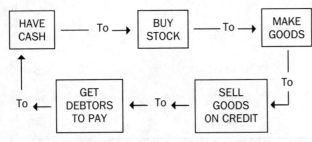

Fig. 6.24 The Working Capital (Cash Flow Cycle)

Inability to pay debts when they are due can have the following consequences for an organisation:

- Difficulty in obtaining credit or further credit from suppliers because of the 'bad feeling' caused by delayed payment.
- Not being able to take advantage of cash discounts.
- Lack of credibility in the eyes of investors or potential investors.
- Not being able to obtain finance for future, profitable expansion programmes.
- In severe cases, having to sell fixed assets to pay off immediate debts and, if additional cash cannot be found, possible bankruptcy (for sole traders and partnerships) or liquidation (for limited companies).

This area is discussed further on page 164.

Did You Know ?

The main reason for small business failure is not a lack of profitability. It is because they have insufficient cash to pay debts.

Current Ratio

The **current ratio** is a measure of whether the company can pay its debts when they are due – in other words, can the company (if it needed to) convert all its current assets into cash and have enough to pay its current liabilities? For example, it could sell its stock, get the money in from debtors and use the cash at the bank.

There is no ideal ratio of current assets to current liabilities, although some say that 2:1 is a healthy figure. However, many organizations run quite happily with a ratio much smaller than this. It is more important that this ratio remains steady over the years – if there is a drastic decrease then this area needs investigating.

The current ratio for Laser Enterprises has decreased from 1.73:1 to 1.11:1 over the period. The organization could convert its current assets into cash to pay its current liabilities at both dates and still have money left over since:

- For every £1.73 of current assets in the year 1992, the Company had £1.00 worth of current liabilities.
- For every £1.11 of current assets in the year 1993 the Company had £1.00 worth of current liabilities.

Of course, it is hoped that this situation will not arise: managers should keep a close watch on when creditors need paying – if things get a little sticky they will need to approach their bank for temporary funding.

A **possible cause** of this fall in the current ratio is that the bank balance has decreased over the time period from surplus into an overdraft situation. It appears that the finance of fixed asset purchases has been made, in part, by a reduction in working capital. Perhaps next year the new fixed assets will earn more profit and then cash?

Acid Test Ratio

The **acid test ratio** is so called because it is said to be a keener measure of the liquidity situation of a company. It is calculated on the same basis as the current ratio but only includes those current assets that can be converted 'quickly' into cash. As there is no guarantee that *stocks* can be sold quickly enough, or at the balance sheet value, this figure is excluded.

A ratio of current assets (– stocks) to current liabilities of 1:1 seems acceptable – any less and there is a danger of a business not being able to pay its debts when due. A large figure would indicate that the company was not making the best use of its funds.

The **acid test ratio** for Laser Enterprises has decreased from 0.99:1 to 0.54:1 over the period.

- For every £0.99 of current assets (excluding stock) in the year 1992, the Company had £1.00 worth of current liabilities.
- For every £0.54 of current assets (excluding stock) in the year 1993, the Company had £1.00 worth of current liabilities.

A **possible cause** of this fall in the acid test ratio is the overdraft situation. Buying fixed assets is leaving the company short of cash. If the overdraft facility is for a sufficiently long period then there may be no problems. On the information given, the management of Laser Enterprises should have considered a longer term method of finance for this purchase.

Activity ratios

The **activity ratios** (sometimes called 'operating ratios') indicate how efficient the managers are in controlling stocks, debtors and creditors and will directly affect the liquidity of the organization. The management of cash flow and methods of avoiding a cash shortage are discussed further on page 164.

Stock Turnover Ratio

The **stock turnover ratio** can be expressed in various ways, one of which is:

$$\text{Stock turnover ratio} = \frac{\text{cost of goods sold}}{\text{average stock}}$$

A rise in this ratio would indicate that less stock is required to support any given cost of sales. Put another way, the stock is held for a shorter period of time before it is sold; it 'turns over' more quickly.

Generally, the quicker the stock turns over the better, but there is a danger in holding too few stocks (see page 164). If stocks are not sold quickly enough, they may become 'out of date' (such as might happen with a fashion store), deteriorate or become damaged.

Holding stocks means money is 'tied up' in the business until they are sold. It also costs money to store the goods and therefore some organizations operate a system called 'just-in-time', where stocks arrive at the place of business 'just in time' for manufacture.

Did You Know ?

The stock turnover of a tin of beans in a supermarket is less than one day?

For Laser Enterprises the stock turnover ratio has *fallen* from 4.12 in 1992 to 3.94 in 1993. In other words the stock is turning over less quickly than before.

The stock turnover can easily be converted to months, weeks or days by dividing 12 or 52 or 365 by your answer.

The stock turnover ratio for Laser Enterprises has decreased from

4.12 times per year   to 3.94 times per year

or the average length of time the stock is held has increased from

once every $\frac{52}{4.12}$ = 12.62 weeks to $\frac{52}{3.94}$ = 13.20 weeks

Possible causes are:

- Poor stock control system.
- Decrease in sales.
- An anticipated increase in sales due early in the next

financial year for which production has to take place this year.
- A new product that takes longer to produce than the existing products.

In the case of Laser Enterprises the second of these possible causes does not apply, as sales have increased.

Debtors Collection Period

The **debtors collection period** is the average length of time it is taking for customers who buy on credit to pay their debts. Time allowed will depend on the organization and the type of goods it is selling. For example, a retail organization will sell goods mainly on a cash basis, the collection period here will be quick.

The credit period allowed varies – sometimes 90 days or more. Most organizations will try to extend their credit payment time period (it is a form of free financing) and so a good credit control system should be in place. Generally, organizations should aim to improve the collection period.

The average time it is taking Laser Enterprises to collect money in from debtors has risen from 8.3 weeks in 1992 to 12.7 weeks at the balance sheet date in 1993.

Possible causes are:

- Poor credit control system.
- A change to a new market area or expansion into an existing market where the customers demand longer payment periods.

Creditors Collection Period

The **creditors collection period** is the average length of time it is taking the organization to pay its debts. This is the other side of the coin. Extend your credit and you are obtaining free finance, but beware – the organization still has to pay for the goods sometime and if there are persistent delays the supplier might withdraw credit facilities!

Generally, a good credit control system would be one where the average collection period for debtors is slightly less than that for creditors – where the organization has received monies due from sales before they pay for the purchases.

The average time it is taking Laser Enterprises to pay creditors for goods has risen from 11.3 weeks in 1992 to 15 weeks in 1993.

Important

When answering questions on cash flow management, liquidity or working capital it is important to use the **liquidity** and **activity ratios**.

Ratios do not tell the complete story

When studying financial statements you must be careful not to take this information in isolation as other information is very useful. Ratios, although being a 'good guide', have limitations since they:

- Only provide past information.
- Do not indicate what is happening or what is expected to happen.

- Cannot be used by management in isolation.
- Are unrealistic when comparing organizations of different size, financed differently or follow different accounting policies.
- Do not give information regarding the management of the organization (see Unit 8).

Cash flow management

Management of the cash flow situation of an organization is very important. To do this we look very closely at the **working capital** (current assets less current liabilities). How this is managed will determine the liquidity of an organization – its ability to pay debts when they fall due. The ways in which a cash flow shortage can be avoided are as follows:

Sources of finance (see also Unit 7)
- Increasing capital – by an issue of shares or debentures to finance longer term projects.
- Delaying the payment of fixed asset purchase, e.g. considering leasing, hire purchase or trade credit.
- Selling fixed assets – as a last resort but sale and lease back is now becoming popular.
- Factoring – selling the value of debtors to a factoring company for a reduced price. A useful way of obtaining cash quicker.

Good control systems

The cash flow forecast illustrates for a period of time the organization's income and expenditure – this should identify any potential cash shortages (see Unit 7, Element 2).

Debtor control

Debtor control is the process by which an organization tries to ensure that debts are paid on time. Not calling in debts is allowing 'free finance' to your customer and costing *you* money. A good control system should:

- Ensure invoices are sent to the customer at the same time that the goods are delivered.
- Prepare an **aged debtor analysis** at the end of each month listing debts outstanding and the period for which they are overdue (see Fig. 6.25).

PERIOD OF DEBT CREDIT TERMS 30 DAYS	AMOUNT OF DEBT £	ACTION	FURTHER ACTION
Less than 1 month	7000	None	
1 months to 2 months	2500	Reminder	
2 months to 3 months	700	Final reminder	Discontinue supply
3 months to 1 year	300	Court action	
TOTAL	10,500		

Fig. 6.25 Aged Debtor Analysis

- Send reminders periodically and, after a period of time, threaten legal action if the debt still remains unpaid.
- Check the creditworthiness of organizations before allowing credit. This can be done by employing an agency who specializes in such actions or by examining the published accounts or by asking for credit references from banks.
- Stop supplies if debts remain unpaid.
- Calculate the debtors collection period.

Creditor control

Creditor control is the process of delaying payments to the suppliers for as long as possible. It will help with the cash flow of the organization but it has its disadvantages such as:

- loss of cash discounts
- suppliers discontinuing supply
- suppliers suing for monies owed

Organizations should prepare an analysis of aged creditors at the end of each month which will list creditors that are due to be paid and act as a reminder to the organization of who needs paying and when.

Did You Know ?

Small business often become the suppliers to large organizations – this helps their profitability. But large organizations often demand a long credit period – 90 days and more. This is often the cause of the small business cash flow problem.

Stock control

Stock control (holding stocks) costs money and therefore many organizations use computers to determine the optimum stock level (see Unit 2). It is essential that organizations have a good stock control system, the objective being to strike a balance between having too few stocks and holding too many stocks – both have disadvantages (Fig. 6.26).

Disadvantages of holding too few stocks	Disadvantages of holding too many stocks
Inadequate stocks to meet an unexpected rise in demand	Too much tied up in stocks that could more usefully be spent on buying fixed assets that would increase future profits
Not being able to take advantage of discounts for bulk purchases	Larger expenses of handling, insurance and storage
More vulnerable to price increases from the supplier	Increased chance that unused stocks may deteriorate, become out of date or damaged
Lost production brought about by a shortage of raw materials	If money has been borrowed to buy the stocks then there will be increased interest to pay

Fig. 6.26 Advantages and disadvantages of holding stock

Further methods of measuring performance

So far, in Unit 6 we have looked at:

- Why it is essential to have a reliable and accurate bookkeeping system.
- How this information is used to monitor and measure the performance of an organization in terms of solvency, profitability and the achievement of targets.

These methods are used as a tool to assess the organization in terms of those products that are already being produced. But what if it is a new product? How can we assess whether the new product will make a profit?

The techniques used to assess the profitability of a new product are **breakeven analysis** and **discounted cash flow**.

Breakeven analysis

To assess whether a new (or existing) product is 'at least covering the costs of producing it', we use breakeven analysis. To use this technique we must first be able to distinguish between 'fixed costs' and 'variable costs'.

We will identify fixed and variable costs by first considering normal household expenses.

Fixed costs are those that do not change according to the number of people living in a household. For instance, the amount paid in mortgage or rent and council tax would be the same whether four people or six people lived in the house. These are the 'fixed costs'. Conversely, the cost of food would alter according to the number of people – this is therefore a 'variable cost'.

Example

Assuming there are four people in a household, fixed costs amount to £100 and variable costs amount to £15 per person, the total cost of running expenses would be

Variable cost (4 × £15 = £60) + fixed cost (£100)

= total cost £160

Therefore

Average cost per person = $\frac{£160}{4}$ = £40

To break even (cover costs), the people in this household would have to earn at least £40 each.

But if there were six people living in the household the cost per person would decrease:

Variable cost (6 × £15 = £90) + fixed cost (£100)

= total cost £190

Average cost per person = $\frac{£190}{6}$ = £31.67

Why? Because the fixed costs are spread over a greater number of people. To break even in this household the people would have to earn £31.67 – if they earned £40 each, they would make a surplus of

6 x £40 = £240 total income

less   £190 total costs

surplus   £50

It is the same for an organization.

Fixed and variable costs of a business

Fixed costs may include rent, rates, heating, lighting, salaries to monthly paid employees. These costs (in the short term) would remain the same whether 1 unit or 100 units were produced.

Variable costs may be the cost of materials for making a product and the cost of wages for employees who are paid on an hourly basis. These costs would increase according to the number of units produced.

Managers would firstly assess:

- how many units it could sell and at what price
- the fixed costs
- the variable cost per unit.

Breakeven point is then calculated.

The definition of *breakeven point* is:

> How many units or products an organization has to produce or sell to make **zero profit**.

The breakeven formula is:

$$\frac{\text{total fixed costs}}{\text{contribution}}$$

where contribution is the selling price less variable cost

The definition of contribution is:

> The amount that each sale contributes towards covering fixed costs.

•Management decisions

If total cost is equal to total income then the product will break even. Managers must then decide whether they can see a longer term benefit from making the product (maybe an increase in sales or a reduction in costs).

If total cost is more than total income then the product will make a loss and the managers would have to decide whether production is worthwhile.

If total cost is less than total income, then the product would be making a profit and managers may decide to commence production.

Example

A company is deciding whether to sell a new type of garden product. Market research and an analysis of costs indicates the following:

Selling price £10 per unit
Variable cost £6 per unit
Fixed costs   £4000

The break even point in units would be

$\frac{\text{fixed costs}}{\text{contribution}}$ = $\frac{£4000}{£10 - £6 = £4}$ = 1000 units

If 1500 units were sold, profit would be

Sales – Variable Costs = Contribution – Fixed Costs =
Profit £15000 – (1500 × £6) = £6000 – £4000 =
£2000

Important

The greater the number of units produced, the lower the cost of producing a unit.

Discounted cash flow (DCF)

Using DCF techniques can be quite complicated and involved. However, in this element we will take a brief look at this method so that you gain a basic understanding. Before an organisation commences with a new project, an investment appraisal is carried out. Questions which should be asked are:

- Will the amount received in income (sales) over the life of the project cover the setting up costs (machinery etc.) and running costs ?
- How much in real terms (taking inflation etc. into account) will we actually receive?
- Will the net amount of sales income receivable amount to

more than any alternative investments, i.e. investing the money and receiving interest?

An organization that uses this method will 'discount' all income and costs of the project starting from the end of the first year and finishing at the end of the project life. By 'discount' we mean that all future values will be expressed in today's (present) values. The discount rate will be a percentage (which may be the current interest rate). Initial costs (setting-up costs) are not discounted because they are paid out at the start of the project. If, after discounting, the net amount receivable is positive, the project is worthwhile. If not, the project is not worthwhile and production should not commence.

Self Check ✔ **Element 3**

6. Limited companies prepare accounts for their shareholders but the accounts are also used by banks and the Inland Revenue. Why would they wish to see them?

7. Some groups of people who are interested in how an organization has performed use the published accounts.
   Explain why this method would be unadvisable on its own to managers of organizations, and state alternative measurements that they might use.

8. In the box below (Box 1), the ratios have been calculated for Laser Enterprises for 1992. Complete any part of the box which has missing information.

9. Has Laser Enterprises made 'more' or 'less' gross profit in 1993? What are the likely causes?

10. Which of the following could cause a decrease in the gross profit percentage?

    (a) Increase in expenses
    (b) Increase in the number of units sold
    (c) Increase in the cost of sales
    (d) The amount of dividends

11. Potential investors use company accounts to decide whether to invest. Give and explain on example of the way in which accounts may help a potential investor to judge performance.

Ratio Calculations for Laser Enterprises

Ratio Category and Type	1992	1993
Profitability		
Gross profit percentage	$\frac{450}{1500} \times \frac{100}{1} = 30\%$	$\frac{480}{?} \times \frac{100}{1} = 24\%$
Net profit percentage	$\frac{165}{1500} \times \frac{100}{1} = 11\%$	$\frac{170}{2000} \times \frac{100}{1} =$
Return on Capital Employed	$\frac{165}{1595} \times \frac{100}{1} = 10.3\%$	$\frac{\quad}{\quad} \times \frac{100}{1} =$
Liquidity (or solvency)		
Current ratio	$\frac{605}{350} = 1.73:1$	$\frac{1000}{900} =$
Acid test ratio	$\frac{605 - 260}{350} = 0.99:1$	$\frac{1000 -}{900} = \quad :1$
Activity		
Stock turnover	$\frac{1050}{255} = 4.12$ times per year	$\frac{1520}{385} = \quad$ times per year
	average stock $= \frac{250 + 260}{2} = 255$	average stock $= \frac{260 +}{2} = 385$
Debtors collection period	$\frac{240}{1500} \times 52 = 8.3$ weeks	$\frac{\quad}{2000} \times \quad = \quad$ weeks
Creditors payment period	$\frac{230}{1060} \times 52 = 11.3$ weeks	$\frac{510}{1770} \times 52 = \quad$ weeks

Box 1

Self Check ✔ **Element 3** *continued*

12. The acid test ratio for an organization was 1:1 in 1992 and 0.33:1 in 1993. Explain the implications of this decline.

13. Which of the following ratios would best assess the profitability of an organization?

    (a) Current ratio
    (b) Net profit ratio
    (c) Stock turnover
    (d) Debtors collection period

14. The management of the cash flow position, often described as the solvency position, in an organization is very important. Which of the following is most likely to improve the solvency position of an organization?

    (a) A fixed asset purchase using funds from the bank
    (b) Allowing debtors more time to pay
    (c) Paying creditors quickly
    (d) Improving the debtors collection period

15. A company has completed its market research and found that it can sell its product at £8 per unit. The variable cost per unit is £4 and fixed costs are £4000.

    (a) What is the contribution per unit?
    (b) What is the breakeven point?

Unit Test
Completion guide: 1 hour plus 5 minutes reading time.

Focus 1

Financial Transactions   10 marks

Questions 1
The purpose of keeping a record of items sold on credit within a business is to:

A Provide detailed records of the amount purchased
B Provide a record of the amount of expenses used
C Provide records of the amount owed to the organization for credit control purposes
D None of the above

Question 2–5 relate to the following information:

An organization sells goods mainly on credit. The following errors have occurred in the last year:

A A purchase invoice has been omitted
B Closing stock has been overvalued
C Some purchase returns have not been recorded
D A credit sale has not been recorded

Which error will have which outcome:

Question 2
The profit figure will be higher

Question 3
The creditors figure will be lower

Question 4
The amount purchased will be too high

Question 5
The total debtors figure will be lower

Question 6
Which document is used internally for recording and checking goods?

A Delivery Note
B Advice Note
C Goods Received Note
D Credit Note

Question 7
An invoice has been sent to an organization for credit purchases. The buying organization has accepted the goods in a good condition. The accounts department in the selling organization will record:

(i)   The amount of sale in the purchase ledger
(ii)   The amount of sale in the sales ledger
(iii) The value of the goods in the sales account
(iv)   The value of the goods in the purchases account

Which option best describes the above statements ?
A (i) and (iii)
B (ii) and (iv)
C (ii) and (iii)
D (i) and (iv)

Question 8
The main purpose of an advice note is to:

A Check that goods are in a good condition
B Advise that payment for goods received is due
C Advise that goods are to be delivered on a specified date
D Provide proof of delivery

Question 9
You have been invoiced for goods bought. On checking the calculations you find that you have been overcharged. You would telephone the selling organization and ask for:

A A debit note
B A delivery note
C An advice note
D A credit note

Question 10
The main purpose of a paying in slip is to:

A Inform the bank of the amount deposited
B Have proof of cheques and cash paid in on specific dates
C Have proof of payments made by cheques on specific dates
D Have proof of the amount paid in by cash

Focus 2

Security   4 marks

Questions 11
On receipt of a cheque for payment of goods bought on credit you should:

A Ensure it is completed correctly
B Carry out a credit check
C Return the cheque as it is not accompanied by a valid cheque card
D Ensure it is dated

Question 12
When using a petty cash system you should

(i) repay upon receipt of a completed petty cash voucher
(ii) ensure you receive a receipt for goods bought

Which option best describes the above statements
A (i) only
B (ii) only
C none of the above
D (i) and (ii)

Question 13
The prime objective of the Cheque Act 1992 was to decrease the risk of fraud.

Mark each of these statements true (T) or false (F).

(i) A crossed cheque with nothing written between the lines is illegal.
(ii) The safest crossing on a cheque is 'account payee only'.

A (i) T   (ii) F
B (i) T   (ii) T
C (i) F   (ii) F
D (i) F   (ii) T

Question 14

A retail business allows a purchase of goods to be made to the value of £150 by a customer with a £50 guarantee card .

Mark each of these statements true (T) or false (F).

(i) The card will guarantee payment will be made to the value of £150.
(ii) It is unwise to accept payment over the guarantee card limit.

A (i) T (ii) F
B (i) T (ii) T
C (i) F (ii) F
D (i) F (ii) T

Focus 3

Accounting Information   10 marks

Questions 15–17 relate to the following information:

Accounting information is used to produce the following:

A Profit and loss account
B Balance sheet
C Cash flow
D Purchase ledger

Which documents will give information on:

Question 15
Assets

Question 16
Expenses

Question 17
Liquidity

Question 18
Potential suppliers of goods to a business are mainly interested in:

A Profitability
B Accurate accounting records
C How well the business is using its assets
D Whether the business is able to pay its debts

Question 19
Effective managers use accounting information to help them plan and control.

Mark each of these statements true (T) or false (F).

(i) The information is best obtained when the year end accounts are produced.
(ii) The information is best obtained from targets and budgets

A (i) T (ii) F
B (i) T (ii) T
C (i) F (ii) F
D (i) F (ii) T

Question 20
A measurement of liquidity is the acid test ratio. This is the relationship between:

A Current assets and current liabilities
B Current assets less stock and current liabilities
C Fixed assets and current liabilities
D Assets and liabilities

Question 21
The final accounts contain costs that can be classified as fixed or variable.

Mark each of these statements true (T) or false (F).

(i) Rates are classified as a variable cost.
(ii) Raw materials are regarded as a variable cost.

A (i) T (ii) F
B (i) T (ii) T
C (i) F (ii) F
D (i) F (ii) T

Question 22
The working capital of a business is the relationship between:

A Assets and liabilities
B Fixed assets and capital
C Current assets and current liabilities
D Total assets and current liabilities

Question 23
Breakeven analysis is used to forecast whether a project is worthwhile.

Mark each of these statements true (T) or false (F).

(i) Breakeven point is $\dfrac{\text{fixed costs}}{\text{contribution}}$

(ii) Break even point is $\dfrac{\text{fixed costs}}{\text{selling price} - \text{variable costs}}$

A (i) T (ii) F
B (i) T (ii) T
C (i) F (ii) F
D (i) F (ii) T

Question 24
The discounted cash flow technique is used to:

A Calculate the amount of cash in the bank
B Forecast expected income and expenditure
C Calculate the amount of cash discounts allowed
D Forecast future sums of money in present day terms

Focus 4

Monitoring   6 marks

Questions 25–27 relate to the following information

The following records on financial information are kept by a business:

A Sales ledger
B Purchase ledger
C Cash budget
D Cash book

Select the procedure that is concerned with:

Question 25
Receipts

Question 26
Creditors

Question 27
Debtors

Question 28
The return on capital employed provides information on:

A Liquidity
B Profitability
C Asset usage
D Capital invested

Question 29
Owners and managers will monitor business performance by the use of ratios

Mark each of these statements is true (T) or false (F).

(i) For a business to survive, it must be profitable.
(ii) For a business to survive it must be liquid.

A (i) T (ii) F
B (i) T (ii) T
C (i) F (ii) F
D (i) F (ii) T

Question 30
The current ratio helps a business to identify its:

A Ability to pay its debts
B Stock turnover
C Use of assets
D Long-term investments

Answers to Self-check Questions (Elements 1 and 3)

1. (a) NO   Organizations using cash to purchase cannot be 'in debt' for that purchase.
   (b) YES An organization that buys on credit will be a debtor (in debt) for that purchase.
   (c) NO   A financial transaction that involves selling goods for cash will be a cash sale.
   (d) NO   See (b).

2. (1)   NO   This is a delivery note.
   (2)   NO   (a) is a security measure for the selling organization – proof that they have delivered the goods.
   (3)   YES As copies of the goods received note are sent to three separate departments. It is a checking procedure that the goods agree with the original order in both quantity and quality. Hence, it is a security measure. Therefore (b) and (c) apply.
   (4), (5) NO   As explained in (3) above

3. Invoice 19501 will become due for payment within 30 days of the invoice date as per terms stated on the invoice. Therefore payment is due 14.1.XX.
   Payment on receipt of a statement of account allows the purchasing organization longer to pay. Invoice 19501 will not appear as due until a statement is issued by Brixton Engineering on 31.1.XX. In total, Laser Enterprises will have received 41 days credit by the due date as per the statement of account.

4. The crossing used by Laser Enterprises is 'Account Payee'. This means that it can only be paid into the bank account of the payee. Account Payee is the safest type of crossing and reduces the risk of fraud.

5.

	VAT	SALE EXCLUSIVE OF VAT
	£ . p	£ . p
(1)	2.98	17.02
(2)	2.01	11.49
(3)	12.92	73.83
(4)	0.56	3.22
(5)	8.15	46.60

6. The final accounts of a limited company tell us how much profit the organization has made for a financial period and the 'balance' between assets and liabilities. By using ratio analysis:

   • Banks can determine whether the organization is both profitable and liquid to determine whether they can continue repayments or can be considered credit-worthy for future loans.
   • Tax authorities will use the information to determine the amount of corporation tax due in that period.

7. Year end financial statements are history, the information is what has happened last year and not what is happening. Managers would not be very effective if they waited until the year end to assess whether they had made a profit. Managers would use ongoing targets and budgets. This would give them the information on which to measure performance monthly or weekly. Interpretation of the information allows managers to identify and correct any problems and identify areas in which improvements on performance can be made.

8. Laser Enterprises ratios for 1993:

Ratio Category and Type	Ratio calculations, 1993
Profitability	
Gross profit percentage	$\frac{480}{2000} \times \frac{100}{1} = 24\%$
Net profit percentage	$\frac{170}{2000} \times \frac{100}{1} = 8.5\%$
Return on capital employed	$\frac{170}{1665} \times \frac{100}{1} = 10.2\%$
Liquidity (or solvency)	
Current ratio	$\frac{1000}{900} = 1.11{:}1$
Acid test ratio	$\frac{1000 - 510}{900} = 0.54{:}1$
Activity	
Stock turnover	$\frac{1520}{385} = 3.94$ times per year $\frac{260 + 510}{2} = 385$
Debtors collection period	$\frac{490 \times 52}{2000} = 12.7$ weeks
Creditor payment period	$\frac{510 \times 52}{1770} = 15$ weeks

9. In financial terms, more profit has been earned in 1993 than in 1992, but the Gross Profit as a % of sales has dropped. Reasons could include a reduction in selling prices to increase turnover, or an increase in purchase prices.

10. (a) NO These expenses are deducted after the gross profit percentage is calculated but will form part of the net profit percentage.
    (b) NO An increase in sales would most probably result in an increase in gross profit.
    (c) YES Profit is sales less the cost of making those sales and therefore an increase in the costs would reduce the gross profit.
    (d) NO Dividends are part of how profits are appropriated (shared out) and are deducted after the net profit is calculated.

11. Potential investors could use ratio analysis from which they can judge profitability and the return on their investment. They could compare the return with that of other organizations and make a decision on whether to invest.

12. The acid test ratio measures the amount of assets that can quickly be turned into cash to pay for debts when they fall due. In 1993 for every £1 of current liabilities the organization only had 33 pence to pay them. This means

that the organization is short on liquid funds and if they cannot pay their debts it could lead to bankruptcy or liquidation. If necessary, the company should approach the bank for some temporary funding.

13. (a) NO   This is a measure of liquidity.
    (b) YES It is a measure of the amount of profit after all costs have been deducted relative to sales.
    (c) NO   This measures the average number of times stock has been sold.
    (d) NO   It indicates how efficient we are at collecting debts. If we have poor control of this area we are affecting our liquidity position.

14. (a) NO   Buying a fixed asset may improve the solvency long term – when the assets help to increase profits. Short term, the level of solvency will deteriorate.
    (b) NO   Debtors owe us money; allowing extra time means we have to wait longer for payment – this would reduce the level of solvency.
    (c) NO   Money would go out of the bank quicker – this would reduce the level of solvency.
    (d) YES It means that we are getting money into the bank quicker.

15. (a) The contribution is £8 – £4 = £4 per unit.
    (b) Breakeven point is:
    $$\frac{£4000}{£4} = 1000 \text{ units}$$

Answers to Tasks (Element 2)

TASK 1

ORDER			
FROM	Laser Enterprises Ltd 21–23 Barkerend Rd Bradstall West Yorkshire WF14 6AY	Tel 0924 603966 Fax 0924 601235 Date 30.12.19XX	**Order No** 6603/1
TO	Brixton Engineering Ltd 201 Frampton Court Birmingham B14 2LZ		

PLEASE SUPPLY

Quantity	Description	Your Cat No	Price Each
300 metres	Cable	C2456	£1.00/metre

Delivered By: Road

To: Laser Enterprises, Unit 6, Grove Industrial Estate, Warefield, West Yorkshire, WF2 3AZ

Signature of approval...Buyer

TASK 2

ADVICE NOTE

Tel 021–456 4891		Fax 021–456 4309		
Invoice To	Laser Enterprises Ltd 21–23 Barkerend Rd Bradstall West Yorkshire WF14 6AY	Deliver To	Laser Enterprises Ltd Unit 6, Grove Ind. Est Warefield West Yorkshire WF2 3AZ	
Your order No 6603/1 Delivery No		Date 3.1.19XX		
Quantity	Description	Cat No	Price/unit	Delivery Date
300 metres	Cable	C2456	£1.00/metre	15.1.19XX

Good Received By ....

Position ....

Signature of approval...

TASK 3

DELIVERY NOTE

Tel 021–456 4891		Fax 021–456 4309		
Invoice To	Laser Enterprises Ltd 21–23 Barkerend Rd Bradstall West Yorkshire WF14 6AY	Deliver To	Laser Enterprises Ltd Unit 6, Grove Ind. Est Warefield West Yorkshire WF2 3AZ	
Your order No 6603/1 Delivery No		Date 3.1.19XX		
Quantity	Description	Cat No	Price/unit	Delivery Date
300 metres	Cable	C2456	£1.00/metre	15.1.19XX

Good Received By ....

Position ....

Signature of approval...

TASK 4

INVOICE

Brixton Engineering Ltd
201 Frampton Court
Birmingham
B14 2LZ

Tel 021–456 4891		Fax 021–456 4309	

To	Laser Enterprises Ltd 21–23 Barkerend Rd Bradstall West Yorkshire WF14 6AY	Deliver To	Laser Enterprises Ltd Unit 6, Grove Ind. Est Warefield West Yorkshire WF2 3AZ

Your order No	6603/1	Invoice Number 19901
Delivery Note No	1256	Date 15.1.19XX

Quantity	Description	Cat No	Price/unit	TOTAL
300 metres	Cable	C2456	£1.00/metre	£300.00

VAT REG NUMBER 398765 567	**VAT AT** 17.5%	£52.50
	AMOUNT DUE	£352.50

E & OE	**PAYMENT WITHIN 30 DAYS OF INVOICE DATE**

TASK 5

LASER ENTERPRISES LTD

GOODS RECEIVED NOTE	Blue Copy Stores Green Copy Purchasing White Copy Accounts

	NAME	SIGNATURE	
Received by	_____	_____	
Checked by	_____	_____	
Carrier	_____	Date received ___15.1.19XX___	

Quantity	Description	Order No	Supplier	Stores Location
300 metres	Cable	6603/1	BRIXTON ENG. LTD	LS2

Comments on condition/amount received

Condition Good, amount as per order 6603/1

Accounts Department

Date Received	Authorisation for payment	Amount of Payment	Cheque No	Payment Sent

TASK 6

STATEMENT						REMITTANCE ADVICE		
Brixton Engineering Ltd 201 Frampton Court Birmingham B14 2LZ						Brixton Engineering Ltd 201 Frampton Court Birmingham B14 2LZ		
Tel 021–456 4891 Fax 021–456 4309						Tel 021–456 4891 Fax 021–456 4309		
TO		Laser Enterprises Ltd 21–23 Barkerend Rd Bradstall West Yorkshire WF14 6AY				FROM	Laser Enterprises Ltd 21–23 Barkerend Rd Bradstall West Yorkshire WF14 6AY	
DATE		ACCOUNT NO 168905/1				DATE	ACCOUNT NO 168905/1	
DATE	INVOICE No	ORDER No	DEBIT £	CREDIT	BALANCE £	DATE	OUR INVOICE No	AMOUNT DUE
31.1.19XX					855.10			
3.1.19XX	Payment			150.10	705.00			
15.1.19XX	19901	6603/1	352.50		1052.00			
CURRENT		**DUE**		60 DAYS AND OVER				
£352.50		£705.00				AMOUNT DUE		£705.00
			AMOUNT DUE			Please return this slip with payment		

TASK 7

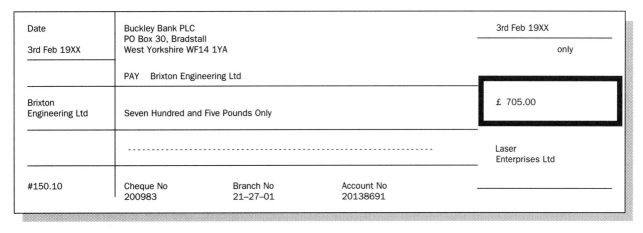

Date 3rd Feb 19XX	Buckley Bank PLC PO Box 30, Bradstall West Yorkshire WF14 1YA			3rd Feb 19XX
				only
	PAY Brixton Engineering Ltd			
Brixton Engineering Ltd	Seven Hundred and Five Pounds Only			£ 705.00
	---			Laser Enterprises Ltd
#150.10	Cheque No 200983	Branch No 21–27–01	Account No 20138691	

Answers to Unit Test

Question	Answer	Question	Answer	Question	Answer	Question	Answer	Question	Answer
1	C	7	C	13	D	19	D	25	D
2	B	8	C	14	D	20	B	26	B
3	A	9	D	15	B	21	D	27	A
4	C	10	B	16	A	22	C	28	C
5	D	11	A	17	C	23	B	29	B
6	C	12	D	18	D	24	D	30	A

Unit Test Comments

Question 1.
If items are sold on credit, it means that businesses or individuals owe the business selling those items money. The name given to these businesses/individuals is **debtors** – they are in debt to the organization. From a selling point of view, it is important to keep control of 'who owes what amount' and by 'when' the debt should be paid. The answer is option C since the other options relate to expense costs incurred and purchases on credit.

Question 2.
Overvaluation of closing stock will reduce the cost of sales which in turn will increase profit – option B

Question 3.
An omitted purchase invoice will reduce the purchases figure and total of creditors – option A.

Question 4.
Since purchase returns are deducted from purchases, omitting the recording of those returns will make the purchases figure too high – option C.

Question 5.
Not recording a credit sale will result in debtors figure being too low – option D.

Question 6.
A NO The delivery note is to give the seller 'proof' that the goods have been delivered.
B NO The advice note is to advise the 'buyer' that the goods will be delivered and that the amount ordered can be delivered.
C YES The goods received note is a document used internally for recording and checking purposes.
D NO A credit note is issued to correct an incorrect invoice.

Question 7.
On acceptance of the goods, the selling organization will record the value of the goods in the sales ledger under the name of the customer and record the amount sold in the sales account. Option C best describes the two statements.

Question 8.
A NO This is part of the procedure of a goods received note.

B NO This will be in the form of a payment reminder.
C YES the advice note states that goods are to be delivered on a specified date.
D NO This is the purpose of a delivery note.

Question 9.
A NO A debit note will increase the amount owed by you to the selling organization.
B NO A delivery note is received when goods are actually delivered.
C NO An advice note states when the goods will be delivered.
D YES A credit note will reduce the amount owed by you to the selling organization.

Question 10.
A NO The actual cash and cheques deposited tells the bank how much has been deposited.
B YES The paying-in slip is your proof of cheques and cash paid in on specific dates.
C NO The cheque stub is proof that cheques have been made out on specific dates.
D NO The paying-in slip does allow for this, but it is only part of its job.

Question 11.
A YES It is important to check that the cheque is completed correctly as incorrect completion will mean delay in payment.
B NO This should be done prior to allowing the purchaser to buy goods on credit – not on receipt of payment.
C NO Although this is very important if you are a retail organization, in the world of businesses a cheque card is not generally used. This is why it is important to carry out a credit check on the buyer first.
D NO Although it is important to check that it is dated, there are other checks that should take place (see page 151).

Question 12.
A good petty cash control system should repay upon receipt of a completed petty cash voucher and receipt for the items bought. Option D best describes the two statements.

Question 13.
A crossed cheque with nothing written between the line is not illegal as businesses can request that it is left blank. However, this is only done in the 'business world' and only by a few organizations. However, the safest crossing on a cheque is 'account payee only'. The most appropriate answer is therefore D.

Question 14.
The card is for £50 and will guarantee payment ONLY to the value of £50 – not £150. It is therefore unwise to accept payment over the guarantee card limit. If goods purchased are over the guarantee card limit – check for approval. The most appropriate answer is D.

Question 15.
The balance sheet gives information on assets and liabilities of the business at a particular point in time. Option B applies.

Question 16.
The profit and loss account lists the expenditure for a particular trading period – option A.

Question 17.
Liquidity is the amount of cash which is available to the company, and is shown in a cash flow forecast, Option C.

Question 18.
Potential suppliers of goods to a business are mainly interested in whether the business is able to repay liabilities. Option D is most appropriate.

Question 19.
Statement (i) is incorrect. If they wait until the year end accounts are produced, then a year will have elapsed before they are aware that they are on target. This is far too late to take corrective measures on things that might have gone wrong in, say, the first and second months of the financial year. Since the budgets and targets are produced 'generally' on a monthly basis, the information is best obtained from this type of financial information. Statement (ii) is correct and option D best describes the two statements.

Question 20.
A NO	Although this is a 'liquidity' ratio, it is not as keen as the asset test ratio which excludes stock from the calculation.	
B YES	As described in A – current assets less stock and current liabilities.	

C NO   The answer to this calculation is not a ratio that is generally used.

D NO   See option C above.

Question 21.
Statement (i) is false – the definition of a variable cost is 'one which alters directly in proportion to production'. This means that, as more units are produced, the cost will increase. Since rates are calculated as being payable on the buildings and not the units produced, rates are classified as a fixed cost. However, statement (ii) is correct. Raw materials will vary according to production – raw materials are therefore a variable cost. Option D is correct.

Question 22.
The working capital of a business is the relationship between current assets and current liabilities. Option C is correct.

Question 23.
Since contribution is fixed costs less variable costs, both of these statements are true and option B applies.

Question 24.
The discounted cash flow technique is used to forecast future sums of money in present day terms – option D.

Question 25.
Receipts (money coming into the business) – D.

Question 26.
Creditors (amounts owed to other businesses – B.

Question 27.
Debtors (amounts owed by other businesses for sales – A.

Question 28.
The return on capital employed provides information on asset usage C.

Question 29.
For a business to survive, it must make profits (which result in future cash at the bank when debtors pay), and be able to pay debts when they fall due (be liquid). Both of these statements are true – option B.

Question 30.
The current ratio is a measure of liquidity and helps identify whether a business can pay its debts when they fall due. Option A is correct.

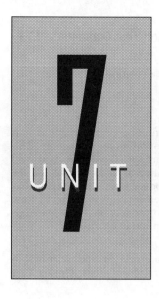

UNIT 7

Financial Resources

Getting Started

Many new businesses start up each year. Some will succeed and become reputable and profitable organizations with sufficient cash to continue and expand. Essential to the success of any new business is forward planning, research and cost estimates prior to the commencement of trading.

The **business plan** contains these elements and you will find that the knowledge and understanding required for its production have been covered throughout most of the units you have studied so far. The actual production of a business plan will be dealt with in Unit 8 but this unit will concentrate on the financial aspects.

Every organization needs finance at the onset to buy **fixed assets** such as:

- land
- buildings
- machinery
- motor vehicles

The fixed assets are those which will be used within the business for a long period of time, some of which must be purchased prior to the commencement of trading.

The business also needs **finance** to support work within the business (working capital – see Unit 6, page 162). This type of finance will be used to buy stocks and enable the business to have money in the bank to pay bills when they fall due. This is especially important since most businesses sell on credit. Funds must be available for it to continue trading, i.e. replenish stocks and pay expenses whilst awaiting payment (see Unit 6).

Once the **market research** has been carried out, the **cash flow forecast** is produced to identify, on a month-by-month basis:

- the value and number of sales to be made
- the purchases made to make those sales
- any other purchases such as expenses
- when debtors will pay
- when the organization will pay its debts to creditors
- purchases of fixed assets

This will result in the identification of the amount of cash available for the next month's purchases.

However, to be able to be successful in business, the cost of producing a product must be calculated to ensure that it is at least making a profit. In Unit 6 we looked at how this can be done using breakeven analysis, but it is necessary to be able to classify further the direct and indirect costs of production.

After a certain period of time, organizations have to produce **final accounts**. The two important documents produced are:

- the **profit and loss account** that will identify the profit made in a particular period of trading, and
- the **balance sheet** that identifies the assets and liabilities at a point in time.

These documents are used:

- To monitor business performance.
- As a base on which an organization may secure finance.

Asset finance Types of finance used primarily for the purchase of fixed assets such as buildings, machinery and motor vehicles.

Balance sheet A statement that lists the assets and liabilities at a particular point in time.

Cash flow forecast A forward plan, usually of one year, that identifies on a monthly basis the income, expenditure and bank balance.

Direct cost A cost of manufacturing that can be directly identified with a unit of production, such as materials.

Indirect cost A cost that cannot be directly identified to a unit of production. These costs are generally overheads, such as rent.

Profit and loss account A statement that lists the income and expenditure incurred for a particular trading period.

Sources of finance Where and how funds can be obtained for different types of purchase.

Working capital finance Types of finance used primarily to fund day-to-day expenses.

Essential Principles

7.1 Sources of Finance for a Business Plan

Many different **types of finance** are available from many different sources. New and existing organizations can obtain finance on a short-, medium- and long-term basis. Further, the methods of finance used will vary according to the purpose and type of business. Therefore, when considering finance for a business, it is important that you are aware of the sources and methods so that the most appropriate choice is made.

In this unit we will concentrate on the sources of finance available for different types of purchase and will identify and explain:

- asset and working capital requirements
- financing methods and sources
- appropriateness of finance methods

Asset and working capital requirements

Assets are those items that are owned by the business. These assets are of two types: **fixed assets** and **current assets**.

Fixed assets

Fixed assets are items which are owned by a business which it expects to keep for some years. They are necessary for the business to trade, but are not bought for stock which is to be sold. Examples would be:

- land
- buildings
- machinery
- office machinery
- delivery van

Current assets

Current assets are items owned by the business where the value is constantly changing. Examples would be:

- stocks
- debtors
- bank and cash

If the business was involved in manufacturing (making) a product, *stocks* would include: raw materials, work in progress (part-made goods) and finished goods.

Working capital

Often called the 'life blood' of the business because without **working capital** a business cannot operate – it will have no funds with which to make the products to sell (see Element 3. Fig. 6.24, in Unit 6). Working capital consists of current assets and current liabilities.

Current liabilities

Liabilities are what you owe and **current liabilities** are amounts owed to other businesses where the value is constantly changing. For example in Element 1, Unit 6, we looked at how we made purchases of stock (a current asset) on credit, which entails owing an amount to a creditor (a current liability).

Examples would be:

- trade creditors (for goods purchased by us)
- other creditors (i.e. the government for taxation and VAT)
- bank overdraft

Case study

Working as a partnership under the name of 'Eazy trapezy' Dale and Karen are trained performers. After attending college and a government start-up scheme, they set up in business three years ago.

One of the services they offer is circus skills. This consists of workshops where people of all ages learn how to juggle, ride unicycles of different heights, play with a diabolo, walk on stilts and perform on the trapeze. Often, they are expected to tour the country and, to do this, they use a camper.

They are often employed by schools, holiday play schemes, colleges and local authorities who pay between 30 and 60 days after the workshop has taken place.

Most of their sales income is put into the bank but a small amount is kept as petty cash. To operate their business, they need to purchase stocks of stationery and publicity material. The stocks of stationery and publicity material are bought on 30 days' credit.

The **fixed assets** they need to run their business are:

- camper motor van
- trapeze that could be demounted
- safety harnesses
- large safety mats
- unicycles of various sizes
- sets of juggles
- sets of diabolos
- telephone answer machine

Their **current assets** consist of:

- stocks of stationery and publicity material
- debtors (i.e. local authority, colleges and schools)
- money in the bank
- cash

Their current liabilities consist of:

- trade creditors

Order of liquidity

The assets and liabilities mentioned above are categorized into '**order of liquidity**'. Those which take longest or are hardest to turn into cash are said to be **least liquid** (such as plant and equipment – or buildings) whilst those which can be turned into cash quickly and easily are said to be **most liquid** (obviously the cash and cash at the bank).

Asset finance methods and sources

A **method** of finance is the **type** of finance used – such as a loan or a mortgage. The source of finance would be where the money was obtained from; in this case the loan may be from a bank whilst the mortgage may be obtained from a building society.

Different methods of finance are available for different types of purchase. For instance, a method used to purchase fixed assets will differ from the method chosen to fund working capital. These are now discussed.

Fixed assets

The method of finance chosen will differ depending on the **life of the fixed asset**. For instance, if it is for the purchase of a building which is intended to have a life of over 50 years, you would choose a different method than if you wished to purchase a computer which has a life of five years.

Methods of finance are therefore categorized into long, medium and short term and the method chosen will 'match' the life of the item being bought.

Long term

Long term refers to sources of finance where the repayment period is normally over ten years.

The long-term finance methods outlined below will be used to build up funds to purchase land and buildings, fixtures and fittings and to finance the growth of a business, i.e. a new extension to a building or updated machinery. Types of long-term finance are as follows:

Equity capital
- *Owners' capital*. This method of finance is regarded as *permanent* and will stay within the business for the life of the business. The amount may have been obtained through savings, loans from relatives or friends or a loan from a financial institution.
- *Share capital*. Again a permanent form of finance from the shareholders of a limited company.
- *Capital and share capital* (**equity**). A new business will fund its initial stocks of raw materials and fixed assets using this method. If, at a later date, the business wishes to expand, further amounts of capital/share capital may be required.
- *Shareholders' funds*. These are the profits made by a limited company from previous years of trading which have been reinvested within the business.

Loan capital
- *Government grants and loans*. Available for businesses that wish to set up in areas of high unemployment (development areas).
- *Debenture*. This is a type of long-term loan used by limited companies where the debenture holder receives interest annually for the life of the debenture.
- *Commercial mortgage*. Available from a building society or a finance institution, this is used for the purchase of a building.
- *Loans*. Loans are available from banks or financial institutions. To obtain a long-term loan businesses must prove that they have a sound business project. Certainly,

no long-term loan will be granted without guarantees as security. Often these types of loans carry a higher rate of interest and so will have to be considered carefully.

Loans can also be obtained from other financial institutions such as:

- EC funds provided to promote the community's objectives like social and regional development funds (usually for areas of high unemployment).
- Venture capital through banks for businesses that may be considered a 'higher risk'.
- The Department of Trade and Industry will provide expertise and financial assistance towards equipment and development costs to encourage research and development into new uses such as computers and fibre optics.
- Local Authorities give assistance for various schemes.

Did You Know **?**

Shareholders' funds (retained profits) are by far the largest source of funds for UK companies, providing around 60% of the total long term finance. Shares (equity capital); debentures and bonds (loan capital) provide a further 10%, and long term loans around 20%.

Medium term

Medium term refers to sources of finance where the repayment period is normally over one year and under ten years. Approximately 40% of all medium term loans are secured against the assets of the business or are guaranteed by the owners of the business. A secured loan means that the lender accepts all or some of the business assets as security on the loan. The lender could reclaim these assets and sell them, should the business fail to repay the loan.

Businesses will use medium term finance to purchase, rent or lease motor vehicles, computer equipment, office machinery or other machinery whose life is less than ten years.

The advantage of this type of borrowing is that it allows the repayments to be spread over a longer period on a monthly or quarterly basis. The loan period given is usually sufficient to allow the business to make profits from the assets purchased by the loan.

Types of medium term loans are as follows:

- **Bank loans from banks or financial institutions.** Generally repayable in monthly periods including an interest charge, over a period of time.

- **Hire purchase.** This allows the organization to buy a fixed asset over a long period of time and so avoid the need to buy it immediately with a large cash payment (money it may need for something else). Here, monthly instalments (including interest) are paid to the finance house which will retain ownership of the asset until the last instalment has been paid.

- **Leasing** (or renting). Equipment from a leasing company has several advantages:

  - It avoids buying the equipment with a large initial cash payment.
  - The leasing company is often responsible for the repair and maintenance of the equipment.

- If the equipment, e.g. a computer, is likely to become obsolete (out of date) within a short period of time, it can be replaced without great cost.

- **Sale and lease back.** This method is becoming an important source of finance. It involves organizations selling fixed assets which they own to a leasing company and then leasing them back.

Did You Know ?

There is a greater reliance on *overdrafts* as a source of medium term finance in the UK than in other countries. A Bank of England report shows that overdrafts account for 56% of small firm debt (> 1 year) in the UK compared to 14% in Germany.

Short-term finance

Short-term finance can be classed as finance needed for up to one year. The following methods are used to fund working capital:

- *Bank overdraft.* This gives the business the right to overdraw from its current account at the bank by a certain amount. Interest will be charged on a day-to-day basis on the amount overdrawn. This method tends to be used if the business finds itself temporarily short of cash to finance its operations.

- *Trade credit.* Refers to credit given by the business's supplier in the normal course of business. They normally allow a firm at least 30 days to pay for the goods or services. This allows the business a form of free finance (see also Element 2 of Unit 6).

Types of finance available for the small business are summarized in Fig. 7.1.

Did You Know ?

Surveys have suggested that companies regard the *cost* of the various types of finance as more of a problem than their *availability*. Around 60% of companies in a recent survey by the Institute of Directors felt that the high cost of finance was the main discouragement to their borrowing more funds.

TYPE	ADVANTAGES	DISADVANTAGES
LONG TERM From banks, financial institutions and EC sources	Greater financial flexibility; inflation lessens real cost	May be borrowing restrictions; more expensive than short term; guarantees required
Share capital	Greater financial flexibility; no repayments	Will reduce shareholders' stake in the business
MEDIUM TERM From banks, financial institutions and EC	Repayment amounts known and can be budgeted for; ideal for financing medium-term fixed assets; inflation lessens real cost	May be restrictions on amount borrowed; more expensive than short-term finance; requirement of guarantees
Hire purchase	Quick and inexpensive to arrange; repayment terms and amounts known; less 'draw' on amount in the bank	Quite expensive; must be sure the amount of interest charged is not too high; the hire purchase company owns the asset until last payment is made
Leasing	As for hire purchase but assets will continue to belong to the lease company; gives the opportunity to replace obsolete assets	Ownership remains with the lease company
SHORT TERM Bank overdraft	Generally, least expensive; quick to obtain; no minimum sum; interest paid on usage only; usually renewable	Temptation to use for the wrong type of purchase because of quickness; guarantees may be required
Short-term loan	Quickly obtainable; repayment period and amount known; improves overdraft flexibility	More expensive than overdraft; must be careful only to obtain the amount required

Fig. 7.1 Finance for the small business

Self Check ✔ **Element 1**

1. Which of the following is a fixed asset?
   A Buildings   B Creditors   C Stocks   D Cash at bank

2. Which is a current liability?
   A Premises   B Mortgage   C Bank overdraft
   D Raw materials

3. Which asset would be seen as most liquid?
   A Stocks of raw materials   B Premises   C Debtors
   D Stocks of finished goods

4. Which of the following is a 'permanent method of finance' for a company?
   A Bank loan   B Debenture   C Equity   D Bank overdraft

5. Craven, a small limited company, has the following sources of finance:
   A Mortgage   B Leasing   C Bank overdraft

   Which of these is the most appropriate source of finance for:
   1 Purchase of a new warehouse
   2 Working capital
   3 Cars that need replacing yearly

7.2 Cash Flow Forecast

In Element 1 we explored the methods and sources of finance available for different types of organizations for different purposes. In this unit we will concentrate on the production of a **cash flow forecast** and will examine:

- The purpose of a cash flow forecast.
- What is contained under the headings of inflows and cash outflows.
- The significance of timing of inflows and outflows.
- Consequences of incorrect forecasting.

The purpose of a cash flow forecast

Individuals who want to start their own business often have some money to put into the business but will need to borrow further amounts. These amounts may be obtained in the form of a government grant or a loan.

Before the grant/loan is allowed, the owners of the new business must demonstrate, in the form of a business plan, that they have a sound business idea. As part of the business plan owners must produce a cash flow forecast. The government and bank/lending institution will be interested in whether:

- The new business will make a profit.
- It will have sufficient cash to continue trading.

What is a cash flow forecast?

The layout of a cash flow forecast can be found in Fig. 7.2; its contents and uses are now discussed. A cash flow forecast is a forward plan, usually on a monthly basis, for a period of one year that identifies:

- *Projected cash inflows:* This will include income from the sale of a product or service, the start-up capital, loans obtained and income from other sources such as rent from property or dividends received from shares.

- *Projected cash outflows:* These include all expenses incurred for making and selling the product/service such as materials, wages, running costs (rent, rates, fuel, power, electric, gas), interest and loan repayments and payments for any fixed assets.

- **Closing balance** (amount in the bank). By deducting total cash outflows from total cash inflows, the balance arrived at will show, on a monthly basis, the amount of cash that is forecast to be in the bank. For the new business the owners can see instantly whether the business is worthwhile.

Existing businesses will use cash flow forecasts to identify varying cash levels throughout the trading year. Any cash shortages can be identified (perhaps when bills must be paid before receiving payment). An advance agreement can then be made with the bank to provide sufficient funds at the times when they are needed.

Monitoring performance

Producing a cash flow forecast on a monthly basis is a useful tool used by the managers/owners of a business. It allows them to monitor performance on a monthly basis.

This is done by comparing what has actually been received in inflows against forecast and what has actually been spent on outflows against forecast. Any identified shortfalls on income or overspends on expenditure will be investigated and, if necessary, corrective measures can be taken.

A cash flow forecast will therefore:

- Identify financial movements of inflows and outflows of cash.
- Help to support the application for finance to a financial institution.
- Promote confidence in the lender by demonstrating that the business can make enough income to repay the loan.
- Provide a forecast on which an application for an overdraft facility can be made.
- Be used as a base on which to monitor performance.

Producing a cash flow forecast

You must first make a list of the forecast **cash inflows**. These will include:

- Amount of capital introduced (start-up capital).
- Forecast amount of income from sales on a monthly basis for a period of 12 months.
- Any other forecast income such as interest received.
- Forecast expenses that have to be paid and when they should be paid. For instance, wages will be paid monthly, whereas rent may be paid quarterly – every three months.

These items are then entered into the cash flow (see Fig. 7.2) as follows:

1. **Cash inflows**
   (a) **Start-up capital:** the amount being introduced into the business. This will be entered into the first month.
   (b) **Sales:** the amounts you have listed as expected to be received on a monthly basis. This amount may vary monthly; for example, an increase may be expected over the months as the business becomes better known or the product being sold may vary according to the season (ice cream in summer?, warm clothes in winter?).
   (c) Enter any other income received in the relevant months.
2. **Total cash inflows:** add a + b + c together.
3. **Cash outflows:** enter each expense individually in the month it is incurred.
4. **Total cash outflows:** add all expenses together.
5. **Movement:** deduct total cash outflows from total cash inflows.
6. **Opening balance:** this is the amount in the bank at the start of the month. As the business has not yet commenced trading, this will be zero for the first month of trading.
7. **Closing balance:** this is the forecast amount in the bank at the end of each month. To arrive at this figure:
   (a) Add movement and opening balance together (if both figures are positive).
   (b) Subtract movement from opening balance (if the movement is a negative figure).
   (c) Add movement and opening balance together and show as a negative (if both figures are negative).

The closing balance for one month becomes the opening balance for the next month.

Case Study 1

Mr Brown is intending to start a business as a sole trader, under the name of Brown's Stationery Suppliers. He has already obtained a loan for the purchase of a delivery van and he has the following list of forecast cash inflows and cash outflows for the 12-month period starting January 19XX.

	£
Start-up capital	6000
Rent received	200 (Jan), 200 (Jul)
Sales	2000 per month from Jan to Jun
	3000 per month from Jul to Oct
	3500 per month for Nov and Dec
Wages	900 per month
Stationery purchases	500 per month from Feb to Jun*
	800 per month from Jul to Oct
	950 per month for Nov and Dec
Travelling	200 per month
Advertising	200 per month
Bank interest	300 per quarter (Mar, Jun, Sep, Dec)
Bank loan	300 per month
Rent of property	1000 per quarter (Jan, Apr, Jul, Oct)
Heat and light	300 per quarter (Mar, Jun, Sep, Dec)
Computer leasing	200 per month
Rates	100 per month

* Purchases are bought on credit and are paid 1 month in arrears.

His cash flow forecast would be as follows.

COMMENTARY

Mr Brown is now in a position to anticipate any cash shortages in advance for his stationery supplies business. The cash flow forecast in Fig 7.2 indicates that:

- total cash outflows are greater than cash inflows for the first ten months of trading.
- Since the start-up capital is being used as a 'buffer' until the business becomes known and forecast sales increase, the business has sufficient funds until October.
- October indicates a negative cash at the bank and Mr Brown should:
  - Ask the bank manager for an overdraft for October to cover the forecast shortage of funds.
  - Prove that it is only short term, as forecast cash inflows exceed cash outflows for November and December.

Notice that the business indicates a cash inflow of rent. This is for a small lock-up room which, at this moment in time, is surplus to requirements of the business; it has therefore been 'let' as storage.

BROWN'S STATIONERY SUPPLIERS JAN–DEC 19XX

	JAN	FEB	MAR	APR	MAY	JUN	JUL	AUG	SEP	OCT	NOV	DEC
CASH INFLOWS												
START UP CAPITAL	6000											
SALES	2000	2000	2000	2000	2000	2000	3000	3000	3000	3000	3500	3500
RENT REC'D	200						200					
TOTAL CASH INFLOWS	8200	2000	2000	2000	2000	2000	3200	3000	3000	3000	3500	3500
CASH OUTFLOWS												
WAGES	900	900	900	900	900	900	900	900	900	900	900	900
STATIONERY PURCHASES		500	500	500	500	500	800	800	800	800	950	950
TRAVELLING	200	200	200	200	200	200	200	200	200	200	200	200
ADVERTISING	200	200	200	200	200	200	200	200	200	200	200	200
BANK INTEREST			300			300			300			300
BANK LOAN	300	300	300	300	300	300	300	300	300	300	300	300
RENT OF PROPERTY	1000			1000			1000			1000		
HEAT & LIGHT			300			300			300			300
COMPUTER LEASING	200	200	200	200	200	200	200	200	200	200	200	200
RATES	100	100	100	100	100	100	100	100	100	100	100	100
TOTAL CASH OUTFLOWS	2900	2400	3000	3400	2400	3000	3700	2700	3300	3700	2850	3450
MOVEMENT	5300	–400	–1000	–1400	–400	–1000	–500	300	–300	–700	650	50
OPENING BALANCE		5300	4900	3900	2500	2100	1100	600	900	600	–100	550
CLOSING BALANCE	5300	4900	3900	2500	2100	1100	600	900	600	–100	550	600

Fig 7.2 Cash flow forecast

Case Study 2

Peter wishes to set up a business making and selling nightwear under the trading name of 'Sleep Tight'. He is to supply retail shops and allow them two months' credit. Purchases of raw materials are also bought on two months' credit. In addition to his start-up capital, Peter hopes to obtain a bank loan to help purchase some fixed assets. Below is a list of Sleep Tight's projected cash inflows and cash outflows for the first 12 months of trading.

Using the list below and the cash flow forecast in Fig. 7.3(a):

(a) Complete the missing spaces in the cash flow forecast.
(b) Comment on the forecast cash flow position of the business.

	£
Start-up capital	7400
Loan received	3600 (Jan)
Sales	4000 per month from Jan to Jun*
	4500 per month from Jul to Dec*
Purchase of fixed assets	5000 (Jan)
Wages	1000 per month
Purchase of raw materials	1000 per month from Jan to Jun*
	1125 per month from Jul to Dec*
Vehicle running costs	400 per month
Advertising	200 per month
Bank interest	300 paid Mar, Jun, Sep, Dec
Bank loan repayments	300 per month
Rent of property	1500 paid Jan, Apr, Jul, Oct
Heat, light, telephone	700 paid Mar, Jun, Sep, Dec
Rates	150 per month

* Items bought and sold are paid for two months in arrears

'SLEEP TIGHT' CASH FLOW FORECAST JAN–DEC 19XX

	JAN	FEB	MAR	APR	MAY	JUN	JUL	AUG	SEP	OCT	NOV	DEC
CASH INFLOWS												
START UP CAPITAL	7400											
SALES	–	–	4000						4500			
LOAN REC'D		–	–	–	–	–	–	–	–	–	–	–
TOTAL CASH INFLOWS	11000	–	4000						4500	4500	4500	4500
CASH OUTFLOWS												
WAGES												
PURCHASE OF RAW MATERIALS	–	–										
VEHICLE RUNNING COSTS	400	400	400	400	400	400	400	400	400	400	400	400
ADVERTISING	200											
BANK INTEREST	–	–	300									
BANK LOAN	300											
RENT OF PROPERTY	1500											
HEAT, LIGHT AND TELEPHONE	–	–	700									
FIXED ASSET PURCHASE	5000											
RATES	150											
TOTAL CASH OUTFLOWS												4175
MOVEMENT	2450									–175		
OPENING BALANCE	–	2450										
CLOSING BALANCE	2450						150					

Fig. 7.3(a)   Cash flow forecast. You can check your workings for Case Study 2 with Fig. 7.3(b).

	JAN	FEB	MAR	APR	MAY	JUN	JUL	AUG	SEP	OCT	NOV	DEC
'Sleep Tight' cash flow forecast Jan–Dec 19XX												
Cash inflows												
Start-up capital	7400	–	–	–	–	–	–	–	–	–	–	–
Sales	–	–	4000	4000	4000	4000	4000	4000	4500	4500	4500	4500
Loan rec'd	3600	–	–	–	–	–	–	–	–	–	–	–
Total cash inflows	11000	–	4000	4000	4000	4000	4000	4000	4500	4500	4500	4500
Cash outflows												
Wages	1000	1000	1000	1000	1000	1000	1000	1000	1000	1000	1000	1000
Purchase of raw materials	–	–	1000	1000	1000	1000	1000	1000	1125	1125	1125	1125
Vehicle running costs	400	400	400	400	400	400	400	400	400	400	400	400
Advertising	200	200	200	200	200	200	200	200	200	200	200	200
Bank interest	–	–	300	–	–	300	–	–	300	–	–	300
Bank loan	300	300	300	300	300	300	300	300	300	300	300	300
Rent of property	1500	–	–	1500	–	–	1500	–	–	1500	–	–
Heat, light and telephone	–	–	700	–	–	700	–	–	700	–	–	700
Fixed asset purchase	5000	–	–	–	–	–	–	–	–	–	–	–
Rates	150	150	150	150	150	150	150	150	150	150	150	150
Total cash outflows	8550	2050	4050	4550	3050	4050	4550	3050	4175	4675	3175	4175
Movement	2450	–2050	–50	–550	950	–50	–550	950	325	–175	1325	325
Opening balance	–	2450	400	350	–200	750	700	150	1100	1425	1250	2575
Closing balance	2450	400	350	–200	750	700	150	1100	1425	1250	2575	2900

Fig. 7.3(b) Completed cash flow forecast, Sleep Tight.

Commentary

The cash flow forecast indicates that:
(a) Cash outflows exceed cash inflows in the earlier part of the year.
(b) The start-up capital is to act as a buffer until the forecast sales increase.
(c) There is a forecast shortage of funds to cover expenses during the month of April.
(d) Peter should approach the bank to ask for an overdraft during April.
(e) The cash flow forecast indicates an increasing bank balance towards the end of the year, helped by the increase in sales.
(f) The forecast indicates Peter's business is in a strong position to afford the loan.

The significance of timing of inflows and outflows

The above examples have highlighted the effect on the bank balance when dealing with inflows and outflows. The *'timing'* of inflows and outflows is very important for the small business. For instance, many large organizations insist on 90 days' credit before payment will be made. Imagine the effect on the nightwear supplier 'Sleep Tight' in the example above if they do not receive any income until after they have had to pay out for their raw materials! The forecast shows an overdraft of £200 is needed for one month, but what if:

• Their customers insist on a credit period of three months or,

• 'Sleep Tight' does not have good credit control and debtors are allowed three months' credit?

The effect on the forecast closing bank balances would be:

Jan	Feb	Mar	Apr	May	Jun
2450	400	–3650	–4200	–3250	–3300

Jul	Aug	Sep	Oct	Nov	Dec
–3850	–2900	–3075	–3250	–1925	–1600

If the credit period was extended to three months 'Sleep Tight' would have a shortage of working capital. If finance could not be arranged the following problems may occur:

• inability to pay creditors
• stoppages on orders for goods bought
• inability to pay wages
• inability to produce goods
• inability to meet orders – lost sales
• insolvency

It is very important that the timing of cash flows is as accurate as possible and that 'guess work' is not used. Credit periods should be identified in advance and a strict credit control system should be implemented (see Element 3, Unit 6, Cash flow management and good control systems).

Consequences of incorrect forecasting

As seen already, one of the consequences of incorrect forecasting – debtors not paying on time – can result in a severe cash flow shortage. However, other errors in forecasting can have similar results. The consequences of **incorrect forecasting** are listed in Table 7.1.

Sales underestimated Expenses overestimated	Surplus cash at the bank
Sales overestimated Expenses underestimated Unexpected expense item	Unplanned overdraft
Unplanned cash shortage	Inability to pay creditors
Poor credit control system	Too much money owed by debtors Debt factoring

Table 7.1 Consequences of incorrect forecasting

Self Check ✔ Element 2

6. Cash inflows in a cash flow forecast for a business may include:
   A Wages
   B Start-up capital
   C Stock purchase
   D Purchase of a motor vehicle

7. When a cash flow forecast is produced, financial movements can be defined as:
   A Opening balance
   B Cash inflows
   C Cash outflow
   D Sometimes a cash inflow, sometimes a cash outflow

8. Decide whether each of the following is true (T) or false (F).
   (i) If debtors do not pay on time, suppliers may refuse to give credit.
   (ii) A business may avoid a cash flow shortage if it takes longer credit periods for purchases than it gives for sales.

   Which option best describes the two statements?

   A (i) T   (ii) F
   B (i) T   (ii) T
   C (i) F   (ii) F
   D (i) F   (ii) T

9. When loans are provided for the finance needs of a business, the amount allowed and repayment timings are based on cash flow forecasts. Some examples of inaccurate forecasting are:

   A Customers do not pay on time
   B Sales are underestimated
   C Rates increase is more than expected
   D Profit margin is less than expected

   Which of the above would result in:

   1 An insufficient borrowing facility
   2 Borrowing is more than required
   3 The amount borrowed is not borrowed soon enough

7.3 Calculating the cost of goods and services

Businesses that are engaged in manufacturing must be able to identify the cost of making the product. This can then be used to determine the selling price, or to identify whether the costs of manufacturing are less than the price customers will pay.

The selling price charged for a product may be determined simply by totalling the costs and adding on a sufficient amount as profit. However, it is usually arrived at by a study of the demand for the product (see Unit 1, supply and demand).

Since the selling price is usually decided by the market, managers will identify the costs of manufacture to:

- Ensure that the amount received in sales income covers the costs of production.
- Control the costs of production so that they can be more competitive and profitable.

To do this, it is important that they understand how costs behave and the ways in which the overheads are spread across the units produced. In this unit we will therefore examine:

- Direct and indirect costs of a unit of product or service.
- The direct and indirect costs in a number of units produced or service provided over a period of time.
- Apportionment of indirect costs.
- Total cost of a unit or service.
- Direct and indirect cost behaviour.

Direct and indirect costs

In Element 3 of Unit 6 we looked at fixed and variable costs: how variable costs per unit increase as output increases and how fixed costs per unit decrease as output increases. Further, breakeven analysis was used to identify whether a business was 'at least covering its costs'. These costs can also be divided up into *direct* and *indirect* costs.

- **Direct costs**, sometimes called **prime costs**, are directly related to the production of an organization's product.

> **Example**
>
> Consider an organization that makes cuddly toys, perhaps teddy bears. To produce the bears, the following **direct costs** will be incurred:
>
> - **Direct materials.** Raw materials used in production such as fur fabric, filling, eyes and nose and thread to sew the bear.
> - **Direct labour.** The cost of wages for employees directly involved in the production process, such as to cut the fabric, to sew the fabric, to fill the bear and for the finishing touches.
> - **Power.** Electricity to make the sewing machines and perhaps cutting machines work.
> - **Depreciation.** On the machines as they become older.

Depreciation

Consider your family car or your friends' family car. Do you think it could be resold for the same amount as it cost to buy? The answer is no (unless it is really unusual). This is because the wear and tear on the car has increased. The reduction in value caused by wear and tear is called **depreciation**. Other machines, such as computers, may depreciate more quickly as they become out of date. The term used for this is 'obsolescence'.

It is the same for businesses. Most fixed assets bought for use within the business will lose value over time – the older they become, or the more they are used, the less is the resale value. The exception to this is usually land and some buildings. Machines bought for the production of a product will lose value and the reduction in value (depreciation) is therefore a direct cost to the organization.

Table 7.2 illustrates the calculation of the direct costs of production.

A company makes 10,000 teddy bears per year. The direct costs of producing the bears are as follows.

Materials/Unit	Cost	Direct cost/ 10,000 units
		£
1 metre fabric	50p/m	5000
1.5 kilo filling	40p/k	6000
Other materials	40p/unit	4000
Labour/unit		
1.00 h cutting/sewing	£3.00/h	30000
0.50 h filling	£2.50/h	12500
0.25 h finishing	£2.50/h	6250
Power	£2000/10,000 units	2000
Depreciation	£2000/year	2000
		67750
Therefore the direct cost per bear is		$\frac{67750}{10000} = £6.78$

Table 7.2   Direct costs of production

Indirect costs, sometimes called **overheads**, are all the remaining costs of a business. These costs do not relate directly to making a product but will be incurred by the making of a number of products.

Example

Assuming a similar organization to the one mentioned above, making cuddly teddy bears, giraffes and pigs, its indirect costs may be:

- Factory overheads
- Management
- Administration
- Marketing
- Running expenses

These 'shared costs' are now discussed:

- **Factory overheads.** Rent, rates, heat and light, maintenance of the factory.

- **Management.** The costs of managers' salaries, depreciation of any cars owned by the business but used by the managers, car expenses etc.

- **Administration.** The costs of administration staff salaries, depreciation on administration machines, fixtures and fittings, the costs of stationery used for processing orders, invoices, cheques etc.

- **Marketing.** Any costs of marketing the cuddly toys

---

including salespersons salaries, depreciation on their cars and car running costs etc.

- **Running expenses.** Any other general running expenses such as rent and rates, heating and lighting of the offices.

The **factory cost** of making the products is therefore an addition of direct costs (which are directly related to a single product) and indirect costs relating to the factory which are spread across a number of products. **Total cost** is arrived at by adding on any other indirect costs as in Table 7.3.

A company has three departments and makes three products. The direct and indirect costs are as follows.

Direct costs	£	£
Dept A	100,000	
Dept B	80,000	
Dept C	60,000	
Prime cost		240,000
Indirect factory costs		
Rent, rates	20,000	
Heat, light	20,000	
Factory maintenance	10,000	50,000
Factory cost		290,000
Indirect costs		
Management	20,000	
Administration	15,000	
Marketing	10,000	
Running expenses	10,000	
Overhead cost		55,000
TOTAL COST		345,000

Table 7.3   Example of direct and indirect costs

But how do we identify the cost of *one single product*?

If an organization makes one product – say teddy bears – the direct and indirect costs can be identified as relating to *that product*. However, if the organization makes three different products, although the direct costs can be identified for each product separately, the indirect costs cover *all three* products. In this case there needs to be some way of apportioning (sharing) the indirect costs in a fair way to each product.

This is done by the following method:

- Identification of cost centres.
- Allocation of costs.
- Apportionment of costs.

- *Cost centres*
  A **cost centre** is a name given to where costs are gathered. This helps managers control the costs of individual areas by being able to identify any overspends. For example, in Table 7.3 above there will be cost centres for each production department, for each factory overhead cost and for each service area – such as management overheads or administration overheads.

  Once the costs have been gathered for each cost centre, the factory overhead and service areas (indirect cost centres) can be shared out to each production cost centre so that a cost per unit produced can be identified. This is done by allocating or apportioning costs.

- *Allocation of costs*
  If a cost can be identified as being specific to a production department cost centre, then the costs can be **allocated** – sent straight to that department. Allocated costs are usually confined to the direct costs only, such as materials or labour.

Apportionment of costs

Costs that are not specific to production are **apportioned** (shared) across each of the production department cost centres. Overheads can be apportioned in many different ways, for example factory overheads may be apportioned using the total number of machine hours or the total number of labour hours used in each department. Alternatively, each factory overhead may be taken separately and apportioned using a different method for each cost. Different organizations choose different methods but the main point to remember is that the method chosen to apportion costs must be fair. Table 7.4 describes the ways in which different overheads can be apportioned.

Overheads	
Factory overheads (one or a combination of the methods in the opposite column)	Machine hours used per department Labour hours used per department Floor space used per department Units produced per department Materials used per department
Other overheads (one or a combination of the methods in the opposite column)	Units produced per department Floor space Number of employees (Could also be labour or machine hours)

Table 7.4 Methods of apportionment of overheads

How apportionment costs are calculated
Whichever method is chosen, the following procedure is followed:

(a) Find the total cost of the overhead to be apportioned.
(b) Find the total units involved in the method chosen, for example total units produced per department will be added together.
(c) Divide total cost by total units of chosen method to get an overhead cost per unit.
(d) Multiply overhead cost per unit by total units in method chosen per department.

The procedure used is illustrated in self-check question 13 at the end of this section. All overheads are apportioned using a labour hour basis.

Direct and indirect cost behaviour

As mentioned earlier, the direct costs can be identified as a cost incurred directly to the production of a unit (if production does not take place the cost will not be incurred). An example would be during a close-down period due to a bank holiday. However, the cost of overheads (indirect costs) would still be incurred. Such costs as rent, rates and salaries still need to be paid regardless of production.

Indirect costs are generally fixed for a period of time, an increase in production would mean a decrease in indirect costs per unit. This is because the indirect costs would be spread over a larger number of units.

The identification of direct and indirect costs
Earlier in this element we described direct costs as those that can be identified as directly relating to the product being made. However, the distinction between direct and indirect costs may alter depending on how the individual organization is able to gather its costs. For example, we identified power and depreciation as being a direct cost. In some instances, it may not be possible to allocate these costs directly to the product being made. In this case, these costs would fall into the indirect cost category and an appropriate apportionment base would be chosen.

Self Check ✔ **Element 3**

10. Mark each of the following statements true (T) or false (F).

    (i) The cost of raw materials used in making a product is a direct cost.
    (ii) Direct costs include the salaries of salespersons.

    Which best describes the above statements?

    A (i) T (ii) T
    B (i) T (ii) F
    C (i) F (ii) T
    D (i) F (ii) F

11. Blue Blouses Ltd. produces one type of blouse. The costs involved are as follows:

Direct materials	3 metres at £15 per metre
Direct labour	0.50 hour at £6.00 per hour
Other direct costs	£1 per hour
Factory overheads	£9 per hour
Other overheads	£220,000
Output for period	10,000 blouses

    The following amounts relate to the above costs:

    A £45   B £58   C £80   D £49

    Which of the above represents:

    1 Total cost per unit
    2 Factory cost per unit
    3 Direct cost per unit

12. Mark each of the following statements true (T) or false (F).

    (i) An organization's costs can be divided into direct and indirect costs.
    (ii) A manufacturing organization will incur both direct and indirect costs during a shut-down for two weeks during a holiday period.

    Which best describes the above statements?

    A (i) T (ii) T
    B (i) T (ii) F
    C (i) F (ii) T
    D (i) F (ii) F

Self Check ✔ Element 3 *continued*

13. A company has three departments and makes three products. The direct and indirect costs are as follows.

Direct costs

Materials/unit	Dept A	Dept B	Dept C
Material	1.00 m at 50p/m	0.75 m at 60p/m	0.50 m at 50p/m
Filling	1.5 kg at 40p/kg	1.00 kg at 40p/kg	0.50 kg at 40p/kg
Others	40p/unit	30p/unit	20p/unit

Labour/unit	Dept A	Dept B	Dept C
Cutting/sewing £3.00/h	1.00 h	1.00 h	0.50 h
Filling £2.50/h	0.50 h	0.50 h	0.50 h
Finishing £2.00/h	0.25 h	0.25 h	0.25 h

	Dept A	Dept B	Dept C
Units produced	10,000	6,000	3,000
Power/units	5,000	4,000	2,000
Depreciation	2,000	1,500	1,000

Indirect costs/units

Factory overheads	40,000	Marketing	30,000
Management	30,000	Running expenses	29,750
Administration	35,000		

1. Calculate the total direct costs per department.
2. Calculate total indirect costs per department apportioning overheads on a labour hour basis.
3. Calculate total cost per unit.

Guide to answering the questions

Labour Hour Basis
The total labour hours used across all production departments are divided into the indirect overhead to give a cost per labour hour. This is then multiplied by the number of labour hours per department to give an apportioned cost per department.

STEP 1 To find direct costs

(a) Multiply the amount of materials used per unit by the unit price to arrive at a price for materials used per unit.
(b) Multiply the amount of labour used per unit by the unit price to arrive at a price for labour used per unit.
(c) Multiply the price per unit by the total units produced to find total per period.
(d) Add the cost of power and depreciation.

STEP 2 To find indirect costs

(a) Multiply the labour hours used per department by the number of units produced to arrive at total labour hours per department for period.
(b) Add together the total labour hours used per department to arrive at total labour hours used for period.
(c) Add together indirect costs to arrive at total indirect overhead costs.
(d) Divide total indirect costs by total labour hours used for period to arrive at indirect overhead cost per labour hour.
(e) Multiply overhead cost per unit by total labour hours used per department to arrive at indirect overhead cost per department.

STEP 3

(a) Lay out the answer in a suitable format.
(b) Divide total units produced per department by total cost to arrive at a cost per unit.

NB YOU WILL NOTICE THAT THE ANSWER INCLUDES NUMBERS ROUNDED TO TWO DECIMAL PLACES

7.4 Profit and loss accounts and balance sheets

In Unit 6 we identified that the profit and loss account and balance sheet have several purposes and are produced for various reasons (see Fig. 6.21). Further, we explored the ways in which we can monitor and measure business performance using information contained in the final accounts of the company.

The results of trading were interpreted and used as a base on which to make decisions about how the organization has performed in terms of profitability and liquidity and how this information could be used as a base on which to secure and maintain finance. Further, through your studies so far you will be aware of the following:

- The purposes of financial documents.
- How financial transactions are produced and recorded.
- Use of day books and the double entry system.
- The sources of finance available to different businesses and the importance of choosing the most appropriate source.

- How the assets of the business can be classified into fixed and current and how current liabilities are deducted to arrive at the working capital figure.
- The distinction between direct and indirect costs and how the cost of a unit produced is calculated.

In this element we will concentrate on 'pulling together' your knowledge and understanding of the above by producing the final accounts of a business. We will examine:

- How the trial balance is produced.
- The purpose of the trial balance.
- How profit and loss accounts are produced.
- How the balance sheet is produced.

Did You Know ?

Don't forget that, as well as the above, there are many useful *external* sources of information on a company's financial situation. For example the Financial Times Share Information Service prints over eighty UK indices of corporate activity, many of a financial nature.

What are the contents of a trial balance?

In Element 1 of Unit 6 we looked at how the day books were used to record, on a daily basis, sales invoices sent and purchase invoices received, and further, how this information was transferred, using double entry, to the ledgers (see Table 7.5). It is the balances left on the ledger accounts that are extracted and used in the production of the trial balance.

Title of Ledger	Contents
Sales Ledger	Accounts of debtors by name A record of sales made on credit A record of sales returns A record of payments made by the debtor
Purchase Ledger	A record of creditors by name A record of purchases made on credit A record of purchase returns A record of payment made to creditors
General Ledger	A record of total sales; purchases; returns; items of expense; assets bought; capital and VAT
Cash Book	A record of receipts and payments made

Table 7.5 The ledgers used within a business

How often trial balances are produced

They can be produced as often as the business requires. However, they are usually produced once per month and definitely at the trading period year end – usually known as 'at the balance sheet date'.

How a trial balance is produced

Periodically the balances left on the ledger account are brought together. These balances will be:

- *Credit balances* for:
  - sales made
  - income received, e.g. from rent or interest from investments
  - any current liabilities (short term), e.g. creditors, bank overdraft, dividends owed to shareholders
  - any long-term liabilities, e.g. capital or share capital, loans or debentures
  - profit made in previous years and left within the business

- *Debit balances* for:
  - purchases made
  - opening stocks of raw materials, finished goods and work in progress for businesses that have been trading for at least one year
  - expenses incurred (including depreciation and bad debts)
  - fixed assets owned, e.g. land, buildings, vehicles
  - current assets, e.g. debtors, bank and cash
  - drawings taken by the owner of the business

Using the double entry system for recording financial transactions means that every transaction is entered twice – once as a debit and once as a credit. By double recording, a

total of the debit less a total of the credit balances should equal zero. In other words, debits should always equal credits.

Worked Example 1

The first step in producing a trial balance is to be able to identify which are credit balances and which are debit balances. B. Brown has completed his first trading year and now needs a trial balance extracted from the list of ledger balances shown below.

- Fill in the missing spaces by writing either CR (for credit) or DR (for debit).
- Transfer the balances to the correct column (either debit or credit).
- Total the debit column.
- Total the credit column.
- Deduct the debit from the credit.

Trial Balance of B. Brown for the year ending 31.12.19XX

	Ledger Balance	DR/CR	Debit	Credit
Capital	3000	CR		3000
Cash	1070			
Bank	1800	DR	1800	
Telephone	50			
Depreciation	100	DR	100	
Motor van	2000			
Creditors	1050	CR		1050
Debtors	30			
Wages	100			
Loan	950	CR		950
Sales	1350			
Purchases	1200	DR		
Total			£6350	

Did you arrive at a zero total? The answer can be found on the next page. It is important that you learn which are debit balances and which are credit balances. Try the next task.

Worked Example 2

Produce a trial balance for J. Black Newsagents for the trading year ending 31.3.19XX from the following information. Don't forget to complete the title. The answer can be found on the next page.

Trial Balance of	for the year ending
	Ledger Balance
	£
Opening stock	300
Drawings	900
Capital	2100
Cash	40
Bank	120
Telephone	50
Light and heat	190
Rent	240
General expenses	130
Buildings	2000
Motor van	750
Creditors	900
Debtors	1200
Wages of sales assistant	520
Loan	1000
Sales	6700
Purchases	4260

What is the purpose of the trial balance?

As the **trial balance** lists all the debit and credit balances it checks the accuracy of the arithmetic in the double entry system. If the trial balance does not agree, then there is an error. In this case, the accounts clerk will check the arithmetic in each ledger account. The information is then used for the production of the profit and loss account and balance sheet.

However, the trial balance does not check whether errors have been made in the recording of a transaction. The following errors are not detected by a trial balance:

- *Commission.* This type is where the correct amount is entered but in the wrong person's account, for example where a sale of £100 is entered into the account of J. Green instead of M. Green in the sales ledger.

- *Omission.* Where a transaction is completely omitted from the books. If we sold £90 of goods to M. Brown, but did not enter it in either the sales or M. Brown's account the trial balance would still agree.

- *Principle.* Where an item is entered into the wrong class of account, for example where a fixed asset purchase such as a motor car is debited to an expenses account. This would falsely reduce the profit figure.

- *Compensating.* Where errors cancel each other out. If the sales account was added up to be £20 too much and the purchases account also added up to be £20 too much, these two errors would cancel out in the trial balance. This is because totals both of the credit side of the trial balance and of the debit side of the trial balance will be £20 too much.

- *Original entry.* Where the original figure is incorrect, for instance a sales invoice was made out for £150 instead of £250 and the £150 had been transferred to the ledger accounts. In this case the trial balance would agree, but sales would be falsely reduced by £100.

- *Reversal of Entries.* Where the correct accounts are used but each item is shown on the wrong side. Assume we had paid a cheque to L. Young for £300. The double entry should be Cr Bank £300, Dr L. Young. In error it is entered as Dr Bank £300, Cr L. Young £300. The trial balance would still agree.

N.B. The initials 'COPCOR' may help you to remember the six types of error.

As you can see it is important that care is taken in recording financial transactions – otherwise, undetected errors will result in inaccurate final accounts (see Element 1 of Unit 6).

Answers to worked examples

Answer to Worked Example 1

Trial Balance of B. Brown for the year ending 31.12.19XX

	Ledger Balance	DR/CR	Debit	Credit
Capital	3000	CR		3000
Cash	1070	DR	1070	
Bank	1800	DR	1800	
Telephone	50	DR	50	
Depreciation	100	DR	100	
Motor van	2000	DR	2000	
Creditors	1050	CR		1050
Debtors	30	DR	30	
Wages	100	DR	100	
Loan	950	CR		950
Sales	1350	CR		1350
Purchases	1200	DR	1200	
Total			£6350	£6350

Answer to Worked Example 2

Trial Balance of J. Black for the year ending 31.3.19XX		
	Debit	Credit
	£	£
Opening stock T	300	
Drawings B	900	
Capital B		2100
Cash B	40	
Bank B	120	
Telephone P/L	50	
Light and heat P/L	190	
Rent P/L	240	
General expenses P/L	130	
Buildings B	2000	
Motor van B	750	
Creditors B		900
Debtors B	1200	
Wages of sales assistant P/L	520	
Loan B		1000
Sales T		6700
Purchases T	4260	
Total	£10700	£10700

Closing stock is valued at £400 (T and B).

As you can see, notations of T, B and P/L have been inserted after each item in the trial balance. These notations have a purpose, as you will see below.

What is the profit and loss account?

The profit and loss account in more detail is called **the trading and profit and loss account**. This is a summary of all the income and expenditure of a business over a period of time. The time period over which the final accounts can be produced vary. They could be produced quarterly, half yearly or annually. However, by law, busi-nesses must produce their final accounts at least once per year. The trading period of a business depends on when their 'year end' falls. If a business commences trading on 1 January, then its 'year end' will be one year later, 31 December. However, if it commences on 1 April, its year end will be 31 March the following year etc.

Table 7.6 identifies which items go into which section. These items have been extracted using the answer to the trial balance you were asked to produce in Worked Example 2. Notice the title: this is always precise – it tells you that it is for the trading year ending 31.3.19XX.

Trading and profit and loss account of J. Black for the year ending 31.3.19XX		
	£	£
Sales		6700
Less cost of goods sold		
Opening Stock	300	
Purchases	4260	
	4560	
Less closing stock	400	
COST OF GOODS SOLD		4160
GROSS PROFIT		2540
Less expenses		
Rent	240	
Light and heat	190	
Telephone	50	
Wages	520	
General expenses	130	1130
NET PROFIT		1410

Table 7.6   Trading and profit and loss account of J. Black for the year ending 31.3.19XX

Producing a trading and profit and loss account

The first step is being able to identify 'which items go where'. To do this, you need to 'get into the habit' of placing notations on the trial balance that separately identify those that form part of the trading account, the profit and loss account and the balance sheet. You may find it useful to use the following notations:

- T   trading account
- P/L   profit and loss account
- B   balance sheet (we will look at these items later)

These notations have been identified in the answer to Worked Example 2. You will also notice that at the foot of the trial balance is an item called 'closing stock'. This is the amount of stock left in the business on the last day of that trading period. This item needs to be entered into the trading account (so the correct amount of stock used is calculated) and into the balance sheet (since it is an item that has value, it is an asset of the business).

How to identify 'which items go where' in the trading and profit and loss account

The trading account

- **Sales**
  This is the total value of credit and cash sales made throughout the trading period.
- **Less cost of goods sold**
  This section lists those items that are directly involved in making (for a manufacturing organization) or reselling (for organizations who do not manufacture). You will notice that these items were identified as the direct costs (see Element 3). This section will therefore include the purchases made. However, for a manufacturing organization it will also include direct labour and indirect factory overheads. Notice that opening and closing stock are entered so that the net amount of stock used during the trading period can be calculated.

- **Gross profit**
  By deducting the costs of sales from the sales figure we arrive at the **gross profit**.
- **Less expenses**
  In this section we deduct any other expenses – in Element 2 we identified these as the *indirect expenses*. These will therefore include overheads such as administration, wages of non-manufacturing staff, rent, telephone, interest paid (say on a loan), travelling or selling expenses.
- **Net profit**
  Gross profit less expenses equals the **net profit** made by the business for the trading period.

What is a balance sheet?

The **balance sheet** of a business is a very important document. It lists the assets, liabilities and capital of the business and summarizes the financial position of the business at a particular date. You will notice the title states 'As at 31.3.19XX'. This is because the balance sheet items are constantly changing. For example, as at 31.3.19XX, J. Black had a bank balance of £120. However, if we were able to look at his financial transactions on 1.4.19XX we might see that one of J. Black's debtors has paid and the money has been put into the bank. This would result in the debtors figure being reduced and the bank increased by the amount paid. This would therefore change the amounts shown in the balance sheet. It is for this reason that it is often said to be 'a snapshot of the business at a particular point in time'.

Producing a balance sheet for a sole trader

Since the sole trader is the owner of the business and is responsible for all profits and losses (see Unit 4), the balance sheet of a sole trader will differ in layout from that of a limited company. The sole trader is not regarded as an employee of the business and cannot therefore take wages. However, as this person still needs money to live, any monies taken from the business will be in the form of drawings. As the sole trader is entitled to all the profits made, these are added to the capital and drawings are deducted. How this is done will be discussed in the 'Financed by' section below.

The balance sheet contains two sections:

- What the business owns – its assets.
- What the business owes – its permanent capital.

As with the trading and profit and loss account it is best to get into the habit of identifying 'which items go where' in the balance sheet. The balance sheet of J. Black can be seen in Table 7.7 and the trial balance from Worked Example 2 is once again reproduced using extra notations to cover the balance sheet items in more detail. The notations used are as follows:

- B FA   Fixed assets such as buildings, fixtures, motor vehicles
- B CA   Current assets such as closing stock, debtors, bank
- B CL   Current liabilities such as creditors, bank overdraft
- B F   'Financed by' section, such as capital, drawings, profit

Balance sheet of J. Black as at 31.3.19XX		
	£	£
Fixed assets		
Buildings		2000
Motor van		750
		2750
Current assets		
Stock	400	
Debtors	1200	
Bank	120	
Cash	40	
	1760	
Less current liabilities		
Creditors	900	
Working capital		860
Total assets less current liabilities		3610
Less long-term liabilities		
Loan		1000
		2610
Financed by		
Capital		2100
Add profit		1410
		3510
Less drawings		900
		2610

Table 7.7   Balance sheet of J. Black as at 31.3.19XX

Fixed and current assets
You will notice that these are shown in order of liquidity – those items that are most difficult to turn into cash are entered first with those that are most liquid, such as the bank and cash items, being entered last. Notice that each 'class' of asset is totalled separately.

Current liabilities
After arriving at a total for current liabilities, deduct this from the current assets to arrive at the **working capital**. For the importance of working capital see Unit 6. Current liabilities are those that are due to be repaid within one year.

Total assets less current liabilities
This figure is arrived at by adding together the fixed assets and working capital. It indicates the total amount of funds tied up in the business prior to the deduction of long-term liabilities.

Long-term liabilities
Long-term liabilities are those that are due to be repaid in a period of longer than one year and will include such things as loans or debentures for a limited company. This total is deducted from the total assets less current liabilities total to arrive at the total of one side of the balance sheet.

Financed by
Here, we indicate how the above assets were financed. It indicates the amount that J. Black's business owes him

personally (£2610). The amount of capital J. Black put into the business is identified and added to this figure is the profit owed to him by his business. However, any drawings he has taken to live on are deducted from this amount.

Limited company accounts

Profit and loss account

The trading account of a limited company is very similar to that of a sole trader. However, the profit and loss account has some differences. Unlike the sole trader, the owners of a limited company (the shareholders) enjoy limited liability. This is because the company is a 'separate entity' distinct from its members and, as such, the owners can also be employees.

Since owners (shareholders) can also be employees (i.e. directors), their salaries and expenses are regarded as an expense. In addition, if debentures are used, the interest payable (like interest on a loan) becomes an expense. In this case, the directors' salaries, expenses and debenture interest are deducted as normal overhead expenses in the profit and loss account.

Appropriation account

The final accounts of a limited company will include an appropriation account. This account, which falls beneath the trading and profit and loss account, shows how the profits have been distributed (shared) (see Table 7.8). Profits are distributed in the following order of priority:

1 Corporation tax – the Inland Revenue is entitled to the first share of the profit. The amount of corporation tax due to be paid is shown as the first deduction.
2 Dividends – this deduction shows any proposed dividends due to shareholders.
3 Reserves – show the amount of profit which the directors and shareholders prefer to leave within the company, perhaps for a specific purpose.
4 Profit and loss account balance – after all deductions from profit have been made, any profit left over from previous years (profit and loss account balance brought forward) is added to the amount left for this year to arrive at the profit and loss account balance carried forward to next year.

	£	£
Net profit		300,000
Less corporation tax		100,000
Profit after taxation		200,000
Less proposed dividends		
Preference shares	20,000	
Ordinary shares	60,000	80,000
		120,000
Less transfer to general reserve		40,000
		80,000
Profit and loss a/c bal b/fwd		30,000
Profit and loss a/c bal c/fwd		110,000

Table 7.8 Appropriation account of a limited company

You will notice that all deductions from profit (as with expenses in the profit and loss account) are debit items and it therefore follows that all additions to profit are shown as credit items. Further, using the double entry rule of 'every item is entered twice', appropriation account items will also appear in the balance sheet.

> **Did You Know ?**
>
> UK companies now tend to distribute a higher proportion of their profits in dividends than do overseas companies. Almost 60% of UK net profits are currently distributed to shareholders as dividends, compared to 40% in France, 30% in Japan and less than 20% in Germany.

Producing a balance sheet for a limited company

The fixed and current items in the balance sheet of a limited company are the same as those of a sole trader. However, the current liabilities will have the extra entries of corporation tax due and amounts to be paid as dividends. Long term liabilities may also include debentures and loans (see Table 7.9).

The 'Financed by' section of the limited company's balance sheet

In Table 7.9 you will notice that the start of the 'financed by' section includes a heading '**Authorized share capital**'. This includes the type and number of shares that the company is allowed to issue. It is for *reference only* and is not included in the balance sheet total. The section headed '**Issued share capital**' identifies the amount of shares actually issued; this amount is included in the balance sheet total.

Notice that the amount of £1 is indicated under both headings. This is the **nominal** value of the share – that is, the original selling price of the shares issued. However, as a company grows so does its share price value. The present value of a share is called the **market value**; this is not shown in the balance sheet. For public limited companies the market value will be determined by the stock market.

Under the heading 'Reserves' we identify the reserves and the retained profit (this is the profit and loss account balance calculated in the appropriation account). This total indicates the amount of funds left within the organization for future growth.

Balance sheet of A. Co. Limited as at 31.3.19XX

	£	£	£
Fixed assets			
Land and buildings		400,000	
Fixtures and fittings		20,000	
Motor vehicles		68,450	
		488,450	
Current assets			
Stock		222,250	
Debtors		117,100	
Bank		25,200	
Cash		500	
		365,050	
Less current liabilities			
Creditors	105,500		
Proposed dividends			
Preference	20,000		
Ordinary	60,000		
Corporation tax	100,000	285,500	
Working capital		79,550	
Total assets less current liabilities		568,000	
Less long-term liabilities			
Loan		8,000	
10% Debentures		10,000	
		18,000	
		550,000	
Financed by			
Authorised share capital			
500,000 ordinary shares of £1 each fully paid		500,000	
200,000 10% preference shares of £1 each fully paid		200,000	
		700,000	
Issued share capital			
200,000 ordinary shares of £1 each fully paid		200,000	
200,000 10% preference shares of £1 each fully paid		200,000	
		400,000	
Reserves			
General reserve	40,000		
Retained profit	110,000		
		150,000	
		550,000	

Table 7.9 The balance sheet of a limited company

Self Check ✔ **Element 4**

14. Mark each of the following statements true (T) or false (F).
 (i) A trial balance cannot detect errors in the double entry system.
 (ii) A trial balance can be used to detect errors in the arthmetic in the double entry system.
 Which best describes the above statements?
 A (i) T (ii) T
 B (i) T (ii) F
 C (i) F (ii) T
 D (i) F (ii) F

15. The trading account will include information from:
 A Drawings account
 B Purchase account
 C Wages account
 D Telephone account

16. A company's profit and loss account will give information on the following:
 A The amount of rent for the year
 B Cash flow for the year
 C Owner's drawings for the year
 D The amount of capital owed to the owner

17. Mark each of the following statements true (T) or false (F).
 (i) The total assets of a company can be found in the profit and loss account.
 (ii) The working capital of a company can be found in the balance sheet.
 Which best describes the above statements?
 A (i) T (ii) T
 B (i) T (ii) F
 C (i) F (ii) T
 D (i) F (ii) F

18. The 'financed by' section of a limited company's balance sheet will show:
 A Market value of a company's assets
 B Market value of a company's shares
 C Nominal value of a company's shares
 D Current assets of the company

Unit Test Completion guide: 1 hour plus 5 minutes reading time

Focus 1

Sources of Finance   10 marks

Question 1
Which of the following is a fixed asset?

A   Machinery
B   Creditors
C   Capital
D   Bank balance

Question 2
Which of the following is a current asset?

A   Motor vehicles
B   Creditors
C   Debtors
D   Equity capital

Question 3
Which of the following is a current liability?

A   Premises
B   Creditors
C   Drawings
D   Capital

Questions 4–6 relate to the following and share options A–D:

Braven Ltd is a small private limited company. Some of its sources of finance are:

A   Commercial mortgage
B   Leasing
C   Hire purchase
D   Overdraft at the bank

Which source of finance is most appropriate for:

Question 4
Purchase of an extension to existing premises

Question 5
Salespersons cars that need changing every two years

Question 6
Working capital

Question 7
In view of a proposed expansion programme, a company needs to increase its working capital.

Mark each of these statements true (T) or false (F).

(i)   It can do this by offering some shares for sale.
(ii) It can do this by increasing stocks.

Which best describes the above statements?

A   (i) T   (ii) F
B   (i) T   (ii) T
C   (i) F   (ii) F
D   (i) F   (ii) T

Question 8
A company, finding itself temporarily short of cash, has arranged an overdraft.

Mark each of these statements true (T) or false (F).

(i)   This is a relatively cheap form of borrowing.
(ii) It is the most appropriate method for this situation.

Which best describes the above statements?

A   (i) T   (ii) F
B   (i) T   (ii) T
C   (i) F   (ii) F
D   (i) F   (ii) T

Question 9
Zenus Enterprises PLC is a large public limited company that wishes to expand. Which is the most appropriate form of finance?

A   Share capital
B   Overdraft
C   Bank loan
D   Hire purchase

Question 10
Which of the following would you consider to be *most important* when deciding to lease rather than purchase an asset?

A   The asset involves rapid technological change
B   Repairs will cost less
C   Leasing is least expensive
D   The asset life has not been determined

Focus 2

Cash flow and cash flow reporting   8 marks

Question 11
A cash flow forecast is a financial document produced by a company.

Mark each of these statements true (T) or false (F).

(i)   It is a forecast of a business's receipts and payments over a future period of time, on a period by period basis.
(ii) It contains predicted information on when debtors will pay.

Which best describes the above statements?

A   (i) T   (ii) F
B   (i) T   (ii) T
C   (i) F   (ii) F
D   (i) F   (ii) T

Question 12
Joseph has just started a small floristry business. His bank requests a cash flow forecast so that it can:

A   Forecast the future profits of the business
B   Assess whether Joseph understands business finance
C   Identify when a bank overdraft may be required
D   Identify the direct costs

Questions 13–15 relate to the following.

Incorrect cash flow forecasting can have the following possible consequences for Joseph:

A Too much is owed to creditors
B Surplus cash at the bank
C Unplanned overdraft
D Overestimated forecast of sales receipts

Which of these could have been caused by:

Question 13
A slump in the trade

Question 14
An unexpected bill for an expensive repair

Question 15
Repayment of a bad debt previously written off

Questions 16–18 relate to the following:

Cash flow forecast (£000's)

	Jun	Jul	Aug	Sep	Oct	Nov	Dec
Total sales receipts	600	600	800	700	900	600	800
Raw materials	450	600	525	675	450	525	700
Wages	90	120	105	135	90	105	140
Running costs	100	110	105	115	100	105	120
Total payments	640	830	735	925	640	735	960
Movement	–40	–230	+65	–225	+260	–135	–160
Opening balance	430	390	160	225	0	260	105
Closing balance	390	160	225	0	260	105	–55

The cash flow forecast is a prediction for the following seven months:

A June
B July
C August
D September
E October
F November
G December

Which of the above months figures indicate that the following situations could arise?

Question 16
An overdraft needs to be arranged

Question 17
An error has been made in calculating the closing balance

Question 18
There is just enough money to pay expenses

Questions 19–21 relate to the following and share options A–D.

A company that makes and sells winter clothes direct to the retailers plans its business on the following annual cycle:

A Spring – receive payment for the product lines
B Summer – marketing the product lines
C Autumn – making the product lines
D Winter – payment to suppliers

Which season will have the following effect on cash flow:

Question 19
A surplus of cash

Question 20
A high demand for cash

Question 21
A stable cash position

Focus 3

Costs   7 marks

Question 22
Which of the following is usually calculated as a direct cost?

A Salaries of administrative staff
B Rent and rates of the office block
C Purchase of raw materials
D Selling expenses

Question 23
The costs involved in manufacturing a product are as follows: direct cost £14, total indirect costs £4000 per year. 8000 units were produced. What was the cost per unit?

A £15   B £14.50   C £14   D £15.50

Questions 24–26 relate to the following.

A company has broken down its costs per unit into the following categories:

Breakdown of costs

	£ p
Materials	4.50
Cutting	1.50
Finishing	1.00
Factory rent	0.50
Factory maintenance	0.10
Other overheads	5.00
Total	12.60

These costs can be subtotalled into the following categories:

A Materials
B Direct
C Indirect
D Factory

Which of the above would produce the following answers:

Question 24
£7.00

Question 25
£7.60

Question 26
£5.60

Question 27
Which of the following is normally calculated as an indirect cost?

A Raw materials
B Advertising
C Wages of production
D Factory rent

Question 28
Mark each of these statements true (T) or false (F).

(i) The cost of raw materials used in making a product is a direct cost.
(ii) direct costs include the depreciation on office machinery.

Which best describes the above statements?

A (i) T (ii) F
B (i) T (ii) T
C (i) F (ii) F
D (i) F (ii) T

Focus 4

Trial Balance, Profit and Loss   9 marks

Question 29
Which account will form part of the profit and loss account?

A Motor vehicles
B Drawings
C Bank
D Rent

Question 30
Which balance would appear in the balance sheet?

A Motor vehicles
B Sales
C Opening stock
D Rates

Question 31
Mark each of these statements true (T) or false (F).

(i) The total value of fixed assets can be found in the balance sheet.
(ii) The total expenditure incurred for the trading period can be found in the balance sheet.

Which best describes the above statements?

A (i) T (ii) F
B (i) T (ii) T
C (i) F (ii) F
D (i) F (ii) T

Question 32
In which account would total sales appear?

A Trading account
B Profit and loss account
C Balance sheet
D Appropriation account

Questions 33—35 relate to the following and share options A–D.

Accounting information includes:

A Creditors
B Overheads
C Cash flow forecast
D Total purchases

Which would appear in the following:

Question 33
Balance sheet

Question 34
Profit and loss account

Question 35
Trading account

Question 36
Mark each of these statements true (T) or false (F).

(i) The information from the trial balance is used as a base on which to produce the final accounts.
(ii) The trial balance will detect inaccuracies in the double entry.

Which best describes the above statements?

A (i) T (ii) F
B (i) T (ii) T
C (i) F (ii) F
D (i) F (ii) T

Question 37
Joanne Craven is a sole trader. Her balance sheet will include:

A Total wages for the year
B Her capital at the beginning of the year
C Overhead cost for the year
D Her shareholding at the beginning of the year

Answers to Self-check Questions

1. A YES Buildings would be bought for use by the business for a long period of time. They would not form part of the stock which is for resale.
    B NO A business will make purchases on credit. As they still owe the money for those purchases, this amount is a liability. Further, as the amount owed is constantly changing, creditors are classed as a current liability.
    C NO Stocks are of value and are therefore an asset to the business. Further, the amount in stock constantly changes. Stocks are therefore a current asset.
    D NO Although cash at the bank is an asset to the business, the amount will change as cheques are deposited and drawn daily. Cash at the bank is therefore a current asset.

2. A NO This is a fixed asset.
    B NO A mortgage is what is owed by a business for the purchase of premises or a factory. Although it is therefore a liability, the amount owed for the mortgage is not constantly changing.
    C YES A bank overdraft is a liability and changes.
    D NO This is a current asset.

3. Most liquid means items that can be converted/sold for cash most easily. The most liquid in the list given is usually considered to be debtors.

4. The description of a permanent method of finance for a business is one which would remain within the business whilst it is in existence. The answer to the alternatives are therefore as follows:

    A NO A bank loan is for a specific period of time, not indefinitely.
    B NO A debenture is a type of loan for a number of years. Although it is usually a long-term method of finance, it is not indefinitely.
    C YES Equity is the share capital of a business and is therefore permanent. What you must remember is that, if shares are sold, it is the ownership of those shares that changes. Finance is not withdrawn from the company but changes hands between the buyer and seller.
    D NO This is a short-term method of finance.

5. It is important that businesses choose the right method of finance according to the type of asset. This is usually dependent on the life of an asset. An asset with a long life would warrant a long-term method of finance. An asset that is short term would require a short-term method of finance. The following would be most appropriately matched:

    1 Purchase of a new warehouse with A Mortgage
    2 Working capital with C Bank overdraft
    3 Cars that need replacing yearly with B Leasing

6. Inflows of cash to a business are money coming into the business. The following would therefore apply:

    A NO This is an expense and therefore a cash outflow.
    B YES Start-up capital is the amount of money put into a business by the owner/s.
    C NO Stock purchases are a cash outflow – they are a trading expense.
    D NO This is cash outflow – a fixed asset expense.

7. Financial movements in cash are either:
    - the amount by which cash inflows exceeds cash outflows or
    - the amount by which cash outflows exceeds cash inflows.

    The answer is therefore option D – sometimes a cash inflow, sometimes a cash outflow.

8. (i) T All organizations should have a good credit control system. As part of this control system, debtors who do not pay regularly may be refused any further credit.
    (ii) T If businesses ensure that payment is received for credit sales then they should have the cash to pay their creditors – providing they have calculated the cost of their product correctly (ensuring that they are at least covering costs). However, the credit period allowed by creditors should be negotiated in advance otherwise the problem in (i) above may apply.

9. A, C, D   2. B   3. A, C, D (see Table 7.1)

10. Answer B.
    (i) T Direct costs are those costs that can be separately identified to a specific product. Raw materials are a direct cost.
    (ii) F Salespeople are employed to sell ALL the products of the business most probably at the same time. These costs cannot be identified to a specific product. This cost is therefore an indirect overhead cost.

11. To answer this question you must first produce a layout of direct, indirect factory overheads and other indirect overhead costs as follows:

Blue Blouses Ltd product costs for period	
	£
Direct materials 3 m × £15	45
Direct labour 0.50 h × £6	3
Other direct expenses	1
Direct cost per unit	49
Factory overheads	9
Factory cost per unit	58
Units produced for period	10,000
Total direct costs	580,000
Other overheads	220,000
Total cost for period	800,000

$$\text{Total cost per unit} = \frac{£800,000}{10,000} = £80$$

Answer
1 C £80
2 B £58
3 D £49

12. Answer B.
    (i) T Direct costs are those costs that can be separately identified to a specific product. Indirect costs are those that cover a number of units. All the costs of a business can be categorized in this way.
    (ii) F As direct costs are directly attributable to a unit of production, these costs will not be incurred when units are not being produced. However, indirect costs such as rent and rates still need to be paid regardless of production.

13. Step 1 (a)

Materials/unit	Dept A		Dept B		Dept C	
		£. p		£. p		£. p
Material	1 m × 50p	0.5	0.75 m × 60p	0.45	0.50 m × 50p	0.25
Filling	1.5 kg × 40p	0.6	1 kg × 40p	0.4	0.50 kg × 40p	0.2
Others		0.4		0.3		0.2
Cost/unit		1.5		1.15		0.65
Multiplied by units produced		10,000		6,000		3,000
Cost/period		15,000.00		6,900.00		1,950.00

Step 1 (b)

Labour/unit	Dept A		Dept B		Dept C	
		£. p		£. p		£. p
Cutting/sewing	1 hr × £3.00	3	1 hr × £3.00p	3	0.50 h × £3.00	1.5
Filling	0.50 h × £2.50	1.25	0.50 h × £2.50	1.25	0.50 h × £2.50	1.25
Finishing	0.25 h × £2.00	0.5	0.25 h × £2.00	0.5	0.25 h × £2.00	0.5
Cost/unit		4.75		4.75		3.25
Multiplied by units produced		10,000		6,000		3,000
Cost/period		47,500.00		28,500.00		9,750.00

Step 1 (c)

Direct costs/unit	Dept A	Dept B	Dept C
	£	£	£
Material cost	15,000	6,900	1,950
Labour cost	47,500	28,500	9,750
Power	5,000	4,000	2,000
Depreciation	2,000	1,500	1,000
Total direct costs	69,500	40,900	14,700

Step 2 (a)

Total labour hours/period	Dept A	Dept B	Dept C
	hours	hours	hours
Cutting/sewing	1	1	0.5
Filling	0.5	0.5	0.5
Finishing	0.25	0.25	0.25
Total labour hours/unit	1.75	1.75	1.25
Multiplied by units produced	10,000	6,000	3,000
Total labour hours/period	17,500	10,500	3,750

Step 2 (b)
Total labour hours for the period

Department A	17,500
Department B	10,500
Department C	3,750
Total	31,750

Step 2 (c)
Total indirect costs for the period

Factory overheads	40,000
Management	30,000
Administration	35,000
Marketing	30,000
Running expenses	29,750
Total	164,750

Step 2 (d)
Overhead cost/labour hour

$$\frac{\text{Total indirect cost}}{\text{Total labour hours}} = \frac{164,750}{31,750}$$

= £5.19 overhead cost per labour hour

Step 2 (e)
Indirect overhead cost/department

Department A	17,500 × £5.19 = £90,825
Department B	10,500 × £5.19 = £54,495
Department C	3,750 × £5.19 = £19,463

Step 3 (a)

Direct costs/unit	Dept A	Dept B	Dept C
£	£		£
Material	15,000	6,900	1,950
Labour	47,500	28,500	9,750
Power	5,000	4,000	2,000
Depreciation	2,000	1,500	1,000
Total direct cost	69,500	40,900	14,700
Indirect costs	90,825	54,495	19,463
Total costs/period	160,325	95,395	34,163

Step 3(b)

Cost per unit	Dept A	Dept B	Dept C
Total costs	£160,325	95,395	34,163
divided by units produced	10,000	6,000	3,000
Cost per unit	£16.03	£15.90	£11.39

14. Answer A.
   (i) T   By producing a trial balance you can check whether the arithmetic of the ledgers in the double entry system is correct. It will not, however, detect errors that do not involve arithmetic – human errors such as not entering a sales invoice at all (see Errors not detected by the trial balance).
   (ii) T   See (i) above.

15. The trading account includes income from sales and items of cost in making those sales. The following answers therefore apply.
   A   NO   The drawings account records the amount the owner has taken for his/her own use throughout the trading period. It is not a cost of making the sales. Drawings are deducted from capital and appear in the 'financed by' section of the balance sheet.
   B   YES   The purchases account records the amount used in making the sales. This is therefore a trading expense and will appear in the trading account.
   C & D NO   These are indirect expenses which appear in the profit and loss account.

16. The profit and loss section records all expenses (other than those relating to trading (answer 16). The following answers therefore apply:
   A   YES   This is an overhead expense.
   B   NO   The amount of cash flowing in and out of the company is not recorded here. This would appear in a cash flow statement.
   C   NO   As mentioned in answer 16A above, drawings will appear in the balance sheet.
   D   NO   This again appears in the 'financed by' section of the balance sheet, (see answer 16A above).

17. Answer C.
   (i) F   The profit and loss account records items of expense whereas the balance sheet provides information on the assets and liabilities of the business. Total assets will therefore be found in the balance sheet.
   (ii) T   As mentioned in (i) above, the balance sheet provides information on the assets and liabilities of a business. As working capital is current assets less current liabilities, this figure will be found in the balance sheet.

18. A   NO   The market value of a company's assets may well appear in the balance sheet, but in the assets section.
   B   NO   It is the nominal value of the shares that is identified in the 'financed by' section.
   C   YES   See A above.
   D   NO   This again appears in the assets section of the balance sheet and forms part of the working capital of the company.

Answers to Unit Test

Question	Answer	Question	Answer	Question	Answer	Question	Answer	Question	Answer
1	A	9	A	17	F	25	D	33	A
2	C	10	A	18	D	26	C	34	B
3	B	11	B	19	A	27	D	35	D
4	A	12	C	20	D	28	A	36	A
5	B	13	D	21	B	29	D	37	B
6	D	14	C	22	C	30	A		
7	A	15	B	23	B	31	A		
8	B	16	G	24	B	32	A		

Unit Test Comments

Question 1

A YES Machinery would be bought for use by the business for a long period of time. It would not form part of the stock which is for resale.

B NO A business will make purchases on credit. As they still owe the money for those purchases, this amount is a liability. Further, as the amount owed is constantly changing, creditors are classed as a current liability.

C NO Capital is the amount put into the business as permanent finance. Capital would therefore appear in the 'financed by' section of the balance sheet.

D NO Although the bank balance is an asset to the business, the amount will change as cheques are deposited and drawn daily. Cash at the bank is therefore a current asset.

Question 2

A NO This is a fixed asset – see question 1 answer A.

B NO Creditors is a liability and constantly changes. It is therefore a current liability.

C YES Debtors owe the business money for sales taken. This is therefore an asset. As the amount owed to the business by debtors constantly changes, it is a current asset.

D NO Equity capital is a method of permanent finance put into a business with limited liability by shareholders. It will therefore appear in the 'financed by' section of the balance sheet.

Question 3

A NO This is a fixed asset – see question 1 answer A.

B YES Creditors is a liability and constantly changes.

C NO Drawings is an amount taken by the owner of the business to 'live on'. This amount is shown as being subtracted from the amount of capital put into the business by the owner. Drawings will therefore appear in the 'financed by' section of the balance sheet.

D NO Capital is a permanent liability – see question 1 answer C.

Question 4–6

It is important that businesses choose the right method of finance according to the type of asset. This is usually on the life of an asset. An asset with a long life would warrant a long-term method of finance. An asset that is short term would require a short-term method of finance. The following would be most appropriately matched.

Question 4

Purchase of an extension with A Commercial mortgage

Question 5

Salespersons' cars that need replacing yearly with B Leasing

Question 6

Working capital with D Bank overdraft

Question 7

A company will need money to increase working capital (the amount left in the business to buy stocks and pay bills etc.). If it has insufficient it will need to raise some. This can be done in many ways but an appropriate way would be to offer some shares for sale. Increasing stocks would be necessary to expand but the company still needs money to buy these stocks. Answer A best describes the two statements.

Question 8

Overdraft on a short-term basis are relatively cheaper and quick to organize. As it is temporary, it would be appropriate; both statements are therefore true.

Question 9

Answer B. It is important that businesses choose the right method of finance according to the purpose. As the expansion of a large public company is intended to be permanent, the method chosen should be permanent. The answer to this question is therefore share capital (A). The other methods are for a period of time.

Question 10

A YES This will avoid the item becoming obsolete (out of date).

B NO An average cost of repairs to the item will be built into the lease cost. However, although it is not the most important in this case, it is a point worth considering. Leasing will allow the business to plan outgoings on a smooth basis and they are less likely to encounter an unexpected bill of expense.

C NO As mentioned in B, costs are 'built in' to the lease price. However, leasing will avoid paying out large amounts of cash in one go.

D NO The asset life must be anticipated so that depreciation can be charged in the profit and loss account. Although asset life determination is not always accurate, it can be done using past information on other assets of the same or a similar nature.

Question 11

The idea of a cash flow forecast is to list all receipts and payments expected over the forthcoming period usually on a monthly basis so that the amount of cash in the bank per month can be identified. The period can vary but generally covers six months to one year. As debtors are a source of future income, when they are expected to pay is entered into the cash flow forecast. Both statements are therefore true (B).

Question 12

The main purpose of a cash flow is to identify the amount of cash at the bank in any one period of time (see answer to question 11). Therefore, C is correct in this case.

Question 13

The correct answer is D as a slump may result in fewer sales than expected.

Question 14

The correct answer is C as an unexpected bill for a major repair can cause an overdraft.

Question 15

If a debt has been written off as bad, the amount should have been received as a source of income will not be included in the cash flow. If the debtor then pays, this income is over and above what has been forecast. This may result in surplus cash at the bank. The answer is therefore B.

Question 16

An overdraft needs to be arranged. The cash flow forecast indicates –£55 for the month of December, answer G.

Question 17

An error has been made in calculating the closing balance.

By checking the additions, you will find that this happened in November: –£135 + £260 = £125, not £105. Answer E.

Question 18
There is just enough money to pay expenses. This happened in the month of September when the closing balance is zero – answer is D.

Question 19
A surplus of cash – this will occur in Spring (A).

Question 20
A high demand for cash – this will occur in Winter (D).

Question 21
A stable cash position – this will occur in Summer (B).

Question 22
A, B and D are costs incurred as a result of *all* the products of the business, not individual products. These costs cannot be identified to a specific product. These costs are therefore indirect. Direct costs are those costs that can be separately identified to a specific product – as in C the purchase of raw materials.

Question 23
The answer is B and cost per unit calculation is as follows:

Direct costs, £14 × 8000 units	£112,000
Indirect costs	£4,000
Total cost of 8000 units	£116,000

$$\text{Cost per unit} \quad \frac{£116,000}{8,000} = £14.50$$

Question 24–26
To answer this question you must first produce a layout of direct, indirect factory overheads and other indirect overhead costs as follows:

	£ p
Direct cost	
Materials	4.50
Cutting	1.50
Finishing	1.00
Total direct cost	7.00
Factory indirect cost	
Factory rent	0.50
Factory maintenance	0.10
Factory cost	7.60
Other overheads	5.00
Total cost	12.60

Question 24
£7.00, B.

Question 25
£7.60, D.

Question 26
£5.60, C (rent, maintenance and overheads).

Question 27
Factory rent cannot be identified directly to the product and is an indirect cost (D).

Question 28
Raw materials (see question 22) are used in making a product and can be identified to a product. It is therefore a direct cost. However, depreciation on office machinery cannot be identified to the product. It is an indirect cost. answer A best describes the two statements.

Question 29
The profit and loss account records all expenses (other than those relating to trading (making the product). The following answers therefore apply.

A	NO	This is a fixed asset used within the business. Fixed assets appear in the balance sheet.
B	NO	The drawings account records the amount the owner has taken for her/his own use throughout the trading period. It is not an expense of the business. Drawings are deducted from capital and appear in the 'financed by' section of the balance sheet.
C	NO	The amount in the bank is a current asset and not a business expense and will appear in the balance sheet since this statement provides information on the assets and liabilities of the business.
D	YES	Rent is a business expense and will therefore appear in the profit and loss account.

Question 30
The answer to this question is option A (see the answer to question 30).

Question 31
The balance sheet lists the assets and liabilities of the business. Fixed assets can therefore be found in the balance sheet. However, trading expenditure will be found in the trading account. Therefore answer A best describes the statements.

Question 32

A	YES	The trading account provides information on sales and the cost of making those sales.
B	NO	The profit and loss account records items of expense.
C	NO	The balance sheet provides information on the assets and liabilities of the business.
D	NO	The appropriation account provides information on how the profit is distributed.

Question 33
Balance sheet (A) since creditors are liabilities.

Question 34
Profit and loss account (B) since overheads are items of expense.

Question 35
Trading account D since purchases form part of the cost of sales.

Question 36
The information from the trial balance is usually used as a base on which to produce the final accounts. However, the production of a trial balance can be used to check whether the arithmetic of the ledgers in the double entry system is correct. It will not detect errors that do not involve arithmetic – human errors such as not entering a sales invoice at all (see Errors not detected by the trial balance). Option A best describes the two statements.

Question 37

A	NO	The total wages for the year are items of expense and will appear in the profit and loss account.
B	YES	Capital at the beginning of the year will appear in the 'financed by' section of the balance sheet.
C	NO	The overhead cost for the year will appear in the profit and loss account.
D	NO	Shareholding relates to a limited company where there are a number of people who have shares. Shareholding does not appear in a sole trader's financial accounts.

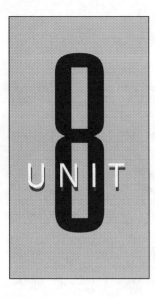

UNIT 8

Business planning

Getting Started

This unit brings together the knowledge, understanding and skills that have been acquired in the previous chapters. The principal objective of Elements 8.1 and 8.2 is to gather all the necessary information for a business plan, and then to produce and present it, bearing in mind a variety of marketing, technological, legal, environmental and social factors. It is the business plan which provides a 'route map' as to how the organization intends to cope with innovation

Batch production The manufacture of a limited number of identical products.

Design brief An outline of the main features of a product, normally formulated as a result of market research.

Externalities They are paid for, or received, by people other than the organization responsible for the activity, e.g. pollution created by a chemical works affecting local residents.

Flow production The mass production of an item using a continually moving process.

Gap analysis A method of reviewing an organization's progress by measuring its actual performance against its objectives. Any difference is known as the *corporate gap*.

Job production The making of a one-off item to a specific design, e.g. a wedding dress.

Mission statement A document detailing the aims of a business which should provide a common purpose and sense of direction.

Objectives A statement of what an organization wants to achieve through its operations.

PEST analysis A systematic method of gathering and analysing changes in the political, economic, social and technological factors which could influence a firm and its products.

Prototype A sample of the proposed product made to test the functional, aesthetic and manufacturing qualities.

Recession Period of slow or no economic growth, often defined as two consecutive periods of falling gross national product.

Satisficing Achieving targets for sales, profits and market share which satisfy the shareholders but do not necessarily produce maximum profits.

Strategic objective A long-term goal, e.g. achieve 15% of the market share by the year 2000.

SWOT analysis A means of analysing a product or a business according to its strengths, weaknesses, opportunities and threats.

Tactical objectives A short-term goal or aim, e.g. increase sales in the third quarter by 2%.

Target market The precise section of the market which a firm wants to aim its product at. The customer profile (sex, age, socio-economic group etc.) will be the result of extensive market research.

Total Quality Management (TQM) A method to ensure that quality is at the forefront of all employee's attitudes and actions. It involves a preventative approach to problems with the aim of getting things right first time through employee co-operation and teamwork.

Training and Enterprise Councils (TECs) These are locally formed, government funded councils which organize training and business start-up programmes in the local area. They are run by local business representatives who authorize colleges or firms to provide appropriate training courses.

Unique Selling Point (USP) A specific feature of a product or organization that differentiates it from its competitors. This can then be emphasized through advertising and promotion.

and change, whether in the *process* of production or in the *product* market itself. In the first part of the unit we examine the establishment of realistic and well-defined objectives for a business idea together with the importance of planning. We will look at how organizations approach the planning process and the various techniques which can be used to survey the market. Once an idea is considered a viable prospect, we must consider the legal implications of implementing that idea and consider how insurance can help offset some of the dangers. Completion of these preliminary activities will allow us to investigate in detail the purpose and content of a business plan. The plan has *five* constituent parts: objectives, a production strategy, a marketing strategy, resource requirements and financial documents. You are requested to formulate your *own* plan for a proposed business or for a new strategy within an established business. The final task is to ascertain whether there is any external assistance available to the business so that the business plan can be put into action. Business can be reasonably straightforward as long as you remember that for any proposed change you must:

Think about it.
Plan it.
Organize it.
Do it.
Review it, *again and again and again!*

There is no external test on this unit. The highly integrated nature of the Elements in the unit are such that we have approached the material in a different way from previous units. By the *end* of the unit, however, you will have covered all that is required of you for providing *evidence* of your competence in this unit. Instead of self-check questions at the end of each Element, as in other units, here you will find such questions at appropriate points throughout the unit.

> Element 1: Produce a business plan to implement innovation or change.
> Element 2: Assess the forces effecting change in organizations and business.
> Element 3: Assess the impact of change on an individual's work and working environment.

Essential Principles

8.1 Objectives of business organizations

Business objectives are a statement of what an organization wants to achieve through its operations. These *goals* or *aims* may differ between businesses for a variety of reasons. Organizations in the private sector may have entirely different objectives from those operating in the public sector, e.g. the Post Office and the National Health Service. *Within* the private sector the particular objectives may be determined by the size and age of the business and the market conditions under which it is trading. In a similar way a charity's objectives when operating within the private sector will differ from those of firms seeking to make a profit.

In this section we will examine business objectives and show how they may differ from sector to sector and organization to organization. A major *reason* for change is, of course, that an organization believes that the proposed innovation will be helping it *achieve* the objectives it is pursuing.

Private sector objectives

For most organizations, excluding charities, the most important long-term objective is to make a *profit*. This is often the reason why companies are formed originally and what motivates existing firms to expand. The traditional economists' view is that firms in the **private sector** are *profit maximizers* where every decision is based on the need to enlarge profits. This view, however, is somewhat simplistic. Firms and their managers may have other objectives, particularly in the short term, as detailed below.

Survival
* *New firms:* In the small firm sector, *survival* is especially important as nearly 60% of all new firms will cease trading within the first three years. This may be due to:

* Lack of resources, particularly finance
* Lack of managerial skill
* Unforeseen problems
* Poor forward planning
* Increased competition
* Lack of satisfied customers.

All new firms face enormous problems in trying to establish themselves profitably in the market. At the outset the owner may be satisfied for the company to survive its early problems while building a reputation and a guaranteed market share. This may only be achieved by offering goods and services at highly competitive prices which, in turn, do not provide maximum profits.
* *Recession:* In difficult trading conditions when demand for the product is low or falling, the main business objective may be to survive. Large firms have high overhead costs which must be financed even when sales are low. In a recession this burden may force the firm into a loss situation which, if prolonged, could lead to collapse. The principal aim in this type of economic climate would be to survive by cutting costs (reducing stock levels, shedding labour, closing factories) and/or reducing prices. In either case profit maximization is of secondary concern. In the recent recession of the late 1980s prominent companies such as Sock Shop, Coloroll and Polly Peck have either ceased trading or undergone major restructuring.

- *Threat of takeover*: Successful firms may become the target of unwelcome predators who want to take it over. In this case the targeted firm needs to convince its shareholders that the current management and structure is best suited to continued success and is sensitive to the changing needs of the business environment in which it operates. To avoid takeover, and ensure survival, the firm may again undertake actions in which profit maximization is of secondary concern, e.g. spend considerable sums on public relations exercises directed towards shareholders, etc.

Breakeven

This applies particularly to *charitable organizations* whose basic aim is to provide the maximum assistance in the chosen area without incurring a loss: e.g. Guide Dogs for the Blind, Save the Children, RSPCA etc. Some firms also may choose to aim for *breakeven* rather than profit as a means of gaining greater market share. In this case they could reduce prices or increase advertising costs in order to generate awareness of their product. Once a larger market share has been secured, the firm has the option to increase prices and return to profitability, particularly if rival firms have ceased trading in the price reduction period.

Reasonable profitability

Most firms aim to make a profit but not necessarily the maximum profit available. H.A. Simon, the Nobel prize-winning economist, used the term 'satisficing' to describe the situation where a firm has several targets, perhaps involving sales, market share and a level of profit which, while not the highest attainable, would satisfy shareholders.

> ### Did You Know ?
>
> Small firms are often unwilling to expand to achieve maximum profits because it means greater risk, dilution of control or increased financial commitment. They may be content with a lower level of profit in return for more leisure or a less pressured lifestyle.

Managerial objectives

In firms where ownership and control are separated, it is possible for the *management* to pursue alternative objectives to profit maximization. Managers may be able to

- Maximize management salaries.
- Increase fringe benefits such as pensions, expense accounts and company cars.
- Increase department budgets to enhance their own status.
- Expand areas and personnel under their personal control.
- Sanction prestige investments, e.g. high profile advertising.

All of these may reduce overall profitability, but as long as sufficient reward is given annually to the shareholders, the management can follow their own individual objectives.

Behavioural objectives

Firms may have objectives which are not only influenced by the owners and managers but also by *all interested parties*.

These 'stakeholders' include the employees, the consumers, the government and active pressure groups. The direction of the company will be determined by the relative strength of each of the interested parties. Each group's objective may be in conflict with that of another group, e.g. the owner's desire for high profits will clash with the employees' aim for higher wages. Similarly the consumer wants a quality product at a reasonable price which may clash with management's desire to cut costs or the government's wish to boost income from indirect taxes. In the end a *compromise* is reached which satisfies the various groups but may, in time, prove to be highly changeable.

Public sector objectives

The **public sector** comprises all the activities performed by the state and its agencies. This sector includes the central government, local government and the nationalized industries.

> ### Did You Know ?
>
> In the period prior to 1979, the nationalized industries accounted for 10% of national output, 7% of all employment and 17% of all new investment. They included industries such as coal, rail, steel, gas, water, electricity, airlines, postal services, telecommunications and bus transport. The state also owned companies which competed in the private sector areas of motor vehicles, broadcasting and aircraft manufacture. Today the nationalized industries account for less than 3% of national output, around 2% of all employment and only 4% of new investment.

Originally the objective of the public sector was to provide a service which satisfied consumer needs while at the same time *breaking even*. This was later amended in 1967 to include a *small surplus* to cover future investment requirements (a rate of return of 8%). These objectives were rarely met and since 1979 the Conservative Government has embarked on a programme of *privatization* whereby the companies and industries are systematically sold off to the private sector.

The remaining public sector is still required to provide essential services for the community but must now do so in an increasingly efficient manner. Some services may still need to be subsidized, e.g. rural rail services. These are financed by government in order to reduce externalities (e.g. congested roads) and not to penalize taxpayers who live in the more remote regions.

The use of objectives

An organization, whether in the private or the public sector, must have clearly defined objectives for the following reasons:

- They focus attention on the ultimate goal of the business.
- They act as a motivator.
- They help effective decision-making.
- They allow management to check the progress of the business.
- They can be used to analyse the performance of individuals and departments.

- They can help to establish secondary targets, e.g. sales per quarter.
- They help to convince outsiders, e.g. banks, suppliers, shareholders etc., about the viability of the business.

Basically the objectives should provide a purpose and direction for the business. They should be quantifiable, measurable and time specific, e.g. to increase overall profits by 85% per annum. In order to help motivate the staff the objectives must be realistic and attainable. It is no use setting a production target beyond the factory's capacity or a sales target in excess of market demand. Whatever the objectives agreed upon, they can only be *achieved* if they are part of a comprehensive and carefully established **business plan**.

8.2 The need for planning

Purpose of a business plan

If an organization is to achieve its primary objectives or to implement change then it must have a **plan** to act as a guide. Trying to operate a business without a plan will result in crisis management. The firm lurches from one problem to the next without direction or focus, often lacking the resources or strategies to deal with the problem. A good plan is required in order to meet the following needs:

Provide direction
The plan should provide the answers to the following questions:

- Can the firm operate within the legal framework?
- Is there a market for the product?
- Can the product be produced profitably?
- Can the product be sold and marketed effectively?
- Does the firm have enough resources: physical, human and financial?
- Is any outside assistance available?

The answers to these questions will form the basis of the business plan and are considered in later sections.

Inform other interested parties about the organization
Firms need to convince outside groups such as bankers, suppliers and prospective investors about the viability of the organization. A well-structured, detailed business plan will help allay fears about the firm.

Did You Know ?

A **stakeholder** is an individual or group with a direct interest in a business's performance. Stakeholders include the employees, shareholders, consumers, suppliers, finance providers and the local community. The firm's long-term interests are best served by acknowledging the needs of these groups.

Anticipate problems and arrange to deal with them
Problems will always occur but many can be adequately dealt with if they are foreseen. Accurate estimates included within the business plan of resources needed in the future (physical, human and financial) will highlight areas of need and allow sufficient time in which to organize such resources.

Planning in organizations
Organizations, particularly large ones, have a systematic approach to long-term and short-term planning. Their overall objective is provided in a **mission statement** which can then be broken down into a *strategic plan* and further still into *annual operating statements*. The planning process can be further enhanced by an analysis of the market, competitors and the economic environment (see SWOT and PEST analysis below). The plan, however, must be flexible and reflect changes in the business environment and the customers' needs. Therefore the plan must be regularly reviewed and evaluated, as must the organization's performance against it (see Gap analysis).

The mission statement
This is a declaration of *intent* designed to motivate staff at all levels to work in a common cause. The **mission statement** should state briefly and clearly the following:

- Primary purpose of the organization
- The sector and industry it is concerned with
- The values of the organization
- The distinctive features of the company

These should be communicated to *all* staff so that there is a unity of purpose and a communal sense of direction. This should then act as a motivating force.

The strategic plan
This stems from the mission statement and details the major objectives and targets for the next three to five years. The **strategic plan** provides a framework within which *specific decisions* can be made about how to achieve the set objectives. Targets can be set for:

- The product
- Product price
- Product quality
- Market share
- Resources required

The operating statement
This is an *action plan*, normally set annually, which details *how* the strategic objectives are to be achieved. It establishes tactical and short-term objectives which must be met in order to achieve the longer-term aims. For example, it may establish annual sales targets for each product and market area in order to reach the longer-term objective of growth in sales and profits.

To assist in the establishment of these strategic and tactical objectives the business can make use of a combination of analytical techniques which aim to focus the firm's attention on problem areas.

SWOT analysis

SWOT analysis is a technique used to examine the internal and external Strengths and Weaknesses of the business, together with the external Opportunities and Threats that exist.

- **Strengths:** These are the advantages which the firm enjoys, e.g. low overheads, a skilled workforce, cheap materials, etc.
- **Weaknesses:** These are the disadvantages as perceived by the company, e.g. lack of market knowledge, outdated technology, poor quality control, etc.
- **Opportunities:** These are situations in the market that could provide an advantage to the firm, e.g. a product gap not yet seen by competitors, poor service offered by rivals, etc.
- **Threats:** These are normally from competitors but may also come from impending legislation by government; examples of threats might include newly arrived foreign competition, changing technology, a rise in interest rates, etc.

This type of analysis will help decide the appropriate marketing strategy to be adopted.

PEST analysis

All firms operate in a business framework which is affected by changes in Political, Economic, Social and Technological factors. **PEST** analysis provides a systematic method of gathering and analysing changes in these four areas which could influence the firm and its produce.

- **Political:** The firm must consider the political stability of the countries in which its product is sold and the government policies being carried out. Changes in taxation, monetary policy and legislation will have an impact on the company: e.g. the current Conservative Government is strongly resisting the Social Chapter of the European Union as they feel it will add to labour costs by enforcing a lower maximum working week.
- **Economic:** The firm must appreciate the general direction of the total economy, with particular reference to growth rates, unemployment, interest rates, inflation and the exchange rate. A small change in interest rates may increase not only the cost of borrowing but also the exchange rate and the relative prices of imports and exports.
- **Social:** Changes in taste and fashion may have a direct effect on a business in the short term. In the longer term, demographic changes, increasing environmental awareness and the growth of pressure groups may also impinge on the business. For instance, the greater consumer awareness of 'green' issues must be addressed by many companies.
- **Technological:** Advancements in science and technology mean that no firm can remain complacent about its product. This was clearly demonstrated by the Swiss who ignored the arrival of the microchip which revolutionized the watch industry. Competitors and consumers may be quick to appreciate the advantages of new processes and products, as evidenced by the growth of the telecommunication and cable industries with mobile phones, answering machines, faxes etc.

PEST analyses can therefore make a company more aware of changes in the business environment and how they may affect the market place in general and the firm's product in particular.

The review process

The strategic and tactical plans are made in the light of current knowledge about a dynamic economic environment. As such they must be consistently *monitored* and *evaluated* to see if they are still effective and appropriate. In some firms this process is a constant one, as information becomes available on a daily basis. For many small companies, however, this may only be an annual event. Whatever the case, the strategic plan and the resultant operating statements must be amended accordingly. Firms who are quick to spot economic changes are often the ones who are quick to exploit gaps in the market and thus improve their profitability.

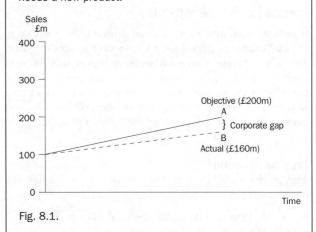

Gap analysis compares the actual results with those predicted. Any shortfall in achieving the original objective is known as the *corporate gap*. In the diagram, AB is the corporate gap for *sales* and highlights a problem area. It may be that the company requires a new advertising campaign to boost sales or to find a new market or even needs a new product.

Fig. 8.1.

8.3 The legal and insurance implications of starting a business

Organizations exist within an economic environment which is regulated by national and international **law**. The business and its owners must operate within that structure or face fines, imprisonment or closure, depending on the severity of the infringement. Legislation has been passed by both the British and European Parliaments to safeguard the employee, the consumer and the public from malpractice of various kinds. These laws can be grouped together into three areas concerning the *premises*, the *product* and the *people employed* to make it. In all cases it will add costs to the business but, if followed, the legislation is aimed at keeping the company out of trouble by prevention. Even where firms are careful and diligently obey the rules and regulations, it is still possible for accidents to occur. The provision of **insurance** enables a business to protect itself from such accidental occurrences and to avoid enormous damages which, without insurance, could threaten the very existence of the firm.

Prior to establishing a business the owners must ensure that they can operate within the existing legal framework.

Legislation and the premises

It is the firm's responsibility to provide a *safe environment* within which employees and, where appropriate, customers can conduct their business. This includes:

- Guaranteeing hygienic conditions
- Provision of adequate washing and toilet facilities
- Provision of adequate work space
- Ensuring all equipment is safe to use
- Provision of, and maintenance of, safety equipment and clothing
- Protection from hazardous substances
- Provision of adequate safety training

It is advantageous for the business to provide a safe environment as this should lead to a more motivated staff. It should also reduce lost production due to staff absence caused by injury and accidents at work. In 1993 over 21 million days of work were lost due to injury in the workplace.

The main legislation governing premises includes the following:

- **The Factories Act 1961**
  Establishes *minimum standards* for cleanliness, space for people to work, lighting, temperature, ventilation, conveniences, clothing, accommodation and first aid facilities. This applies to any premises employing two or more people in manual work.

- **The Offices, Shops and Railway Premises Act 1963**
  This extended the protection for factories, as outlined above, to other buildings.

- **The Fire Precaution Act 1971**
  This lists the *type* of premises for which a fire certificate is required. This ensures that premises have adequate means of escape, fire prevention equipment, instruction and training for employees in the event of a fire.

- **The Health and Safety at Work Act 1974**
  This requires the management to:

  - Establish a written policy on health and safety.
  - Ensure that all employees know the policy and follow its instructions.
  - Provide training, instruction and supervision on health and safety.

- **Control of Substances Hazardous to Health Regulations 1988**
  This regulates how hazardous materials are handled, used and controlled.

- **Health and Safety (General Regulation) 1993**
  This Act introduced major changes to Health and Safety legislation following the imposition of six new EU Directives. These covered the areas of

  - Workplace conditions
  - Work equipment safety
  - Health and safety management
  - Personal protective equipment
  - Manual handling of loads
  - Display screen equipment

To ensure that firms comply with these regulations a Health and Safety Commission was established with a force of inspectors who regularly inspect premises. They are empowered to give advice and issue *improvement orders* (for compliance within 21 days) or *prohibition orders* (stopping unsafe practices immediately). Law breakers can face fines of up to £20,000 or imprisonment of up to six months.

Legislation and the employees

The business must ensure that its dealings with the *workforce* are legally correct. Employment legislation ensures that the employee is protected by law in the following areas:

Terms of employment
The **Contract of Employment Acts 1972–1982** state that all workers are entitled to a *written statement* of the terms and conditions of employment. This should include details of:

- Job title
- Rates of pay
- Commencement date
- Details of payment
- Hours of work and holiday
- Grievance procedures
- Sickness benefits
- Dismissal rules and procedures
- Period of notice required

Additional points may be covered by the Company Rule Book as well as by agreements reached through collective bargaining with trade unions.

Health and safety
The **Health and Safety Act 1994** requires firms to formulate a written safety policy and to obey safety regulations (see details above). A Health and Safety Inspectorate exists to enforce the Act.

Discrimination
It is now illegal for employers to *discriminate* against employees on the grounds of race or sex. Protection was awarded by the following Acts:

- **Equal Pay Acts 1990 and 1983** – women to receive equal pay with men for equal work.
- **Sex Discrimination Acts 1976 and 1986** – discrimination on the basis of sex made unlawful in the areas of recruitment, selection and promotion.
- **Race Relations Act 1976** – prohibits discrimination on the grounds of colour, race, ethnic or national origin.

To ensure that these laws are applied two bodies were established to help employees to fight cases of discrimination. In 1975 the *Equal Opportunities Commission* was formed to advise people of their legal rights and in some cases to provide financial help when a case goes to court. For cases of racial discrimination the *Commission for Racial Equality* will help investigate unfair practices.

Unfair dismissal
The *Employment Protection Act of 1978* and the *Employment Act of 1980* established a framework within which dismissal was considered 'fair', e.g. for gross

misconduct, incompetence, redundancy, illegal employment, etc. In these cases it laid down procedures which must be followed. These consist of oral and written warnings, with the right to appeal.

If employees feel they have been unfairly treated, an appeal can be made to an Industrial Tribunal, an independent judicial body established to deal with employee complaints. In the case of redundancy, the employer may be obliged to pay compensation in the form of redundancy payments. Compensation will depend on age, length of service and final salary.

Legislation and the product

In the past, business was best summarized by the legal maxim *'caveat emptor'* or 'let the buyer beware'. This indicated that buyers had to use common sense when entering into a *purchase contract*. The onus was on the buyer to ensure that everything was satisfactory and functioning as claimed. This view left the consumer wide open to abuse, especially when *products* became more complicated and technical. Today the consumer is in a much stronger position and the supplier must abide by a series of Acts designed to protect the purchaser. The consumer is protected in a series of ways, ranging from the initial advertising of the product, its description, the quality and quantity of the product and its purchase on credit. The business must ensure that its product and marketing fall within these guidelines. The main areas of protection and the appropriate legislation are as follows.

Advertising and description
The **Trade Descriptions Acts 1968 and 1972** make it illegal for a trader to give a false or misleading description of the products on offer. This includes claims about the composition and performance of goods as well as the manner and timing of services. It also regulates claims about price reductions. A 'sale price' can only be claimed if it has been offered at a higher price for 28 consecutive days in the previous six months.

The Advertising Standards Authority (ASA) operates the British Code of Advertising Practice which requires all adverts to be 'legal, decent, honest and truthful'.

Did You Know ?

Recent cases before the ASA have included the range of Benetton adverts aimed at 'shocking' the public into an awareness of the Benetton name, e.g. an advert depicting a newly born baby was banned by the ASA in 1991. Other 'shocking' pictures have included a hanging horse, an empty electric chair and a bird covered in oil. Benetton claim that such advertising methods are successful, as sales increased by 12% after a series of such adverts in 1992.

Quality and quantity of the product
The **Sale of Goods Act 1979** protects the consumer by insisting that the product is

- of merchantable quality
- fit for its purpose
- as described

The **Consumer Protection Act 1989** governs the safety requirements of dangerous goods, such as chemicals and electrical equipment, as well as toys and inflammable clothing. It is necessary to provide warnings, safety advice and safety instructions for these goods.

The **Weights and Measures Act 1985** makes it an offence to give short weight or measure. Inspectors visit premises to ensure that the correct measure is being delivered.

The **Food and Drinks Act 1955, 1976 and 1982** regulate the hygiene, composition and labelling of food products.

The **Food Safety Act 1990** regulates the manner in which food is handled from the manufacturer, including stages involving transport, storage, preparation and final sale.

The **Consumer Credit Act 1974** protects the consumer involved in credit agreements. It ensures that credit can be provided only by licensed credit brokers sanctioned by the Office of Fair Trading. Consumers must be provided with a written statement of the true cost of borrowing known as the annual percentage rate (APR).

The **Fair Trading Act 1973** established the Office of Fair Trading to oversee the rights of consumers by checking and enforcing all laws relating to fair trading, in particular those pertaining to consumer credit.

The **Environmental Protection Act 1990** introduced measures to control the pollution of land, water or air by products or processing. It requires firms not to create a public nuisance (from smoke, litter, fumes or noise) or damage the environment by the waste disposal of dangerous substances.

Insurance

Insurance is essential for any business as it provides protection from the outset against a wide range of unforeseen events. Although some firms may resent paying high insurance premiums they are relatively small compared with the cost of a major accident where the business is at fault or the cost of a major incident such as fire. The main *types* of business insurance are as follows.

- *Asset insurance:* This protects the business against fire, theft or damage. As well as providing rebuilding and replacement cover the policy can be extended to include 'consequential loss'. This takes into account the loss of business suffered in the period between the event and the resumption of normal trading.

- *Employers liability:* This covers claims for compensation by staff who have been injured at work. It is compulsory by law to have sufficient insurance.

- *Public liability:* This type of insurance covers non-employees who may have an accident while visiting the premises, e.g. customers, suppliers or government inspectors.

- *Motor vehicle insurance:* It is unlawful not to have at least third party insurance so that passengers, other road users and pedestrians are covered in case of accident.

- *Fidelity guarantee:* This protects the business against any dishonesty by employees, e.g. the embezzlement of funds or theft of goods.

- *Product liability:* Legal insurance can protect the business against prosecution under the various Acts of Parliament regarding fair trading, employment and sales of goods etc.

Once the owners have satisfied themselves that the venture can be performed legally they can proceed with the establishment of a detailed business plan.

Self Check

1. Decide which stakeholders would be in favour of the following objectives. Then explain, in one or two sentences, the reasons why (there may be more than one supporter for each option).

	Govern- ment	Share- holders	Employees	Salaried managers	Consumers
To make a profit					
To expand					
To control costs					
To raise wages					
To reward decision takers					
To improve productivity					
To increase market share					
To maintain dividend growth					
To invest in new technology					

2. Conduct an assessment of a fast food outlet (or a business of your choice) in your area using the SWOT analysis approach. The 'strengths and weaknesses' are the actual position of the outlet at the present time. The 'opportunities and threats' represent the outlook in the future.

Strengths	Weaknesses
Opportunities	Threats

3. Compare your results with those of another student. Discuss the areas of disagreement.

4. Which act covers the following situations:
   1. The number of hours an employee is required to work.
   2. A written policy concerning safety precautions.
   3. The handling of substances such as acid.
   4. The temperature of an office.
   5. The provision of exit notices and routes.
   6. The refusal to employ workers of a foreign origin.
   7. The wage rates of women.
   8. The dismissal of a worker.
   9. The rules regarding the promotion of a 'sale'.
   10. The contents of food items.
   11. The discharge of waste into a river.
   12. The sale of faulty equipment.

5. Find out what the college regulations are for health and safety in the area where you work most. How have these added to the costs of running the college?

8.4 The business plan: characteristics and objectives

Characteristics of a business plan

A **business plan** has both internal and external uses. It is relevant both for start-up of the company as a whole and for planning major changes in the corporate strategy. *Internally* it acts as a focus for all concerned in the business in that it provides a purpose, a direction and a set of targets to achieve. It also allows management to check and monitor progress as the business implements change. *Externally* the plan is needed to convince others, such as banks, suppliers and prospective investors, about the viability of the company and any new projects it is proposing. To help convince these groups that the business is properly organized and has a chance to succeed, the business plan should incorporate the following six features:

- **Identification of business objectives:** This should include a summary of the business idea, personal details, the product, type of business organization and management structure.

- **A production plan:** A list of premises, plant and machinery, raw materials and labour required for the initial production. The design and layout of the production process should also be included, with due regard to legal requirements.

- **A marketing plan:** A comprehensive review of the marketing mix.

- **Identification of the physical, human and financial resources required and time constraints.**

- **A financial forecast:** This will involve the start-up capital needed for fixed assets together with operating budgets and cash flow forecasts.

- **A monitoring and review procedure:** A system of control mechanisms to ensure the business is progressing according to plan.

Let us explore these six characteristics as though we needed to convince a bank manager about the viability of the product, the business and the personnel controlling it.

Earlier in the unit we detailed the importance of well focused objectives. In this section we commit our ideas about the business to paper in as concise and quantifiable a manner as possible.

Did You Know

Many banks offer business advice for new companies. The National Westminster Bank produces a 'business start-up guide' for prospective entrepreneurs. In 1993, according to the Federation of Small Businesses, 400,000 people set up their own firm. Unfortunately 55,000 small firms also went bust. This highlights the need for careful and thorough planning in order to reduce the possibility of failure by foreseeing and avoiding problems.

Business objectives

These should include:

- Description of the product and its special features
- A brief outline of the business idea
- Its long-term and short-term objectives, e.g. sales of 8000 units per month at an average price of £7.50.
- Brief personal details: education, experience and skills of key personnel
- Business name and address
- Business organization, i.e. type of business format (partnership, private limited company)
- Management structure and key personnel

Once this outline has been established, work can be done on producing a detailed plan for marketing, production and resource requirements (see below).

The business plan: production

The **production** part of the business plan is an explanation of how you intend to design and make your product. You must address the following important questions:

- What goods to produce?
- Where to produce them?
- How to produce them?
- How many to make of each type (the scale of production)?
- How to ensure quality?

The solutions to these questions require inputs (premises, raw materials, machinery and labour) to be converted into outputs in the most effective manner. You must consider how best to *combine* the factors of production and in what proportion. A prospective investor would have to be convinced that the production system had been well thought out. It should show the design requirements of any new product and how that design is to be converted into a finished article.

Design strategy

The starting point is to formulate a **design brief**. This is an outline of the main features of any new product, which should be guided by the results of previous market research.

- **Design brief:**
  This should detail.

  - General features of the product
  - The desired shape and appearance
  - The market it is aimed at
  - The cost of manufacture
  - The image to be created, e.g. a quality product, value for money, safety, etc.

  The overall aim of the brief is to guide the designers towards producing the desired good at minimum cost without compromising quality.

- **Design specification**
  The design team must transform the concept into a physical reality. To do this they make a detailed list of the *technical specifications* required such as:

  - Materials to be used
  - Cost range

- Quality and reliability of end product
- Shape, size and styling of the product
- Appearance and image
- Safety according to legislation
- Time limits

- **Prototypes**
  Using assembly and component drawings made from the specifications, several models of the new product can be constructed. These may be scale models or models made from different materials so that modifications and final styling can be done. From these various solutions a particular design will be favoured and a number of samples can be made for full testing and consumer reaction.

- **Testing and inspection:** The samples are thoroughly tested under a range of conditions to ensure the product fully meets its original brief. After careful inspection, the final approval for full production can be made.
- **Production:** The new product is launched, possibly at a specialist trade fair or at some media event. Even at this stage the company must be prepared for teething problems and for feedback from early sales.

Production strategy

This involves the choice of a *production method* and the selection of the *correct combination* of resources.

- **Production method**
  There are principally three types to choose from.

  - **Job production:** for unique items with little chance of an exact repeat order, e.g. Channel Tunnel, QE2, tailored suit, portrait etc. This requires a skilled workforce with a wide range of tools and machinery.
  - **Batch production:** for items required in a significant number and which can be made in distinct operations. Each batch passes from one operation to the next where specialist machinery is used by semi-skilled labour, e.g. shift manufacture.
  - **Flow production:** a continuous sequence of operations where the product moves constantly from start to finish, e.g. car assembly. This is only feasible for goods in constant high demand as the investment in machinery is substantial.

  The type of production method (process) selected will depend on the level of demand, the type of product and the finances available for investment.

  Having chosen the most appropriate method you must arrange the *factors of production* in the best combination. These factors of production are principally premises, machinery and equipment, raw materials and labour.

- **Premises**
  In choosing the right premises and location for production, you must consider the following:

  - **Size of premises:** is there enough room for present production and for expansion?
  - **Location of premises:** do you have easy access to the market and a suitable pool of labour? Is it convenient for delivery of raw materials?
  - **Facilities:** are these sufficient for the intended

production, e.g. power supply, telecommunications, drainage, office space, toilets and washing areas?
- **Legal requirements:** do the premises comply with all regulations with respect to the type of production (e.g. food) and the workforce (e.g. health and safety)?
- **Local regulations:** do you satisfy requirements of the local authority (advertising, noise levels, hours of opening etc.)?

- **Machinery and equipment**
  You must be able to show that the plant and machinery are fit for the intended purpose. A prospective investor would need to know:

  - Type of machinery and equipment required
  - Age and condition (new or second-hand)
  - Output specifications
  - Running costs
  - Present value and rate of depreciation
  - Cost of maintenance
  - Cost of replacement

- **Raw materials**
  It is important that you not only order the correct quantity of raw materials but also that they are of the right quality and they arrive on time. The level of stocks must be sufficient to keep production going but not excessive so that valuable finance is tied up.

- **Labour**
  'Behind every good product is a good workforce'. You must ensure that you have selected the most appropriate workers with regard to both skill level and motivation. Some of the labour will need to be full-time but others, particularly at the start of a business, may be part-time. As each company is different in its labour requirements you may have to budget for the specific training needs of your workforce. Finally, you must ensure that all legal requirements with regard to employment, health and safety are carried out.

The overall aim of the production plan is to make a product which doesn't come back, for customers who do.

Production layout

The final part of the production plan is to determine the type of **plant layout** that is required. There are principally two main alternatives:

- **Process layout:** This method is generally associated with batch production where the work space is divided into distinct areas. Within these areas one *particular function* is carried out, e.g. cutting, milling, drilling, welding, pressing, grinding and polishing in an engineering workshop. Different products will use different functions for different lengths of time. The main problem will be in scheduling the work so that all functional areas are kept busy. The main advantage is its flexibility.
- **Product layout:** In this method you design the work space so that the product passes from one function to another in a *continuous* process. The time between operations is kept to a minimum in order to maximize throughput and keep costs down. This is often associated with flow production techniques, e.g. car assembly, bottling plants etc.

Quality control

Quality control involves ensuring that the product and its features entirely satisfy the consumer. In the past, in the UK, we attempted to 'inspect in' quality by testing the end-product. This was wasteful and time consuming as the errors had already been made. Today we attempt to 'build in' quality by inspection at each stage of the production process. This is known as **total quality management** (TQM). It is important that you describe the methods by which you will ensure that the product reaches the end consumer in first-class condition, i.e. a policy of zero defects. It is imperative that managers switch from a philosophy of 'right most of the time' to 'right every time'.

The business plan: marketing

A **marketing plan** should be a written document showing where a business is at present with regard to its marketing, where it is aiming to be in the future and how it proposes to get there. In order to achieve this the business must

- Conduct market research.
- Determine a target market.
- Apply a marketing strategy.

The main points and conclusions from each section then form the marketing element of the overall business plan.

Market research

This is the collection, collation and analysis of data relating to the market and the consumption of the proposed product. Whichever method of collection is used the data should provide the answers to the following questions:

- Do the consumers want the proposed product?
- Why will they buy it?
- What special functions should the product have?
- What quantity will they buy?
- What price are the consumers prepared to pay?
- What shape, style and colour should it take?
- Who are the typical consumers of the product (age, sex, lifestyle etc.)?
- Where are the consumers likely to buy it?
- When are the consumers likely to buy it?
- Are there any competitors at present?

The objective of this research is to make the product 'market oriented'. The business must be market driven, that is, be involved in producing what the consumer wants, not what the business wants to sell. This is an important distinction often overlooked by new and old companies alike.

This information can be gathered by either *desk research* using secondary data or *field research* using primary data.

- **Desk research:** This involves using *secondary data*. These are data which originally have been collated for other purposes but which can be reinterpreted to provide useful information for the product and its potential market.

  This information may exist *internally* within the organization in the form of sales figures, market profiles, reports from sales representatives etc. More probably the information can be extracted from *external* sources such as published reports. The government produces reports on Social Trends, Census of Population and an Annual Abstract of Statistics. Commercial companies such as the Economist Intelligence Unit also publish business data. These sources can be used to build up consumer and market profiles for the product without taking too much time or involving too much cost.

- **Field research:** This involves the business in collecting its own data (i.e. *primary data*) directly from the public. The main advantage is that it is specifically designed to provide the exact data required and only the organization conducting the research will have access to the information. Unfortunately it is also more expensive and time consuming. The majority of methods use a *questionnaire* and this can be completed by:

  - Personal interview
  - Postal survey
  - Telephone survey

Other methods include:

- *Consumer panels:* A selected group of consumers who use and test the product over a period of time.
- *Direct observation:* Watching how consumers behave in the market place, e.g. reactions to a new display.
- *Test marketing:* Selecting a restricted geographical area to conduct a pre-launch test of the product.

When all the data have been gathered, they can be collated and analysed to determine a consumer and market profile.

Target market
The initial research should provide clues as to the nature of the potential customer. It should help to determine:

- Age and sex of customer
- Life of customer
- Income group of customer
- Target price
- Target quantity
- Target retail outlet
- Dominant features of the product as required by customer
- Competition in the market
- Strengths and weaknesses of competitors (SWOT analysis)

Having obtained this information the business can adopt a suitable marketing strategy.

Did You Know ?
If you are going to succeed in your target market it requires a USP (unique selling point) to differentiate it from other similar goods. This can be either a feature of the product (faster, longer lasting, smoother etc.) or a feature of your business (better service, more convenient, faster delivery, after-sales service etc.).

Marketing strategy
A **marketing strategy** is based on a *marketing mix* of the four P's, product, price, place and promotion. These must be related to the needs of the consumer so that the business ensures that it delivers the right product, at the right price, in the right place and that customers know of it through the right promotion. The main points of each element are:

- **Product** *Appearance:* shape, colour, size, design, packaging
  Function: technical dimensions with regard to performance
  Other benefits: after-sales service, guarantee, credit facilities
- **Price** This is only partly determined by *production costs* which essentially set a 'floor' to the pricing policy in order to break even. More often than not the actual price will be determined by the *number of competitors* in the market and the *market segment* which has been targeted; e.g. high fashion items can command a price well in excess of production costs because this is regarded as an exclusive, high quality market.
- **Place** This involves *distribution*, which is the process of moving the products to the place where consumers require them. Channels of distribution vary significantly and include direct mail order, wholesalers, individual retailers, retail chains, door to door and tele-sales. The business must choose the most appropriate channel to keep costs to a minimum yet ensuring maximum exposure of the product.
- **Promotion** The objective of promotion is to gain and retain customers. It can be achieved indirectly through *advertising*, using any of the following forms of media.
  - Television
  - National newspapers
  - Regional newspapers
  - Magazines
  - Radio
  - Cinema
  - Posters

More direct methods include:

- Mail shots to likely customers
- Promotion and special offers (free gifts, competitions) etc.
- In-store displays, especially at point of sale
- Exhibitions and trade fairs
- Branding in order to differentiate the product from its rivals
- Personal selling (door to door, in store, telephone sales etc.)
- Packaging – to create an awareness of the product and its quality or special features

The marketing mix should therefore be a carefully constructed combination of techniques and tactics. Different mixes can be aimed at different segments of the market or for different periods of the year. The mix should be periodically reviewed in the light of sales information.

Business plan: resource requirements

In this section you must list and detail all the **resources** your business will require to cope with any proposed change. The three major groups of resources are physical, human and financial. There is a fourth resource which is often neglected, however, and that is time. The business will only be a success if it can organize the resources into an effective productive unit and delivers the goods at the right time. Each resource component must not only be described but also be quantified as accurately as possible. The main sections and components of resource planning are given below, with important questions for consideration. The answers to these will form the resource requirement part of the business plan.

Physical resources

Important *physical* resources include the following:

- **Premises** Purchase or rental
  Cost of mortgage/rent per month
  Freehold or leasehold
  Local rates
  Production/office space
  Service costs for heating, lighting and security
  Alterations required to comply with employment, health and safety legislation. Estimated cost?
  Insurance for premises and public liability

- **Machinery** Type, model
  Output capacity
  Purchase, hire or lease
  New or second-hand
  Maintenance cost
  Labour requirement: numbers and skill level
  Running costs

- **Vehicles** Number, type, make
  New or second-hand
  Insurance, road tax
  Maintenance

- **Raw materials** Type and quality required
  Quality specifications
  List of suppliers
  Advantages of using each supplier
  Supplier quality assurance
  Lead time between ordering and delivery
  Discounts available
  Storage space required
  Storage conditions needed, e.g. refrigeration

- **Finished goods** Storage required
  Security
  Access to loading area

Human resources

The success of a firm undertaking change often revolves around the skill and motivation of its *workforce*. It is important that you put as much effort into selecting, training and retaining your staff as you do in choosing any other assets. When identifying labour needs, the following must be considered:

- **Key personnel** Identify those posts which are critical to the smooth operation of the business or the new activity. Give details of:

  - Job description and responsibilities
  - Skills required
  - Experience needed
  - Health requirements

- **Other personnel** Follow same procedure as above. These personnel will also form part of the team and must be felt to be equally valued. The difference, however, is the amount of time and money you are prepared to spend in 'search costs' to fill such non-key posts.

- **Recruitment**
  - Identify methods and costs of each type of recruitment method to be used, e.g. advert in local paper, national employment agency etc.
  - Consider interview arrangements and costs.

- **Training** Specify a budget for any training requirements.

- **Insurance**
  - Identify types of insurance required for production and service staff.
  - Consider costs of insurance.

Financial resources

Each of the resources detailed above requires *financing* by the business. There are principally two types of cost involved, fixed cost and variable cost.

Fixed costs: These are costs which are incurred irrespective of the volume of production. They will comprise a large section of the initial set-up costs of a new business or new activity. Examples of fixed costs are:

Premises	Rent, rates and interest on loans
Machinery	Insurance
Vehicles	Heating
Fixtures and fittings	Depreciation

Variable costs: These are costs which fluctuate with the level of activity. Examples include:

Raw materials
Fuel
Packaging
Wages of direct labour

Some production costs do not fit neatly into either definition. This is because they comprise both a fixed element and a variable element. A good example would be telephone costs where there is a fixed charge for rental plus a variable charge for usage. Other examples include electricity, gas and overtime for fixed salary workers. These costs are known as **semi-variable costs.**

Once the fixed and variable costs have been established it is possible to calculate the total costs of the business or the new activity proposed by the business. The next problem is to determine what type of finance is required and who is going to supply it. The type of finance can be divided into two components, fixed capital and working capital.

- **Fixed capital:** This is finance needed for the *purchase* of assets which are for continual use in the business, e.g. land, premises, machinery and vehicles. The cost of these is written off against profits over their anticipated life.

  This *use* of assets is an expense and is therefore charged annually under the title of *depreciation.*

  The finance options open to a business for the acquisition of fixed assets are:

- *Purchase:* This can be done by using the company's own capital or borrowing from a financial institution such as a bank, finance house or building society. Whichever source is used, the loan should match the life of the asset, e.g. a machine with a six-year working life requires a loan over a six-year period.
- *Hire purchase:* Often used for plant and machinery and negotiated usually with a finance house which specializes in providing such finance. The purchaser pays a deposit and regular instalments (including a service charge) to the finance house. In exchange the finance house pays the supplier the full amount. The goods bought do not become the property of the buyer until the final instalment has been paid.
- *Leasing:* This involves the firm (the lessee) paying an agreed rental to the leasing company (lessor) for specific equipment over a period of time. At the end of the period the equipment is returned (or negotiations are entered into for purchase). This enables the company to avoid large capital payments at the outset plus the opportunity to upgrade the equipment regularly.

- **Working capital:** This is the day-to-day finance required for running the business. It is needed to pay for:

Raw materials
Running costs
Debtors, e.g. credit offered to customers
Stocks of finished goods

Some of this will be generated from sales but it is not guaranteed that the inflow from sales will occur at the same time as funds are needed. This is a problem particularly when the business is expanding and it requires extra stocks and more credit for the increased number of customers.

The main sources of finance for working capital are:

Bank overdraft: A facility that allows the business to overdraw funds in excess of its bank balance up to an agreed limit. This type of variable loan is advantageous in that interest is only paid on the amount actually overdrawn.
Trade credit: Suppliers may grant periods of credit of between 30 and 90 days before payment is requested for goods delivered. It is, in effect, an interest-free loan for the period of credit.
Debt factoring: Where a business is already operating it can 'sell' its debt to a factoring company who will advance up to 85% of debts outstanding. This improves the cash flow at the cost of a small commission.

If these services are insufficient to finance the working capital needed, then the business must obtain an injection of permanent capital from an external source, e.g. the owner, shareholders or through a bank loan.

Time

It is essential that a business is able to *co-ordinate* the demand for its goods with the supply of its goods. On the *demand* side the marketing policy will generate consumer interest through its advertising and promotion. This will create sales orders from which a future sales forecast can be made. On the *supply* side the design and process planning will need to be completed before final production can be established. It is imperative that these two elements come together and are effectively controlled and monitored. This is the purpose of **production control.**

Objectives of production control
- To convert sales forecasts or orders into an achievable manufacturing programme, i.e. to ensure that it is within the capacity of the machinery, labour force, etc.
- To supply and co-ordinate information between departments, e.g. future raw material requirements for the production department
- To monitor the throughput of goods in the manufacturing process so that orders are met on time.

Elements of production control
- *Capacity planning:* This will be determined by the number of machine hours available, the output per machine and the availability of labour. (Account must be taken for time lost in maintenance, re-tooling, resetting and statutory labour breaks)
- *Master schedule:* An overall plan of future requirements of machine time, materials and labour, based on sales forecasts
- *Loading:* The allocation of production hours to specific jobs or orders
- *Scheduling:* This specifies the sequence in which the jobs are performed. Critical path analysis can be used for complicated operations.
- *Materials planning:* Based on the sales forecasts and the production schedule, a plan can be established for the ordering, delivery and usage of raw materials.

This is a dynamic process which changes constantly as fresh orders are received, new products are designed and problems are encountered (e.g. late delivery of materials or machine breakdown). As an effective manager you must be able to plan ahead and anticipate problems rather than wait for them to occur, i.e. be proactive rather than reactive.

Self Check ✔

6. Choose a business from one of the following (or an idea of your own) and provide a set of business objectives. Use the outline given above as a guide. This will form section 1 of your business plan as required in Element 2.

   Hairdressing salon
   Restaurant
   Picture frame manufacture
   Landscape gardening
   Local parcel delivery
   Removal service
   Office cleaning service

7. What decisions are you going to take in the following areas:

   Design strategy for the product
   Production strategy
     Production method
     Premises
     Machinery required
     Raw materials
     Production layout
     Quality control

   Briefly describe the proposed action in each of these areas using the above as headings where appropriate. Incorporate this as section 2 of your business plan. Include also a scale drawing of the work area showing process layout and employee facilities.

8. Market research:

   What information do you need?
   How are you going to get it?
   How long will it take to get?
   How much will it cost?

   Answer these questions with respect to your chosen business and identify the type of information you want, where it exists and how to get it within a given time period.

9. Prepare an outline marketing plan for your product using the four P's and add it to your business plan as section 3.

Product	Describe the appearance, function and benefits of the product or service.
Price	Determine a price range in which you are going to trade in the short run (getting established) and the long run.
Place	Choose a channel of distribution most suited for your business.
Promotion	Outline the direct and indirect methods to be used to promote your product.

Self Check ✔ *continued*

10. Complete a table with headings such as these for your own proposed business and estimate the total annual cost of your resource requirements for the first year of operation.

	Description	Annual financial cost
Fixed costs		
Premises		
Machinery		
Vehicles		
Working capital		
Raw materials		
Stock		
Other		
Human capital		
Administrative staff		
Production staff		
Other staff		
	Total	

8.5 Financial data and forecasts

In order to convince prospective investors or lenders, you must be able to demonstrate effective **financial planning and control** of your business. This basically requires a realistic and detailed view of the profitability of the enterprise together with an accurate assessment of its cash requirements. To achieve this you must produce five financial statements:

- Opening balance sheet
- Operating budget
- Projected profit and loss
- Projected balance sheet
- Cash flow forecast

The objective of these is to show:

- The starting position of the business with regard to its assets and liabilities.
- The projected revenue and costs on a monthly basis.
- The projected final position of the business with regard to its assets and liabilities.
- The timing of cash inflows and outflows.

At this point, review the information in Unit 7 dealing with cash flow forecasting, balance sheets and profit and loss accounts so that you can concentrate on the *use* of the statements rather than their technical content.

The opening balance sheet

At the beginning of an accounting period, normally a year, the business draws up a record of its assets and liabilities which shows the overall financial health of the company. It is common practice nowadays to present this **opening balance sheet** in *column* form, showing the total net assets of the company and how these have been financed by funds

Operating Budget

		JAN		FEB		MAR		APR		MAY		JUN		JUL		AUG		SEP		OCT		NOV		DEC	
		Budget	Actual	Budget	Actual	Budget	Actual	Budget	Actual	Budget	Actual	Budget	Actual	Budget	Actual	Budget	Actual	Budget	Actual	Budget	Actual	Budget	Actual	Budget	Actual
1	Sales																								
2	**Less Cost of Sales**																								
	Opening stock																								
	plus Purchases																								
	Total stock																								
	less Closing stock																								
3	Stock used																								
4	**Gross Profit (1–2–3)**																								
	Less																								
	Admin. expenses																								
	Selling expenses																								
	Distribution expenses																								
	Depreciation																								
	Finance charges																								
5	Total expenses																								
	Net Profit before tax (4–5)																								

Fig 8.2 Operating Budget

from either shareholders or long-term liabilities. This statement is your starting point. The aim is to improve the value of the company by adding to the assets, thus increasing its net worth.

The operating budget

An **operating budget** is a forecast of the predicted sales revenue and costs for the next accounting period. It will be based on various assumptions with regard to:

- Level of sales
- Direct production costs
- Overhead costs

The format should be as in Fig. 8.2. It will provide a month-by-month analysis of the expected revenue and costs thus allowing the business to predict a profit. This, however, is not the only use of the operating budget. It is also meant as a control mechanism. Each month the actual figures can be compared with the budgeted figures to determine any differences. These differences or variances can be analysed and reasons determined for their occurrence, e.g. lower predicted profit in a month due to higher than expected material costs. In the light of this information the business can take action to remedy any problem, e.g. search for a cheaper source of raw materials, investigate alternative materials or control wastage. As such the operating budget acts as a monitoring device and a trigger for remedial action. It can also act as a motivator in that each person in control of part of the budget has a goal to achieve, i.e. a target output at a target cost.

Projected profit and loss statement

A projected **profit and loss statement** is formed from a combination of the information from the operating budget and the current tax regulations. It shows what the assumed profit will be before and after tax has been paid. It will be in the form of Fig. 8.3. This then is the ultimate target of the business for the current year. As time progresses the operating budget may be adjusted for changes in revenue and costs which will then have a knock-on effect to the projected profit and loss account. It is important that the

Profit and loss statement

	£	£
Sales revenue		A
LESS Cost of goods sold		
Materials	B	
Direct labour	C	
Production overheads	D	
	B+C+D	= E / F
Gross profit	A–E	
LESS Selling expenses	G	
Administrative costs	H	
	G+H	= I / J
		F–I
Operating profit		
LESS Interest	K	
Profit before tax	J–K	L

Fig 8.3   Profit and Loss Statement

business knows what it is aiming at and strives for that target, rather than waiting for the year-end to discover what they have achieved.

The projected balance sheet

The opening balance sheet can now be *altered* using the information from the operating budget, the projected profit and loss and changes in the cash position of the firm. This will demonstrate if the business is capable of increasing its net worth, i.e. the original aim at the start of the period.

The cash flow statement

Perhaps the most important financial statement and the one most overlooked by new businesses is the **cash flow statement**. This records the inflow and outflow of the business on a monthly basis. It is set out as in Fig. 8.4.

The statement helps to identify periods when there will be cash shortages. Cash flow problems can occur for a variety of reasons:

- Overtrading, i.e. inadequate working capital in times of expansion
- Too much investment in fixed assets
- Stockpiling

CASHFLOW FORECAST

		JAN	FEB	MAR	APR	MAY	JUN	JUL	AUG	SEP	OCT	NOV	DEC	TOTAL
	Cash inflows													
1	Sales	800	1200	1800	1890	1985	2084							
2	Capital introduced	10000												
3	Loans received	5000												
4	Other income	0		250										
A	**Total receipts**	15800	1200	2050	1890	1985	2084							
	CASH OUTFLOWS													
5	Purchases	400	600	900	945	992	1042							
6	Salaries	450	450	450	450	450	450							
7	Equipment	7500							3500					
8	Rent + rates	300	300	300	300	300	300							
9	Transport	100	100	100	100	100	100							
10	Promotion	50	50	50	50	50	50							
11	Services	100	100	100	100	100	100							
12	Insurance	80	80	80	80	80	80							
B	**Total payments**	8980	1680	1980	2025	2072	2122							
C	**Net cash flow (A–B)**	6820	–480	70	–135	–88	–38							
D	**Opening bank balance**	0	6820	6340	6410	6275	6187							
	Closing bank balance (C+D)	6820	6340	6410	6275	6187	6149							

Fig 8.4   Cash Flow Statement

- Granting too much credit or offering easy credit terms
- Over borrowing
- Unforeseen expenses
- Changes in demand not anticipated
- Seasonal variations in demand

By forward planning these problems can be identified and corrective action can be taken *before* the event, i.e. the business is being proactive instead of reactive. The actual statement will consist of an opening cash balance adjusted each month by receipts and payments. This becomes more complicated when suppliers extend credit to the business and the business offers credit terms to its customers.

It is vital that the cash flow statement is regularly reviewed because more businesses fail through poor financial management than any other single cause. Not only must the figures be updated but so too must the probability of their occurring. It is possible that not all of the debtors will eventually pay up and not all the estimated costs and revenue will be 100% accurate. The economy is a dynamic system and as such the financial records must reflect changes to the business as and when they occur. Periods identified as having a cash flow problem can be covered by making prior arrangements for extra financing, e.g. an overdraft for the period concerned. The problem has been foreseen and a solution planned into the programme.

Financial modelling

All of the projected financial statements can be used to explore outcomes under different market conditions. This is the application of 'what if' **scenarios**.

- what if sales fall by 5%
- what if machine productivity improved by 10%
- what if material costs were reduced by £X per unit
- what if new machinery was purchased in March

All of these situations can be examined and their impact on the cash flow and other budgets estimated. This type of *modelling* is made easier by the use of computers and some suitable spreadsheet software. This allows the management to explore the various options and to have contingency plans, already established, for likely changes in business performance.

8.6 External assistance available

The completed business plan is a plan of campaign which details the requirements for the coming year and the near future. During the compilation of the plan a list of required resources has been made. The final step for the business is to determine who is going to *supply* these resources.

The *business itself* may have capital reserves which have been earned in the past and can be used for the coming period. A new company may have to rely on the owners' original injection of funds which, more than likely, will be insufficient for all of its needs.

There are various *external groups* which are available for either advice, funds or expertise. These sources are:

- **Individuals**
  - *Business advice:* Other people in the area or in a similar venture may be able to assist with advice about typical problems and solutions they have tried. You may be able to learn from the mistakes of others and so avoid similar mishaps.
  - *Technical advice:* The services of an accountant, solicitor and insurance broker are required if the firm is too small to employ its own specialists.
  - *Investment funds:* Prospective investors will need to be convinced of the viability of the product, your potential to gain market share and the efficiency of the business. This is one of the objectives of the

business plan. In small firms, serious investors may be willing to become partners.

- **Banks**

  Most of the main lending banks offer a small business advisory service, e.g. NatWest Start-up service. They offer not only banking services, such as accounts and loans, but also advice and experience. The NatWest Business Start-up Guide is an excellent example of business literature which explains the fundamentals of starting an enterprise. Shortfalls in cash flow or fixed capital funding can be provided by the banks through overdraft facilities, loans and mortgages. They also offer comprehensive business insurance.

- **Other financial institutions**
  - Building societies can provide mortgage loans for the purchase of premises.
  - Finance houses provide funds for the purchase or leasing of machinery and equipment.
  - Merchant banks may specialize in the provision of venture capital.

- **Government**

  Both central and local government provide a variety of services through the following institutions:
  - *Training and Enterprise Councils (TECs)* provide locally based training plus business start-up support. The TECs decide what the skill needs are for the locality and then commission colleges or firms to provide appropriate courses. They are funded by central government but run by local business representatives.
  - *The Department of Trade and Industry (DTI)* is in charge of the government's regional policy which aims to correct imbalances of income and employment by stimulating the local economy of depressed regions. If the business is in a development area or an enterprise zone it may be eligible for government grants, rates assistance or tax allowances. The DTI also provides consultancy help under the Enterprise Initiative. They will pay up to half of the cost of specialist help for projects involving
    - business planning
    - design
    - financial and management information systems
    - manufacturing and services systems
    - marketing
    - quality
  - *Local authorities* – since 1979 local authorities have been encouraged to promote business location and development in their areas as a means of solving local unemployment and revitalizing run-down areas. This assistance has included:
  - business advice
  - grants and loans
  - subsidized rents and rates
  - training and education facilities geared to the needs of the business
  - re-location and job-creation grants
  - financial and advisory assistance for business start-up

- **European Union**

  Funds from the European Union have been available to UK firms through several institutions such as:

- *European Regional Development Fund (ERDF):* This provides assistance for businesses and for infrastructure improvements.
- *European Social Fund (ESF):* This concentrates on helping in areas of high unemployment through the provision of training and related labour schemes.
- *European Investment Bank:* This provides loans at attractive rates to firms in development areas.

Once the required advice and finance has been arranged and the business plan has won approval, the firm can go ahead with its proposal. All that is required now is to monitor the progress of the business against the project plan.

8.7 Impacts of change

Many of the possible impacts of change on the individual's work and working environment (Element 3) have already been considered elsewhere in this book. Look back to the materials in Units 3, 4 and 5 for examples. Of course in this unit we have also touched on the impacts of change in a number of respects.

Self Check ✔

11. Complete Fig. 8.4 (p.218) using the following assumptions:
    - Sales continue to increase by 5% each month in the first year (rounded to nearest whole £).
    - Purchases are 50% of sales (rounded to nearest whole £).
    - An extra machine is bought in August for £3500.
    - Transport costs double in July onwards.
    - Promotion increases to £90 per month from September onwards.
    - Hiring out spare storage space brings in other income of £150 in November and December.
    - All other costs remain unchanged.

    What is the closing bank balance at the end of December?

12. Prepare similar financial statements for your *own* business. Add these to the business plan.

13. Write to your local authority requesting information about assistance for the establishment of new firms in the area. Would your firm qualify for any help?

14. Contact the Department of Trade and Industry about central government assistance. Does your area qualify for regional help?

15. For your own plan, identify the following items for inclusion in the business plan:
    - total financial resources needed
    - amount to be raised internally from the owners
    - sources of finance available from external providers, e.g. banks, local authority, central government and European Union.

Answers to self-check questions

Most answers to questions 1–15 are a matter of your interpretation. However here is an answer to Question 11.

CASHFLOW FORECAST ANSWER

		JAN	FEB	MAR	APR	MAY	JUN	JUL	AUG	SEP	OCT	NOV	DEC	TOTAL
	Cash inflows													
1	Sales	800	1200	1800	1890	1985	2084	2188	2297	2412	2533	2659	2792	24640
2	Capital introduced	10000												10000
3	Loans received	5000												5000
4	Other income	0		250								150	150	550
A	**Total receipts**	15800	1200	2050	1890	1985	2084	2188	2297	2412	2533	2809	2942	40190
	CASH OUTFLOWS													
5	Purchases	400	600	900	945	992	1042	1094	1149	1206	1266	1330	1396	12320
6	Salaries	450	450	450	450	450	450	450	450	450	450	450	450	5400
7	Equipment	7500							3500					11000
8	Rent + rates	300	300	300	300	300	300	300	300	300	300	300	300	3600
9	Transport	100	100	100	100	100	100	200	200	200	200	200	200	1800
10	Promotion	50	50	50	50	50	50	50	50	90	90	90	90	760
11	Services	100	100	100	100	100	100	100	100	100	100	100	100	1200
12	Insurance	80	80	80	80	80	80	80	80	80	80	80	80	960
B	**Total payments**	8980	1680	1980	2025	2072	2122	2274	5829	2426	2486	2550	2616	37040
C	**Net cash flow (A–B)**	6820	–480	70	–135	–88	–38	–86	–3531	–14	46	260	326	3150
D	**Opening bank balance**	0	6820	6340	6410	6275	6187	6149	6063	2532	2518	2564	2824	3150
	Closing bank balance (C+D)	6820	6340	6410	6275	6187	6149	6063	2532	2518	2564	2824	3150	

*Note: answers are occasionally rounded to the nearest whole number

B PART

The Portfolio

This final chapter of the book is devoted to the **portfolio of evidence** that you will compile in order to achieve your GNVQ. Most of the chapter examines closely the various skills that might be involved in putting together a portfolio.

Remember that many of the skills and approaches needed in the portfolio will have been considered in Units 1 to 8 of this book. For example, Unit 3 has looked at different sources of market information, at different types of survey method, sampling design, construction of questionnaires, and so on. Unit 8 has looked more closely at constructing a Business Plan. Many of the documents and procedures involved in setting up, and running, the business are covered in Unit 6; and so on.

Nature of the portfolio

Once the evidence you have collected for a unit has been assessed as satisfactory and you have passed the external test (if any), you will be credited with a pass in that particular unit. Passing all eight mandatory, four optional and the three core skill units will give you your Advanced GNVQ in Business. Individual units on the GNVQ are not graded; i.e. you either have or have not reached the required standard for the unit, but a *grade is awarded for the overall qualification*, at pass, merit or distinction level. This is where the **portfolio of evidence** comes in.

Throughout your GNVQ course, you will be collecting many different types of evidence to show that you have successfully completed elements and units. This all needs to be stored in your portfolio in such a way as to allow your tutors or teachers (and staff from the awarding bodies) to decide whether the grade you receive for the Advanced GNVQ should be at pass, merit or distinction level. In coming to a decision on what overall grade to award, they will judge your work against three important *themes*:

- **Planning** – how you have set out the way in which you will approach particular tasks and activities.

- **Information-seeking and handling** – how well you have identified and used information sources.

- **Evaluation** – how you have reflected on the tasks that you have undertaken and suggested alternative courses of action and their implications.

We shall look at these three important areas in more detail later in the chapter (see page 241).

Your portfolio will contain evidence relating to:

- Mandatory units
- Optional units
- Core skill units
- Grading activity
- Performance in external tests
- Comments from your tutors or teachers

In order to give yourself the chance of getting the best possible grade, make sure that your portfolio is well structured, with a clear index. Your tutors or teachers will provide you with the necessary forms and charts to complete and insert into your portfolio.

What will a portfolio contain?

The portfolio is likely to contain a *variety* of evidence. Listed below are some of the most common forms of evidence:

- Assignments
- Projects
- Observations by your tutor
- Written tasks and oral questioning
- Work placement tasks
- Case studies
- Group work
- Practical work
- Surveys
- Reports
- Diagrams/charts/graphs
- Displays/exhibitions
- Computer work
- Certificates from other sources
- Role plays
- Audio and video tapes
- Records of visitors to business organizations
- Tests set by tutors
- Log books and records of achievement

Whatever type of evidence you choose to put forward to claim credit for an element or a unit, you will need to remember a number of important points:

1 That the evidence is **valid**, i.e. fit for its purpose. In other words, does the evidence you are submitting *really* satisfy the performance criteria laid down in the element? If not, you will need to change some of the evidence or add to it and re-submit it for assessment. Use the performance criteria as a checklist against which you compile your evidence.

2 That the evidence is **authentic**. Your tutors will check to see that the evidence you submit is genuine and that it is all your own work. This will be especially important when it comes to group work. Working as part of a team is an essential skill that you will need to develop, but you must be able to provide evidence to show that you have played a full part in the working of the group.

3 That there is **sufficient** evidence to be able to claim full credit for the element or unit. Your tutor will give guidance on whether or not you have collected enough evidence to satisfy the requirements.

4 That you have got **permission** to use evidence from other people. There shouldn't be a problem recording and using information that is collected in your school or college, but when you are using data and information from outside sources, perhaps from a part-time job or work placement, you must make sure that you have permission before the evidence is used.

The stages in continuous assessment

Although the exact nature of a piece of assessed work will vary between one school or college and another, there are a number of clearly defined **stages** that you will go through when carrying out continuous assessment, namely:

Stage 1: Receiving written and/or verbal instructions from your tutor about an assessment that will provide evidence to meet the requirements of a particular element or group of elements.

Stage 2: Discussing the practicalities of carrying out the work with your teacher or tutor and perhaps with other members of your group.

Stage 3: Devising an 'action plan' (see Fig. 9.10) for the assessment, indicating time deadlines, tasks and sources of information.

Stage 4: Discussing the action plan with your teacher or tutor, who may suggest alterations or improvements to make your task easier.

Stage 5: Carrying out the assessment in line with your action plan.

Stage 6: Having your written and/or oral work checked by your tutor, who will either confirm that it is of the required standard or indicate that more needs to be done to reach the standard.

Stage 7: When completed, claiming from your teacher or tutor for the particular element or elements covered, and filing your evidence in your portfolio.

Who marks the assessments?

You will find that studying for a GNVQ is quite different from any other courses of study you may have done. You will be expected to take responsibility for setting your own realistic timescales for achieving tasks and handing in evidence to your tutors. Under the GNVQ system, the person who checks to see that your evidence is of the right quality and quantity is called an **assessor**. This will usually be the teacher or tutor who set the assignment or task. In order to make sure that all the assessors in your school or college are assessing at the same level, one of the team of staff teaching you will take on the role of an *internal verifier*. The internal verifier is often the course tutor or course co-ordinator for the *Advanced GNVQ in Business* at your school or college, who oversees the smooth operation of your course and maintains fairness in the assessment process. If you don't feel that your work has been fairly assessed, you can appeal to the internal verifier to look at your work again. He or she will also look at a sample of assessment work from different students at regular intervals to see that standards are consistent across all units and between all assessors. All assessors and internal verifiers have to be trained in the operation of GNVQ assessments so as to ensure consistency of standards throughout the country.

In addition to staff from your own school or college who check your evidence and assess your work, there is another independent check by a person known as an *external verifier*. External verifiers are employed by the awarding bodies (BTEC, RSA or City & Guilds) to see that the methods of assessing GNVQ students at your school or college are working properly. They will visit your school or college from time to time to check that the assessment system is fair and in line with other centres running GNVQs throughout the country. They will want to talk to students about how the GNVQ is running and whether there are any concerns that can be investigated. Don't be afraid of telling the external verifier what you think of the course; they welcome feedback just as much as you do.

We now look at how the **core skills** mentioned in the introduction to this book can be demonstrated within the portfolio.

Core skills

GNVQs have been developed to provide a broad education which may be used as a basis for employment or entry into higher education. This is done by ensuring that students develop:

* A knowledge and understanding of business subject matter.
* A wide range of skills which underpin many different jobs.

Apart from the evidence of achievement you will be required to produce in order to pass the eight mandatory units and the four optional units, you will also need to produce *evidence of achievement* in the three **core skill** unit areas of:

* Communication
* Application of number
* Information technology

Unlike the mandatory and optional units, you will not find the core skill units taught as separate subjects. As far as is possible the teaching, development and assessment of the core skill units will be integrated into the teaching and assessment of these other units.

In order to claim that you have developed certain skills, you will have to provide **evidence** of achievement. Many schools and colleges provide students with a *log book* (detailing the skills performance criteria) for this purpose. This will be incorporated into your portfolio of evidence at the end of the course. While assessment will often be the method by which you will demonstrate that you have acquired certain skills, there are other possibilities. These would include:

- Work experience
- Audio-visual presentations
- Your domestic situation
- Social or leisure activities
- Previous study

During your Advanced GNVQ course you will find that many of the skills listed in the following pages are covered by your assessments or other evidence of achievement several times. This is no bad thing, since it allows you to improve on these skills and thus claim a merit or distinction rather than a pass. From time to time it is also useful to review your progress in the core skills and, in conjunction with your tutor, develop an action plan to remedy deficiencies or improve on the minimum pass grade.

In the following pages we state the *performance criteria* for each of the skills and how you could provide evidence of their achievement. To help you build up your portfolio of evidence we also provide space for you to record *how* you have achieved, or intend to achieve, these skill criteria. These statements may eventually be included in your portfolio of evidence.

It is very important to ensure that your portfolio of evidence shows your full abilities in these **core skill** areas. Some aspects of the presentation and handling of data relevant to all three core skills will be considered in the next section of this chapter.

Communication

Element 3.1

Take part in discussions with a range of people on a range of matters.

This means you should:

Make contributions in discussions which are relevant and expressed effectively.

Make contributions in a tone and manner which is suited to the audience.

Encourage others to contribute, and listen carefully to what they say.

Clarify any points which others make if you do not understand.

Possible evidence:

Discussions may take place, face-to-face or over the telephone with:

tutors	colleagues
peer group	family
customers/clients	etc.

when dealing with routine tasks, solving problems or dealing with sensitive issues.

Date	Evidence	Page reference in portfolio

Element 3.2

Prepare written material on a range of matters.

This means you should ensure that:

Any information you provide is accurate and meets the requirements of the audience.

All documents are easily read. You should use highlighting and indentation to enhance meaning.

Sentence construction, paragraphs, spelling and punctuation are correct.

A suitable format for presentation is used.

Possible evidence:

Responding to tutors, colleagues, family or customers by producing:

Assessments	Booklets
Memoranda	Log book entries
Letters	Publicity material
Leaflets	etc.

Date	Evidence	Page reference in portfolio

Element 3.3

Use images to illustrate points made in writing and in discussions with a range of people on a range of matters.

You should ensure that:

A range of illustrative material is used to improve other people's understanding of the points you made.

Illustrative material clarifies the points you wish to make.

Illustrative material is used at appropriate points in your work.

Possible evidence:

Organization charts	Photographs	Pictographs
Diagnostic and flow charts	Graphs	Tables
Pie and bar charts	Sketches	Histograms

Date	Evidence	Page reference in portfolio

Element 3.4

Read and respond to written material and images on a range of matters.

You should:

Identify accurately the main points in the text.

Discover the meaning of unfamiliar words, phrases or illustrative material.

Refer to appropriate sources for help.

Possible evidence:

Sources to use include:

manuals, dictionaries, tutors, supervisors, colleagues,

when dealing with reports, memos, letters, assessments.

Date	Evidence	Page reference in portfolio

Information technology

Element 3.1

Set system options, set up storage systems and input technology.

You should:

Enter information using the correct procedures.

Enter information so that editing may be carried out efficiently.

Keep copies of source information and drafts.

Save and store information so that it is easily retrieved.

Use security routines to avoid loss of work or unauthorized access.

Select changes in systems operations which result in more efficient working.

Ensure that changes in system operations do not adversely affect other users.

Possible evidence:

Copies of information produced showing IT applications such as documents created or saved.

Report on evaluation of IT used, including systems options such as:

    Mouse speed
    Changing cursor
    Changing screen colours.

Date	Evidence	Page reference in portfolio

Element 3.2

Edit, organize and integrate complex information from different sources.

You should:

Retrieve information using retrieval routines effectively.

Protect information from accidental deletion.

Use edit, search or calculation routines to minimize the number of steps taken.

Use editing, moving and copying routines so as to minimize the likelihood of deleting or disrupting information.

Save or arrange information in such a way that it is easy to transfer.

Correct any discrepancies which arise between source material and new files/records.

Possible evidence:

Using IT applications such as databases, wordprocessing or spreadsheets produce:

    Reports with chapters and subsections
    Tables of figures
    Complex graphical information
    Databases (e.g. employee details)
    Documents incorporating different IT applications (e.g. graphs and wordprocessing)

Date	Evidence	Page reference in portfolio

Element 3.3

Select and use formats for presenting complex information.

You should be able to:

Provide print-outs of information which are legible, accurate and complete.

Provide print-outs of information that meet user requirements.

Ensure waste is minimized.

Ensure that information is presented effectively using format options.

Provide a final version of information drawn from different sources that is clear and easy to understand.

Possible evidence:

Using IT applications such as databases, spreadsheets, wordprocessing and desktop publishing, produce:

  Documents with page numbers, indexes, justified paragraphs, different character styles etc.
  Documents with imported tables, graphs etc.
  Tables of figures.

Date	Evidence	Page reference in portfolio

Element 3.4

Evaluate features and facilities of applications already available in the setting.

You should be able to:

Explain the importance of accuracy and precision when using IT.

Explain the importance of using procedures designed to protect information from deletion or unauthorized use.

Describe and evaluate the use of IT applications in the workplace.

Describe and evaluate some IT applications used to improve day-to-day working.

Compare and evaluate the above applications with other non-IT means of information handling.

Possible evidence:

Using IT applications such as databases, wordprocessing or spreadsheets, produce:

Reports on the use of IT in an organization.
Reports into the feasibility of introducing IT into an organization.

Date	Evidence	Page reference in portfolio

Element 3.5

Deal with errors and faults at level 3 (Advanced)

You should be able to:

Use IT equipment in accordance with health and safety requirements.

Identify simple errors and faults and take action to rectify them.

Identify more complex errors and faults and report them to an appropriate member of staff.

Avoid harm to persons or equipment when errors or faults occur.

Warn others of IT problems so as to prevent disruption of their activities.

Possible evidence:

Arising out of the use of IT equipment in school/college workshop or work experience, produce:

A report on health and safety procedures to note when using IT.
A statement of a problem experienced with IT equipment and procedures followed.
A copy of a fault report made in a log book.

Date	Evidence	Page reference in portfolio

Application of number

Element 3.1

Gather and process data at core skill level 3 (Advanced)

You will ensure that:

Correct techniques are selected.

The techniques are used properly.

Mathematical terms are interpreted correctly.

Data are recorded in the correct units and format.

Records are accurate and complete.

Possible evidence:

Making and checking estimates using measures such as lengths, weights, speeds etc.

Converting between different measurement systems (e.g. £ and $ or yards and metres) using tables, graphs, scales.

Design and use a form to collect and record data.

Design and use a questionnaire to survey opinion.

Classify data into different groups.

Date	Evidence	Page reference in portfolio

Element 3.2

Represent and tackle problems at core skill level 3 (Advanced)

You will ensure that:

Appropriate methods are used to solve problems.

The problem solving technique adopted is used properly and to an appropriate level of precision so as to obtain the correct answer.

Mathematical terms are explained in layman's language.

Rough estimates are used to check calculations.

Mathematical aids (e.g. rulers, calculators, compasses) are used correctly.

Conclusions drawn from results are well founded.

Explanations for your conclusions can be given.

Possible evidence:

Solving problems using simple arithmetic.

The correct use of fractions, decimals, ratios and percentages to describe facts such as profitability, absenteeism etc.

The correct use of simple formulae or equations (e.g. to calculate return on capital investment projects or economic order quantities).

The use of diagrams to solve problems (e.g. breakeven charts, flow diagrams, decision trees).

Solving geometrical problems such as finding areas, volumes or perimeters for various shapes and solids (e.g. product packaging, product transportation).

Use of shorthand symbols to express series of numbers that are arranged in a particular way.

Solving more complicated equations.

Date	Evidence	Page reference in portfolio

Element 3.3

Interpret and explain mathematical data at core skill level 3 (Advanced)

You should be able to:

Identify trends or significant features in data.

Draw the correct conclusions or make the correct predictions from data.

Explain the mathematical terms used.

Justify the conclusions or predictions you have made.

Follow conventions or standard rules for presenting data.

Represent data accurately using symbols and diagrams.

Possible evidence:

Using mathematical terms to describe common shapes (e.g. cylinders for cans, cubes for blocks).

Construct and explain statistical diagrams (e.g. pie or bar charts).

Calculate and explain the arithmetic mean of a set of figures.

Explain the implications of combining two separate events (e.g. age structure:activity ratios).

Calculate the probability of an event given the probability of other events.

Date	Evidence	Page reference in portfolio

Presenting and analysing data

In many assignments you can demonstrate *evidence* of the 'core skills' and of the other skills required for a merit/distinction grade by the way in which you present and analyse data.

Presenting information and data

We shall first look at some of the ways in which information can be **presented** in your assignments. The visual presentation of research results in the form of tables, charts or diagrams can make *patterns* in the research stand out more forcefully. It therefore helps you to see what your research has discovered, as well as enabling anyone who reads the assignment to grasp more clearly the results of your research. The ability to construct and interpret statistical diagrams is also a requirement of the Core Skills Unit 'Application of number'. It is important, however, to choose the right form of presentation. You should consider the advantages and disadvantages of the alternatives available to you and decide which method of presentation is the most appropriate for the findings you have to present.

Grouping data

Data need to be **grouped** and classified before they can be analysed. This means sorting the bits of information you have obtained into logical groupings. If a small range of figures or responses is involved this is usually straightforward. If, for instance, you asked visitors to a resort to grade the quality of information they had received *before* reaching their destination on a scale of 1 (inadequate) to 4 (excellent), you would only need to sort the responses into these four categories. Here the groupings suggest themselves, but if a large range of figures is involved you need to reduce them to a smaller number of groupings.

Imagine for instance that, in a survey, 1000 adults were asked to fill in a questionnaire. Their responses would be easier to analyse if you put them into groups according to age. Usually you need around 5–10 groupings. Fewer than this may mean you are generalizing too much and obscuring the details of your findings; more than this and the purpose of grouping the data (which is to make it more manageable by summarizing it) begins to be lost. You also need to ensure that each grouping covers a similar range. In this case you might use the following groupings:

18 and under 30 years
30 and under 40 years
40 and under 50 years
50 and under 60 years
60 and under 70 years
70 and under 80 years
80 years and above

Tables

A **table** is defined as an arrangement of data in labelled rows and columns. The main purposes of presenting data using a table format are:

1 To present crude data in an orderly manner
2 To make it easier to identify trends
3 To summarize different types of information

Each table should include all that is relevant but exclude anything which is unnecessary. All tables must be clearly labelled, units marked and the source of data given, as in the table below looking at the age distribution of different ethnic groups in Great Britain.

Great Britain

Ethnic Group	Age group (percentages)				
	0–15	16–29	30–44	45–59	60 and over
West Indian or Guyanese	24	30	19	19	9
Indian	29	25	25	14	6
Pakistani	44	23	20	11	3
Bangladeshi	46	26	15	11	3
Chinese	25	28	29	13	5
African	31	28	28	10	2
Arab	23	30	33	9	5
Mixed	54	24	13	6	3
Other	27	27	31	10	4
All ethnic minority groups	34	26	22	13	5
White	19	21	21	17	21
Not stated	36	22	16	11	15
All ethnic groups[a]	20	22	21	17	20

[a]Including White and Not stated.

(*Social Trends* 1993)

Table 9.1 Ethnic Groups in Great Britain

From this table we can immediately see that 46% of all ethnic Bangladeshi people are aged between 0 and 15 years, compared to only 24% of all ethnic West Indian or Guyanese people. Remember: whenever you present a table, make *use* of the information contained in the table when you discuss your findings.

Line graphs

Line graphs are one way of showing changes and trends more clearly. They can be used to indicate the relationship between two variables. In the case of a teenage drinking survey, for example, you may want to establish if there is any significant relationship between the ages of teenagers and the amount that they drink. A line graph will help you to see if your findings suggest that there is such a relationship.

The first stage in constructing a line graph is to sort your data into two groups of figures. One of these groups will be plotted on the horizontal axis (known as the x axis) and the other on the vertical axis (known as the y axis). It is usual to place the *dependent variable* on the y axis and the *independent variable* on the x axis. Essentially, the dependent variable is something that is determined by, or depends upon, another variable. In the case of the teenage drinking survey, the dependent variable is the amount of alcohol consumed because its value depends upon the age of the teenagers concerned. The opposite is clearly not true – the age of the teenagers does not in any way depend upon the amount that they drink. The age of the teenagers is therefore the independent variable and is plotted along the horizontal axis (Fig. 9.1(a)).

Next you must choose a *scale* for each of your axes. The point at which your axes cross is referred to as the *origin* and it is usual for all variables to have a value of zero at the origin. Bearing this in mind your scale should be large enough to make clear the way in which the variable you are

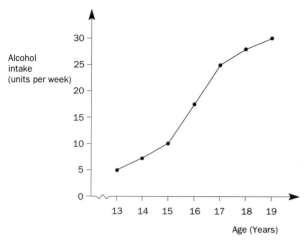

Fig. 9.1(a) Line graph of age of teenagers and amount of alcohol consumed

plotting has behaved over time. Sometimes the choice of a scale is easy, but what if the first observation you wish to plot has a value of several thousand million pounds? This would be the case if you were plotting UK expenditure on consumer goods and services over time. Some information on the way this has changed over time is given in Fig. 9.1(b). Note the use of a zig-zag to break the y axis, enabling us to show the range £62m–£76m. Without the zig-zag, our line graph would occupy such a small proportion of the diagram it would be less clear and considerably more difficult to interpret.

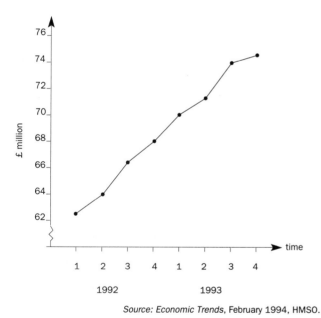

Source: *Economic Trends*, February 1994, HMSO.

Fig. 9.1(b) Line graph of quarterly expenditure of UK consumers

Line graphs are popular because they highlight *trends* and *relationships* in data that are not so easy to spot if data are simply presented in the form of a table. When constructing your own line graphs remember the following points of good practice:

- Label your axes showing clearly the units of measurement. For example, the variable on your x axis might be time and this might be measured in quarters of a year, as in Fig. 9.1(b).

- Give the original source of the information plotted.
- Give the graph a title indicating what it shows.
- Plot the *independent variable* on the x axis. This variable should be the one that is changed to assess the impact on a different (*dependent*) variable.
- Plot the *dependent variable* on the y axis.
- Choose a scale that enables you to identify changes in the dependent variable.
- Use a dot (or cross) to mark each item of data on your graph. Connect these points with a straight line.
- When the same axes are used to plot more than one graph, draw each graph in a *different colour* so that they are easily distinguished. Remember to include a *key* showing which variable is shown by which graph.

Of course, as with tables, make sure you *use* any line graphs you have presented. For example, in Fig. 9.1(a) we see that the most rapid increase in weekly units of alcohol consumed occurs between the ages of 15 and 17 years, a rise of some 15 units per week over this 2 year period.

Bar charts

These are one of the most widely used techniques for presenting economic data. It is possible that you will want to use a **bar chart** in your assignment. It is therefore important for you to understand how to *construct* one. However, it is also important for you to understand how to *interpret* a bar chart, since you are almost certain to come across them when you examine economic data.

Bar charts can either be drawn vertically or horizontally. Which is preferable is a matter of personal choice, though vertical bar charts are more commonly used. Whichever way you present information, it is important that you give your diagram a *title* and a *scale*. You should also ensure that the original source of your information is given.

A bar chart can be used to show the importance of the *different components of a given aggregate*. For example, we could use a bar chart to show the *proportion* of an individual's expenditure on a given day on different goods and services purchased. Thus, an individual's total purchases can be itemized as:

Bus fares	£1.20
Lunch	£0.80
Stationery	£1.25
Refreshments	£0.75

This can be represented in the form of a bar chart, as in Fig. 9.2.

Fig. 9.2 Bar chart

More usually, there are three main *types* of bar chart you can use:

1 Simple bar chart
2 Component bar chart
3 Multiple bar chart.

A **simple bar chart** is a set of non-joining bars of equal width whose length or height is proportional to the

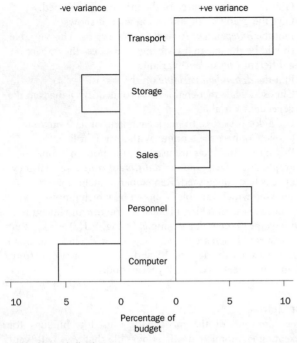

(a) Horizontal display

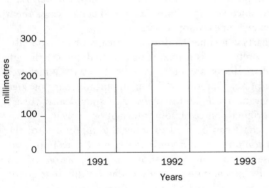

(b) Vertical display

Fig. 9.3 Simple Bar charts

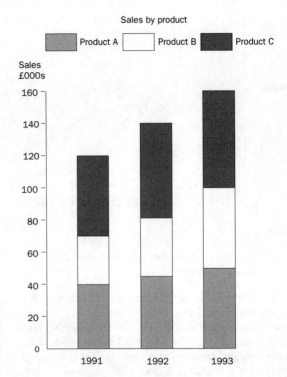

Fig. 9.4 Component bar chart

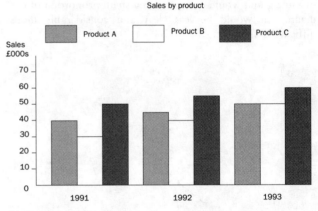

Fig. 9.5 Multiple bar chart

frequency it is representing. They can be drawn in a horizontal or vertical format and can show negative as well as positive values (Fig. 9.3).

A **component** or **segmented bar chart** is useful to illustrate a breakdown in the figures, e.g. the total sales of XYZ Co. could be broken down into sales by product (see Fig. 9.4). The constituent parts of each bar are always stacked in the same order with the height of each part representing the values of sales of that product.

A **multiple bar chart** uses a separate bar to represent each constituent part of the total. The data in Fig. 9.4 can be represented in multiple bar chart form, (see Fig. 9.5).

Pie charts

A **pie chart** is a circle divided into segments. The circle represents a whole number, and each segment represents a share or proportion of that number. We can use the information in Fig. 9.2 above and show it this time as a pie chart so that at a glance you can see the proportion of the individual's expenditure going on each item.

To construct a pie chart you will need a compass and a protractor. Let us use the information about personal expenditure given on page 237 as an example. First you must draw a circle of any radius – it must, of course, be big enough to enable you to display clearly the information you intend to illustrate! The circle represents the total. In our case it represents total spending by an individual on a given day. The problem now is to divide the circle into its component parts, i.e. expenditure on bus fares, lunch and so on. This is where you will need your protractor. There are 360° in a circle, and therefore each component of the circle has to be represented as a *proportion* of 360°. Refer to the information given on page 237 and you will see that total spending on this day was £4 of which £1.20 was spent on bus fares. We can calculate what *percentage* of total spending this represents:

$$\frac{£1.20}{£4.00} \times 100 = 30\%$$

This means that the segment of our pie chart which represents expenditure on *bus fares* is equal to 30% of the area of the circle. To be able to draw this segment we must first multiply 360° by 30%:

$$\frac{30}{100} \times 360° = 108°$$

Now find the mid-point of the circle and draw a radius. Next, use your protractor to mark off an angle of 108° and draw another radius such that the angle between the two radii you have drawn is 108°.

To obtain the next segment of the pie chart simply repeat the procedure. For example, as a *percentage* of total expenditure, *lunch* is equal to £0.80/£4.00 × 100 = 20%. This means we require an angle of 20/100 × 360° = 72°. Taking your protractor and using one of the radii you have already drawn, mark off an angle of 72°. Draw another radius such that the angle between the radius you have constructed and the one you have previously drawn is 72°.

Fig. 9.6 represents the expenditure of our individual on various goods and services as a pie chart. To help you we show the *angles* as well as the *percentage contribution* of each component. Remember to check that all the *percentages* total to 100, and all the *angles* total to 360°.

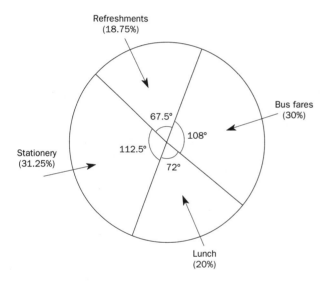

Fig. 9.6 Pie chart to show expenditure on various goods and services

Histograms
Visually, **histograms** are similar to bar charts except the bars connect together rather than having spaces between them. They are used to present *continuous data* rather than data that have been divided into *categories*, such as products A, B and C. The histogram is a set of *rectangles*, with the *area* of each rectangle in proportion to the frequency of a particular class interval. The *base* of each rectangle represents the class interval; in Fig. 9.7 each class interval is 10 miles. The *height* of each rectangle represents the class frequency; in Fig. 9.7 this is the number of people travelling that (10 mile) distance. From the histogram we can gain a quick visual impression as to where the bulk of the distribution lies. For example, in Fig. 9.7 we can see that most people (50) in the survey have travelled between 30 and 40 miles to visit the Safari Park.

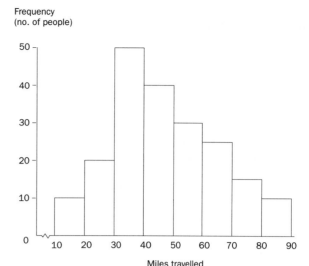

Fig. 9.7 Histogram of miles travelled to visit safari park

Because the *areas* of each rectangle are proportional to the class frequencies, you must remember to adjust the *height* of any rectangle where the *base* (class interval) is different from that of the other rectangles. For example, if one rectangle had 20 miles instead of 10 miles for its base, then you would need to *halve* the height (frequency) of the rectangle since the base is *double* that of other rectangles.

Scattergrams and correlation
A **scattergram** is a useful diagram for indicating the type of relationship (if any) between two variables. Each point on the scattergram is a *co-ordinate* i.e. the value of *x* and *y* represented as a point on the diagram. If variables *are* related, we often say that there is a **correlation** between the variables.

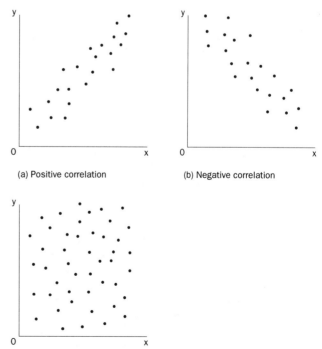

Fig. 9.8 Types of scattergram

In Fig. 9.8(a) there is a *positive correlation* between the two variables: both tend to rise (or fall) together. In Fig. 9.8(b) there is a *negative correlation* between the two variables: as one variable rises, the other falls. In Fig. 9.8(c) there is *no correlation* between the two variables.

Scattergrams are useful because they can give a quick visual impression of the relationship between two variables. However, you should remember that a strong correlation between two variables does not necessarily mean that the relationship between them is one of cause and effect – an increase in one variable is not necessarily the *reason* for the increase or decrease in the other. The correlation may be the results of other factors or of coincidence.

Analysing information and data

Once you have undertaken research and collected together relevant data for an assignment, you need to **analyse** the results of your research and present your findings in a logical and coherent manner. While you will hope in your completed assignment to display your writing skills, some of your assignments will also need to incorporate diagrams and statistical analysis. Here we concentrate on some of the numerical and statistical ways in which you can make sense of your information and data.

Fractions, decimals and percentages

Fractions, decimals and percentages are all ways of expressing parts or divisions of a whole.

Fractions are calculated by dividing the number that refers to the part by the number that refers to the whole. Thus if a survey found that one out of four patients in a hospital ward was dissatisfied with the meals served in the hospital, we can express this as a fraction: $\frac{1}{4}$. If the number referring to the part and the number referring to the whole have a *common denominator*; i.e. a number by which both can be divided, we divide the two numbers by the common denominator. Thus if instead of one out of four patients our findings involved three out of twelve patients, we would first express this in fraction form as $\frac{3}{12}$. As 3 is the common denominator of 3 and 12 we divide both numbers by 3 and arrive again at $\frac{1}{4}$. The fraction is the same in both cases because the *proportion* of patients expressing dissatisfaction (i.e. the part or division of the whole) is the same in both instances.

Fractions can be a useful way of simplifying your findings or of making a trend or pattern in the findings more obvious. If you conducted a survey in a holiday resort, for example, and found that 37 out of 72 people questioned considered the leisure information they had received to be inadequate, you might observe in your discussion of the findings that 'around half of the people interviewed felt that the leisure information they had received had been inadequate'.

A **decimal** is a fraction with a denominator of 10, or of some power of 10 such as 100, 1000 and so on. A decimal is calculated by dividing the upper part of a fraction by the lower part, adding noughts to the upper number as required. When the first nought is added a decimal point is inserted in your answer and for each additional nought the point is moved one place further to the left. Thus $\frac{1}{4}$ can be converted to a decimal as follows:

$$\frac{1}{4} = \frac{10}{4} = \frac{100}{4} = 0.25$$

Percentages

We find a **percentage** by multiplying the decimal (or fraction) by 100.

$$0.25 \times 100 = 25\%$$

Again these calculations can easily be performed on a calculator. In the first of the above examples the stages in the calculation are:

$$1 \div 4 \times 100 = 25$$

Percentages are useful in analysing the responses to questions in a questionnaire. If for example a survey found that seven out of thirty-two mothers questioned at a play-group find the facilities unsatisfactory, this could be expressed as a percentage. The part (7) is divided by the whole (32) and the resulting fraction is multiplied by 100:

$$\frac{7}{32} \times 100 = 21.875\%$$

It is the usual practice to express such percentages to the nearest whole number, or to one decimal place. This is done by rounding figures of 5 or more up, and figures that are less than 5 down. The above percentage therefore becomes:

22% to the nearest whole number
21.9% to one decimal place

Percentages can also be used to express the response rate to a questionnaire. If you distribute 100 questionnaires and 83 are returned, the response rate would be 83%. A further use of percentages is to make your findings easier to comprehend. Imagine, for example, that you have found out from your local authority that the most recent estimate of the population of the borough in which you live is 115,073. These are distributed among the following types of property:

52,203	owner-occupied properties
37,411	council-owned properties
21,879	private rented accommodation
3,580	other accommodation/unaccounted for

These figures might be easier to grasp if they were expressed as percentages:

45%	owner-occupied properties
33%	council-owned properties
19%	private rented accommodation
3%	other accommodation/unaccounted for

Averages

When you have a group of figures or scores it is often useful to have one figure which indicates the overall tendency. In everyday language this is known as an **average**, but in statistics there are different kinds of average, including *mean*, *median* and *mode*.

- *Mean:* The most commonly used is the *mean*, which is the simple arithmetic average. It is calculated by adding up all the scores and dividing the total by the number of scores. Imagine for example that you asked 10 teenage smokers to record how many cigarettes they smoked on a particular day and the reported totals were as follows:

5, 15, 12, 40, 10, 10, 4, 9, 5, 10

The mean is calculated by adding these scores up and dividing by the number of scores:

120 ÷ 10 = 12

An advantage of the mean is that it takes into account *all* the individual scores. A disadvantage is that extreme scores can influence the mean so that the mean actually gives a misleading impression. In the above example, there is one extreme score – 40 – and this makes the mean greater than it would otherwise be. If the score of 40 were omitted, the mean of the other scores would be 9 (to the nearest whole number). If a report on these findings stated 'On average the teenagers in the survey smoked 12 cigarettes a day' this would be quite misleading as in fact only three of the teenagers smoked 12 or more cigarettes.

- *Median:* The *median* is the middle score of a group of scores. It is found by placing the scores in numerical order and identifying the number that is in the middle. Thus if eleven scores were arranged in numerical order the median would be the sixth score because this would have five scores to the left of it and five scores to the right. If there is an even number of scores the median is the arithmetic average (the mean) of the two middle numbers. To return to the above example, if we place the scores in numerical order we have the following:

4, 5, 5, 9, 10, 10, 10, 12, 15, 40

As there is an even number of scores there is not a single middle number but two (10 and 10). The mean of these two numbers is 10, which is therefore the median. (If the middle numbers were 10 and 12, the median would be 11; if they were 10 and 11, the median would be 10.5)

An advantage of the median is that it is less influenced than the mean by extreme scores and is therefore more representative than the mean when there are extreme scores. In the example of the smoking survey, 10 cigarettes per day is a more representative average score than 12 cigarettes per day. A disadvantage, however, is that it is mathematically less precise than the mean and does not give a true arithmetic average.

- *Mode:* The *mode* is simply the number that occurs most frequently in any given set of scores. Thus if we take the original set of scores in the smoking survey

5, 15, 12, 40, 10, 10, 4, 9, 5, 10

the mode is 10, because this score occurs three times, which is more frequently than any of the other scores. An advantage of the mode is that it is usually easy to find. However, difficulties arise if the same frequency is shared by more than one number. It is also a crude measure of the average score, especially if there is not a great difference in the frequencies of the scores (in the above example, 5 occurs almost as frequently as 10).

If you mention an average in an assignment, always explain whether it is a mean, median or mode. If the average seems in any way unrepresentative or misleading (if it has been distorted by any extreme score, for example) point this out also.

Range and standard deviation

As well as the *average* we are often interested in how the data are distributed (or *dispersed*) around the average. The *range* and *standard deviation* are ways of indicating how scores are distributed within a set of figures. They are useful because they can show if the scores are close together or far apart.

- *Range:* The *range* is the difference between the highest and lowest scores. In the smoking survey the highest score was 40 and the lowest 5, so the range was 35:

40 – 5 = 35

A disadvantage of the range is that it only uses the extreme scores and so can give a misleading impression if one number is markedly higher or lower than the rest. In the smoking survey, the range becomes very different if we omit 40 from the list of scores. The lowest number is still 5 but the highest now is 15, so the range drops to 10. The original range (35) was misleading because it implied that the scores were more highly scattered than they in fact are.

- *Standard deviation:* A more satisfactory measure of distribution is the *standard deviation*. This is a measure of the spread of scores around the mean value. If the scores are grouped closely around the mean value, the standard deviation is small. If the scores are widely distributed, the standard deviation is large. The distribution curves in Fig. 9.9 represent large and small standard deviations. The small standard deviation curve indicates that most of the scores are close together around the mean; the large standard deviation curve indicates that they are spread quite widely around the mean.

Although a knowledge of range is a GNVQ requirement, a knowledge of standard deviation is not. However, you may wish to make use of the concept of standard deviation in your assignments. You should be able to find a more detailed explanation of standard deviation in any book on statistics, or your teacher may be able to help.

Spreadsheets

Many of the calculations we have been discussing in this 'Analysing information and data' section can be performed on a computer using a **spreadsheet** program. A **spreadsheet** is a program for handling numerical information. On screen it appears as a grid of boxes or 'cells', each of which can contain a number or a formula to act upon the contents of other cells. For example, a very simple calculation would be to add the numbers in two cells together; another would be to express one number as a percentage of another, or as a percentage of the total of all the numbers on the spreadsheet. Not only can a spreadsheet perform a large range of calculations, it can also present numerical information that has been entered, and the results of calculations that have been carried out, as charts and graphs.

This section on presenting and analysing data is by no means exhaustive of all the possibilities. Nevertheless it has covered many of the ways in which you can provide *evidence* of the *core skills* of communication, application of number and information technology. Using such techniques can also help in providing evidence of the *themes* required if you are to be awarded a merit or distinction. It is to these that we now turn.

Assessment criteria for merit and distinction

To achieve a merit or distinction, your portfolio must contain consistent evidence which covers the following three **themes**:

- Planning
- Information seeking and handling
- Evaluation

You will be given the chance to develop these skills throughout your programme of study and should be given the opportunity to add further evidence to your portfolio.

Some of the assessments you are given to complete may not be appropriate for obtaining a merit or distinction. For example, if all of the activities that you need to complete are listed clearly for you and do not require you to obtain any further information, then this may not fall into the category of a graded assessment. Although some of your assessments may be categorized as 'pass only', your tutor will give you sufficient opportunities to allow you to obtain a *merit* or *distinction* grade overall.

For an assessment to be of **merit standard**, the tasks you undertake must be *discrete* and for a **distinction** the tasks must be *complex*.

'Discrete' means that:

- The tasks are self-contained.
- The overall method of working is well defined.
- The number of different things you have to do within the task is limited.

'**Complex**', on the other hand, means that:

- You are often asked to deal with a number of interrelated tasks.
- You will be expected to define the problem, method of working, targets, timescale etc., rather than having this information presented to you.
- The problem you are asked to work on will contain a number of complicated activities.

Your tutor will tell you whether the assessment you are given will qualify for a merit or distinction. The criteria or standards needed for you to obtain a merit or distinction in your assessments are shown in the table below (Table 9.2). Apart from the tasks themselves being rather more complex for a distinction, the words in italics also help you see the different emphasis needed for a distinction.

You will notice from the table that one of the main differences between merit and distinction grading is the ability of a student to work on his or her *own initiative* and to use more of his or her *own judgement*. Grading at merit level implies a greater input to your work from your tutors than is the case with grading at distinction level, where more independent action is rewarded. Also you need to apply a *broader range* of skills, techniques and sources of information in order to qualify for a distinction.

Planning

In **planning** your work you must write down how you intend to approach and monitor the tasks given, *before* you start on the tasks. To begin with, we suggest that you:

Merit (discrete tasks)	Distinction (complex tasks)
Planning	
1 Draw up plans and prioritize your work on your own.	Draw up plans and prioritize your work on your own.
2 Be able to monitor and perhaps revise your plan of action *with the guidance of your tutor.*	Be able to monitor and perhaps revise your plan of action *on your own.*
Information seeking and handling	
3 On your own be able to identify, access and collect information from *main sources* and use *additional sources provided by your tutor.*	On your own be able to identify, access and collect information *from a range of sources and justify your selection.*
4 On your own check the validity of the information *using methods given to you.*	On your own check the validity of the information *applying your own methods.*
Evaluation	
5 You must be able to judge outcomes and identify and apply alternative criteria.	You must be able to judge outcomes and identify and apply a *range* of alternative criteria.
6 You must be able to justify how you have approached the assessment.	You must be able to justify your approaches *pointing out the advantages and disadvantages.*

Table 9.2 Achieving merit or distinction

1 Read carefully through the activity/tasks that you have to complete.
2 Read through the material again and start to think about what it entails.
3 Have a short break and, at the same time, continue to think about what is required.
4 Get a piece of paper and write down the following:
   (i) The type of information you need to find out.
   (ii) What you need to do to get that information.
   (iii) In what order – some tasks will take longer than others. For instance you may have to write to an organization to ask for information. If so, you need to allow plenty of time for the information to be sent. Writing a letter of this type will need to be one of your earlier activities.
5 Having compiled your initial list, think about what you have written; have you missed anything out? Are you sure that you have done them in the right order?
6 When you feel happy that everything is in order, rewrite your list in date order. To do this we suggest that you:
   (i) Work out the number of weeks you have been given to complete the tasks/activities.
   (ii) Make the last date your assignment 'hand in' date.
   (iii) Place the first task in your 'log' or 'action plan' and realistically estimate the time it will take to complete.
   (iv) Place the other tasks in order of priority.
   (v) Ensure you allow sufficient time to check your assignment before the 'hand in' date.
   (vi) Check your plan and ask yourself the following questions:

   - Have I allowed sufficient time for the tasks?

- Have I listed the tasks in the correct order?
- Have I allowed time to check my work?

It is imperative that you allow yourself sufficient time to check through your work, to correct any minor errors which could count against you. Many students receive lower grades because they do not plan their work. They think that they have 'lots of time' to complete the tasks and leave them to the 'last minute'. This results in them rushing the work, leaving things out or making silly mistakes.

Remember, you will be assessed on skills as well as performance criteria. Allow sufficient time to check your grammar, punctuation and spelling.

If you are asked to use information technology in the production of the activities/tasks, make sure that you build in 'hands on' time. Many students who have not planned their work effectively will make a 'last minute dash' to the IT workshops to wordprocess their work. This causes a great deal of anxiety and frustration as they often find that they cannot get access to a computer. Tutors often hear the following phrases.

I could not get onto a computer.

There was no printer paper left.

There was a 'bug' on the machine and I lost my work.

The printer ribbon/cartridge ran out and a replacement is not available until tomorrow.

I thought I could work on the computer today, but all the second-year students were there.

Colleges and schools have a limited number of computers to cater for their students' needs. The number they have is calculated on an even throughput of student usage. If, for instance, 40 first-year GNVQ advanced students all demand access to them at the same time, there is likely to be insufficient computer space, especially considering the other courses that need to use them and that are perhaps timetabled in to use them on that day. We cannot stress enough:

- ALLOW SUFFICENT TIME TO COMPLETE ALL TASKS
- BUILD IN AN ACCURATE AMOUNT OF TIME FOR USING I.T. FACILITIES
- BUILD IN TIME TO CHECK YOUR WORK BEFORE THE 'HAND IN' DATE

7 Once you are sure of the above, build into your plan a column that will allow you to *monitor* your courses of action. You will need to state, against each activity or task, whether you have achieved your completion date. If not, you need to identify the reasons why and decide what you must now do to overcome this problem.

Figure 9.10 overleaf shows a complete **action plan** for a group assignment which involved developing a business plan to set up a business. The students had to identify what informa-tion was needed to carry out the task, what they had to do to obtain the information, who was going to undertake which task and by when they expected to complete the tasks. Each member of the group had £20,000 to put into the venture; if they needed more, they could obtain a bank loan for up to half of the capital invested.

Action plans are an ideal way of keeping track of the progress of an assessment and checking that tasks are being completed on time.

Information seeking and information handling

A good way of identifying possible **sources of information** is to write down any that immediately spring to mind. This is called 'brainstorming' and is often used in the business world. The idea is to list anything that comes to mind; don't think about it too much or this may limit the exercise. Having completed your brainstorming session, you can start to identify (or dismiss) the relevant or irrelevant sources. It is then time for a short break to clear your mind. Come back to the task and carefully check your list until you are happy that the relevant sources have been included. Below we have identified some of the sources that we think may help you in the skill of information seeking:

Library	Business and work placement providers	Home Environment	College	Public
Librarian	Supervisors	Parents and relatives	Lecturers/ tutors	Questionnaires
Books Magazines Dictionaries	Trade catalogues	Radio/TV	Observation	Observation
Business directories	Induction booklet	Yellow pages/ telephone directory	Brochures Leaflets	
Newspapers Periodicals	Annual report	Observation	Exhibitions Open days	
Database CD ROM	Trade exhibitions	Newspapers		

Table 9.3 Information sources

The important points to remember about any information you collect are that it must be relevant, it must be valid and it must be current. You will need to consult your information sources regularly to ensure that you have collected sufficient to enable you to complete the tasks. Quite often, students leave this part of their assessments until it is too late; you must make sure that you sustain the momentum of information collection and do not just rely on an initial burst of enthusiasm. It's no good realizing that you are missing vital information the day the assessment has to completed. Tutors often hear these sorts of comments from their students:

I thought I had all the information I needed.

I didn't realize that I needed to collect information on that task.

I collected lots of information, but when it came to completing the tasks I was missing some.

How to list research and information sources
You must *list* all the sources of information you use, whether from a book, an interview or a television programme, for example. Remember, this will form part of your evidence for your grading themes and will be used by your tutor and the external verifier in the assessment of your work. It is a good idea to make use of a *diary* for this

Action Plan Group members: Kay Smith, John Ford, Indira Singh

What we need to find out	What we need to do	Date to be completed	Date completed	Completed by
Business activity we could run	Brainstorm – business ideas, taking into account our skills and expertise	Jan 26	Jan 26	All
Types of business formations	Decide on the formation of the organization	Jan 27	Jan 27	All
How to produce CV	Produce CVs – book I.T. time	Feb 3	Feb 2	All
Whether business is feasible	Talk to organizations	Feb 4	Feb 14	All
Business formation for our group	Write up the introduction	Feb 5	Feb 15	Kay
Memorandum of association	Visit library, use class notes, write up memorandum	Feb 5	Feb 15	John
Articles of association	As above	Feb 5	Feb 15	Indira
Market research	Research, class notes, look at types of methods used	Feb 19	Feb 21	Indira
Questionnaires	Produce draft questionnaire	Feb 21	Feb 28	Kay and John
I.T. availability for questionnaires	Check work – produce questionnaires using IT	Feb 25	Mar 1	Indira
If our business idea has potential	Get the questionnaires completed by the public	Mar 1	Mar 4	All
As above	Analyse questionnaires	Mar 4	Mar 6	Kay
Research for suitable premises	Look in newspapers, commercial estate agents	Mar 9	Mar 12	Indira and John
Advertising techniques	Class notes, results of questionnaires, books, look at types of advertising used by other companies	Mar 12	Mar 18	Indira and John
Find out costs of advertising	Find price of radio, newspaper, leaflet drops, hoardings, bus advertising	Mar 14	Mar 19	Kay
Contents of a projected cash flow	Draw on formal input, class notes, obtain bank 'start your own business' pack	Mar 14	Mar 18	Kay
How to create a corporate image	Produce business cards, decide on logo, decide on letter heads	Mar 14	Mar 14	Indira
Best way of producing posters etc.	Produce posters etc. for advertising	Mar 14	Mar 14	John
Costs associated with above	Use information already obtained for premises, find costs of heat and light, wages. Trade catalogues for cost of office equipment. Use other sources of cost of producing service	Mar 19	Mar 19	All
Cash flow production	Produce projected cash flow	Mar 25	Mar 26	Kay
Profit and loss and balance sheet production	Draw on formal input, class notes	Mar 28	Mar 28	Kay
Potential of business	Produce an evaluation – identify whether business is profitable and liquid. Decide on potential and write conclusion	Mar 30	March 30	All

Fig. 9.10 A Typical Action Plan for an Assessment: setting up a business

part of your work, listing information sources on a day-by-day basis. You should record your information sources for inclusion in your portfolio in the following manner:

- **Book** – state the name of the author, title of the book, date of publication and the name of the publisher.

- **Newspapers and magazines** – state the name of the author, title of the article, name of the newspaper/magazine, date of publication.

- **Quotes** – in addition to the above information, quotes must include the page number of the publications from which they are taken.

- **Interviews** – state the name of the person with whom the interview took place, the reason for the interview, the date it took place and where the interview was carried out. Remember that interviews and discussions can take place with many different people, e.g. owners of businesses, public sector officials, parents, tutors etc.

- **Radio and television** – state the programme name, the channel or radio station, the date and time, as well as the nature of the programme and details of any relevant individuals who took part.

Quite often you will need to write to various organizations to collect information to help you with your assessments. Make sure you include copies of any letters you send and any replies you get back. Even if you don't manage to receive any information back, the fact that you have tried will count in your favour.

Evaluation

Evaluation is the third of the grading themes that your evidence will be assessed against. While planning and information seeking/handling are relatively easy to understand, evaluating the work that you have done can sometimes be a little daunting. You may find yourself thinking:

> How can I evaluate my work when I don't know where I may have gone wrong?

This is a natural reaction and one which you should not become worried about. It is important to remember that you are expected to develop the skill areas of planning, in-formation seeking/handling and evaluating throughout your course of study; nobody expects you to get everything right first time! To begin with, you will be guided by your tutors and teachers who will help you with evaluation and the other grading themes. As time progresses, you will gradually take on this responsibility yourself, so that you can work towards completing all tasks efficiently on your own.

What is evaluation?

In terms of your Advanced GNVQ in Business, *evaluation* is the way you look back at:

- The tasks you have completed.
- The activities you have undertaken.
- The decisions you have taken in the course of your work.
- Any alternative courses of action open to you.
- The implications of the particular actions you carried out.

When evaluating your work, you must be able to justify *how* you have approached the tasks. You should get into the habit of writing down *why* you thought it was necessary to complete tasks in a particular way and how you expected to achieve those tasks. You should ask yourself questions, such as:

- What were the advantages in tackling the assessment in this way?
- What were the disadvantages?
- If I was given the chance to do the work again, what would I change?
- What areas need improvement?
- How could the improvements be implemented?
- Which areas am I satisfied with and why?
- Which areas am I dissatisfied with and why?
- Would I complete the tasks in the same order?
- Did I allow myself enough time for information collection?
- Did I allow myself sufficient time for I.T. inputs to the work?
- Did I check my sources of information?
- Would I try to obtain further or different information next time?

Being able to critically evaluate your own work requires time and training; many senior managers working in business find it a very difficult task! If you adopt a structured approach to the problem, using the types of questions listed above, you will be a long way towards developing your skills of evaluation.

Sample Assessments

This section will give you an understanding of how assessments are structured and how you can ensure the best possible grade for your own pieces of work. Completing assessments shows that you have met the requirements of mandatory, optional and additional units in your GNVQ. Although the external tests for the mandatory units are important and must be passed, most of the evidence that you put forward for your portfolio will revolve around the types of assessments we will be looking at in this section. In particular we will look at the following:

- The structure of typical assessments.
- Identification of how the assessments meet the requirements of the performance criteria and skills.
- Actual students' answers to these assessments.
- Tutors' comments.

We will look in detail at three sample assessments covering the following mandatory units:

- Unit 8 Business planning
- Unit 2 Business systems
- Unit 6 Financial transactions and monitoring

The information and tutor guidance given in these units will help you to develop the skills of planning, information seeking and handling, and evaluation.

In each of the assessments, the following are identified:

1. **Activity information** (assignment front sheet)
   - *Elements and performance criteria* – this sheet will identify the elements and performance criteria that can be achieved by completing the assessment. At the side of each performance criterion, the evidence to be produced will be identified.
   - *Skills* – in the same format as the above, the skills achievable and the evidence required to achieve those skills are identified.

2. **The Assessment** – the assessment itself which will contain written guidelines to help you complete it.

3. The **student's activity action plan**.

4. The **student's answer** to the assessment with **tutor comments**.

5. The **students' evaluation** of their work.

6. The assessment activity **feedback sheet** which will identify performance criteria achieved and tutor comments.

Unit 8 Business Planning: Sample Assessment

You will notice from the unit specification that this unit *overlaps* with some of the other mandatory units in certain areas. This is because business planning entails looking broadly at the business world. In many respects, *business planning* is a summary unit which allows you to *apply* previous knowledge and understanding of units studied so far on your GNVQ programme.

1 Activity information

Business Planning: Assessment 3. The sales and marketing plan. Table 9.4 identifies the planned assessment opportunities.

2 The assessment

The Sales and Marketing Plan

Now that you have completed a cash flow forecast for your business, the next stage is to develop a sales and marketing plan.

This is different from your original market research because you are now producing a product or a service and are attempting to expand your sales and/or your market areas.

In your plan you should concentrate upon the different marketing mixes which you intend to use – product, place, price, publicity etc. This gives you an opportunity to look at expanding your business; to develop an advertising campaign; to review your pricing strategy; and to produce a plan to cover the next period (one year?).

Included in the plan should be a budget of how much this is going to cost and a timing schedule to indicate 'roughly' when the various measures/targets are to be achieved. You should also show how you intend to monitor this process.

You are:

1 To produce an action plan by Tuesday 17.3.19XX.
2 Recommended to use flow charts and a calendar or a timing schedule to supplement your main sales and marketing plan.
3 Wordprocess and/or use graphics packages to present this assignment.
4 Advised to read the skills and the assessment guidelines carefully.

Assessment Guidelines

One neat copy of the assessment is to be produced per group, although it is envisaged that:

- Each group will share out the work evenly.
- Perhaps you may wish to indicate which person has done what!
- You include 'rough drafts' of your work to show how your ideas have developed and progressed throughout the course of this assessment.
- The sales and marketing plan will cover the 4 P's to a satisfactory standard and that these areas are applied to your business plan.
- Evidence will be given of research into costs and your ability to set realistic deadlines and targets for the progress of your plans.

(Courtesy of John Cowans and Richard Ingham)

Unit: Business Planning

Activity Title: Sales and marketing plan

Unit/Element and performance criteria	Evidence to be produced
8.1.5	Sales and marketing plan
8.1.6	Timing schedules
8.2.3	Sales and marketing plan
8.2.7	Monitoring performance
8.3.1	Sales and marketing plan
8.3.2	Action plan/group work
8.3.3	Budget, costs
8.3.4	Timing schedules
8.3.5	Sales and marketing plan
Skills	
Communication	
3.1.1	Group work
3.1.2	Leaflets
3.1.3	Discussion
3.2.2	Clear or wordprocessed
3.3.1	Graphs/schedules
3.3.2	Flow charts
Number	
3.3.1	Costs/prices/flow charts
3.3.2	Graphs/conclusions
IT	
3.1.1	Use of wordprocessing/graphics packages
3.3.1	Final drafts

Grading themes achievable in this assessment:

Planning 1 & 2
Information seeking 3 & 4
Evaluation 5 & 6

Table 9.4 Planned Assessment Opportunities

2 Devise a sales and marketing plan.
3 Research the costs of a marketing campaign.
4 Include a realistic timing schedule and flow chart.
5 Identify the budget needed for our proposed campaign.
6 Identify plans for reviewing and monitoring progress.

- *Areas of difficulty*
  1 Being able to apply the theory to our business plan.
  2 Obtaining costs of advertising.
  3 Completing the reviewing and monitoring section.
  4 Being able to identify an appropriate calendar for advertising.

- *Standards*
  We will know we have achieved the required standard when we have checked, ticked off, and completed the evidence required to meet the performance criteria, using information technology to complete the assignment.

3 The student's activity action plan

- *The purpose of the activity*
  By producing a sales and marketing plan for our original business plan, we hope to be able to expand our original idea.

- *What is needed*
  In our group we need to, in order of priority:

  1 Look at the marketing mixes and apply appropriately to our original idea.

4 The student's answer to the assessment with tutor comments

The marketing mix contains four main areas – product, promotion, price and place. These are now applied to our original business plan.

Product

There are a wide variety of products available at our toy and babywear parties. Our products are classified as durable consumer goods. This means that they are used by consumers in everyday life. For example, childrens' toys and babywear is played with, and worn by, children every day.

We intend to sell our products mainly at the customers' homes. When buying toys, the purchaser will receive the following benefits:

1 Hassle-free shopping – we will sell at house parties.
2 Value for money – since we have less overheads, our toys can and will be priced below those in departmental and other stores.
3 Socializing – a chance for viewers to meet new people.
4 Child development – our toys will help the child develop skills and dexterity.
5 Child contentment – the toys will keep the child occupied and offer mental stimulation (both 4 and 5 are also advantages for the mother or person caring for the child).
6 Toys will be hard wearing and of good quality.

On buying babywear products the purchaser receives the following benefits:

1 Hassle-free shopping.
2 Value for money.
3 Increased social life.
4 Their child looking neat and presentable.
5 Babywear products that are hard wearing and of good quality.

The products will succeed owing to the following factors:

- *Lifestyle*
  The majority of children have a large number of toys to play with and, as they grow older, their toys change to match their age and ability. Therefore, toys are a necessary part of their lifestyle. Likewise with babywear, clothes are a necessity for everyone – but parents need to change babies' clothes often due to growth and changes in taste.

- *Population structure*
  Our original survey identified a very large number of mothers/guardians whom we could invite to our toy and babywear parties who have children of various ages. There are a lot of children in today's population.

Tutor comment

Do you have evidence of this? Generally, there has been an increase in the population of older people (living longer), rather than young people.

Competition
There is no/little competition with our toy and babywear parties that we know about.

Tutor comment

Have you done any research?

However, competition exists between companies who make toys and babywear. There is a wide variety of companies with toys on the market such as Fisher Price, Tony Fisher and Matchbox who are always developing new products. The type of toys each company makes and the price charged will help to determine the prices charged at our parties.

Packaging
The packaging used for our product will help our business succeed for the following reasons:

- The packaging will protect the toy or clothing.
- The toy or clothing will be packaged in 'see through' material (this allows people to be able to see what they are buying).
- If the product is not displayed in 'see through' packaging, a picture of the product will be clearly identified on the covering.
- Clear instructions will be stated on the packaging concerning the material, safety standards and, if a toy, what it is expected to do.

Distribution
Toys and babywear will be taken from the cash and carry to the location of the party. Purchasers who are not able to take purchased products away with them will have the benefit of a free, next day delivery service.

Price Determination

Objective
Price MUST be less than in retail establishments but sufficient to cover costs and make a profit. Therefore we should try to ensure our costs are kept to a minimum.

Estimated Demand
Estimated demand for the product is as follows:

(a) Product features:
   (i) Better/more features means a higher cost.
   (ii) Distribution channels – the more channels, the greater distribution cost.
   (iii) Advertising – increased advertising means increased price to recoup costs.

Tutor comment

You should have applied this section to your own business.

(b) *Determination of expected price:*
   (i) It must be lower than the shops to remain competitive.
   (ii) It must be high enough to cover costs and make a profit.

(c) *Competitor reaction:*
   Due to our size, we feel that there will be little reaction from the retail establishments. However, should some other businesses start up in competition, offering a similar service, we must be able to remain competitive – reducing our price accordingly and still ensuring we cover costs and make a profit.

(d) *Share of the market:*
   If we provide brand-named goods that already have a large market share, we will make more sales as our selling price will be less than that of the retail establishments.

(e) *Marketing policies:*
Exchanges or refunds are available when people bring back goods that they are dissatisfied with. However, they must also bring back the promotional gift received.

Tutor comment

Do not forget to refer your reader to the section where you have discussed your promotional gifts.

Place

We intend to hold our parties at the following places:

- Pub
- Homes
- Community halls etc.

Initially the parties will be held in our own homes. As the business becomes more established, venues will switch to other people's homes and halls etc. The houses in which we will hold our parties will be in easy reach of those we intend to invite.

Our products will be purchased locally from businesses based in the Newcastle, Durham and Washington areas. The following is just a small number of outlets available to us in these areas:

- Macro (Washington)
- Earlsway (Gateshead, Team Valley)
- Bookers (Gateshead, Team Valley)
- Peter Lowry (Tyne Tunnel Industrial Estate)

Since the above businesses are cash-and-carries and are classed as middle men, the distrubition channel for our business is as follows:

Producers	→	Wholesalers	→	Consumers
Toys and				
babywear		Cash and carries		Those invited

Tutor comment

This section has been explained well; however, in your diagram of distribution channels, you should have placed your business before the consumer.

Promotion

The promotion of our products will be by the following means:

- Leaflets – giving details of our parties
- Invitations – for those who know of our services

The leaflets are designed to help the guest in deciding to come to the party (see Appendix 1). This is followed up by the invitation showing details of where, when and at what time the party will start (see Appendix 2). However, as the business becomes established, the leaflets will not always be sent to guests who have previously attended one of our parties.

Both leaflets and invitations are sent to all our guests. In August, invitations will be distributed with a range of different dates to allow us to arrange several parties at one time.

- The sales of 'brand named' products in the above information since our market research (for part 1 of the assignment) indicated that people preferred these type of products.

Tutor comment

Does your research relate to both toys and babywear?

- Free gifts – such as a height chart on purchases of more than £10. This will hopefully stimulate extra spending. For example, if someone sees two items they desire for £8 and £3, they are more likely to buy both if they can obtain a free gift worth £4.99. It is the case of 'getting an excellent bargain'.

The party guest is informed of our 'freebies' by means of a small card which is enclosed with the leaflet (see Appendix 3). These promotional free products will be given for approximately five months.

Tutor comment

Will you have to pay £4.99 for each chart you intend to give away? Will the promotion be worthwhile in terms of extra sales versus increased costs? If so, you should either contain the evidence here or refer the reader to the relevant section in your report.

- Helium filled balloons will be issued free with any purchase made. The balloons will carry our logo and become a form of advertizing as the children carry them around.

Tutor comment

How much will this cost? Will the cost be offset by an expected increase in sales?

Personal Recommendation

We feel confident that once people have been to our parties, they will recommend us to their friends so that most of our advertising will be spread by word of mouth. We believe that too much advertising will push up costs that we will need to recover through an increase in price. Therefore, we would not be able to remain competitive and the business may fail.

Tutor comment

A well thought out conclusion to this section.

Timing Schedule

The timing schedule and flow chart for our promotional campaign can be seen in Appendices 4 and 5.

Budget and costs

The following costs have been researched and relate to our promotional campaign:

1000 leaflets (set and printed)	£500
1000 invitations (set and printed)	£650
200 balloons printed with logo	£250
200 height chargs (designed and printed)	£750
200 fliers (designed and printed)	£500
TOTAL	£2650

This cost can be spread over a period of five months. Within these five months, it may become necessary to make extra purchases of balloons, height charts and fliers. However, since the design is already set, these will be at a reduced cost.

Tutor comment

The above costs seem realistic; however, it would have been advisable to obtain at least two estimates/quotes, to give details of your supplier and, if given, the actual quotation as evidence.

Further, how do these costs affect your cash flow as produced in assignment 2. It would have been advisable to show the revised business cash flow forecast here taking into account the above promotional costs.

Plans for reviewing and monitoring

(a) Constant monitoring of the budget to ensure we do not overspend and create cash flow problems. This will be done by a comparison of actual sales/costs compared with forecast sales/costs.

(b) Record the number of sales made during year 1 which will help us in our second year of trading. By doing this, we will be able to identify, more accurately, changes in sales on a monthly basis and purchase accordingly. During months of high sales we aim to capitalize on them by doing one or more of the following:

- Carry out a stronger advertising campaign
- Promote using various methods
- Use a larger venue than individual homes, i.e. a community or public hall.

The aim is to increase sales in those months when trade is slow.

(c) Review promotion methods after the first five months have finished. If these methods are found to be successful, we will intensify them at various times throughout the year. Success of the promotion will be evident during the months of September to December (pre Christmas) and June and July.

If the methods are found to be unsuccessful we need to change the campaign and increase advertising which will result in an increased advertising budget. Slower trading months are expected post Christmas.

(d) Keep a constant check on all cash-and-carry prices to obtain the keenest price available at the time. Ensure enough cash is available to take advantage of any special offers and during the traditional 'sales' periods.

(e) Monitor prices of goods purchased so that we ensure sufficient is added to make a profit. The exact 'mark-up' on our products will be recalculated regularly when 'real costs' are more accurately identified.

(f) Constant review of the timing schedule to ensure adequate times have been allowed for the smooth running of our operation – in terms of preparing for parties too early or too late and to check that the invitation replies are arriving at the correct times.

Tutor comment

This is a very good section, well thought through and explained.

Diary of completion

This has been omitted but it included a day-by-day account of the tasks and sub-tasks required for the completion of the assessment.

5 The student's evaluation

For this assessment we were required to design a sales and marketing plan. We checked our work regularly against the performance criteria to ensure that we had met the requirements. We felt that the time allocated to this assessment was insufficient and had we had more time we would:

- Research price determination more thoroughly and try to apply it to our business. The problem that occurred here was that the textbooks used did not explain this area clearly.
- Identify ideas for a 'back-up' promotional policy should the one we identified not be successful.
- Gather more evidence as to the costs of advertising via different suppliers – and identify other methods of advertising.
- Complete a revised cash flow that will identify the new projected cash flow position over the period in question.
- Upon completion of the cash flow we would estimate whether any further funding will be required and, where necessary, approach our financial sources in advance.
- Research in more detail into our suppliers – for instance to see if it were possible for us to go direct to the manufacturers for some of the products rather than cash and carry. Cutting out the 'middle man' would allow us to offer our products at a reduced price.
- Consider inducements that we could offer to the 'party host' to encourage them to use their own homes for the selling of our goods. Perhaps a percentage discount on any purchases made to be used against products sold at the party. Or free special offers to encourage them to be a 'party host' during those months when we feel trade will be slow – i.e. post Christmas. These costs would be built into a revised cash flow forecast.
- Plan our time more effectively so that the above could have been considered during production of the plan.

Tutor comment

Your evaluation is thorough and, in conjunction with your section on reviewing and monitoring your work, the evidence you have put forward for grading is of a distinction standard.

6 Assessment Activity Feedback Sheet

Activity feedback

Unit: Business Planning

Activity Title: Sales and marketing plan

Unit/Element and performance criteria	Signed as achieved	Assessor's comments
8.1.5 8.1.6 8.2.3 8.2.7 8.3.1 8.3.2 8.3.3 8.3.4 8.3.5		Overall a very good piece of work. Some of the promotional ideas that you suggest are good. Your flow chart identifies that you have planned your promotion campaign well but it appears that you will take a lot of time before you get the business running. Some sections need to show more evidence of market research. What variety of toys/clothes will you sell (product lines and ranges)? Price needs more work for your final plan; it needs to be more precisely linked to your own business.
Skills		
Communications 3.1.1 3.1.2 3.1.3 3.2.2 3.3.1 3.3.2 Number 3.3.1 3.3.2 IT 3.1.1 3.3.1		In presenting your work, you should include a contents page and an introduction. Make sure your final plan and flow chart are wordprocessed and include the use of graphics packages so that you can claim some of these skills. However, you can claim communication skills and IT skills against your leaflet.

Grading Themes

Planning	1 Merit 2 Merit	
Information seeking	3 Merit 4 Merit	
Evaluation	5 Distinction 6 Distinction	

Note

The performance criteria on the above assessment feedback sheet is not signed as being achieved. However, the students who completed this assessment did provide sufficient evidence and did achieve the performance criteria stated.

You can see some examples of the types of support materials presented in this assessment in the following 5 appendices.

Appendices 1–5

Appendix 1

Toy and Babywear Parties

As someone we know Joanne and myself would like to invite you to one of our many Toy and Babywear Parties

We hope that this leaflet will tell you a little more about our Toy and Babywear Parties

We look forward to seeing you in the near future.

Joanne Johnson
Vicki Hollinshead

Toy and Babywear party organizers

Toy and Babywear Parties

At our topy and babywear parties we sell a wide variety of products.

Both toys and babywear to cater for all the age groups which you may be buying for.

At our toy and babywear parties all of our toys are of brand names: Tomy, Fisher Price etc. Therefore they will comply with European safety standards.

What's more – All of our toy and babywear is cheaper than that of any department store.

Toy and Babywear Parties

Invitations

We would appreciate it if you could reply to us as soon as possible.

All that is needed from you is the invitation reply slip (invitation is enclosed in this package).

On replying please state the ages of those who you may be buying for and if you will be bringing a friend along with you. There will be plenty of people at this venue and so there will be no problems if friend is unable to attend.

Telephone calls

A quick telephone call can confirm your invite. If you are not attending then it is vital that we know.

If you are attending then please tell us the following information on your short call.

P.T.O

Appendix 1 cont.

Toy and Babywear Parties

Telephone calls

continued.

* ★ Your name

* ★ If you will be bringing a friend along with you.

* ★ The age of those you will be buying for.

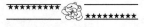

If there is no reply on calling us then our answering amchine will be switched on. Please do not hesitate to leave a message.

Replying is vital to us as if we know the correct number of people then it can help us determine which products to buy. It will also help us with other preparations.

Please come along

We will not pressure you into buying.

You will see the price differences, and notice the value for money.

We hope that this leaflet has given you an insight into our parties and encouraged you to come along at the date stated on the invitation.

V Hollinshead

and

J. Johnson

We would like to introduce the new service offered to you. It is offered by ourselves for the HASSLE-FREE SHOPPER.

Please read this leaflet to find out more about it.

Toy and Babywear Parties

Tutor Comment

This leaflet is a good example of IT Skills & Element 3.2 Communication Skills

Appendix 2

PLEASE COME
ALONG TO OUR TOY
AND BABYWEAR
PARTY

ON: _____

TIME: _____

AT: _____
_____
_____
_____

TEL no: _____

- -

The ages you will be
buying for are:

Will you be bringing a
friend
yes _____ no _____
(please tick).

- -

I will/will not be able to
come along to your toy
and babywear party.

(Please send invitation
reply to the above address)

The Guest will
keep this part of
the invitation.

The Guest will
send this part of
the invitation back
to us.

This is the standard invitation, it will be sent to all those
who we choose to invite.

Tutor Comment
Another claim for element 3.2
Communication Skills

✓ *Good*

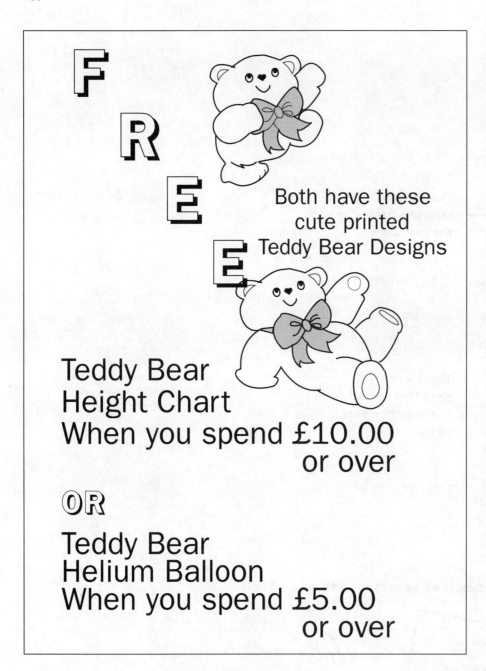

F R E E

Both have these
cute printed
Teddy Bear Designs

Teddy Bear
Height Chart
When you spend £10.00
or over

OR

Teddy Bear
Helium Balloon
When you spend £5.00
or over

Appendix 4

May

1	sun	Prepare invitations and leaflets
2	mon	
3	tue	
4	wed	
5	thu	
6	fri	
7	sat	
8	sun	
9	mon	
10	tue	
11	wed	
12	thu	
13	fri	
14	sat	
15	sun	
16	mon	
17	tue	
18	wed	
19	thu	
20	fri	
21	sat	
22	sun	
23	mon	
24	tue	
25	wed	
26	thu	
27	fri	
28	sat	
29	sun	
30	mon	
31	tue	

June

1	wed	Get invitations printed
2	thu	
3	fri	
4	sat	
5	sun	
6	mon	
7	tue	
8	wed	
9	thu	
10	fri	Decide on numbers
11	sat	
12	sun	
13	mon	
14	tue	
15	wed	
16	thu	
17	fri	
18	sat	
19	sun	
20	mon	
21	tue	
22	wed	
23	thu	
24	fri	
25	sat	
26	sun	
27	mon	
28	tue	
29	wed	
30	thu	

July

1	fri	Get height charts
2	sat	
3	sun	
4	mon	
5	tue	
6	wed	
7	thu	
8	fri	
9	sat	
10	sun	
11	mon	
12	tue	
13	wed	
14	thu	
15	fri	
16	sat	
17	sun	
18	mon	
19	tue	
20	wed	
21	thu	
22	fri	
23	sat	
24	sun	
25	mon	
26	tue	
27	wed	
28	thu	
29	fri	
30	sat	
31	sun	

August

1	mon	
2	tue	Write invitations
3	wed	
4	thu	
5	fri	Distribute them
6	sat	
7	sun	
8	mon	
9	tue	
10	wed	
11	thu	
12	fri	
13	sat	
14	sun	
15	mon	
16	tue	
17	wed	
18	thu	
19	fri	
20	sat	
21	sun	
22	mon	
23	tue	
24	wed	
25	thu	
26	fri	
27	sat	
28	sun	
29	mon	
30	tue	
31	wed	

TIMING SCHEDULE SHOWN ON CALENDAR

Appendix 4 contd.

September	October	November	December
1 thu	**1** sat	**1** tue	**1** thu
2 fri	**2** sun	**2** wed	**2** fri
3 sat	**3** mon	**3** thu	**3** sat
4 sun	**4** tue	**4** fri	**4** sun
5 mon	**5** wed	**5** sat	**5** mon
6 tue	**6** thu	**6** sun	**6** tue
7 wed	**7** fri	**7** mon	**7** wed
8 thu	**8** sat	**8** tue	**8** thu
9 fri	**9** sun	**9** wed	**9** fri
10 sat	**10** mon *Get balloons printed*	**10** thu	**10** sat
11 sun	**11** tue *Purchase toys and babywear*	**11** fri	**11** sun
12 mon	**12** wed	**12** sat	**12** mon
13 tue	**13** thu	**13** sun	**13** tue
14 wed	**14** fri	**14** mon	**14** wed
15 thu	**15** sat *Hold 1st party*	**15** tue	**15** thu
16 fri	**16** sun *Deliver products from party*	**16** wed	**16** fri
17 sat	**17** mon	**17** thu	**17** sat
18 sun	**18** tue *Make arrangements*	**18** fri	**18** sun
19 mon	**19** wed *for the next party!!*	**19** sat	**19** mon
20 tue *Sort through replies*	**20** thu	**20** sun	**20** tue
21 wed	**21** fri	**21** mon	**21** wed
22 thu	**22** sat	**22** tue	**22** thu
23 fri	**23** sun	**23** wed	**23** fri
24 sat	**24** mon	**24** thu	**24** sat
25 sun	**25** tue	**25** fri	**25** sun
26 mon	**26** wed	**26** sat	**26** mon
27 tue	**27** thu	**27** sun	**27** tue
28 wed	**28** fri	**28** mon	
29 thu	**29** sat	**29** tue	
30 fri	**30** sun	**30** we	
	31 mon		

Tutor Comment
Very good idea and well presented, but it is going to take you nearly 6 months before you have your first party.

TIMING SCHEDULE SHOWN ON CALENDAR

Appendix 5

FLOW CHART

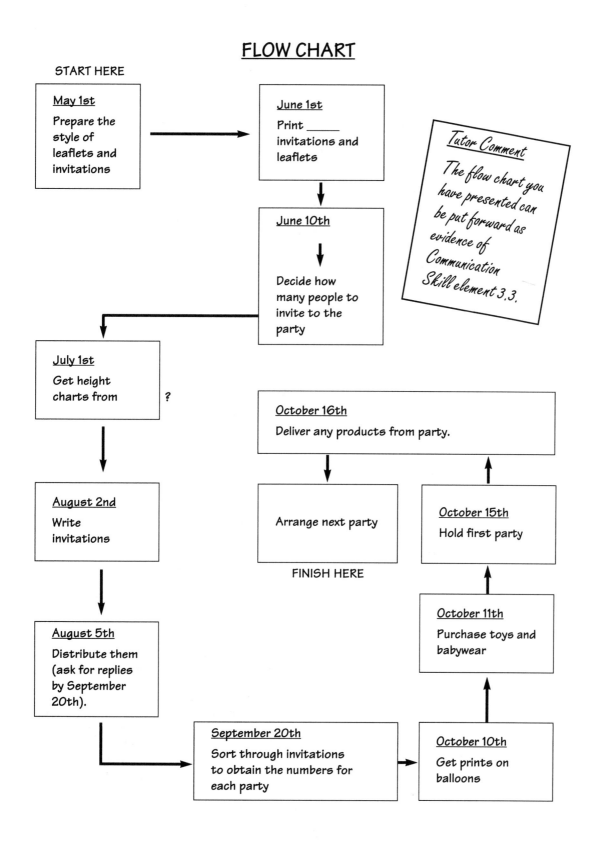

START HERE

May 1st

Prepare the style of leaflets and invitations

June 1st

Print _____ invitations and leaflets

June 10th

Decide how many people to invite to the party

Tutor Comment

The flow chart you have presented can be put forward as evidence of Communication Skill element 3.3.

July 1st

Get height charts from _____ ?

August 2nd

Write invitations

August 5th

Distribute them (ask for replies by September 20th).

September 20th

Sort through invitations to obtain the numbers for each party

October 10th

Get prints on balloons

October 11th

Purchase toys and babywear

October 15th

Hold first party

October 16th

Deliver any products from party.

Arrange next party

FINISH HERE

*There will be sufficient numbers of leaflets and invitations printed for several parties.
They will all be distributed at the same time, although there will be several different dates.
i.e. 20 invitations may have 15th Oct. and 20 invitations may have 21st Oct. etc.

Unit 2 Business Systems

This unit is concerned with the administrative, communication and information processing systems within a business organization. The assessment shown below will concentrate on the *administrative* systems.

1 Activity Information

Business systems: Assignment 1. Investigate administrative systems used within the organization.

Planned assessment opportunities	
Unit: Business systems	
Activity Title: Investigate administrative systems	
Unit/Element and performance criteria	**Evidence to be produced**
2.1.1	Sections within report and accompanied by relevant appendices
2.1.2	Section identifying health and safety; Companies Act (e.g. annual reports; employment law; fiscal – VAT, PAYE, pensions)
2.1.3	Contact with a business, list of questions, information obtained used as the basis of the report
2.1.4 2.1.5	Report conclusion and recommendation
Skills Communication 3.2.1 3.2.2 3.2.3 3.2.4	The production of the report to a satisfactory standard in conventional business format. Grammar, punctuation and spelling will have been corrected
3.3.1 3.3.2	Appropriate appendices and references made to these in the report
IT (textual) 3.1.1 3.1.2 3.1.3 3.1.4 3.1.5	Use of wordprocessing facilities to produce the final draft

Grading themes achievable in this assessment:

Planning 1 & 2
Information seeking 3 & 4
Evaluation 5 & 6

2 The assessment

Investigate Administrative Systems

Within organizations there are various departments/ sections, e.g. finance, personnel, warehousing, marketing, administration. As part of this assessment you are required to SELECT and INVESTIGATE ONE department/section within an organization.

The following areas may be covered by your research:

- Function of the department/secton
- Filing systems used
- Stock control system
- Types of written communication used etc.

When collecting information you should refer to the RANGE for Element 2.1.

Task

Compile a report on the administration system in your selected department/section, showing how the system is appropriate to the needs of the organization.

You should report on users' opinions of the system in your findings.

Your report must be correctly presented, include headings/sections, have an appendix (if necessary) of examples/evidence and, finally, must be signed and dated by you.

(Courtesy of Maureen Douglas and Sue Farrell)

3 The student's activity action plan

The purpose of the activity

By producing a report on the administrative system within an organization, I hope to identify whether the system meets the needs of those who work for the organization.

- **What is needed**
  I need to, in order of priority:

  1 Contact a business organization, tell them what I am doing and ask permission to come into their organization to find out about one of its departments.
  2 Make sure that my report:
    (a) Provides evidence of research and planning.
    (b) Demonstrates that I understand the functions of the system.
    (c) Identifies how the system meets the needs of the organization.
    (d) Gives an account of how effective I consider the system to be and make reference to the opinions of those who use it.
    (e) Is structured correctly.
    (f) Includes an evaluation of the system investigated.
    (g) Wordprocess throughout the assessment and check for spelling and grammatical errors.

- **Areas of difficulty**
  1 Being able to obtain permission from the organzation.
  2 Obtaining the relevant information.
  3 Completing the conclusions and recommendations section.
  4 Being able to obtain all the information on time.

- **Standards**
  I must check the range of Element 2.1 against my work to ensure I have met the performance criteria.

4 The student's answer to the assessment with tutor comments

A report into the administrative systems of an organization

1.0 Terms of reference

1.1 This report was requested by Richard Ingham and is to investigate the administrative systems within an organization. The report shows how the system is appropriate to the needs of the organization.

2.0 Procedure

2.1 To make contact with the organization via telephone. The department chosen was the Personnel Department of a large organization based at Newcastle.

2.2 To research the following areas:

(i) The function of the personnel department.
(ii) The filing systems used.
(iii) Stock control system.
(iv) Forms of written communication used.

3.0 Findings

3.1 Function of the department:
(a) Responsible for the recruitment and training of staff.
(b) To be responsive, flexible and forward-looking personnel policies and practices are essential in an organization.
(c) The personnel Information/Recruitment Officer uses a computerized personnel system to provide statistical data on manpower issues. The system also contributes to the recruitment and selection process.

3.2 Filing systems:

A personal file is held on every member of the organization and contains the following information:

Start note
Application form (and subsequent internal applications)
References
Appointment letter
Childcare/next of kin proforma
Equal opportunities proforma
Staff handbook proforma
Change notes
Maternity forms
Letters, i.e. promotion
Written warnings
Salary sheets
Finish note

(a) The start note, change notes and finish notes are the basic filing information.
(b) The start note is completed when a contract begins and contains the following information:

Full name	Division
Address	Date contract begins
Date of birth	Grade
Marital status	Payroll No.

A copy is inserted into the personal file and a copy is also held by the finance section.

(c) The change note is completed when a change to the person's file is to be made, e.g. when a person marries, marital status changes as do some surnames. As with the start note, a copy is kept on file and a copy is sent to the finance

section. A change note is completed every time a change is made.

(d) The finish note is completed when a person's contract ends. As with other notes, a copy is sent to the finance section so that they know when to stop paying the individual.

(e) Records of employees are kept on file for three years after they have finished at the organization. After this time, they are sent to a warehouse and stored safely.

Tutor comment

What you have written in this section is very informative, however there are areas that you have omitted to describe – even if briefly. I note that some of these are contained as appendices. After a brief description (even if you choose to describe them as a group), you should refer the reader of this report to the relevant appendix numbers.

3.3 Stock control

The personnel department does not really deal with stock control; the only stock they hold is stationery etc. The personnel department orders stock from the stock department (Appendix 7).

3.4 Types of written communication

(a) There is no standard style of written communication within the organization.
(b) When mail is received, a form is filled out containing a brief of the post. Each piece of correspondence has to be date stamped. It is then given to the Director of Personnel who marks it out to her staff. After this, the post is distributed and the form is filed for future reference (Appendix 8).
(c) A copy of everything to be sent out by post is taken and entered into the 'Day File', which then has to be checked and signed by every member of staff whose name appears on the 'Day File' form (Appendix 9).

Tutor comment

Some important systems have been omitted, such as the recruitment procedure used within this personnel department, the health and safety aspects and the drawing up of contracts (see your Appendix 2) from an administrative point of view.

4.0 Conclusions

4.1 Effectiveness

(a) The filing system that the Personnel Department use is very effective. The procedures are easy to understand and although there are many people working at this organization the system still remains uncomplicated.
(b) When the information is finally transferred completely onto the computerized system PS2000, then the information will be much easier to handle and more accessible. At present, there is not much space as there are many filing cabinets.

(c) The system ensures that every aspect of personal information is covered fully and confidentially.

(d) The idea of briefly noting every piece of correspondence which is received into personnel (and who this correspondence is marked out to) is a very effective way of tracing anything which is needed quickly.

(e) It seems good practice to have a 'Day File' in circulation through the department as this helps staff keep in touch with their colleagues' work.

5.0 Recommendations

5.1 The staff feel that it would be better and more effective if the filing system procedure was written out. This is because they have had a lot of problems in the past, e.g. when a woman married and changed to her husband's name, the staff changed all the details on the file except the surname. Hence when staff came along at a later date to find the file, it was filed under the wrong name.

5.2 It is also felt that there should be more space to store the files and that larger offices are therefore needed. Many people work in the personnel department and working conditions are therefore cramped. Staff generally feel that a separate room to store the files would improve their working conditions.

Tutor comment

Your recorded observations are described well. However, more areas may have come to your attention had the omitted areas mentioned previously been included.

List of appendices

Appendix	Description
1	Organization Structure
2	Statement of terms and conditions of employment
3	New employee information form
4	Equal opportunities form
5	Staff handbook form
6	Promotion form
7	Order form
8	Mail received form
9	Day File (mail sent out)

The appendices are not included since they contain confidential information

Tutor comment

The evidence you gathered and presented as appendices will allow you to claim skills towards communication Element 3.2.

5 The student's evaluation

For this assessment I investigated the functions of a personnel department. I felt that I researched my work well and obtained a lot of relevant information. Whilst producing the assessment I felt that I concentrated too much on my presentation and did not allow sufficient time to check my

work against the evidence required to cover the performance criteria. As a result, I did not supply evidence to cover Element 2.1.3. If I had the opportunity to do this assessment again I would do the following:

- check my work more regularly against the performance criteria to ensure that I had provided evidence to cover all of the performance criteria.
- ensure that the evidence supplied is in sufficient depth (e.g. to cover recruitment and selection procedure).
- use the library to provide evidence to cover the law relating to the health and safety aspects and the drawing up of contracts from an administrative point of view.
- plan my work more thoroughly – then I would have noticed the omission.
- produce a questionnaire concerning the functions of a personnel department. The personnel staff would complete this and, on analysis, would have helped in putting forward evidence.

I feel that I now need to research the areas omitted and produce an account to put forward as evidence to cover Element 2.1.3.

Tutor comment

This is a very good evaluation. You have identified areas that could be improved upon and how you may overcome these.

Always remember, careful planning = a good result

You may carry out your suggestion to provide evidence for PC 2.1.3.

6 Assessment Activity Feedback Sheet

Activity feedback

Unit: Business systems

Activity Title: Investigate administrative systems

Unit/Element and performance critera	Signed as achieved	Assessor's comments
2.1.1. 2.1.2 2.3.4 2.3.5		A well presented assessment demonstrating that you have investigated and provided evidence for the performance criteria marked.
2.1.3		Your assessment does not contain satisfactory evidence that you understand the areas mentioned in 2.1.3. Please contact your organization again to arrange for the collection and presentation of this evidence.

Skills

Communication 3.2.1 3.2.2 3.2.3 3.2.4 3.2.5		Your presentation provides satisfactory evidence that you can claim these skills.

IT (textual)
3.1.1
3.1.2
3.1.3
3.1.4
3.1.5

Satisfactory evidence that
these skills have been
achieved can be claimed.

Grading Themes		
Planning	Although an action plan is included, a review of your tasks – perhaps with the guidance of your tutor – would have helped you to identify the areas omitted from the assessment.	
Information Seeking	3 Merit 4 Merit	
Evaluation	5 Distinction 6 Distinction	

Unit 6 Financial transactions and monitoring

This unit is concerned with the financial transactions that occur within a business, the systems used to record these transactions and the measures that can be used to monitor performance.

Pass assessments

Referring back to p241 of the Portfolio, we described a Merit assessment as one where the tasks are *discrete* and a Distinction/Merit assignment as one where the tasks would be *complex*. The assessment given for this element is quite different from the two we have already studied. This is because it is what has been deemed as a 'Pass' assessment, because:

- The tasks are stated clearly and precisely.
- It does not involve any planning – this is done for you by the way the tasks are written.
- It does not involve any research.
- It may allow the students to evaluate their work, but it would only be a minor part of the activity.

Your tutors may often issue you with *pass only* assessments to cover perhaps a small number of performance criteria, or to ensure that you have the basic knowledge and understanding of certain performance criteria. Pass only assessments may often be given as class exercises, given out on entry and collected at the end of the session.

1 Activity information

Successful completion of this assessment is for the coverage of element and performance criteria:

6.3.4 A given a set of accounting information is examined to judge the performance of the business.

The themes of planning, information seeking and evaluation are not covered by this assessment.

2 The Assessment

Below are the final accounts for Zenus, a limited company engaged in manufacturing.

Summarised P/L A/C for Zenus Limited for the years 31.12.92 and 31.12.93

	1992 £000s		1993 £000s	
Sales		600		748
Less cost of sales				
Opening stock	100		120	
Purchases	492		664	
Less closing stock	120		188	
Cost of sales		472		596
Gross profit		128		152
Less expenses		88		108
Net profit before tax		40		44
Corporation tax		10		10
Net profit after tax		30		34
Dividends		10		10
Profit and loss A/C bal. c/fwd		20		24

Zenus Limited summarized balance sheets

	As at 31.12.92 £000 £000 £000			As at 31.12.93 £000 £000 £000		
Fixed Assets						
at net book value			60			80
Current Assets						
Stock		120			188	
Debtors		100			164	
Bank		20			14	
		240			366	
Less Current Liabilities						
Creditors	90			152		
Corporation tax	10			10		
Dividends	10	110		10	172	
Working capital			130			194
			190			274
Less Long-term Liabilites						
10% Debentures			–			60
			190			214
Financed by						
Authorized Share Capital						
150,000 Ordinary Shares of £1 each			150			150
Issued Share Capital						
150,000 Ordinary Shares fully paid			150			150
Reserves						
P/Loss A/C bal. b/fwd			20			40
P/Loss Retained			20			24
			190			214

Using the information contained above, answer the following questions:

1. Is the organization more or less profitable than last year?
2. Using the current ratio and acid test ratio, describe the organization's solvency position.
3. How useful is the information contained in the final accounts to managers of the organization?

Student's answer

1. Using the gross and net profit percentages the organization has the following gross and net profit percentages:

Gross profit percentage   1992   1993

$$\frac{\text{Gross profit} \times 100}{\text{Sales}} \qquad \frac{128}{600} = 21.3\% \quad \frac{152}{748} = 20.3\%$$

$$\frac{\text{Net profit before tax}}{\text{Sales}} \qquad \frac{40}{600} = 6.7\% \quad \frac{44}{748} = 5.9\%$$

The organization has decreased in gross and net profitability by 1% and 0.08% respectively over the two-year period.

Tutor comment

Well laid out. Good answer.

2. These two ratios assess an organization's ability to pay its debts. The results of the ratios are as follows:

$$\text{current ratio} = \frac{\text{current assets}}{\text{current liabilities}}$$

$$1992 \quad \frac{240}{180} = 1.33:1 \qquad 1993 \quad \frac{366}{172} = 2.13:1$$

$$\text{acid test} = \frac{\text{current assets} - \text{stock}}{\text{current liabilities}}$$

$$1992 \quad \frac{240 - 120}{180} = 0.67:1 \quad 1993 \quad \frac{366 - 188}{172} = 1.03:1$$

As a general rule, 2:1 is expected for the current ratio and 1:1 for the acid test. However, it depends on the organization; what is more important is whether there are any large variations in the results.

In 1992, the acid test indicates that, had all of its current liabilities needed paying at one time, it would not have been able to pay them all without selling stock. It only had 67 pence to pay every £1 of current liabilities.

However, it could have sold some stock and covered its liabilities as the current ratio tells us that it had £1.33 of current assets for every £1 of current liabilities.

Tutor comment

Your written analysis is correct according to the ratios you have calculated. However, you have used an incorrect figure in the production of the 1992 current ratio and acid test ratio.

The figure used in your calculation was 180 instead of 110. The new calculation will alter the outcome and, subsequently, your interpretation. Please recalculate and, using the correct information, provide an assessment of the company's position.

According to the results the solvency position of Zeus Limited has improved in 1993. Both the current ratio and the acid test ratio indicate that, if it needed to, it could liquify its current assets without selling stock and still pay its debts when they fall due. The acid test ratio indicates that it had £1.03 to pay every £1 of current liabilities.

3. The financial accounts of an organization at the year-end give out-of-date information and report what has happened and not what is happening. Managers need to know what is happening throughout the year so that they can put right what has gone wrong.

Tutor comment

This area needs expanding. You need to identify what other information a manager would use to monitor performance and mention that he needs to identify areas where improvements in performance can be made.

Other types of evidence

So far we have concentrated on assessments making most use of *written* and *visual* types of evidence. As we noted on p.221 there are other types of evidence which you might incorporate into your portfolio. Here we briefly suggest some hints on the following:

- Presentations
- Group discussions
- Meetings
- One-to-one conversations and interviews
- Telephone skills.

Presentations

You may feel nervous if asked to give a **presentation** to the rest of the group, but you should remember that most if not all of the other members of the group will almost certainly feel just as nervous as you when it is their turn. There are two practical ways of reducing your nerves and increasing your confidence before a presentation: you can make sure that you are thoroughly prepared and you can practise what you are going to say.

Listed below are some tips which might help you to give a successful presentation:

- *Good preparation* ensures that you have enough to say, that you know what you are talking about and that you are unlikely to be thrown by any questions that might be asked.
- Be *realistic* in terms of what you intend to say. Although you should prepare fully, do not try to cram too much into the time you have been given. If you rattle through your material, your listeners will find it hard to follow and will soon stop trying. When you plan what you are going to say, think of your *audience*: they will probably not be as familiar with the subject as you and your presentation needs to take this into account.
- The presentation will be more effective if it has a *clear structure*. Concentrate on a few key aspects of the subject and arrange them in a logical order.
- Prepare a *set of notes* which you can speak from during the presentation. A common method is to have a series of *numbered cards*, each dealing with a section of the presentation and containing a few headings or key words. Do not write your speech out in full and simply read it out to the audience. If you do this you will be looking down the whole time and the presentation will sound stiff and unnatural.
- Make use of *visual aids* such as flip charts and overhead projector transparencies. It can be a mistake to use too many however and you should remember that they should support your presentation rather than dominate it. They should also, of course, be big enough for everyone in the room to see. If you have photographs or other items which you wish to pass around the group, do so when you have finished talking so that the attention of the audience is not distracted.

- *Practise* your presentation at least once, either on your own or with friends or family. This has several advantages. It will help to lessen your nerves and make your delivery more confident and relaxed. It will make it less likely that you have to keep looking down at your notes. Finally, it will give you an idea of timing and indicate whether you have prepared too little or too much. However, do not practise to the point that the presentation becomes over-rehearsed – you do not want it to sound like a recitation.
- During the presentation itself try to be *natural* and relaxed. Try to vary the tone, speed and pitch of your voice so that the delivery is lively and interesting. Make use of non-verbal communication: maintain good eye contact with all of the audience (don't just look at the teacher or close friends), and accompany what you have to say with the appropriate gestures. Be careful though to avoid distracting mannerisms such as shifting from foot to foot.

Evaluating a presentation

After giving a presentation you might be asked to write an *evaluation* for inclusion in your portfolio. Below is a checklist of questions that can be asked when deciding what to write:

- Do you feel the amount of information you included in your presentation was about right?
- Was the amount of information included too little, so that you seemed to finsh too quickly?
- Was the amount of information included too much, so that you had to rush parts of the presentation, or didn't manage to finish it?
- Was your estimate of how long the presentation would last accurate?
- Was the information arranged in a logical order and presented in a comprehensive manner? (Did the audience seem to understand what you were saying?)
- Were your notes useful and effective? (You didn't forget what to say at any point!)
- Do you feel your use of visual aids was successful? Could everybody see them and understand them? Did they prove a distraction at any point?
- Did you *talk* to the audience at all times, rather than *reading* from your notes?
- Did you address all members of the group and maintain good eye contact with them?
- Do you think you handled questions well?
- Did you anticipate possible questions?
- Did the audience seem to enjoy the presentation, and find it interesting?
- Did the presentation initiate an interesting discussion?
- Were you confident and relaxed during the presentation?
- Did your preparation for the evaluation increase your knowledge of the topic?
- If you gave a presentation again, is there anything about your approach to both the preparation and delivery of the presentation that you would change?

Group discussions

As with presentations, *good preparation* is an important element in ensuring effective participation in a **group discussion**. If you prepare well, you will not run out of things to say. Preparation is also important because it means

you will not enter the discussion with views that are not based on a sound knowledge of the facts. If you don't have this underlying knowledge, you are likely to find it difficult when others challenge your opinions.

It is therefore a good idea to prepare a set of *notes* for the discussion, to remind yourself of the main points you wish to make, the evidence to support them and relevant factual information. During the discussion itself, however, do not stick rigidly to your notes and ignore what others are saying. Follow the direction of the discussion and make sure that your contributions are *relevant* to what is being said. Remember that listening to others and responding appropriately is an important communication skill.

At the same time, if the discussion seems to be going around in circles do not be afraid to introduce *new ideas* or a fresh angle on the subject. If opposing views are being expressed, it is fruitless for the participants in the discussion simply to go on repeating these views – try instead to look for common ground between those who are in disagreement and build upon it.

If you are nervous about taking part in the discussions, try to make your first contribution early on – *early participation* helps to build confidence and makes it easier to continue to play an important role in the discussion. At the same time, *do not dominate* the discussion by interrupting others and by saying far more than anyone else does. If any members of the group are not participating, invite them to do so by asking for their views.

If you are *leading* the discussion, you have a special responsibility to ensure that everyone is given an opportunity to contribute. You also need to keep the discussion on course and prevent it drifting into irrelevancy. If one aspect of the subject has been exhausted, move the group on to another, perhaps after summarising the main views expressed, or the consensus if one has emerged. The leader of a discussion should usually be impartial and not express his or her own views.

Evaluating a group discussion

If you are writing an *evaluation* of a group discussion, bear all of the above points in mind and consider how far the behaviour and contributions of yourself and others created an effective discussion. The following checklist may help in your evaluation.

A good group:	A bad group:
– Has clear objectives	– Lacks clear objectives
– Is organized in a way that helps it to achieve these objectives	– Is disorganized: group activity is muddled and chaotic
– Has an atmosphere which is friendly and relaxed but also purposeful	– Has a tense, argumentative atmosphere or one which is friendly and relaxed but non-productive
– Has participation by all members	– Is dominated by one or more members and has some members who contribute little or nothing
– Encourages frank discussion and the open expression of opinion	– Has members who are reluctant to question the views of others

– Has a leader who encourages all members to contribute but who also directs and co-ordinates in a constructive way	– Has a leader who is dominant and dictatorial or who offers no guidance or co-ordination
– Has members who feel a high level of motivation, commitment and satisfaction	– Has members who are discontented and uninterested and who feel they are achieving little
– Completes tasks effectively and fulfils its objectives	– Fails to carry out tasks efficiently and to fulfil its objectives

Meetings

You may be asked to take part in a **meeting**, possibly as a role play exercise. This is similar to a group discussion, but more formally structured. The meeting is likely to have a chairperson, and will probably work through the items on an agenda.

Most of the advice given above about group discussions applies to meetings:

- *Prepare* what you are going to say but do not adhere rigidly to a predetermined line of argument.
- Make sure that what you say is relevant to the topic under discussion.
- *Listen carefully* to what others say and respond appropriately. Do not dominate the proceedings.
- If you are *chairing* the discussion, it is your particular responsibility to:
  - encourage all present to contribute;
  - direct and co-ordinate the business of the meeting, moving on to the next item of the agenda when appropriate;
  - prevent the discussion becoming repetitive and straying into irrelevancy.

One of the more formal aspects of meetings is that proposals are put in the form of *motions*. A motion suggests decisions that should be taken by the meeting and courses of action that should be followed. When a motion is passed, it becomes a resolution. Usually a motion has a proposer (the person who puts the motion before the meeting) and a seconder (another person present at the meeting who formally indicates his or her support for the motion). The names of proposer and seconder will usually be recorded in the minutes of the meeting. The wording of motions always begin with 'That ...', as in the following example:

> *That residents of the care unit be allowed to visit the town centre on Saturday afternoons provided they are accompanied by a member of staff.*

Lengthy motions are to be avoided. Clarity is essential because resolutions provide the basis for future action. The wording should therefore be precise and unambiguous.

When a motion is being discussed, a member of the meeting may propose a change or *amendment* to the motion. Again a proposer and a seconder are needed. An amendment does not contradict a motion, but may propose significant alterations to it. An amendment usually does one of the following:

- deletes words from the motion;

- adds words to the motion;
- substitutes different words for part of the motion;
- combines any of the above.

Like motions, the wording of amendments always begins with 'That ...':

> *That the words after 'provided' be deleted and replaced by 'there is one accompanying member of staff for every five residents'.*

Evaluating meetings

When writing an *evaluation* of a meeting you might refer back to the points made above about meetings and about group discussions, and consider whether the meeting you attended had the characteristics of a meeting that was effective and properly conducted. In particular, you might consider the following:

- Was the business of the meeting completed? (Were all agenda items covered – if not, why not?)
- How was the meeting conducted? Were correct rules of procedure (regarding motions, for example) followed?
- Did all present contribute sensibly and effectively? Did everyone participate and allow others to express their views?
- Was the meeting effectively chaired? (Were those present encouraged to participate? Was the discussion that took place relevant and purposeful? Should the person chairing the meeting have acted differently at any point?)
- What changes, if any, to the way the meeting was conducted might have improved its effectiveness?

One-to-one conversations and interviews

Non-verbal types of communication, such as those considered in Unit 4, will be important here, as well as verbal communication.

- *Paralanguage*
  Paralanguage is a term used for the additional information conveyed in a spoken message by the *way* in which the speech is delivered. Aspects of paralanguage include the following.
  - *Volume.* For example, if "Pass the salt, please" is said quietly it is likely to be a polite request; shouted loudly it will sound more like an angry demand.
  - *Emphasis.* Note in the following sentence how placing the emphasis on a different word each time significantly alters the meaning that is conveyed:

    HE gave the money to me.
    He GAVE the money to me.
    He gave the money to ME.

  - *Tone.* This can also alter meaning. "Well done!" can be made to sound like sarcasm or genuine praise. Variation of tone enlivens our speech, making different shades of meaning or emotion more distinct and helping to retain a listener's attention. Contrastingly, a flat monotone will not engage the listener and will lessen the listener's ability to comprehend fully what is being said.
  - *Speed of delivery.* Slow, measured speech can convey calmness and reassurance, while interest or enthusiasm are often reflected in more rapid delivery. Fast, muddled speech may be the result of anxiety or panic.

- *Distribution of pauses*. Pauses in a conversation may reflect awkwardness between the participants and can even have a menacing effect, but they can also suggest that you are relaxed and tension-free. Hesitation in speech may be an indication of uncertainty, stress or fatigue.

- *Posture/Body position*
Moods, emotions and attitudes are often reflected in a person's **body position**. For example, a slouched position may indicate depression, while tightly clenched hands and a tense, upright position may show anxiety. Noting body position can therefore help us to gauge a person's mental and emotional state.

At the same time, it is important for interviewers to be conscious of the messages that their own body language conveys. Generally, you should seek to show that you are relaxed, accessible and attentive. Experts suggest that this is achieved when standing by allowing the arms and hands to hang loosely along the sides, and when sitting by resting the hands loosely in the lap. Folded arms are seen as a defensive gesture that inhibits free and open communication. If the body position is *too* relaxed (feet up on an adjacent chair!) this is likely to suggest laziness or inattention, though deliberately informal positions are sometimes appropriate.

If you are seated, leaning forward towards a person can be an appropriate way of communicating interest and concern, especially if the interviewee is anxious or distressed. Sensitivity is needed here, however, as some individuals may be unsettled by this and consider it intrusive. Seating positions should also be considered. Sitting directly opposite another (especially on either side of a table) can imply competition and may cause others to feel intimidated. Sitting side-by-side implies co-operation: students working together on a project, for example, will often sit like this. The position often favoured by interviewers when meeting people is to sit at an angle (roughly ninety degrees) to the other person. Research suggests that this makes conversation easier, and it also enables the person being interviewed to look at or away from the interviewer as desired.

- *Eye contact*
Eye contact is usually a sign of friendliness and a willingness to communicate. It helps to initiate a conversation and regular eye contact during the course of the conversation is a way of showing attention and interest. Too much eye contact, however, can appear hostile or intrusive; a person who is stared at is likely to feel uneasy, angry or embarrassed.

- *Facial expression/movements of the head*
The **face** is the most expressive part of the body. It is capable of suggesting an enormous range of emotions but is also on occasion used to disguise how we truly feel. Changes in facial expression may be voluntary or (as in the case of blushing) involuntary. Research suggests that when a person's facial expression contradicts what he or she is saying, others are likely to believe what they see rather than what they hear. This has important implications for those who are involved in personal interaction, and emphasizes again that what is said to a listener should be accompanied by non-verbal signals that are consistent with the verbal message. More

positively, appropriate facial expressions can support and reinforce what is said: a smile can help to reassure an anxious listener.

Facial expression and movement – especially smiles and nods of the head – are also important in sustaining conversation. Smiling and nodding during a conversation usually indicate agreement and understanding, and can be used to encourage a person to continue speaking. A rapid succession of nods can indicate especially vigorous agreement but is also often a sign that the person nodding now wishes to speak.

- *Gestures*
Gestures may be used to replace speech (as in sign language) or may serve to clarify or emphasize what is said (as when the words "I don't know" are accompanied by a shrugging of the shoulders). Many gestures are spontaneous and involuntary, and they may help to indicate a person's emotional state. Nailbiting, for example, might suggest nervousness and a hand over the mouth when speaking might be a sign of embarrassment. Correspondingly, the interviewer should be aware of what might be conveyed by his or her own gestures. Drumming one's fingers on a table during an interview, for example, is bound to suggest impatience. Some gestures (scratching the nose, pulling on an ear) can be a distraction and may therefore inhibit conversation.

- *Touch*
In some contexts **touch** is an important means of expressing warmth, reassurance and understanding. A touch on the arm, a pat on the shoulder or a squeeze of the hand can be very effective ways of showing support and understanding, and can give a person a sense of being valued.

Evaluating conversations and interviews
If you are writing an *evaluation* of a conversation or interview you should refer to these aspects and consider your own performance in the light of them. In particular, you might ask yourself the following questions:

- Was I relaxed and did I help the other person to feel at ease?
- Did I adopt an appropriate posture and make good eye contact with the other person?
- Was it apparent that the other person clearly understood everything I was saying:
- Did I take account of the particular needs and circumstances of the person I was speaking to? (e.g. if the person had a disability such as visual impairment.)
- Did I elicit a full and positive response from the other person? (If not, why not?)
- Did I show active listening skills?
- Did the conversation flow freely?
- Were there any awkward moments during the conversation? If so, why did they occur and how did I overcome them?
- If I were conducting the conversation again, are there any aspects of my own performance I would particularly want to change or improve?

Telephone skills

Speaking to another person on the **telephone** is a form of conversation which involves certain specific skills. Some of the main points that you should bear in mind are listed below.

- At the beginning of the call, identify yourself and, if applicable, your position and/or organization.
- Make sure you know who you are speaking to.
- If you are making the call, have a clear idea before you pick up the telephone of the purpose you want the call to achieve. Is there information you need to obtain? Do you want to pass some information on, or instigate a course of action?
- When you are speaking to the other person, explain briefly and clearly during the early stages of the conversation why you have made the telephone call.

- If you have a few points to cover during the call, it will help to have a note of these with you before you begin.
- Speak clearly and at a measured pace. Remember that the non-verbal communication which aids understanding in a face-to-face conversation is absent.
- Have a pen handy to make notes during the conversation. It can sometimes be difficult to remember later details of names, dates and times and exactly what was decided or agreed upon.
- Don't be afraid to ask the other person politely to repeat points if anything is unclear or you do not catch something that is said.
- At the close of the call, end the conversation in a polite and friendly way. It might also be appropriate to confirm a course of action that is to be taken (either by yourself or the other caller) or to sum up what has been agreed.

Index